A History of

BARBADOS

1625–1685

TO

MY FATHER AND MOTHER

FOREWORD

THERE is one reflection which must give satisfaction to all in Great Britain who are interested in colonial history. At one time it seemed possible that, when they had well-nigh exhausted the ground of their own colonial history, American writers might proceed to monopolize the field of the British West Indies. Fortunately the labours of Dr. Lillian Penson, Messrs. Williamson, Higham, and Harlow (to mention the names of those with whose work I am most familiar) have made altogether impossible such a consummation.

The amount of material that has become available since the publication of Sir R. Schomburgk's *History of Barbados* fully justifies the issue of a new account of its beginnings, based on the original documents.

Moreover, the story in many ways appeals to the modern reader. It is noteworthy to find some two hundred and seventy-five years ago the claim to dominion status set up in a tiny island in the West Indies ; and Mr. Harlow's narrative shows that *Latifundia perdidere* other countries besides Italy. Considering the part played by the West Indian trade in the events that led to the American Revolution, the careful and well-documented chapter in this book on the earlier trade relations between Barbados and New England is of especial interest. Indeed we may go further and say that, whoever would understand the English colonial policy of the seventeenth century in its strong points, as well as in its weak, should find a remarkable microcosm of it in the story of Barbados.

H. E. EGERTON.

AUTHOR'S PREFACE

A PREFACE is like a chairman's remarks, very apt to weary the audience before the speaker is allowed to begin. Its proper function, perhaps, is rather that of a vote of thanks, and its right place accordingly at the end of the discourse. However that may be, I owe a very deep debt of gratitude.

The present work originated in a thesis written for the B.LITT. degree at Oxford. During that time I was fortunate enough to have as my supervisor, Mr. H. E. Egerton (sometime Beit Professor of Colonial History in the University of Oxford); and to him my warmest thanks are due for unfailing support and valuable guidance.

To the Principal and Fellows of Brasenose College, Oxford, I am indebted for many things; encouragement at all times and generous assistance both during the period of research and again when the time came for publication.

Finally I have to thank the Government and people of Barbados who so readily came forward to combine with my old College in making the publication of this work possible.

V. T. H.

UNIVERSITY COLLEGE,
SOUTHAMPTON, 1925.

CONTENTS

BIBLIOGRAPHY

(i) MANUSCRIPTS

(a) IN THE PUBLIC RECORD OFFICE

Colonial Papers. Consists of correspondence between colonial governments and the successive Councils and Committees set up to
administer colonial affairs, together with reports and other
relative documents.

Colonial Entry Books. Miscellaneous papers referring to the colonies
are occasionally bound in with these entry books.

(Where I have consulted the original manuscript—as has been
done in the great majority of cases—I give the call-number at the
Record Office in the foot-note. Otherwise the page reference in
the printed calendar, abbreviated as *Cal. Col.*, is given.)

Chancery Proceedings. Charles I. Bundles C. 60/38, C. 58/4.

(Depositions and breviats similar to those in the Rawlinson and
Trinity College, Dublin, collections.)

Ledgers and Files of the Royal African Company.

T. 70/15, 16, and 238 (letters from the Company's factors at
Barbados, 1679–81).

T. 70/646 (statement of negroes sold in Barbados, 1662–3).

T. 70/936, 937, 938, 939, 940, 941, and 314 (statement of sales,
1673–84).

(b) IN THE BRITISH MUSEUM

Sloane MSS. 159, ff. 20–1. (Details of Francis Lord Willoughby's
settlement at Surinam in Guiana.)

Sloane MSS. 1519, fo. 19 et seq. (A letter of Lord Willoughby
referring to Scottish servants.)

Sloane MSS. 2441, ff. 1–22. 'An account of His Ma^{tys} Island of
Barbados, and the Governm^t thereof.' (1684.)

Sloane MSS. 2902. (Economic and judicial material.)

Sloane MSS. 3662, fo. 62 et seq. John Scott, 'Description of Barbados '.

Sloane MSS. 3984. (Mainly details of the Barbadian sugar trade, 1685.)

Additional MSS. 11411. An out-letter book of Thomas Povey, 1655–61. (Of the first importance for Barbadian history during this period.)

Additional MSS. 25120. 'The Coventry Papers.' (1676–9.) (Contains a number of letters from Coventry to Governor Sir Jonathan Atkins.)

Additional MSS. 30307. Prince Rupert's Voyage to the West Indies. (1651–2.)

Additional MSS. 35251. Modiford's protestation. (1655.)

Additional MSS. 28089. Details of the farming of the 4½ per cent. duty in Barbados.

Egerton MSS. 2395. (This famous collection is a mine of economic and political information relating to the West Indies and particularly to Barbados during the period 1653–79.)

Egerton MSS. 2543, fo. 123. 'A state of yor ma^{ts} Interest in the West Indies,' 1660–1 (probably by Sir Thomas Modiford).

Stowe MSS. 184, ff. 124a–127a. (Letters of Robert Rich, Earl of Warwick, to Governor Bell and others, urging submission to Parliament.)

Stowe MSS. 324, fo. 4. (Account of the establishment of the 4½ per cent. duty in Barbados.)

(c) IN THE BODLEIAN LIBRARY

Rawlinson MSS. A., vol. 3, fo. 135 ; vol. 62, fo. 638 ; vol. 257, fo. 109 ; vol. 478, fo. 48.

Rawlinson MSS. C., vol. 94, fo. 33 et seq. (A collection of petitions and depositions in connexion with the Carlisle-Courteen dispute, which together with the Chancery and Trinity College, Dublin, documents are invaluable for the history of the original settlement of Barbados.)

Clarendon MSS., vols. 71, 72, 80, 81, 82, 84, 85. (Correspondence between the Earl of Clarendon and Lord Francis Willoughby, Lord William Willoughby, and others, 1660–7.)

Clarendon MSS., vol. 87. (Details of Sir Richard Dutton's misgovernment, 1683.)

Tanner MSS., vols. 54, 55, 56. (Numerous letters between officials in England and the Barbadian Government, particularly the Ayscue-Willoughby correspondence, during the years 1650–60.)

Tanner MSS., vol. 36, fo. 36. (Referring to Sir Richard Dutton's policy, 1681.)

(d) ELSEWHERE

Trinity College, Dublin, MSS. G. 4, 15. (In addition to evidence concerning the first settlement, this collection includes the original deed of demise from the Earl of Carlisle to Lord Willoughby of the Caribbee Islands, Lord Willoughby's letters patent as Lieutenant-General, letters of Wolverston, a description of Barbados, and other documents referring to the early period.)

' Davis Collection ', Royal Colonial Institute, London. (Transcripts made by the late N. Darnell Davis of Barbadian deeds of sale, parochial minutes, and other valuable local documents of the seventeenth century. The originals have since been destroyed by fire.)

(ii) EARLY PRINTED NARRATIVES

Foster, Nicholas. *A Briefe Relation of the late Horrid Rebellion in Barbados.* (London, 1650. Thomason Tracts, E. 1388 (433).)

Bradford, W. *History of the Plymouth Plantation.* (*c.* 1650, reprinted in the Massachusetts Historical Collections, 4th series, vol. iii, 1856. Contains useful information concerning New England–Barbados trade.)

Ligon, Richard. *A True and Exact History of the Island of Barbados.* (London, 1657.)

England's Slavery or Barbados Merchandize : Represented in a Petition to the High and Honourable Court of Parliament, by M. Rivers and O. Foyle. (London, 1659.)

Davies, John. *The History of the Caribby Islands.* (London, 1666.)

Great Newes from Barbados : A True and Faithfull Account of the Grand Conspiracy of the Negroes against the English, and the happy Discovery of the same. (London, 1676.)

An Abstract of all the Statutes made Concerning Aliens Trading in England, by S. Hayne, Ryding-Surveyor for His Majesty's Customs. (London, 1685.)

ttleton, Edward. *The Groans of the Plantations.* (London, 1688.)

Dalby, Thomas. *An Historicall Account of the Rise and Growth of the West India Colonies.* (1690. Reprinted *Harleian Misc.*, vii, pp. 340–69.)

(The accounts of Hayne, the Customs officer, with those of the planters, Dalby and Lyttleton, together provide a detailed study of the influence of the economic legislation under the later Stuarts upon the West Indian, and particularly the Barbadian, sugar industry.)

Some Memoirs of the First Settlement of Barbados, . . . *Extracted from Ancient Records.* (Barbados, 1741.) (Although these records contain some serious chronological mistakes, they are based on original documents which are now lost.)

Frere, George. *Short History of Barbados.* (London, 1768.) (A brief, and sometimes inaccurate account, but contains useful quotations from early statutes, &c.)

(iii) PRINTED DOCUMENTS

Calendar of State Papers. Colonial Series (America and West Indies). Vol. i, 1574–1660 ; vol. ii, 1661–8 ; vol. iii, 1669–74 ; vol. iv, 1675–6 ; vol. v, 1677–80 ; vol. vi, 1681–5.

Calendar of State Papers. Domestic Series. Charles I, Charles II. (Contains occasional references to colonial affairs.)

Acts of the Privy Council. Colonial Series. Vol. i, 1613–80 ; vol. ii, 1680–1720.

Calendar of Treasury Papers. Vol. i, 1599–1696.

Acts and Statutes of Barbados, made and Enacted since the Reducement of the same unto the authority of the Commonwealth of England. (London, 1654.)

Acts of Barbados, ed. J. Jennings. (London, 1673.)

Acts of Barbados, 1648–1718, ed. J. Baskett. (London, 1732.)

Historical Manuscripts Commission Reports. Calendars of the Rye and Hereford, Lord Muncaster, Duke of Portland, Loder and Symond, Lord Braye, Le Fleming, House of Lords, Ormonde, Round, MSS. (The Harley Papers, Duke of Portland's collection, are particularly important.)

Journal of the House of Lords, vols. v, vi, vii, ix, xi.

Journal of the House of Commons, vols. iii, v, vi.

Thurloe, John. *A Collection of State Papers of J. T. To which is prefixed a life of Mr. Thurloe by Thomas Birch.* (7 vols. London 1742.) (The main source of information for Barbadian relations with the Home Government during the Protectorate.)

Force, Peter. *Tracts and other Papers*. (4 vols. Washington, 1836–46.) Vol. ii, nos. 2 and 7 ; vol. iii, no. 14 ; vol. iv, no. 11.

Massachusetts Historical Society Collections. (Particularly, 2nd series, vol. vii ; 3rd series, vol. ix ; 4th series, vol. vi ; 5th series, vols. i, vii, viii ; 6th series, vol. i.)

Records of the Governor and Company of the Massachusetts Bay in New England, ed. N. B. Shurtleef. (Boston, 1853.)

Plymouth Colony Records, ed. W. White. (Boston, 1859.)

Records of the Court of Assistants of the Colony of the Massachusetts Bay. (Boston, 1862.) Vol. i.

Records and Files of the Quarterly Court of Essex County, Mass., ed. G. F. How. (Boston, 1897.)

The Papers of Edward Randolph, ed. Toppan (vols. i–v), ed. Goodrick (vols. vi–vii). (Boston, 1898 and 1909.)

(The Collections marked with an asterisk contain statistics and other information referring to Barbadian trade relations with the North American Colonies.)

' The Calvert Papers ', No. 3. (Baltimore, 1899.)

' The narrative of General Venables ', ed. C. H. Firth. (Royal Historical Society, 1900.)

' Colonizing Expeditions to the West Indies and Guiana, 1623–67 ', ed. V. T. Harlow. (Hakluyt Society, Series II, vol. lvi.)

(iv) MODERN WORKS

Schomburgk, R. H. *The History of Barbados*. (London, 1782.)

Bryan Edwards. *The History, Civil and Commercial, of the British Colonies in the West Indies*. 5 vols. (5th ed. London, 1819.)

Darnell Davis, N. *Cavaliers and Roundheads in Barbados*. (Georgetown, British Guiana, 1887.) (A well-documented account of the Civil War in Barbados.)

Weeden. *The Economic and Social History of New England*, 1620–1789. (Cambridge, U.S.A., 1890.)

Osgood. *The American Colonies in the Seventeenth Century*. (New York, 1904.)

Beer, G. L. *The Origins of the British Colonial System*, 1578–1660. (New York, 1908.)

—— *The Old Colonial System*. (New York, 1912.)

BIBLIOGRAPHY

Edmundson, G. Articles on Guiana in the *English Historical Review*. (Vols. xvi, xix.)

Mims, S. L. *Colbert's West India Policy*. (Yale Historical Publications, i, 1912.)

Newton, A. P. *The Colonising Activities of the English Puritans*. (Yale Historical Publications : Miscellany i, 1914.)

Pitman, F. W. *The Development of the British West Indies*, 1700–63. (Yale Historical Publications, iv, 1917.)

Higham, C. S. S. *The Development of the Leeward Islands under the Restoration*. (Cambridge, 1921.)

Wrong, Hume. *Government of the West Indies*. (Oxford, 1923.)

Williamson, J. A. *English Colonies in Guiana and on the Amazon*, 1604–68. (Oxford, 1923.)

—— *The Caribbee Islands under the Proprietary Patents*. (Oxford, 1926.)

Penson, L. M. *The Colonial Agents of the British West Indies*. (London, 1924.)

I

EARLY YEARS (1625-40)

EASTWARD of all the West Indian group the island of Barbados [1] lies alone, fronting the long unceasing roll of the Atlantic. Thrust up in some far distant age from the deep ocean bed, it lay for many dreaming centuries untenanted and silent, save for the boom of the surf on the encircling coral reef and the scream of wheeling birds among the tropic woods.[2]

And then the European world began to stir, moved by a new impulse. Heralded by Don Christoval Colon adventurers came, full of greed and mysticism, to probe, and wonder at, and desecrate. The long sleep of the Western Paradise was over. Fortunately for the islands they came, and saw—and passed on ; seeking the greater glories of the Main. Occasionally some mighty galleon, beating up to the north to catch the Trade Winds, might have been observed from the Barbadian beach, but nothing more.

[1] The derivation of the name is uncertain. Some suggest that it arose from a Spanish word meaning a kind of bearded fig-tree, owing to the shaggy appearance of the wooded slopes. Another suggestion is a Spanish word for the hanging branches of a vine which strike root in the ground. On the other hand, it may well be a corruption for *St. Bernard*, a name given to an unknown island in approximately the same latitude and longitude as Barbados. Variants in Spanish maps include the following : St. Barnado, Bernados, Barbudoso, Barnodos, and Barnodo.

[2] In spite of Schomburgk's assertion to the contrary (*History of Barbados*, London, 1782, pp. 254-7) the island was not regularly inhabited by native tribes. In 1536 Pedro a Campos found it entirely deserted, and left hogs to breed there for future wanderers (John Scott's ' Description of Barbados ', Sloane MSS., Brit. Mus. 3662, f. 62).

Nearly a century passed before the English found
their way to this gem of the so-called Indies. They,
too, brought in their wake much evil-doing and sordid
discord. Time, it is true, has done much for the healing of these wounds, although a scar remains in the form
of a complex racial problem. The wild luxuriance of
the olden time is gone : in its room is an ordered
beauty of man's fashioning.

Steaming into Carlisle Bay on a modern liner a
striking scene presents itself. Girt about with azure
water, and fringed with a broad line of creaming foam
and sand, the island looks for all the world like a well-
kept garden. Terrace by terrace it rises in gentle
gradients to the chalky marl of Mount Hillaby in the
centre, sloping away as gently again to the Atlantic
shore on the other side. Every available foot of the
ground, with its black volcanic soil and reddish clay
from the ocean floor, is carefully cultivated. Fringing
the beach are coco-nut trees, leaning this way and
that : behind and above groves of tall, straight-
stemmed palms, orange, lemon, bread-fruit, and other
tropical trees. But the feature that chiefly makes for
the garden-like appearance is that of the green sugar-
canes, clothing the rising terraces row on row.

Dotted about are the white stately houses of the
planters, built of coral, and the little villages of log
cabins belonging to the negro labourers. In the fore-
ground lies the port of Bridgetown ; approached
through the outer bay, where the ocean-going vessels
anchor, past the breakwater, and into the inner
harbour. Here there is usually a throng of smaller
craft, some from America and others from neighbouring islands ; and on the quay a crowd of negro women
and boys clamouring for the patronage of the new-
comer.

The town itself is a pleasing sight in the clear West
Indian atmosphere, aflame with flowers, and nestling

at the foot of the hills with its narrow streets, shops, pleasure grounds, squares, and military parade. Along the coast a railway runs for twenty-eight miles, linking up the capital with Speightstown and the watering places, Fontabelle and Hastings. In Bridgetown itself there is a tramway system. Indeed a curious mixture of the languid loveliness of the tropics and the swift stir of modern life.

The first Englishman to visit Barbados was probably one Captain Simon Gordon, who claimed to have landed there in the year 1620, and to have found the island uninhabited. It was not, however, until five years later that any definite steps were taken to effect a settlement. In 1625 one John Powell, the elder, on board the good ship *Olive*, touched at Barbados on his return voyage from Pernambuco to England. ' And landing some men ', we are told, ' they set up a Cross in or about St. James's Town, now called the Hole, and inscrib'd on a Tree adjoyning *James K. of E. and this Island*. Having thus done they came along-shore to the Indian River, and left there also some marks of their Possession for the Crown of England.' [1] Having ascertained that the island was

---

[1] *Memoirs of the First Settlement* . . ., p. 1 (Barbados, 1741). Cf. Sloane MSS. 3662, ff. 62–54; Ligon's, *True and Exact Account of Barbados* (London, 1657); C.O. 1/14, No. 37, Public Record Office. Dr. James A. Williamson in his recent work, *The Caribbee Islands under the Proprietary Patents*, has, I think, proved conclusively that the date of 1605, given to this incident in the *Memoirs*, and copied by Bryan Edwards (*History of the West Indies*) and by subsequent writers, is a compiler's mistake for 1625. It may be said here that since writing this first chapter I have been privileged to read Dr. Williamson's scholarly work before it was printed. Therein he traces in detail the complicated story of the Carlisle proprietorship and the injustice done to Sir William Courteen, the actual founder of the Barbadian colony, and in doing so makes use of Chancery Records with which I was unacquainted. Moreover, the question of the proprietary patents is one which affects the English Caribee Islands generally, and not Barbadian history in particular. I have, therefore, while benefiting from Dr. Williamson's researches, reduced

untenanted, Powell returned home by way of St. Christopher to report the important discovery to his shrewd and wealthy employer, Sir William Courteen.

The latter, who with his brother Sir Peter, controlled a powerful trading company operating both from London and Middleburg in the United Provinces, was not slow to appreciate the value of the information thus afforded. Straightway he fitted out an expedition under Powell to occupy and plant the island. Owing, however, to an ' accident at sea ', the voyage was abandoned, and Powell put back to Cowes.¹ A second expedition, financed by a syndicate consisting of the Courteens, their brother-in-law John Mounsey, John Powell the elder, and Henry Powell, was more effective. After capturing a prize, from which ten negro slaves were taken, the *William and John*, commanded by Captain Henry Powell, reached Barbados on 17th February 1627, when eighty settlers were disembarked to try their fortune.²

The landing took place on the leeward (that is, the western) side of the island, at a spot which they named Jamestown ; and there the royal standard was unfurled. Setting to work with a will, these pioneers hewed down trees and built themselves log houses near

my own account of this intricate matter to a minimum, only mentioning the incidents which directly influenced the development of Barbados itself.

¹ Rawlinson MSS. (Bodleian) C. 94, f. 33. This collection of petitions and depositions by mariners and colonists who took part in the original settlement, together with similar documents in the Chancery Proceedings (Charles I, Bundles C. 60, No. 38, and C. 58, No. 4, &c.), forms an invaluable authority for the first years of Barbadian history. Copies of these and similar depositions are to be found in the Trinity College, Dublin, MSS. (G. 4. 15, No. 736, pp. 77–118). Powell had obtained letters of marque against the Spaniards, and the ' accident' here referred to was probably the capture of a Spanish vessel, which he brought back with him to Cowes (Additional MSS. 37, 816, f. 135b).

² T.C.D. MSS., op. cit., pp. 157–63 ; cf. C.O. 1/14, No. 39.

the sea-shore.[1] At that stage they remained for some time, working their little clearings and leaving the virgin forest of the hinterland untouched.[2] The strain of labouring under a tropical sun was relieved by hunting wild hogs, in which the woods abounded. Unfortunately, they killed them off in such numbers that within three years there were none left.[3]

Captain Henry Powell now bethought himself of an old friend named Groenewegen, Governor of the Dutch settlement by 'the River Dissekeeb on the maine of Guyana', with whom he had previously served in the West Indies for the King of Spain.[4] Leaving the settlers to subsist on the wild game and fruits of the island, Captain Henry Powell, with his nephew John, sailed to Guiana to obtain roots and seeds for crops best suited to the climate. Groene-wegen, who received them kindly, persuaded the Indian tribe of the Arawacoes to barter with them for yams, cassava, Indian corn, plantains, 'and for the Produce of Trade — Tobacco, Cotton, and Annotte'.[5] Powell relates how the natives 'had a desire to goe wth me as ffree people to manure those fruits, and that I should allow them a piece of Land, the which I did'.[6] With Groenewegen's sanction,

---

[1] Rawlinson MSS. C. 94, f. 13a.

[2] Cf. *The Calvert Papers* (Baltimore, 1899), No. 3, pp. 26–31 : '. . . the place is a plaine ground, growne over with trees and under-shrubs, without passage, except where the Planters have cleared'.

[3] See 'Voyage of Sir Henry Colt, Kt., . . . to the Islands of the Antilles in the ship called the Alexander, Anno 1631' MSS. in the University Library, Cambridge. Printed in *Colonizing Expeditions to the West Indies and Guiana, 1623–1667* ; ed. V. T. Harlow, pp. 54–102, Hakluyt Society, vol. lvi.

[4] Sloane MSS. 3662, f. 62 (op. cit.). Major John Scott, the writer of this narrative, has frequently been derided as being wholly untrustworthy. Dr. Edmundson (*E. H. R.*, vol. xvi) has, however, by reference to Dutch and Spanish contemporary documents, made out a very strong case in support of the general authenticity of his statements.

[5] Ibid.   [6] Rawlinson MSS. C. 94, f. 33.

about forty Indians, including the wives and children
of men who intended to follow the next year, went
back to Barbados with the Powells. Subsequently,
they were betrayed and reduced to slavery there by
those who robbed the Courteens of their Barbadian
interests ; a piece of treachery which aroused bitter
hatred against the English, and which nearly cost
Groenewegen and the Dutchmen of Guiana their lives.

Within a few days of their return to Barbados, in
May 1627, Henry's brother, Captain John Powell,
senior, arrived from England on board the *Peter*,
bringing a cargo and nearly ninety men and women.[1]
Thus doubly reinforced with numbers and supplies
the work of planting proceeded quickly. More ground
was cleared, and about twelve estates marked out and
planted, where the industry and experience of the
Indians soon produced a profusion of foodstuffs.
' Oranges, lemons, limes, pomegrandes, peeches, and
such other fruites there are ', a visitor reported—' but
not in any great plentie as yet.' [2] It was not long
before the planters began to export an increasing
quantity of cotton, cotton-wool, and tobacco, although
this last appears to have been of a poor and earthy
variety.[3] By 1629 there were between sixteen and
eighteen hundred people on the island.

The entire expense of this promising venture
was being borne by Sir William Courteen and his
associates. He himself paid wages to the colonists, who
received from him all necessaries, and returned all
profits.[4] Neither the land nor the stock was their

[1] His departure from England had been delayed by the Lord High
Admiral—possibly because his cargo included commodities, the
exportation of which was normally forbidden. See *Acts of the Privy
Council*, I, No. 136 (5th April 1627).

[2] *Calvert Papers*, No. 3, p. 80.

[3] See Letters of Henry Winthrop from Barbados in 1627 (*Winthrop
Papers*, viii, pp. 285-9.

[4] Rawlinson MSS. C. 94, f. 13a, ut supra.

own ; they were merely his tenants at will, working
the demesne of the lord of the manor. Indeed, it
was a form of that exclusive government by merchants which Adam Smith stigmatizes as ' the worst
of all governments for any country whatever '.[1] Of
this truth the unhappy condition of settlers under the
Bermuda Company is a sufficiently striking example.
Nevertheless, in the case of an infant community,
absolute control of some kind may be a necessity.
Without the means of protection and the resources
of a merchant prince like Courteen, or an exclusive
company of merchants, no group of settlers could have
succeeded in such an enterprise. So great in those
days were the financial risks incident to maritime
communications, disease, attacks by natives, and the
slowness of returns on money invested, that joint-
stock companies became the recognized instrument
in developing overseas trade and colonization. This
task no national Government in the seventeenth
century, except the Spanish, was strong enough to
undertake.[2]

But between the proprietorship of a merchant,
intimately acquainted with the needs and resources of
his settlement, and that of a spendthrift courtier,
whose ignorance compels him to leave the colony at
the mercy of subordinates, there is a vital difference.
A long period of injustice and misgovernment under
a ruler of the latter sort was now Barbados' fortune.

James Hay, Earl of Carlisle, was a Scot, who by
following King James to his English throne, had
gained thereby an earldom. An incorrigible spendthrift, he soon became involved in difficulties with
his creditors, chief of whom was a syndicate of London
merchants, headed by Colonel (later Sir) Marmaduke

[1] *Wealth of Nations*, Book IV, chap. 7.
[2] Witness the French, Dutch, Danish, and English East India
Companies.

Royden.[1] These latter now decided to utilize their
hold over Carlisle in order to gain a footing in the new
and lucrative business of exploiting the Lesser Antilles.[2] Negotiations were set afoot with the result
that, on 2nd July 1627, Carlisle received a formal
grant of the Caribee Islands, among which (despite
geographical ignorance) Barbados was certainly included. Forthwith, the Earl in liquidation of his
debts leased 10,000 acres in Barbados to Royden and
his associates, with full taxative and judicial authority.[3]
Throughout the negotiations no word of protest, so
far as is known, was raised by Courteen; a circumstance
which seems to indicate that Carlisle deliberately
misled his rivals into thinking that he was making
no claim upon Barbados until the patent was safely
passed. Such hoodwinking would not be difficult, for
Charles I notoriously cared for none of these things.[4]

Realizing that he had been tricked, Courteen sought
the protection of a powerful courtier in the person of
Philip Herbert, Earl of Pembroke. The latter, who
claimed this and other islands by virtue of a promise

[1] Cf. *Dict. Nat. Biog.*

[2] Another group of merchants, headed by Ralph Merrifield and
Edward Warner, had already in 1625 successfully planted St. Christopher. They also probably approached Carlisle with a view to accepting
his overlordship, should a patent be obtained.

[3] 'Ten thousand acres granted to Marmaduke Rawdon (Royden),
&c., by the Earl of Carlisle on 22nd February 1629-30—being that
Plantation which hath been already partly measured and marked out
by Charles Wolverston and yᵉ said Captain Wheatley. . . .' Boundaries
are then detailed. Copy of actual document, *Deeds of Barbados*,
vol. i, p. 483. These invaluable deeds, since destroyed by fire at
Barbados, have been carefully transcribed by the late Mr. Darnell-
Davis, and deposited in the library of the Royal Colonial Institute,
London. These transcripts are henceforward referred to as the
'Davis Collection'. Cf. also Rawlinson MSS. C. 94, f. 28.

[4] As Williamson points out, the patent was passed before the
Powells had returned to England with the news of the successful
settlement of Barbados ; but Carlisle must have known of the departure
of Courteen's expedition in 1626.

from James I, accordingly intervened. On 25th February 1628, during the absence of Carlisle from court on an embassy, he induced the King to grant him the islands of 'Trinidado, Tabago, Barbudos, and Fonseca', in trust for his friend Courteen.[1] Carlisle, however, was the more popular man. On his return a further grant was obtained from the complacent Charles, in which Barbados was definitely confirmed to him as one of the Caribee Islands.[2] The chief lawyers of the day considered that the right lay with Pembroke and Courteen, by priority of claim and being 'first in Occupancie'.[3] But when the dispute was referred to Lord Keeper Coventry he concluded that, despite obvious confusion between Barbados and the barren rock of Barbuda, the inclusion of the former in Carlisle's first patent had been intended, and was therefore his. Royal instructions were thereupon dispatched in May 1629 to the Governor of Barbados, declaring the Earl of Carlisle's title to the island to be of full strength and virtue, and none other to have force.[4] It was a typical court intrigue, and the game had been won by the more skilful courtier. The resultant strife in the colony itself between the followers of the two claimants seriously retarded its development.[5]

Barbados was now to be subject to a ruler with sovereign rights modelled on those of the Palatine

[1] *Cal. Col.* 1574–1660, p. 87 ; Rawlinson MSS. C. 94, f. 27.

[2] *Cal. Col.* 1574–1660, p. 91 (7th April 1629). Also in T.C.D. MSS. (G. 4. 15), p. 57.

[3] Sloane MSS. 3662, f. 60a.

[4] *Cal. Col.* 1574–1660, p. 97 (18th April 1629).

[5] Sir Henry Colt (*Voyage*, ut supra) gives a graphic picture of the backward state of the island in 1630. ' Your ground and plantations show what you are, they lie like the ruins of some village lately burned ; here a great timber tree half burned, in another place a rafter singed all black . . . nothing is clear(ed) ; what digged or weeded for beauty ? All are bushes and long grass, all things carrying the face of a desolate and disorderly show to the beholder '

Bishop of Durham. Just as the Conqueror had granted exclusive authority to that potentate in his northern outpost, because he himself was not strong enough to exercise it, so Charles I granted to the Earl of Carlisle in the far off Indies similar powers and for the same reason.[1]

Although the Carlisle charter declared that the settlers were possessed of every right and privilege proper to freeborn Englishmen, it nevertheless precluded any real measure of representative government.[2] All subsidies, customs, and impositions were granted for ten years to the Earl, who was also empowered to choose what manors were to be included in his private demesne, and to fix his own rents.

Subject to a feudal tenant-in-chief of almost unlimited power it remained to be seen how the colony would fare. If employed with knowledge and sympathy such extensive authority would have been an effective bulwark against foreign interference and internal faction. In less than twenty years, however, the harassed settlers were petitioning the King to relieve them of this 'Transcendente Authoritie', which had brought them 'to slavery worse than villanay'.[3]

Meanwhile, even before this barefaced robbery had received official sanction, the merchants behind Carlisle had launched their attack upon the rightful owner of Barbados. The respective invasions and counter-invasions of the Carlislists and Courteenists are intimately linked up with the maze of intrigue and litigation which went on in London. Sometimes the centre of interest is in England, sometimes in Barbados,

---

[1] T.C.D. MSS. (G. 4. 15), p. 40, ' The Power of the Courts of the Bishoprick of Durham '.

[2] The Earl of Carlisle's first patent, T.C.D. MSS., p. 42 (op. cit.). It is quoted verbatim by Bryan Edwards, *History of the West Indies* (London, 1819 edition), vol. i, p. 320 ; cf. also Rawlinson MSS. C. 94, f. 6.   [3] Rawlinson MSS. C. 94, f. 22.

and at others in the Leeward Islands. For our present purpose it is only necessary to touch on those events which directly affected the development of the Barbadian colony.

In June 1628 one Captain Wolverston, who had been appointed by the Royden syndicate to assume the management of their 10,000 acres and to be Governor for three years, arrived at the island with sixty-four men.[1] Though armed with a formal commission from Carlisle,[2] he had been carefully instructed to gain possession, if it were possible, without using violence.[3] John Powell and his men allowed these newcomers to land and take up their abode. But when Wolverston, after settling down and organizing his forces, claimed jurisdiction over the Courteen planters, open war was narrowly averted. What followed is uncertain. But it was afterwards stated that Wolverston ' seduced the people, imprisoned the Gouvenor (Powell), and tooke the Govern[mt] upon himselfe for the Earl of Carlisle '.[4]

By way of backing up these proceedings and also founding a plantation of his own, Carlisle in the same year sent out to the island two merchants named Havercamp and Mole. Arriving in October they set twenty men, whom they had brought with them, to

[1] Chancery Proceedings, C. 60/38 (1), quoted by Williamson.

[2] After his election by the merchants, Carlisle (as proprietor) gave Wolverston a Commission to be Governor and Commander-in-Chief of Barbados (29th March 1628) for three years. If he died within that time the settlers transported by the London merchants—i. e. not the Courteen settlers—were to elect his successor. See *Some Memoirs of the First Settlement. . . . Extracted from Ancient Records, Papers, and Accounts taken from . . . some of the First Settlers*, p. 9, Barbados, 1741.

[3] ' Letter to Captains John Powell and Wm. Deane, and other his Ma[ties]. Loveing Subiects upon y[e] Iland of Barbados ' (4th April 1628). Rawlinson MSS. C. 94, f. 31.

[4] Rawlinson MSS. C. 94, f. 29. For further details see C.O. 1/14, No. 31.

open up a new estate under the direction of a certain Richard Leonard, to whom they farmed the profits of the first year for £1,000. They then induced the Courteen planters, who seem to have lost faith in their previous employers, formally to acknowledge the Carlisle régime, and to submit to the payment of heavy dues.[1]

Violence thus begun bred further violence. No sooner would one party gain control over the island than an expedition sent by the other would execute a *coup d'état* and the position would be reversed. Thus feud and faction became the order of the day in a little community that was faced by perils enough already from hurricanes, starvation, and probable attacks from the Spaniard. On 26th February 1629 Henry Powell arrived on the scene with a cargo of supplies, and nearly one hundred men and women. Wolverston and Deane [2] were enticed to a conference, seized and manacled ; John Powell was released from prison and reinstated as Governor, and all the servants, possessions, and tobacco belonging to Royden & Co., to the value of £10,000, were confiscated, together with tobacco worth £2,000 from Carlisle's own plantation. Then, after having received a further 100,000 lb. weight of tobacco from the Courteen planters and a general promise of allegiance to the Pembroke patent, Henry Powell sailed away to England, taking with him Wolverston and Deane as prisoners.[3]

The counter-stroke took place on the arrival in the following August of Henry Hawley, the new Carlisle

[1] After a few months Havercamp and Mole returned to England, leaving Wolverston in charge of the planters on the 10,000 acres, and Leonard over Carlisle's private plantation.

[2] William Deane had gone out to Barbados under John Powell, but had deserted him for Wolverston, with whom he had been previously acquainted at Bermuda. He was now running an independent plantation of his own.

[3] Chancery Proceedings, ut supra, and Egerton MSS. 2395, f. 602.

Governor, a man who quickly became notorious for unscrupulous audacity. John and William Powell and the leading men of the Courteen party foolishly accepted Hawley's invitation to dine on board his ship the *Carlisle*. The unsuspecting guests were promptly seized, stripped, and chained to the mainmast, where they remained for nearly a month, exposed to the glare of a tropical sun, until the ship itself was captured by a Spanish force off St. Christopher.[1] Within a week the *coup d'état* was complete, and Hawley departed to the Leeward Islands, leaving Robert Wheatley as Deputy Governor. The latter had to face an armed attack from the enraged Courteen men. The rising was crushed, and Wheatley took the opportunity of driving his opponents from all of their plantations which happened to fall within the limits of the 10,000 acres—regardless of the fact that the plantations in question had been carved out of the virgin forest before the London adventurers had been heard of.

The duel was now over : Carlisle had triumphed both at Whitehall and in the island itself. For many years Sir William Courteen, and later his descendants, made repeated efforts to secure compensation for their loss, but without success. The period of invasion and counter-invasion was passed, but there was neither peace nor prosperity in the island. It was no coincidence that the years 1630 and 1631 were remembered among Barbadians as 'the Starving Time', when hunger threatened to extinguish the troubled colony.[2] Not only that, but a spirit of cruelty and

[1] Hawley, who was on board, was also taken prisoner, but with his usual adroitness succeeded in gaining his release. Cf. Egerton MSS. 2395, ff. 503–7 (John Hilton's narrative). Printed in *Colonizing Expeditions to the West Indies*, ut supra, pp. 1–17.

[2] *Memoirs*, p. 14. Cf. *Acts of the Privy Council*, I, No. 266 (4th February 1631) : 'the Board was thus made acquainted as well by

lawlessness had been bred among the planters. Of
this fact the case of Sir William Tufton affords a
striking example.

Arriving at Barbados in September 1629 with a commission from Carlisle to be Governor for four years,
he set to work (with more energy than tact) to extirpate
the prevalent confusion and brutality. In particular
he attacked the barbarous treatment meted out to
Christian servants by their masters, and threatened
to transfer sufferers from the worse sort of planters
to more humane employers. Immediately Pierce, a
brother-in-law of the dispossessed Hawley, seized the
opportunity of stirring up a mutiny against him ; and
although the rebels were suppressed with leniency,
they subjected Tufton to continuous persecution, in-
tercepting his letters and sending scandalous reports
of him home to Carlisle. These representations,
together with Hawley's own manoeuvres in England,
produced the desired effect. Despite much good work
done,[1] he was replaced by Hawley, who was instructed
by Carlisle to depose him ' by force if need be '. Nor
does the tale of violence end here.

Although he peaceably handed over his office on
Hawley's arrival, the latter soon afterwards goaded
Tufton into protesting against his arbitrary rule, and
then seized him and his chief supporters by armed
force. After a farcical trial seven of them were condemned to death. Lots were drawn ; Tufton being
shot and the rest hanged.[2] ' This was done ', wrote

the humble petition of the Planters and Adventurers to the Caribee
Islands as by the Earl of Carlisle present in Councell of the greate
distresse wherein the said Planters and theire servants were at this
present, by reason of the greate want of bread and other victualls
there. . . .' Twenty hogsheads of meal and other foodstuffs were
ordered to be sent for their relief.

[1] Such as dividing the island into six parishes, establishing vestries
therein to conduct local affairs, and building churches.

[2] Rawlinson MSS. C. 94, ff. 12a, and 15b, op. cit.

Lord Dorchester, 'uppon p^{re} meditate malice in the beginning, prosequntion, and the end.'[1]

Meanwhile, events that were destined to exert a considerable influence upon Barbadian affairs were taking place in England. In 1636 the Earl of Carlisle died, having previously made over all his proprietary rights in the Caribee Islands to three trustees, Sir James Hay, Archibald Hay, and Richard Hurst, who were to pay off the creditors and then hand over the remaining assets to his son, the young second Earl. The arrangement, if not deliberately dishonest, was doubly unfortunate. Not only did the unhappy creditors fail to recover a penny of their debts until after the Restoration, but the Earl persistently strove, until the outbreak of the Civil War, by intrigue and litigation to secure the full exercise of the proprietary rights for himself in place of the trustees.[2] Neither of these circumstances were calculated to promote stability and prosperity in Barbados.

Hawley, as might be expected, decided to fish on his own account in these troubled waters. He had been in England since 1634, and now obtained a renewal of his commission from the trustees, returning to Barbados in July 1636. Within two months he opened his campaign by refusing to acknowledge the authority of Captain Thomas Warner, now appointed not only Governor of St. Christopher but also Lieutenant-General of all the colonies under the Carlisle patent, and prevented him from obtaining volunteers at Barbados for his projected settlement of Metalina. The latter replied by appealing to the Secretary of State, describing Hawley's conduct as obstinate and rebellious.[3]

---

[1] Lord Dorchester's account, C.O. 1/15, No. 30, P.R.O. The above account is based on this relation except where otherwise stated.

[2] Cf. Chancery documents, quoted by Williamson (ut supra), chap. vi.   [3] *Cal. Col.* 1574–1660, p. 240.

Opposition thus being doubly quelled, as well among the Carlisle as among the Courteen settlers, Hawley proceeded to rule according to his own ideas. One of his more extraordinary acts was to return to the medieval system of land tenure, whereby mesne-tenants and villeins were obliged to devote a proportion of their time to working the lord's private demesne. He and his council ' endeavoured to have the fifth part of ye peoples Labours, and uppon dis-contente they tooke Armes; and ever since (the inhabitants) have paid 40^lb weight a head and a hen a head, or in stead thereof 20^lb weight in cotton or tobacco '.[1] Other exactions were rigorously enforced, the most important and the best hated being the poll tax, levied of every inhabitant, men, women, and children. No risks were taken: for as soon as the cotton and tobacco crops were gathered in, officers came round and attached them until all taxes and duties had been paid.[2] The ostensible object of the poll tax was the fortification of the island. But, as one planter remarked eight years after Hawley's reign, ' the Island is not yet fortified, nor gunnes mounted '.[3] Arbitrary fines, some as much as 50 lb. of tobacco (then worth about £6 sterling) were also imposed by the Governor and Council. Taxes were laid for ' killing pidgeons ', keeping storehouses, and so forth.

[1] Rawlinson MSS. C. 94, f. 5b. Cf. the following clause in a deed of lease in 1636: ' yieldinge and paying therefor yearly and every year unto the said Earl of Carlisle his heires and assignes, on the five and twentieth of March, the full some of twenty pounds of cleane Cotton, or the value thereof for each man, woman or boys of or above the age of fourteen yeares, inhabiting or living in or upon the afore-said Land and premises . . .', *Deeds of Barbados*, vol. i, p. 534 (Davis Collection, Box 2, R. C. I.). For similar examples see vol. i, pp. 126, 176, and 538—all in Box 2.

[2] Rawlinson MSS. C. 94, ff. 4b, 5, and 10b. Peter Strong, a planter who lived in Barbados from 1634 to 1641, declared that he was com-pelled to pay all these taxes during the years he was there.

[3] Ibid., f. 12a (deposition of Thomas Batten).

As an example of parental care an ordinance was passed ' that noe strong beere should be sold but to the Governor and Councell, and such as he pleased '.[1] Again, in 1639 an Alienation Court was established for regulating the transfer of land. On each contract a commission of 5 lb. of cotton-wool or 20 lb. of tobacco per acre was exacted, ' and other oppressive ffees, which wee but for speaking against have been Imprisoned, and put in irons '.[2] Obedience to the Carlisle government was further maintained by obliging all settlers to accept new patents for their estates, under threat of immediate dispossession; oaths of fealty and personal homage to the feudal proprietor being exacted.

Two years later Hawley's intrigues took definite shape. In 1638 Robert Rich, Earl of Warwick, a prominent figure in many colonizing and privateering enterprises, bought the Earl of Pembroke's unused patent of 1628. With characteristic energy he immediately prepared expeditions for the settlement of Tobago and Trinidad.[3] At the same time, as heir to the Pembroke-Courteen claims, he evidently hoped to secure a reversal of the previous decision in favour of Carlisle, and himself become proprietor of the Caribee Islands.[4] Exactly when and how Hawley threw

[1] Ibid., ff. 5a and 11a, statement of several planters.

[2] Such fees were, of course, extortionate, but the establishment of a system of recording sales seemed to have been necessary, considering the frequent changes of ownership which took place during this period.

[3] See *Colonizing Expeditions to the West Indies* (ut supra), introd., pp. lviii–lxiv.

[4] There was quite a good chance of success. Owing to the difficulties in which Charles I had become involved, both at home and abroad, he might easily have been prepared to conciliate so prominent a member of the opposition as Warwick in this way. Cf. Williamson, op. cit., chap. vi. Also Thomas Verney to Sir Edmund Verney (10th Feb. 1638/9): ' I hope, if my Lord of Warwick hath bought the Island (Barbados) that we shall have better orders in the

in his lot with Warwick is uncertain. But before the end of 1638 he was evidently allowing agents to entice the islanders to desert Barbados and join with Warwick's men at Tobago, and after his departure for England (where he arrived early in 1639) his brother William, the Deputy-Governor, continued the intrigue.[1] Hawley would realize that sooner or later Carlisle and the trustees, now temporarily reconciled, would hear of the business, and act accordingly. It was important, therefore, that he should visit England in order to consolidate the position with his new patron. As usual his forecast proved correct. Carlisle had already obtained a royal commission for his recall,[2] and was securing the King's assent to the appointment of one Sergeant-Major Henry Huncks as Governor in his stead.

Hawley acted with characteristic promptitude. Counting on the slipshod methods of the King and his officials he posed as being still Governor of Barbados, and succeeded in obtaining a special commission of inquiry to all plantations as to the excessive quantity of tobacco grown there, a matter of particular interest to Charles I.[3] Furnished with this expedient he departed in haste for Barbados, arriving, as he had hoped, before Governor Huncks. Straightway he sought to gain the planters by adopting the surprising role of a champion of democracy. After purging the island officials of potential enemies he chose a number of burgesses to represent the freeholders, ' and settled a Parliament '.[4] A day of mercy, too, was decreed,

island then we have hitherto had ; ' Letters and Papers of the Verney Family (copy, Davis Collection, Box 6, R. C. I.). Lord Dorchester's suggestion, written after the Restoration, that Warwick claimed as a trustee of the first Earl, is obviously incorrect.

[1] C.O. 1/10, Nos. 12 and 13 (P. R. O.).

[2] *Cal. Col.* 1574–1660, p. 292 (Petition of Hawley's wife to the King). [3] Ibid. 1574–1660 (27th March); p. 291.

[4] It is noteworthy that from that day until this Barbadians have continuously enjoyed representative government.

and all prisoners awaiting trial were released. It is hardly surprising that the Parliament thus chosen elected Hawley as Governor, nor that the name and authority of the Earl of Carlisle was forthwith treated 'with the utmost scorn'. Hawley, in fact, was using the name of Warwick, and the detestation with which the settlers regarded the Carlisle proprietorship, to make himself absolute.

When, therefore, Huncks arrived in June 1639 his reception was anything but cordial. His demand to be allowed to read his commission before the Assembly of freeholders was refused. Permission to address a select company of Hawley's adherents was all that he could secure : as to his commission, 'they would take tyme to think of it'. 'I presented them', reported Huncks, 'ye Kinges Letter, wch they did extremely slight, bidding me lay it on the Table.' When Huncks refused to part with his commission, Hawley ordered it to be taken from him by force, declaring that the propriety belonged to the Earl of Warwick.[1] Realizing that the position was temporarily hopeless, Huncks sailed to Antigua, leaving Hawley to consolidate his position.[2]

Warwick, however, had not 'made good' at home, and retribution swiftly fell upon the head of his lieutenant. In reply to a list of thirteen charges against Hawley, presented by the Carlisle trustees, the King, in December 1639, appointed four commissioners, to whom were entrusted royal letters declaring the validity of Hunck's commission, and requiring Hawley to surrender his office forthwith.[3]

[1] C.O. 1/10, No. 27. 'Copy of Sar^nt Mai^or Huncks, his lre to my Lord ye Ea. of Carlisle, dated 11th July 1639' (P. R. O.).

[2] *Cal. Col.* 1574–1660, pp. 299–300.

[3] Ibid., p. 305. Among the thirteen charges against Hawley it was stated that he had deprived Peter Hay, the Receiver-General of taxes for the Earl of Carlisle, of 6,300 lb. of tobacco which he had collected, threatning him 'that if he would not submitt to the

Upon the arrival of the commissioners in June 1640 Hawley realized that the game was up, and quietly resigned the government with an acknowledgement of his offence. His estates were sequestrated, and he himself sent home as a prisoner in the custody of Commissioner John Hammer. The planters themselves viewed his departure with regret : they had no love for the Carlisle régime, and had been prepared to stand by him as a constitutional ruler.[1]

Major Huncks, summoned from Antigua, was received and settled in office. His reign, however, was a short one. In 1641 he was recalled to England to answer certain charges, and died shortly afterwards.[2]

It was only to be expected that the foregoing years of feud and conspiracy would seriously hamper the development of the young colony. The chief resulting handicap was the scarcity of provisions. Sir William Courteen had regularly supplied his settlers with cargoes of food ; but under the Carlisle proprietorship the colony fared very badly in this respect. 'A pigge six weekes old', wrote a visitor in 1634, 'was at £5 sterling, a turke 50s., and a chicken at 6s. Beefe or

Orders, then newly made at the said Assembly, he should be served as Sr. William Tufton was wth a Bullett in his bosome'. Another charge was to the effect that he had boasted 'that he had more authority on the said Island wth his Staffe wch hee bore in his hand on ye way, then y^or ma^tre the Kinge of England' (C.O. 1/10, No. 28, P. R. O.).

¹ Cf. *Acts of the Privy Council*, I, No. 448 (Petition of the Barbadian planters). After trial by the Privy Council Hawley was by order of the Board reinstated in his possessions, and returned to take an active part as a councillor in island affairs. He died in July 1677 at the ripe age of 80 (*Cal. Col.* 1574–1660, p. 313) ; 1677–1680, No. 317. Cf. 'Deeds', Nos. 1 and 2. The Commissioners at Barbados discovered that during his governorship he had gradually sold 5,000 acres of the Carlisle demesne land (Davis Collection, Box 6, R. C. I.).

² These charges Huncks seems to have refuted. 'He had returned', wrote John Scott, 'in the same quallity had not death p^revented' Sloane MSS. 3662, f. 60b).

Mutton they have none.'[1] Moreover, demoralization
was apparent. In 1631 another visitor had remarked,
' You are all younge men and of good desent, if you
would but bridle ye excess of drinking together w^th
ye quarrelsome conditions of your fyery spiritts. . . .
Ye worst of all was your manifold quarrells. Your
younge and hott bloods, should nott have oyle added
to encrease ye flame, but rather cold water to quench it.'
Their servants, too, he added, were a lazy lot, ready for
any excuse to hang round his ship ' to avoyde labour '.[2]

Yet despite such difficulties Barbados was within
ten years of its settlement a flourishing plantation,
producing large crops of tobacco, cotton, and indigo.
Even in 1628 Robert Alsopp was able to inform the
Earl of Carlisle that Barbados and St. Christopher
had already exported 100,000 lb. of tobacco, in
addition to 2,700 lb. from the Earl's private estates.[3]
Cotton growing came into prominence about two
years later,[4] and increased so rapidly that by about 1640
cotton and cotton-wool ranked equal with tobacco
among Barbadian exports.[5]

[1] *The Calvert Papers*, iii, p. 26.

[2] ' Voyage of Sir Henry Colt ', printed in *Colonizing Expeditions to
the West Indies* (ut supra).

[3] *Cal. Dom.* i, p. 411. This crop sold for £37 10s. per 1,000 lb.

[4] ' But now the trade of cotton fills them all with hope.' ' Voyage
of Sir Henry Colt ' (1631), op. cit.

[5] The extent of cotton growing may be estimated from the following deeds of sale :

    (i) Sale of 100 Acres of land by J. Perrott to Capt. Richard Peirce
        for 10,000 lb. of Cotton. June 25, 1641 (Deeds, vol. ii,
        pp. 422–3, Davis Collection, Box 1, R. C. I.).

    (ii) Sale of 50 Acres for ' eleven thousand five hundred pounds
        of merchantable cotton wooll '. Feb. 25, 1641 (Deeds, vol. i,
        p. 270), ibid.

    (iii) On 23rd June 1640 a plantation was appraised at 36,000 lb.
        of cotton, the dwelling house at 2,000 lb., and ' the Cotton
        House, boarded all over ' at 4,000 lb. (vol. i, p. 13).

Tobacco and cotton were accepted as equivalent currency at this
time, all fines and taxes being payable in either commodity.

This rapid expansion had been largely due to the trade facilities provided by Dutch and other European merchants, who supplied Barbados with salted provisions, clothing, and equipment at cheaper rates than the traders from England. Such intercourse between an English colony and foreign powers was directly opposed to the nationalistic conceptions of the age, but it continued in the case of Barbados, despite the efforts of the home authorities to prevent it. The latter considered reasonably enough that since the planting of a colony required great expense and trouble, its produce should be exclusively enjoyed by the Mother Country. The idea of excluding the foreigner had not yet been elaborated into a Navigation Act, but already spasmodic efforts were made to enforce the principle. In 1634, for example, an attempt was made to drive out the foreign trader from Barbados by means of high tariffs. Acting under instructions from home Governor Hawley issued an Order in Council, ' That all Dutch, French and other strange ships that come to Anchor here, for Relief, Refreshment or Trade should pay to the Governor twenty shillings in money, or goods to the value, and seaven per cent on all the Goods which they vended '.[1]

Frequent orders also were issued to naval commanders to compel all captains of ships coming from the plantations ' to give bond to bring their vessels and lading, without breaking bulk, into the port of London, or some other port of the kingdom, there to enter and unlade their goods '.[2] Thus, in the logbook of Sir John Pennington for 1634 there is the following entry : ' Wee sent one of our Master Mates and 6 men aboarde the *Alexander* that came from the Barbados, with order to carry her up to London, the

[1] *Memoirs*, p. 18 ; Sir John Harvey in 1630 discovered forty Dutch vessels at the Cape de Verd Islands, bound for the West Indies (*Cal. Col.* 1574–1660, p. 113). [2] *Cal. Col.* 1574–1660, p. 125.

Captain beinge minded notwithstandinge his bond to goe over for Holland.' Again a year later he wrote : ' The Master of a ship coming from the Barbadoes, with fusticke and cotton entered into a bond to carry her with all her goods to London.' [1]

This policy of concentrating the colonial trade into the home market was one of the reasons why the English Government so strongly discouraged the cultivation of tobacco in the plantations. It was realized that the production of crops other than foodstuffs, made the colonists dependent on the Dutch and other strangers for their provisions. In 1637 the King wrote pointing this out to the Carlisle trustees, and ordering them to prohibit all trade with strangers.[2] That this step produced the desired result is evident from a statement by Sir Thomas Warner two years later. ' Through the restraint on tobacco ', he wrote, ' the poor planters are debarred from free trade, and unable to furnish themselves with necessaries, much less to buy ammunition.' [3]

Restrictions, indeed, were numerous and imposts heavy. Already, in 1631, an Order in Council had required the Earl of Carlisle to limit the planting of tobacco in St. Christopher and Barbados until such time as more staple commodities might be raised there. None other than sweet, wholesome, and well-packed tobacco was to be exported, and that to London alone.[4] The severe limitation of the market quickly

---

[1] H.M.C. x., Lord Muncaster's MSS., Part IV, pp. 285–6 and 292. Cf. *Acts of the Privy Council*, I, No. 292 (6th April 1632) : ' Whereas we have beene informed that divers shipps and vessells comeing from St. Christophers and Barbathoes, the Caribee Islands etc. . . . doe goe into forraingne Countries with theire goods and marchandize to his Majesties great losse and preiudice in his Customes. . . , the Lords of the Admiralty are required to take effective measures to compel such ships to come to London, or some other of the Ports of this Kingdome.'

[2] *Cal. Col.* 1574–1660, p. 251.   [3] Ibid., p. 295.

[4] In 1631 heavy import duties were also imposed—2*s.* per lb. on

lowered the value of tobacco to ' so base a price ', that the Barbadian planters were in considerable distress. But appeals to the home authorities for an alteration in their policy met with no response. The statesmen of the time considered that the welfare of the colonies as well as that of the Mother Country demanded the suppression of tobacco. The young colony must be made strong and self-sufficient for its own sake in order that it might best contribute to the strength and self-sufficiency of the Empire as a whole. It was the parental coercion of the mercantile policy.

Thus, distracted by internal dissension, with a limited home market and free trade with foreigners prohibited, the Barbadian planters were working under great difficulties, and development was retarded. But the cloud of civil war, about to burst over England, was to prove a blessing in disguise to the island colony. The temporary disappearance of England as a market for her goods allowed Barbados fully to avail herself of the trading facilities offered by the Dutch. With their aid she became in less than ten years one of the chief sugar-producing colonies in the New World. At the same time the fortune of war brought to the island Roundhead and Cavalier gentlemen, seeking peace and an opportunity to repair shattered fortunes ; a type of colonist which soon raised Barbados to a position of political as well as economic importance. There was much truth in the name of ' Little England ' which these refugees gave to their new home. Unfortunately, they brought with them the problems and the strife of the old country no less than its brains and activity.

Spanish tobacco, 1s. on Barbadian, and 9d. on Virginian. A year later, however, that on Barbadian tobacco was reduced to 6d., and Virginian to 4d., because these varieties were ' but of a meane condition ' (*Acts of the Privy Council*, I, No. 291). For restrictions on the importation of tobacco, see ibid., Nos. 269, 270, and 380.

II

KING OR PARLIAMENT ?

§ 1. *Barbados as an Independent State* (1641–50)

As already noted the first Barbadian ' Parliament ',
to which elected burgesses were summoned, had been
established by Hawley in 1639. The earlier assemblies
called by Henry Powell and others had been primary
meetings of all freeholders, not of elected representatives.[1] Thus the statement, frequently repeated, that
Philip Bell, who became Governor in 1641, was the
founder of the elective chamber in Barbados is incorrect. What he actually did do was to raise the assembly
from being a merely advisory body into one which
possessed the right of initiating legislation.

Hawley too had been responsible for important
judicial organization. In respect of civil causes the
island had been divided by him into four precincts,
each with a court of Common Pleas presided over by
a judge and four assistants. From these, cases could
be transferred to the Governor's Court of Appeal.
Minor offences were dealt with by Justices of the
Peace at their Quarter Sessions, while more important
criminal causes were tried at the Grand Sessions, held
at Bridgetown three times a year.[2]

Thus the work of Philip Bell was the consolidation
and expansion of an executive and judicial system
already in existence. The six large parishes into which
the island had been divided by Sir William Tufton,

[1] Cf. Election of Councils by G. Powell, junior, and Henry Hawley
(Rawlinson MSS. C. 94, ff. 1 and 4b respectively).

[2] *Memoirs of the First Settlement*, pp. 15–16.

were now split up into eleven smaller parishes.
Churches were built, and the vestries empowered to
nominate and displace their ministers, allowing them
a yearly salary from a parochial levy of one pound of
tobacco per acre.[1] These eleven divisions also formed
convenient political units. Bell ordained that each
parish should elect two burgesses for the Assembly.
The new chamber was recognized as a component of
the legislature, with definite powers and rules of procedure.[2] The powers of a Court of Chancery were
reserved to the Governor and Council alone, ' to hear
and determine all writs of errors, petitions of grievances, and all other equitable matters whatsoever '.[3]
Other laws enumerated fines, specified the security to
be given against fraud by public officials, and laid a
mass of local business on the shoulders of the parochial
Justices.[4] The militia too was reorganized, and a
proportional land tax levied to pay for the upkeep ;
with the result that within a few years Ligon was able
to write of ' 10,000 foot, as good men and as resolute
as any in the world and a 1,000 good horse '.[5]

As regards his ecclesiastical policy Bell imitated the
unbending attitude of the Anglican Church at home.
About the year 1647 an Act was passed condemning
unorthodox conventicles, held by ' divers opinionated
and self conceited persons ', and calling upon the
people to ' conform to the government and discipline
of the Church of England ' as by law established.[6]

[1] Ligon's *Account*, p. 100, ut supra. See Appendix B.
[2] *Memoirs*, p. 24 (London, 1732). In 1634 the church at Barbados,
as in the other plantations, had been placed under the jurisdiction of
the Bishop of London, at the suggestion of Archbishop Laud. Cf.
Ligon's *Account*, pp. 100-1 ; also *Laws of Barbados*, ed. Rawlins,
London, 1669.
[3] *Laws of Barbados*, No. 8, London (1855 edition).
[4] Ibid., Nos. 3, 4, and 5.   [5] Ligon, p. 100.
[6] *Laws of Barbados*, No. 15 (published by J. Barlett, by order of
the Lords Commissioners of Trade and Plantations, London, 1732).

Turbulent schismatics were shown the error of their ways at the whipping-stool.[1] By another enactment, very much on the lines of the later Clarendon Code,[2] regular church services and catechizing of the youth by the parochial clergy was insisted on. Family prayers every morning and evening, and attendance twice every Sunday at church for all within a radius of two miles, and twice a month for those beyond, was ordered under heavy fines. The absence of a white servant from service was punished according as the fault lay with himself or with his master. Constables and churchwardens were required, ' in some time of Divine Service any Sunday, to walk and search Taverns, alehouses, victualling houses, or other houses, where they doe suspect lewd and debauched company to frequent. And if they shall find any drinking, swearing, gameing or otherwise misdemeaning themselves, that forthwith they shall apprehend such Persons, and bring them to the Stocks there to be imprisoned the space of Four Hours.' [3]

While this process of regulation and co-ordination was being slowly effected the Governor was steering a most difficult course in the external relations of the island. For some years the friction between Charles I and his parliaments had been steadily increasing, until matters were brought to a crisis in 1642 by the action of the Long Parliament in taking the customs-duties out of the hands of the King.[4] When open

[1] ' All this time our governor received letters from Philip Bell, Esq., Governor of Barbados, complaining of the distracted condition of that Island in regard of divers sects of formalists sprung up there and their turbulent practices, which had forced him to proceed against some of them by banishment and others of mean quality by whipping . . . ' (Winthrop's *Journal*, 1620–49, pp. 142–3).

[2] I continue to use this convenient name for the ecclesiastical legislation of 1661–5, though it is now well recognized that much of it was distasteful to the Lord Chancellor.

[3] *Laws*, No. 16.

[4] *Cal. Dom.* 1641–3, p. 460. Also *Lords Journal*, v, p. 401a.

hostilities broke out, both parties immediately endeavoured to obtain control over the colonial empire.
But while their energies were absorbed in the campaigns at home, neither side was in a position to
coerce ; and this the colonies fully realized.

Parliament on its side applied itself to the problem
at an early stage. As colonial questions cropped up
temporary committees were appointed to consider
them and to report. On 20th October 1643 a petition
of merchants trading to Barbados was ' referred to
a Cōmitee, and (order made) that Mr. Philip Bell,
now governor there, be continued Governor there,
till the House take further order '.[1] As the Earl of
Carlisle was a royalist his estates were sequestrated,
and the proprietorship of the Caribees assumed by
Parliament,[2] who on 2nd November 1643 appointed
a standing committee with comprehensive powers.[3]
At the head of the committee was the Earl of Warwick, as Governor-in-Chief and Lord High Admiral
of all islands and plantations ' within the bounds and
upon the coasts of America '. The committee itself
consisted of five members of the House of Lords and
twelve of the House of Commons, the latter including
such famous names as Sir Henry Vane, Sir Arthur
Heselrigg, John Pym, and Oliver Cromwell. Parliament at the same time endeavoured to secure obedience
to the committee by granting the colonies a large
measure of self-government.[4] This combined show of
coercion with promise of privilege was, as the ordinance
admitted, the outcome of information received ' that
there hath been lately procured from his majesty
several grants under the Great seal for erecting some
new Governors and Commanders ', in the West

[1] *Commons Journals*, iii, p. 283.
[2] Cf. ibid., pp. 291 and 294.
[3] *Lords Journals*, vi, p. 291a and b (' Ordinance Concerning the
Govt. of the Plantations in the West Indies ').
[4] Ibid.

Indies. It was about this time that Charles I issued a commission to the Earl of Marlborough as his representative in those parts, which was accepted at St. Christopher and Antigua.

Philip Bell however at Barbados was not so easily enticed. A policy of strict neutrality was felt to be the only possible one by planters who depended for their existence on supplies from England. 'And therefore,' writes John Scott, 'like subtil Statesmen they temporised with al new Commissions, came they either from the Parliament or late King.'[1] The royal commission brought by Marlborough was therefore respectfully refused,[2] while the attentions of Parliament met with no better reception.

Within a few weeks of its establishment the Warwick Committee opened its campaign by passing 'several Acts under their Hands and Seals for exempting the Inhabitants of the Caribee Islands from all Taxes and common charges, other than what should be necessary for the support of the Government, and defraying the Public Occasions of the Islands'. The inhabitants were also authorized to elect their respective Governors, subject to the committee's approval; and were ordered to oppose the admittance of any unauthorized Governor.[3] The next step was taken on 1st December 1643, when Warwick dispatched a letter to the Governor and Council of Barbados, demanding their allegiance, and enclosing copies of the ordinance which established the Warwick Committee, and of their subsequent enactments.

The Barbadian reply stated their case explicitly. They were not in a position to aid either of the

---

[1] Egerton MSS. (Brit. Mus.) 2395, f. 48 : 'A Briefe Relation of the Beginning and Ending of the Troubles of the Barbados, wth the true Causes thereof', by A. B.

[2] *Lords Journals*, ix, p. 51b, 'Report concerning the Caribee Islands'.   [3] Ibid., p. 51a.

contending parties in England ; yet they themselves depended for their existence on the supply of provisions and other necessaries from the home market. They wished therefore to be entirely impartial. They had not accepted the commission brought by the Earl of Marlborough from his Majesty ; and at the same time they were ' giving all favourable and friendly reception unto all Merchants, and seamen which arrived here from any of the Parliament's Ports '.[1] And with this adroit delivery of ' an answer answerless', the harassed Parliament had to be content.

On 23rd December 1644 the Commons agreed that upon payment of a fine of £800 the sequestration of the Earl of Carlisle's estate should be taken off ;[2] and an ordinance to that effect passed the Lords on 13th February 1645.[3] After some debate a declaration was approved on 5th September of the same year confirming the Earl's rights to the Caribee Islands.[4] With Carlisle's authority now allied to its own the Warwick Committee, on 27th March 1646, wrote to Barbados commanding obedience to the reinstated proprietor and an open profession of allegiance to the Parliament.

The second answer of the Governor and Council was no less emphatic than the first had been. They expressed their willingness to be serviceable to the kingdom, their honour for the Parliament, ' but their yet allegiance to the King ' ; and therefore desired to be spared a little till things were settled. They added that now they were even less in a position to submit than formerly, ' by reason of a general Declaration of the Inhabitants subscribed by every Parish, wherein they express their several Resolutions, not to receive any Alteration of Government, until God

---

[1] *Lords Journals*, ix, p. 51b.
[2] *Commons Journals*, iii, pp. 709 and 732.
[3] *Lords Journals*, vii, p. 192b.
[4] Ibid., ix, p. 49a.

should be so merciful unto us as to unite the King and Parliament '.[1] This Declaration, they observed, had been occasioned by a rumour that fresh commissions were about to be sent out from both the Parliament and his Majesty.

The further proceedings of Warwick and his commissioners were not calculated to mollify the Barbadian Government. The parliamentary envoys who had brought over this new demand at the same time presented two other commissions, one of which purported to be a grant of liberty of conscience to all inhabitants in matters of religion. The Governor and Council replied that the freedom of worship therein provided had always been allowed in Barbados. ' And if any man here have suffered (Minister or lay) either by Deprivation, Banishment, or Imprisonment, it hath been for preaching Blasphemies or Heresies, or for maintaining or promulgating known Errors in the Fundamentals of Faith.' [1]   But because there were many sects in the island which under pretence of liberty might take occasion to deny all ordinances, including the observances of the Lord's Day, they therefore required all to come to the public preaching ; and that was deemed sufficient.[2] In other words they had laid down their own system of limited toleration and they meant to stick to it, despite the Roundheads of Whitehall.

The third commission presented by the envoys was even more tactless. Certain masters of ships, who had arrived at Barbados, were authorized to co-operate with such in the island as should declare for the Parliament, in order to deny Trade with all who ' had fallen to the Enemy '.   They were further commissioned ' to call the Governor and some of the

---

[1] *Lords Journals*, ix, p. 51b.

[2] *Hutchinson Papers*, i, p. 175. The Rev. James Parker, Minister of Barbados, to Governor Winthrop of Massachusetts.

Council into question, for some pretended acts of injustice here past'.[1] As a Barbadian minister remarked at the time, the establishment of such ' inferior ' and biased characters as a court of inquiry exasperated instead of conciliating the colonists, who were predominately royalist in sentiment.

Writing in 1646 to Governor Bell, with whom he had long been acquainted, Warwick laid before him the triumphant position of the Parliament, pressing him ' to consider seriously of what is propounded in ye generall letter, ye holding out an oportunitie to procure the former neutralitye of the Barbados to be forgotten ; wch if it should continue will not possibly admit at this time a tolerable Interpretation'.[2]

Much less dictatorial in tone had been an earlier letter by the same writer.

' The fruites of o^r ancient acquaintance will best appeare now on y^{or} part by comunicating y^{or} knowledge of me and some other persons of hono^r joyned wth me, to those in y^{or} Island to whom we may be lesse knowne. I doubt not but you will easily admit an assurance of the Parliament's faithfull and hono^{ble} Intencons both to his Mat^{ie} and the Plantacons in the Course by them now settled.'[3]

The sweeping victories gained by the Parliament forces in the 1645 campaign had thus made the Council of State feel more sure of itself when dealing with the colonies.

Later in 1646 Warwick made another effort. ' I was in hopes,' he wrote to Governor Bell, ' ere this

[1] *Hutchinson Papers*, I, p. 175, and *Lords Journals*, ix, p. 51a. Similar orders were sent to Nevis, Antigua, and Santa Cruz, and were returned unanswered.

[2] Stowe MSS. (Brit. Mus.) 184, f. 124a. This and other letters between the Earl of Warwick and the Barbadian Government provide invaluable information for these first years of the Civil War, and do not appear to have been hitherto published.

[3] Ibid. The majority of these letters are undated, but internal evidence determines the matter within a few months in each case.

time to have received advertisem^t of the Islands
rendring a perfect obedience to the Parliament, w^{ch}
woulde certainly have much advantaged and secured
the Interest and Trade of the Inhabitants.' After
assuring Bell that his friendship for him and for
Barbados in general makes him desire nothing but
their true happiness and prosperity, he concludes on
a sterner note. 'You will I suppose by those that are
now going from hence be informed of the true State
of Affaires here, wch if well considered may rationally
and stronglie advise the deserting of what ever may
disoblige the Parliament's Care and respect towards
yo^u, whereof I have you seriously to consider.' [1]

Towards the end of 1646 Mr. Drax, a Roundhead
and one of the foremost planters in the island, wrote
to the Earl of Warwick describing the fixed resolution
of Barbados to abide by its neutrality, and affirming
his own loyalty to the parliamentary cause. In reply
Warwick expressed the hope that the hopeless position
of the royalists in England would induce the island to
submit. In that case Parliament would consider
'how to raise the Island to a more improved and
flourishing condition '.[2]

Meanwhile, events vitally affecting Barbados were
taking place in London. On 2nd March 1647 a pass
was granted for the Earl of Carlisle to go over and
assume the rule of the Caribee Islands,[3] a step which
would have terminated the neutrality hitherto preserved by Barbados. With the arrival of the proprietor,
backed by the authority of Parliament, the planters
would have been forced to one side or the other ;
hostilities would have broken out and trade been
brought to a standstill. The re-establishment of the
Carlisle proprietorship was also feared by certain
parties in England. On the day when the pass was

---

[1] Stowe MSS. 184, ff. 124b–125a.　　[2] Ibid., 125a.
[3] *Lords Journals*, ix, p. 49b.

granted, two petitions were presented to the Committee for Foreign Plantations. In one of these over eighty creditors of the first Earl of Carlisle stated that, in spite of a decree in Chancery obtained over twenty years ago, no satisfaction had been given by the young Earl for the debts due to them from his father. If the Earl transports himself to Barbados, it ' will be the utter undoing of your Petitioners '. ' The Earl endeavours to go beyond Sea, as Governor of the Islands ; and thereby it will be in his power to divert the whole Profits to what Use he pleaseth, and all the Profits received from many years are not yet accounted for.' [1] The departure of Carlisle was no less dreaded by the merchants and planters in London, whose fortunes were sunk in the Barbadian trade. In their petition they stated that the island had been settled at great hazard and cost to themselves, and now that it had come to some maturity the kingdom might expect considerable benefit from the customs there, and the petitioners some reward for their labours. ' But on the contrary, the whole Plantation would in likelihood perish if Disorders should there arise.' [2]

In conclusion, the merchants went to the root of the matter by attacking the Carlisle proprietorship. They called upon the committee to settle the land tenure of Barbados in free and common socage ; ' and also to hear the Petitioners to offer their Reasons touching the manner of the Government, as may best stand with the quiet of the Peace '.

The truth was that both planter and merchant wished to get rid of any jurisdiction or authority which tended to prejudice their trade interests. It mattered little whether the Earl of Carlisle was a King or

---

[1] *Lords Journals*, ix, p. 49b. By a decree of 20 Charles I the profits of the Caribee Islands had been ordered to be handed over yearly to the Carlisle creditors. ' The humble Petition of William Latham and Eighty other Creditors of the Earl of Carlisle.'

[2] *Lords Journals*, ix, p. 50a ; also Rawlinson MSS. C. 94, f. 22.

Parliament man. The important fact was that proprietary government had exerted a restrictive influence
on the colony's development, and the planters, now
a virtually independent community, had no mind to
return to it.

In consequence of the present agitation the Parliament in March 1647 referred the whole question to
the Plantations Committee, with power to use all
necessary means to examine the validity of the Carlisle
patent, and whether according to a recent Act the late
delinquency of the Earl debarred him from holding
a position of trust, such as Governor of the Caribee
Islands.[1] The merchants and planters then in England
seized the opportunity thus offered ; and proceeded
to build up an elaborate case against the Carlisle
claim.[2] Sworn depositions were obtained from as
many of the original settlers as could be found, by
means of which it was proved that Sir William Courteen
had been first in occupation, and that the proprietors
had never afforded ' the least helpe safety or protection ',[3] but on the contrary had oppressed them by
sending over arbitrary rulers. The committee came
to the unanimous conclusion that the proprietary
right lay with Courteen and his heirs ; but ' noe bodie
moveing in his behalfe [4] they wondered and looked
amazedly one upon another, and being fullie and
sufficiently sattisfied on that particular pointe ', went
on to examine the allegations of misgovernment.

[1] *Commons Journals*, v, p. 105.
[2] Rawlinson MSS. C. 94, ut supra. The proceedings are to be found
in ' Brief Collection of the Depositions of Witnesses . . . in a difference
depending between the merchants and inhabitants of Barbados . . .
and the E. of Carlisle '. Another account which gives in addition the
speech of the counsel in defence of the patent is in Trinity College
Library, Dublin (ut supra).   [3] Rawlinson MSS. C. 94, ff. 4b–5a.
[4] Sir William Courteen had died in 1636, and his son was wandering
in great poverty on the Continent at this time. Egerton MSS. 2395,
f. 602.

The committee's report to Parliament finally advised the concession of only half the planters' demands. They resolved, ' that the going of the Earl of Carlisle to the Charibee Islands will tend to the disturbance thereof, the Hindrance of Trade, and the Discouragem^t of the Planters, and will endanger the Defection of the Planters from the Parliament '.[1] His proprietary title was left undisturbed, but actual control was still in the hands of the Committee for Plantations.

Meanwhile, in spite of all efforts to continue trade relations with royalists and parliamentarians alike, Barbados found her commerce with England seriously curtailed. Capital usually invested in ventures overseas was now concentrated on war expenditure at home. The labour which normally produced foodstuffs or manufactured clothing and implements for the colonies, was now engaged in fighting battles. Limited production accordingly forced the colonist to buy at high rates.[2] Moreover, the attempt to trade with two hostile parties inevitably proved a failure. Cavalier and Roundhead traders fought on the high seas, with the result that few of either side ever reached Barbados.

In 1644 Warwick issued letters of marque authorizing not only the seizure of royalist ships, but of all vessels found trading with places which had not accepted the Parliament's authority.[3] And in 1646 he appointed a number of master mariners and others at Barbados to see that there was no trade there ' with such as had fallen to the enemy '.[4] On the other hand, in January 1644, a parliamentarian named Miles Causton, master of the ship *George*, was seized by royalist vessels on his way from the West Indies, and taken to Dartmouth, where his ship and goods were

---

[1] *Lords Journals*, ix, p. 53d.   [2] Cf. H.M.C. vi, 1, p. 58.
[3] *Cal. Dom.* 1644–5, pp. 627–8.
[4] *Lords Journals*, ix, p. 51a.

confiscated as prize—' they saying that all Londoners were rebels '. Whilst at Dartmouth he saw a fleet of royalist men-of-war ready to put out to sea on a raid against parliament shipping at the Canary Islands and the Azores, and thence to Barbados and the other Caribee Islands.[1]

The regular trade routes between the plantations and the Mother Country being thus thrown into confusion, Barbados was obliged to find other marts for its merchandize, in order to obtain commodities which the island itself did not produce. The most urgent need was for provisions. The island, being devoted to other crops, only produced sufficient food to supply a fraction of its population. This difficulty was solved by opening up trade with New England [2] and by increasing the connexion with the Dutch.

From the time when the Dutch Governor Groenewegen assisted Henry Powell to plant the island, a profitable connexion had been steadily maintained with the merchants of Holland and Zeeland, in spite of the efforts of the English men-of-war to compel West Indian ships to fulfil their bonds to go for London.[3]

The close ties, both economic and political, with which the Mother Country had endeavoured to bind the colonies to herself in order to build up a centralized, self-contained empire, were now quickly broken. To the no small chagrin of the English merchants free trade was established with foreign nations. As early as February 1645 the former complained to the Council of State that ' divers Worldly-minded Persons, wilfully neglect to ship their Merchandize in English Vessels, but imploy House-Moores and Danes, and drive their

[1] H.M.C. xiii, 1, Portland MSS., i, p. 168.
[2] Trade with New England rapidly became one of the prime factors in the commercial life of the island. See chapter vii, below.
[3] See chapter i.

Trade in Foreign Vessells'.[1] [English merchants for their own interest should have agreed, under the circumstances, to receive colonial produce through any channel.

In 1647 the direct trade between Holland and Barbados provoked the Earl of Warwick to address a letter of protest to the Governor and Council, though his obvious weakness obliged him to confine himself to a general admonition. After pointing out the damage inflicted on English trade by 'ye trade and habitācon of the Dutch in y^or Island', he continued : 'I shall not for the psent prescribe any positive rule for the remedying of this inconvenience.' He would only persuade them to consider the situation and report their desires to the Plantation Committee who would manage the business, 'wth all due respect to that nacon and to the good correspondence wch we desire to maintaine each wth other'.   He concludes with what was little more than a pious hope ; ' For the mean time you doe well to cherish y^or oune countrymen by giveing them all just advantage of Trade before Strangers.' [2]   Under the circumstances it is hardly surprising that such injunctions were ignored. The Dutch traders were the planters' only hope ; and such was their monopoly during the Civil War that even when charging high prices, they could still undersell the scarce commodities from England.[3]

[1] *Lords Journals*, ix, p. 185a and b.
[2] Stowe MSS. 184 (Warwick Correspondence), f. 126b.
[3] A Barbadian planter, writing in 1651, gives the following price-list : ' The Dutch sell their Commodityes after ye rate of a penny for a pound of sugar, browd-brimd white or black hatts yields here 120 lb. of sugar, and 140 lb. and some 160 lb. ; Browne-thred is at 36 or 40 lb. of sugar a pound ; thred stockens will yield 40 lb. of sugar a paire ; mens shoes 16 lb. new fashioned shoes 25 or 30 lb. ye paire ; pinnes at great rates and much desyred, a man may have for them what he desyreth ; an Ancher of Brandewyn 300 lb. of sugar . . . a yard of good whyted osenbridge linnen at 6 or 7 lb. of sugar. Holland of twelve pence, if fyne, will yeeld 12 or 14 lb. of sugar a yard ; and

The extent of the foreign traffic may be estimated from Ligon's description in 1647 of the Barbadian imports. He speaks of biscuits and barrels of meal from Holland, of French and Spanish wines from the Madeiras and the Azores, 'and from France Brandy, which is extream strong'; beef also from Holland, from New England, Virginia, 'and some from Russia', and 'Pork from all these places, with the most sortes of salt fish'.[1]

Hitherto the economic growth of Barbados had been retarded by the fact that the staple commodity was tobacco, in respect of which Barbados laboured under peculiar disabilities. In addition to the restrictive policy dictated by popular opinion against tobacco in the time of Charles I, the island (together with St. Christopher) had been subjected to heavier duties than those levied on American tobacco. It is true that Spanish and other foreign tobaccos were virtually excluded by a combined duty of 2s. per lb.; yet the Caribee Islands, as the home Government had intended, could not long face the competition of the northern plantations. And although the Long Parliament, on assuming control over the customs in 1642, assessed all colonial tobacco at a uniform rate of fourpence a pound,[2] other considerations had in the meantime relegated the tobacco industry to a subordinate position among the productions of the island.

Furthermore, the value of all tobaccos was falling so rapidly, owing to increasing output from America, that in 1646 the average price was only three farthings a pound.[3]

all Commodytyes are accordingly.' Any one investing £300 in such goods for Barbados makes a profit of 'three for one'. Tanner MSS. (Bodleian) 54, ff. 153–4.

[1] Ligon's *True and Exact Account*, pp. 33 and 37.

[2] *Lords Journals*, vi, pp. 351b, 352b; *Commons Journals*, vi, pp. 333–4.

[3] Sloane MSS. 3662, f. 59, 'John Scott's Description'; cf. J. Davies,

Under these conditions the planters suffered considerably, their mode of life being one of poverty and indigence. 'Hard labour and want of victuals had so much depressed their spirits, as they were come to a declining and yielding condition.'[1]

Learning from the Spanish Main that an acre of land would normally produce three times as much sugar as tobacco, the planters at Barbados determined to devote their energies to this profitable manufacture. The sugar cane had been known in the island since the days of the Powells ; but hitherto it had only been used for brewing ' fire water '.

The first Barbadian to plant his fields with canes seems to have been Colonel Holdip, about the beginning of the fourth decade.[2] Others, in similar difficulties with their tobacco crops, followed his example, obtaining cane shoots, implements, and general instructions from Brazil, then in the hands of the Dutch. Their first efforts however were discouraging ; ' the secrets of the work being not well understood, the Sugars they made were very inconsiderable, and little worth for two or three years '.[3] [Enterprising planters now wisely betook themselves to Brazil, where long experience had taught the best methods of manufacture. Here they learnt how to rectify their first blunders. Instead of planting the canes upright in separate holes they were shown how to lay the canes along shallow trenches. Each knot in this way produced an independent shoot ; while the continuous root offered much greater resistance to gales. Other points, such as the right time and the proper method

History of the Caribee Islands, London, 1666. ' At the beginning, all the forreign Inhabitants of the Caribbees apply'd themselves wholly to the culture of Tobacco, whereby they made a shift to get a competent livelihood, but afterwards the abundance that was made bringing down the price of it ', they turned to other manufactures (p. 187, chapter iv, Book II). [1] Ligon's *Account*, p. 41.
[2] Sloane MSS. 3662, f. 60b. [3] Ligon's *Account*, p. 85.

of cutting the canes ; the type of grinding process which obtained the maximum quantity of sugar juice ; and the arrangement of the coppers for boiling and purifying, were observed and put into practice on the plantations in Barbados. The inspiring force of the enterprise seems to have been ' the great industry and more thriving Genious of Sr James Drax '.[1]

In September 1647 Ligon reported, ' we found many sugar works set up and at work ; but yet the sugars they made were but bare Muscavadoes,[2] and few of them merchantable commodities ; so moist and full of molasses, and so ill cured as they were hardly worth the bringing home for England '.[3] By the year 1650, however, considerable experience had been gained, and a rapidly increasing quantity of sugar was exported to European markets. Indeed, the development of the island between 1640–50, a period in which the trade and industry of the Mother Country was almost at a standstill, was phenomenal. After examining the import and export records of Barbados for twenty years, John Scott computed that in 1666 the island was seventeen times as rich as she was before the planting of sugar.[4] Emphasizing the same fact Ligon instances the land value of 500 acres belonging to Major Hilliard. Before the introduction of the new manufacture the plantation was worth £400 ; yet in 1648 one half of it was sold for £7,000. ' And it is evident all the land here, which has been employed to that work, hath found the like improvement.'[5] In 1650 the total value of the crops for a season of twenty months was calculated at £3,097,800.[6]

---

[1] Sloane MSS. 3662, f. 60b. Drax was knighted by authority of the Parliament in 1659.

[2] Muscavadoes was the name applied to brown unrefined sugar.

[3] Ligon's *Account*, pp. 85–8.

[4] ' John Scott's Description ', Sloane MSS. 3662, f. 59a.

[5] Ligon, p. 86, op. cit.

[6] Ibid., p. 96. The growing prosperity of the island is also

These were the days when fortunes were made rapidly.[1] Later when the supply approximated more nearly to the demand, and competition became keener, planters were glad to get a quarter of that price.

This sudden expansion of a poverty-stricken island into one of the wealthiest English plantations in the New World, at a time when the Mother Country was in the throes of civil war, was made possible by the extensive employment of Dutch capital.

' The Holland^{ers} ', we are told, ' that are great encouragers of Plantāçons, did at the first attempt of makeing sugar give great Credit to the most sober Inhabitants, and upon the unhappie Civill warr that brake out in England, they managed the whole Trade in o^r Westerne Collonies, and furnished the Island wth Negroes, Coppers, Stills, and all other things Appertaining to the Ingenious ' (ingenios—sugar works) ' for making of sugar.' [2]

Moreover, these Dutchmen provided the necessary stock and negro labour on credit, and were content to wait for their returns till a crop had been planted, gathered, and converted into merchantable sugar. ' And this I take to bee the True and originall cause of y^e Riches of that Collonie.' [3] As an added advantage the English, on 19th December 1649, fixed a preferential scale of sugar duties in favour of the colonies. Whereas foreigners were to pay an import of $3\frac{1}{2}d$. per lb. on ' whites ', and $2\frac{1}{2}d$. per lb. on ' muscavadoes ', the English planters only paid $3d$. and $2d$. respectively.[4] The home market, however, owing to political events, was about to be entirely closed to Barbados.

remarked on by a visitor there in 1648 : ' Barbadoes have some rich men, having sugar mils, Indico, Ginger, Suchets of Oranges and Lemmons, and bad Tobacco : . . . this Isle is full of gallant people, very civill and well governed, and now no fear of the Spaniard being so populous ' (*Force Tracts*, ii, No. 7, p. 5).
[1] Cf. *History of the Caribee Islands* by J. Davies (London, 1666), p. 9, chap. i, Book I.   [2] Sloane MSS. 3662, f. 59a.
[3] Ibid., f. 59b ; cf. f. 54a.   [4] *Commons Journals*, vi, pp. 333-4.

Curiously enough this access of prosperity, advantageous as it was from an economic point of view, eventually proved to be the main cause of the island's decline. In the days when a variety of small crops were grown the land was occupied in small holdings by a large number of tenants. This system, usual in most young colonies, was partly the result of the original grants of small allotments to the first settlers, and partly owing to the established custom of bestowing ten or twenty acres on each time-expired servant, with which to set up as an independent planter.[1] In this way the island was possessed of a numerous and sturdy ' yeoman ' class, who swelled the ranks of the militia and were indeed the backbone of the colony. With the advent of the sugar industry this healthy condition of affairs was altered. Sugar planting to be successful requires large acres of land and a plentiful supply of cheap labour : the Dutch system of long credits provided the more affluent with the means to obtain both. But the small planter with his few acres and little capital could not face the considerable initial expense of setting up a sugar factory. The land in consequence fell more and more into the hands of a coterie of magnates,[2] whose appropriations ' strangely Depopulated the Island, for the People thus supplanted took all opportunities of transporting themselves to other places ' [3]—to the irreparable loss of the colony. An example of the process was to be found in Captain Waterman's estate, comprising 800 acres, which at one time had been split up among no less than forty proprietors. On the other hand, negro

[1] See chapter vi, ' The Labour Problem '.

[2] Sloane MSS. 3662, f. 59a, ut supra. Cf. the following statement : The richer sort ' by giving Credit to their profuse and sometimes necessitous neighbours on severe Termes, insensibly in few yeares wormed out the greatest p̄t of yᵉ small proprietors '. *Thomason Tracts* (Brit. Mus.) 669, 11 (115).

[3] Sloane MSS. 3662, f. 59a. Chiefly to Carolina.

labour, which was cheaper and more suited to the arduous toil of a sugar plantation than that of Europeans, was increasing at a great pace. In 1645 it was stated that the Barbadians ' have bought this year no lesse than a thousand negroes, and the more they buie, the more they are able to buye, for in a yeare and a halfe they will earne with God's blessing as much as they cost '.[1] The negro population, a source of anxiety and weakness to every colony in which they were introduced, in 1645 numbered 5,680. In 1667 the number had risen to 82,023. This two-fold process, whereby a sturdy English colony was converted into little more than one large sugar factory, owned by a few absentee proprietors and worked by a mass of alien labour, constitutes the main feature of Barbadian history.

Meanwhile, Philip Bell's policy of strict neutrality was becoming increasingly difficult to maintain. As long as the struggle in England was undecided it was possible for a colonial government to keep both parties more or less at arm's length. Hitherto Governor Bell and the more level-headed of the inhabitants had succeeded in preventing disorder. ' And though they are of several persuasions, yet, their discretions ordered everything so well as there never were any fallings out between them.' An unwritten law was observed that, ' whoever nam'd the word " Roundhead " or " Cavalier " should give to all those that heard him a shot and a Turkey, to be eaten at his house that made the forfeit.' [2] Until about the year 1648 generosity and good will were the characteristics of the planters.

Dinner parties, where the best food and wines of

---

[1] Sir George Downing to J. Winthrop, junior (*Winthrop Papers*, p. 536, vol. vi, 4th Series, Massachusetts Hist. Soc.). Also cf. H.M.C. xiii. 1, Portland MSS. i, p. 29. Order of the directors of the English Guinea Company to one of their merchants, to exchange a cargo of spirits at the River Gambia for ' as many lusty negroes or cattle as possible, and send them to the Barbadoes ' (9 Dec. 1651).

[2] Ligon, p. 57.

Europe were to be seen, were the order of the day.[1]
But after the collapse of the royalist cause in 1646 this
happy state of affairs came to an end ; for the storm
centre was to a certain extent transferred to Barbados.

During the years of active warfare there had been
a small but regular stream of immigrants to the island,
consisting chiefly of gentry from the southern counties,
' who had retired thither only to be quiet and to be
free from the noise and oppressions of England '.[2]
As the Mother Country became too hot for unre-
pentant royalists, emigration to Barbados became
the recognized course. Officers also of the King's
army, captured after a battle or at the fall of a town,
regularly preferred the option of going to Barbados
to imprisonment in the Tower.[3] The same course
was more ruthlessly forced upon the royalist rank and
file, and to such an extent that the phrase ' to Barbados
a man ' became proverbial. These unfortunates were
shipped over as servants to a virtual slavery. During
their term of service (usually about five years) they
were the chattels of the planters who had bought
them. Even officers were sometimes included in the
batches of prisoners so transported.[4] The volume of
this tide of immigration to Barbados may be estimated
by the fact that the white population there in 1645
was between eighteen and twenty thousand,[5] and that
five years later it had risen to over thirty thousand.[6]

[1] Davies, *History of the Caribee Islands*, pp. 128–9 (London, 1666).

[2] Clarendon, *History of the Rebellion*, iii, p. 416.

[3] Major Byam and the two Walronds, afterwards so prominent in
the affairs of the island, came over after the capture of Bridgewater.

[4] See *Cal. Col.* 1574–1600, p. 360. After the Restoration numbers
of gentlemen, including such senior officers as colonels, were redeemed
from slavery in Barbados. (For further details of this traffic in political
prisoners see chapter vi, ' The Labour Problem '.)

[5] Sloane MSS. 3662, f. 54a : Davies, *History of the Caribee Islands*,
p. 9, chap. i, Book I.

[6] T.C.D. MSS. (G. 4. 15), p. 182 : 'A brief Description of Barbadoes.'

The influence of the newcomers soon made itself felt. Sprung for the most part from families that were taking a leading part in English politics, and smarting under a sense of personal wrong, they were as determined to enforce and maintain their political principles in Barbados as they had been on the battlefield in England. As a Roundhead contemporary puts it, 'they got into the Principall Offices of that Government, and by degrees drew the People, if not absolutely to decline their former Peaceable Resolutions, yet in great measure to incline to the lost Cavalier party, by making the Current of all Preferments and Authority to stream to those that way affected '.[1] Being apprised of this movement, which was undermining Bell's position of neutrality as well as driving away all hope of a peaceable submission to Parliament, the Earl of Warwick in 1648, by authority of the Plantation Committee, wrote a warning letter to the Council of Barbados. 'I shall expect,' he declared, ' and hereby require that if any persons be removed from theire place of Councell or Comand or otherwise molested in theire estate or liberties upon any apprehension that they had inclinations to submit to that authority' (of Parliament), 'you doe take order for the restitution of theire place.' He concluded with the significant remark, that, 'By y^or conforming hereunto an estimate will be made of y^or love to peace and justice, w^ch ·you seem to ayme at in y^or waiving of all Declaracons on either side in the publique, quarrel of this Nacon.' [2]

The leader of these royalist 'Die-Hards' was Colonel Humphrey Walrond, who had spent a considerable fortune in the King's cause. In all activities

---

[1] Egerton MSS. 2395 (Brit. Mus.), f. 48 : 'A Brief Relation of the Beginning and Ending of the Troubles of the Barbados . . .,' set forth by A. B., a diligent observer of the times (1653).

[2] Stowe MSS. (Brit. Mus.) 184, f. 125b.

he was ably seconded by his brother Edward, a lawyer of the Temple. Endowed with strong personalities, undoubted talents, and a turbulent impatience of all authority but their own, they were a disruptive element in Barbados for the next twenty years. Over the aged Governor and his lady, ' in whom by reason of her quick and industrious spirit lay a great stroak of the Government,' [1] they succeeded in acquiring considerable influence. Their ardour and loyalty to King Charles was perfectly sincere ; but at the same time they were determined, that they, and no other, would sit on his right hand and on his left—on the Barbadian throne at any rate.[2]

One of their first steps was to bring about the banishment of Colonel Guy Molesworth, a dangerous rival in their own party. In order to stir up opposition against him the Walronds played on the fears of Colonel Drax and other Roundhead leaders, by representing Molesworth as a fire-eating royalist, who had declared that ' it would never be well in this island, until the Roundheads Estates were given to the poor Cavaliers '. The plot had the desired effect; Drax and the others combined with the Walronds, and overawing the Governor constituted themselves a court martial. Molesworth was imprisoned for three months, while the court ' endeavoured by tortures and other barbarous proceedings used towards certain persons, to compel them to accuse the petitioner in order that they might have some pretence to take away his life '.[3] Such methods did not produce the required evidence, and the Court had to be content

[1] Egerton MSS. 2395 : A. B.'s ' Relation ', p. 2.

[2] Owing to the fact that all the available authorities for the years 1647–50 are strongly Roundhead in sympathy, it is somewhat difficult to arrive at a just appreciation of the characters and aims of the Walronds, against whom, as the leaders of the ' malignants ', no imputation was considered too bad to be entertained.

[3] *Lords Journals*, xi, p. 297a.

with a sentence of immediate banishment.[1]   The
next step of the royalists towards control of the
government was to procure for their nominee, Major
Byam, the important offices of Treasurer and Master
of the Magazine and Defences.

Such was the situation in 1649 when an envoy from
the Bermudas arrived at the island. Hitherto the
Bermudan colonists had stood neutral, but recently
they had banished all supporters of the Parliament ;
much in the same way as the Guelphs of the fourteenth
century drove out the imperial Ghibellines from
Florence. The Bermudan envoy now proposed an
alliance, offensive and defensive, with Barbados, and
asked for a supply of arms and ammunition, in order
to uphold the royalist cause. The Walrond party
naturally urged the government to accede to the
proposals, for such an action would have committed
Barbados irretrievably. They were faced, however,
with the vehement opposition of Colonel Drax and
the Parliament men. After long debate a compromise was decided upon : the official alliance was
refused, but the envoy was allowed to buy what
ammunition he could get for his money.[2] It was
a decision which reflected the general sentiment of the
inhabitants at that time. Public opinion, while pre-
dominantly royalist, was imbued with a strong desire
for peace and the preservation of the newly acquired
prosperity.

Not content with such moderation, the extremists
now set themselves to frighten the inhabitants into
open hostility by pretending the discovery of a

[1] The small ship in which he and his household departed was seized
at sea by a pirate, ' to his utter undoing and damage of twenty
thousand pounds'. In 1649 he laid a petition before the Council
of State for compensation from Drax and the others, but without
success (*Lords Journals*, xi, p. 297a).

[2] Egerton MSS. 2395, A. B.'s ' Relation ', p. 2.

Roundhead plot. Making use of his influence with Governor Bell, Edward Walrond in his name summoned a number of carefully chosen gentlemen upon whom he could depend as a Committee of Public Safety. Before this gathering he delivered an elaborate speech, in which he alleged the existence of a plot by the 'malignant' or Roundhead party, to drive all royalists from the island and declare for the Parliament.[1] Excited by fears for their personal safety, the members of the committee, adopting Walrond's suggestion, took an oath of secrecy, and by a large majority passed a resolution that all Parliament men must be banished forthwith, and their estates confiscated. After Bell had likewise been sworn to secrecy he was informed of what had passed.

The remaining task was to win over the Assembly, which was known to contain a majority of moderate King's men. At their next sitting the same oath was imposed upon them, and the resolution submitted, which after some debate was confirmed. A joint committee was appointed by the Council and Assembly ' to consider of the quietest and most peaceable wayes of sending these malignants into Exile '.[2]

The general body, however, began to feel that things were going too far. Extirpation of the Roundheads would only weaken the island, and in all probability incur the vengeance of the Parliament. The astute Colonel Modiford, a lawyer and planter, and a politician destined to play a very prominent part in West Indian affairs for the next twenty years, characteristically suggested a policy of moderation. Before the committee was ready with its report on the banishment of Roundheads, he submitted a bill, ' for

[1] Ibid., p. 3. Also, ' A Briefe Relation of the late Horrid Rebellion . . . written at sea by Nicholas Foster ', p. 6, London, 1650 (*Thomason Tracts*, E. 1388–(433)).
[2] A. B.'s ' Relation ', p. 3.

the unity of the Inhabitants of the Island under the Government thereof '.[1]

In an eloquent speech he cited the woes of England, when religious difference had ' given her up as a prey to the rude souldiery ; '[2] and in fine, urged ' so many reasons in order to the peace and plenty of this place, that they all unanimously were so apprehensive of it, as they quite retracted their first Votes, and agreed to the latter way, at wch every man seemed well contented '.[3] According to the compromise thus agreed on, all coercive ecclesiastical legislation was repealed, and whoever henceforth opposed the authority of the Barbadian Government was declared to be ' an enemy to this island and the peace thereof '.[4]

The Walronds, however, did not own themselves so easily beaten. The younger brother, with a lawyer's cunning, persuaded the Council and Assembly to add ' such a misterious oath to the law and such severe caution, and clauses against non conformists and private conventicles '[5] that the peaceful purpose of the Act was nullified. The terms of the oath which was to be subscribed by all whom the Government should select were made intentionally offensive to Commonwealth principles.[6] Furthermore, such heavy penalties were added to the Act, for attending Conventicles, that the breach between Anglican and Independent instead of being healed was made wider than ever.

Hearing of these proceedings by the royalist govern-

---

[1] ' A Briefe Relation ', by Captain Nicholas Foster, gives the full text of the Act, pp. 9–15.

[2] Foster's ' Relation ', p. 8. [3] A. B.'s ' Relation ', p. 3.

[4] Foster's ' Relation ', p. 7. Cf. *Cal. Col.* 1574–1660, p. 341.

[5] A. B.'s ' Relation '.

[6] The oath is printed in full in Nicholas Foster's ' Relation ', p. 10 (' A. B.' gives a garbled version of the oath, making the terms more violently royalist than they actually were.)

ment, the parliamentary section of the inhabitants roused themselves to action. James Drax and the other leaders organized a general petition from each parish, which was presented to the Governor on 23rd April 1650. Therein the petitioners asserted their right, according to the privileges of English freeholders, to elect a new Assembly once a year—' none having sat so long as the Assembly that now is '.[1] They further observed that, to their great grief, the original intention of the ' Act for uniting the Inhabitants ' had been overruled, and that the present royalist Assembly was endeavouring to perpetuate itself. They therefore called upon Bell to order an immediate election ; a course which, if adopted, they promised to support by all the means at their disposal. Meanwhile, Drax and his associates had interviewed Philip Bell and persuaded him to suspend the publication of the fateful Act, which he did on the ostensible ground of a technical flaw in its wording. When therefore the petitioners formally presented their demands before the Governor while presiding at a Council meeting his mind was made up.

Although himself a strict Anglican and a believer in limited monarchy he realized that the only hope of maintaining peace in the island lay in withstanding all extreme measures. To oppose the Walronds meant trouble ; but to give way to them meant certain war. Bell there and then declared his assent to the election of a new Assembly ; ' at which the Walronds in a rage rose up and divers of the Council with them, and disserted the Governor, leaving only two to sit with him '.[2] The rupture had come at last.

The royalists now openly declared the Governor a Roundhead, and instituted what was becoming so familiar a feature in England—a pamphlet war. At

---

[1] Nicholas Foster's ' Relation ', p. 11.
[2] A. B.'s ' Relation ', p. 3. Cf. Foster's ' Relation ', p. 19.

the moment this party had an almost unanimous
Assembly at its back. But if the promised general
election took place the Roundhead minority, and the
numerous body of moderate royalists, would in all
probability combine and assume control of affairs.
The inflammatory pamphlets therefore which were
nailed up in conspicuous places throughout the island
endeavoured, as before, to frighten the Moderates into
extreme measures by stories of a Roundhead plot
organized by James Drax, ' who as by letters appears,
is factor for the Rebells in England '.[1] The pamph-
leteers one and all called in passionate phrases for
an armed rising to put down this pretence of liberty,
' for thereby is meant slavery and tyranny '.

The call for bloodshed was soon to be answered.
In the parish of St. Philip, which included Walrond's
plantation, a number of young Cavaliers lately come
from England collected themselves. ' They sweare
God Damn 'em they will sheath their swords in the
hearts of all those that will not drink a health to the
Figure II (Charles II), and another to the confusion
of the Independent doggs.' [2]

Making a final attempt to maintain order, Governor
Bell issued a sternly worded proclamation. After
condemning the pamphlet war, ' raised on purpose to
beget intestine and civil broyles,' he ordained that all
so offending in the future were to be seized, ' and
punished as Enemies to the public peace of this
Island '. All persons were likewise forbidden to take
up arms upon pain of death.[3] In order to enforce his
authority, Bell issued commissions to Drax and others
to raise the militia. Drax lost no time, and arrested
Major Byam and Edward Walrond. But he had not
raised more than a hundred men when there was a

---

[1] From one of the pamphlets, several of which Nicholas Foster
quotes verbatim, ' Briefe Relation ', pp. 24–34.
[2] Ibid., p. 36.   [3] Ibid., p. 37.

night alarm that the Cavaliers were up and advancing on Bridgetown. Bell immediately issued another commission for Drax to seize the ringleaders as rebels. Unfortunately, the numerical inferiority of his supporters and his own lack of firmness caused him to waver and agree to a parley.[1] With that extraordinary persuasiveness of which he was master, Humphrey Walrond seems to have convinced Bell of his honesty and loyalty to the existing government, and was allowed to depart. Consequently, on 1st May 1650 the royalists leaders were able to dictate terms of peace to the now helpless Governor.

Following a profession of loyalty to Governor Bell the ' Propositions ' which they presented provided that all Independents should be disarmed, and the magazine at Bridgetown placed in the ' trust and guard ' of the Cavaliers. Still more drastic was the clause which provided for the punishment of all who had ' laboured the ruine of those loyally affected to his Majesty '. Twenty persons, whom they would nominate, were to be put on a speedy trial ' because our forces cannot disband till it be effected '. Roundhead participation in the government of the island was definitely excluded. In order to make their position impregnable the memorialists obliged the Governor to consent to place himself under their charge, coming ' without any known disaffected person ' in his company. In the tone of these Propositions there is something peculiarly reminiscent of the ' Lords Appellant ' in their dealings with Richard II. In both cases the magnates constituted themselves the guardians of the ruler, the defenders of the people, and established a close oligarchy. And in both cases the motive was largely self interest.

On 3rd May 1650 Charles Stuart was ' with great solemnity proclaimed King of England, Scotland,

[1] Nicholas Foster quotes the Propositions verbatim, pp. 40–3.

France and Ireland,'[1] and the Book of Common Prayer declared to be the only pattern of true worship. The Cavaliers were supreme.

It was not long before Philip Bell realized that he was a mere *roi fainéant*, and repented of his weakness in being so easily browbeaten. Moreover, the same feeling of reaction was present in the minds of Colonel Modiford and the Moderates. They were for the rule of the King, and not for that of the Walronds. Modiford therefore, although he had been a signatory of the Propositions, accepted a commission from Bell to raise the Windward Regiment of militia, for the restoration of the Governor's authority. He immediately issued orders to his second in command, Lt.-Colonel Birch, who in one night mobilized 1,500 infantry and 120 horse, and marched to the Governor's relief, ' and became very terrible to the Walronds '.[2] The result of the campaign was just about to be reversed when Humphrey Walrond's personal influence over the Governor saved the day for his party. A Roundhead writer remarks in disgust that Modiford's action ' would undoubtedly have turned the Scale, had not the elder Walrond by commanding tears to wait upon his deceitful professions of Zeal, Faith, and Honesty to the Governor, prevailed with him '. Birch was ordered to disband his forces. A *volte-face* so easily gained, naturally inspired distrust of a Governor, ' that would upon the persuasions of his Enemies be induced to Disarm himself and his friends '.[3]

Bell's credit with the Roundheads and the royalist Moderates was gone ; and his person was in the hands of the extremists. Backed by a subservient Assembly the latter organized a body of cavalry to overawe

---

[1] Nicholas Foster's ' Relation ', p. 44.

[2] A. B.'s ' Relation ', p. 4.

[3] Ibid. Foster gives another and less probable version of this incident.

possible opposition. The concessions also in the Propositions, which Bell had striven for, were forgotten; they 'keeping only such as were for their Advantage, impudently alleadging, That no other Promises ought to be kept by Persons in their Condition'.

The reign of the Walronds, however, was a short one. To their consternation about 5th May there landed at Bridgetown Francis Lord Willoughby of Parham, who presented to Philip Bell two commissions; one from the second Earl of Carlisle, appointing Willoughby his Lieut.-General in the Caribee Islands,[1] and another from the exiled Charles Stuart appointing him as Governor of Barbados. The ship *Elizabeth*, which had brought him, had anchored in Carlisle harbour on 29th April. But Willoughby had elected to remain quietly on board for a few days, till the tumultuous proceedings then on foot were over.

§ 2. *The Coming of Francis Lord Willoughby* (1650–2)

THE arrival of Lord Willoughby at Barbados marked the beginning of a new epoch for that island, and for the British West Indies in general. He was by nature a pioneer, with much of the untiring activity and impulsive pursuit of grandiose schemes which characterized Sir Walter Ralegh and Sir Humphrey Gilbert. He attempted too much, and expended his fortune on the planting of colonies from which he himself reaped little benefit. Yet in British Guiana and Carolina, as well as in the West Indies, his short, stormy career was responsible for a permanent advance in Anglo-Saxon expansion in the New World.

On the outbreak of the Civil War Willoughby had

[1] T.C.D. MSS. (G. 4. 15), pp. 1–28. Commission copied verbatim. Cf. *Cal. Col.* 1574–1660, p. 327. Commission is here dated Feb. 26/1647.

found himself in the difficult position of one whose
loyalty to the kingship was tempered by dislike of
arbitrary rule.   After some hesitation he threw in his
lot with the Parliament, for whom he mustered the
train-bands of Lincolnshire.[1]   Throughout the cam-
paigning he acquitted himself with energy and skill.
But the growing power of the extremists in the
parliamentary ranks caused him, with many others, to
react to the royalist side.   In 1647 he fled to Holland
and openly espoused the cause of Charles, serving for
some time as Vice-Admiral in the royalist fleet under
Prince Rupert.   But some months before this change
of sides took place Willoughby had signed a contract
that was destined to alter the whole course of his
subsequent career.   On 17th February the Earl of
Carlisle leased to him the proprietorship of the
Caribee Islands for twenty-one years.   In return for
a nominal rent Willoughby was to receive one half of
the gross rent of the province.   The reason for what
seems at first sight to be so one-sided a bargain seems
to be that Carlisle was really safeguarding the proprietorship by securing as an ally a prominent member
of the Presbyterian party, who were at that time on
the point of making peace with the King and estab-

[1] See ' Ten Matters Worthy of Note ' (Correspondence of Francis
Willoughby), London, 1642.   Letter from Charles I to Willoughby
(June 4/1642) : ' We do, by these our Letters, Command and
Charge you, upon your Allegiance, to desist and forbear to Raise,
Muster, Train, Exercise, or Assemble together any part of the Trained
Bands of that our County of Lincoln. . . .'   Willoughby replied,
' Sir, As there can be nothing of greater unhappiness to me, then to
receive a Command from your Majesty, whereunto my endeavours
cannot give so ready an obedience as my affections ; so I must con-
fesse the difficulty at this time not a little how to expresse that duty
which I owe to your Majestys late Commands and not falsifie that
Trust reposed in me by your High Court of Parliament '.   Cf. H.M.C.
xiii, Portland MSS., Part I, p. 707, Captain J. Hotham to the Earl
of Newcastle (4th May 1643) : ' . . . my Lord Willoughby hangs
most off '.

lishing a tolerant parliamentary monarchy.[1] Carlisle had however miscalculated, for the Presbyterian negotiations with the King fell through ; and he had to pay for the miscalculation when the unforeseen restoration took place and Willoughby's lease had still eight years to run. While serving under Rupert Willoughby secured from Prince Charles (acting under instructions from his father in England) confirmation of his lease and was appointed as royal governor.

Willoughby's advent therefore as representative of the King whom they had so loudly championed was a bitter pill for the Walronds. And a hard task they found it to discover a plausible excuse for opposing the unexpected rival. ' This new Pageant ', we are told, ' gave a mortal wound to the ill-gotten Principallity of the Brothers ; for this man they could not oppose, without going against their declared Principles of Loyalty to their Kingly stalking horse.' [2] Their only hope was to undermine his influence with the inhabitants by questioning his loyalty. Making capital out of his previous record they insinuated ' that he was once a Roundhead, and might be again '.[3]

To some extent their intrigues met with success. On 7th May 1650 Willoughby formally presented his credentials to the Governor, Council, and Assembly, who ' willingly and humbly ' received him, acknowledging his commission. But the influence of the Walronds proved so strong that Willoughby was

---

[1] Carlisle also signed two other documents, one annulling the commissions of all Governors in the province, and authorizing Willoughby to fill the office as he thought fit, and the other appointing him as *his own* Lieutenant-General of the Caribee Islands. As Williamson (ut supra, chap. vi, § 2) points out, these two documents were made public, but the transference of the proprietorship was carefully kept secret, until the appropriate time for publishing the fact should arise. But when the expected attack upon the Carlisle patent took place in 1647, naturally nothing was said about the matter, as Willoughby was by that time an avowed royalist.

[2] A. B.'s ' Relation ', p. 5.   [3] Ibíd.

obliged to agree to a three months' suspension of his authority, during which their government was to continue in office.[1] Such a breathing-space would give the brothers time to consolidate their position, and reduce Governor Willoughby to the subordinate position previously occupied by Philip Bell.

The Walronds now speeded up their plans to destroy the Roundhead party in Barbados, in order to leave Willoughby no alternative at the end of the three months but to comply with their wishes. Their first step was to carry out the terms of the ' Propositions '. Twenty Parliament men were nominated and ordered for trial ;[2] some of whom, knowing what to expect, wisely left the island. The remainder were arraigned on the charge of endeavouring the ruin of those well affected to his Majesty, the alteration of the government of Church and State, and the establishment of the parliamentary régime. The accused pleaded ' not guilty ', and asked to be allowed to answer the three counts separately at a legal trial. This request, however, was evaded. A guard was placed over them for the night ; and the following morning they were summarily condemned to pay fines ranging from 80,000 lb. to 5,000 lb. sugar. On 11th and 23rd May Acts were passed ordering nearly a hundred Independents to leave the island.[3] Fines were followed up by sequestration of estates, for which purpose the royalist leaders constituted themselves a sequestration committee. At the same time a tax of 50 lb. of sugar per acre was exacted from every Nonconformist to pay for the upkeep of the royalist army. So active were they

[1] Foster's ' Relation ', p. 110. The proclamation giving effect to this decision is here given verbatim.

[2] The names of the twenty are given in Foster's ' Relation ', p. 48.

[3] On 3rd Aug. it was enacted that no Nonconformist or sectary ' shall inhabit or dwell within this Island, after conviction thereof by the Oath of two Credible Witnesses. . . .' (C.O. 1/11, No. 17, P. R. O.). See list of the fines in Foster's ' Relation ', pp. 67–70.

that in twelve months' time an Independent wrote to
England that, ' because they could not Come to their
desyne, they went and broke their act of oblivyon, and
Sequestred 52 Gallandt plantations, who are as much
Werth as all yᵉ yland besydes '.[1] At the same time
the Walronds did their utmost to undermine Willoughby's position, and win support to themselves from
every section. ' To some that were poor and covetous
they promised shares of the Roundhead Estates, to
others that were blindfold Cavaliers, they pressed the
danger of Willoughby ; To others who most regarded
their Liberty, they prest the setting up of a Popular
Government,' which they did not hesitate to say had
been their intention from the beginning.[2]

Meanwhile, Lord Willoughby entered into negotiations with the Leeward Islands with a view to going
there and spending his three months' leisure in establishing his authority under the royal and proprietary
commissions. He met, however, as stubborn a neutrality
as that formerly maintained by Barbados.[3] On 1st
June 1650 he wrote to the Council and Assembly of
St. Christopher, stating that he had at last accomplished his long-intended journey into these parts,
and that he had been received and acknowledged by
the Barbadians.[4] He made no doubt but that ' the
whole Province will make itt an unanimous shrifᵗ in
their endeavours to preserve the Kinges Honnoʳ,' and
his undoubted right to those parts, derived by letters

[1] Tanner MSS. (Bodleian) 54, ff. 153–4 : ' A Lᵗʳ from Barbados
by yᵉ Way of Holland c̄n̄g yᵉ Condic̄on of Honest men there ' (9th
Aug. 1651).

[2] A. B.'s ' Relation ', p. 5.

[3] Darnell Davis in his book *Cavaliers and Roundheads in Barbados*
states that Willoughby spent his three months actually at the Leeward
Islands ; but contemporary evidence proves this erroneous.

[4] Tanner MSS. (Bodleian) 56, f. 209a : Willoughby to Council
and Assembly of St. Christopher, 1st June/50. The letter is dated
' Barbados, this first of June 1650 '.

patent to the Earl of Carlisle.[1]   In their reply of
13th July the St. Christopher Government reaffirmed
their determination to stand neutral.[2]   On 23rd
December 1650 Willoughby wrote again, urging the
formation of a league of the Leeward Islands with
Barbados for both political and economic purposes.[3]
But they were not to be moved ; and on 31st January
1651 Willoughby's commissioners were ordered to
leave St. Christopher.[4]

Lord Willoughby in the meantime was endeavouring
to counter the intrigues of the Walronds. He quickly
realized that the only policy which could save both
himself and Barbados in general from destruction was
one of moderation. Sending for Colonel Modiford,
the leader of the Moderate party, he assured him that
all his counsels would be employed in composing the
existing distractions, and in preventing future differences between Barbados and the Mother Country.
For this purpose he sent Captain George Martin into
England ; ' not onely to satisfie the whole Nation of
the Proceedings before my comeinge hither, but allsoe
of what hath been done since and to prevent all mis-
understanding and to settle a perfect and free trade
wth them '.[5]   This was a policy calculated to win the
support of all sober-minded planters with fortunes at
stake ; and it succeeded admirably. With the enthusi-

---

[1] Tanner MSS. (Bodleian) 56, f. 209a. Willoughby to Council
and Assembly of St. Christopher, 1st June/50.

[2] Ibid., f. 209b.   [3] Ibid., f. 240.

[4] Ibid., f. 211. Antigua, however, was strongly royalist. '... Ashton
whoe is governor of Antigua hath proclaymed Charles there, King
of England, Scotland, and Ireland, and courted very strongly Nevis
and St. Christophers to doe the like by letters to that very effect from
Willoughby, whoe have returned this reply both to Ashton and
Willoughby that they will take neither partye but allowe free trade
to all commers. Ashton hath a maine desiyne to put Barbados upon
forming a fleete of Shippes. . . .' (H.M.C. xiii, Rye and Hereford MSS.
4, p. 387).

[5] Tanner MSS. 56, f. 240.

astic support of the Roundheads and the moderate
Cavaliers, he took the bold course of depriving Colonel
Walrond of all power and authority in the island. The
Act of Sequestrations was repealed and an Act of
Indemnity passed ; he himself bestowing ' many
marks of Favor upon the former Sufferers, and their
remaining Families, in so much, That men generally
looked on him as a blessing sent from God to preserve
them against the tyranny of the two Brothers '.[1]
About this time Colonel James Colleton, a man of
considerable wealth and influence, came out to Barbados. In this man Willoughby confided, assuring
him of his moderating intentions, and desiring him to
write to the London merchants that they might
procure for him a commission from the Council of
State.[2]

It is hardly surprising, however, that the Parliament
was not to be thus easily mollified, considering the
persistent and increasing defiance which Barbados had
offered. Already Colonel Alleyne and a number of
other Roundhead planters had arrived in England for
the purpose of urging the Parliament to avenge their
wrongs by reducing the Barbadian royalists by armed
force. The proclamation of Prince Charles, the
sentences of banishment and confiscation of estates
by the Cavaliers, and the trade *entente* between Barbados and Holland, were all represented in a series
of urgent petitions.[3]

The Parliament was not slow in taking action. On

---

[1] A. B.'s ' Relation ' (Egerton MSS. 2395), p. 6.   [2] Ibid.
[3] *Cal. Col.* 1574–1660, pp. 344 and 388. Cf. Lord Willoughby's
letter to his Lady : Feb. 1651. ' And I hope they will reward those
runaway bankrupt rogues, who durst stay no longer here for fear of
a gaol, wereof learned Mr. Bayes is one having by their villainy done
what in them lies to ruine one of the best and sweetest islands in the
British possession ' (Tanner MSS. 54, ff. 147–9) ; printed by Schomburgk (*History of Barbados*), Appendix X ; calendered in H.M.C.
xiii, c ; Portland MSS. i, p. 558.

23rd August the Admiralty Commissioners ordered that a special committee be appointed to consider the contumacy of Barbados, and that an Act prohibiting all trade with the island should be drawn up. On 31st August the customs officers at Bristol and Plymouth were ordered to make stay of all vessels bound to Barbados; all cargoes were to be examined, and those ' belonging to persons who stand out in rebellion to the Commonwealth' confiscated.[1] Attempts were also made to prevent ships sailing thither from Amsterdam.[2]

Indeed, the English merchants, who had formerly controlled the trade with Barbados, were glad enough that the plantation had abandoned its former neutrality. It gave them a weapon to compel the already harassed Parliament to turn its attention to the open trade of that colony with Holland, from which they were suffering severely. The proposed Act ' prohibiting trade and commerce to Barbados, Antigua, Virginia, and the Somers Islands, because of their rebellion against the Commonwealth and Government of England,' was passed after some delay and emendation on 3rd October 1650.[3] All ' Generals at Sea ' were commanded to seize ships endeavouring to carry on trade with the ostracized colonies.

The London merchants were determined to drive the matter still farther. They reported that the trade ban would be ineffective unless enforced by an expedition thither; and did not rest until the dispatch of an armed force had been definitely voted.[4]

This energetic action on the part of Parliament aroused protests from several quarters. The Puritans

---

[1] *Cal. Col.* 1574–1660, pp. 342–3.   [2] Ibid. (10th Sept.).

[3] C.O. 1/11, No. 21, P. R. O. *Commons Journals*, vi, p. 478. The rebellious colonists were stigmatized in the Act as ' notorious Robbers and Traitors and such as by yᵉ Lawe of Nations are not to be p̄mitted any manner of Comerce or Traffique with any people whatsoever '.

[4] *Cal. Col.* 1574–1660, p. 343.

of New England, whose chief industry of late years had been the supply of provisions to Barbados, laid a petition before the Plantation Committee, desiring permission to continue their trade with the prohibited islands. But their request was refused.[1] A month later the Proconsul and Senate of Hamburg wrote to the Parliament, urging ' that their citizens might be allowed the freedom of trade to those places to which they had been accustomed, and that in particular the ships already laden might be allowed to trade there '.[2]

Meanwhile, the Roundhead planters from Barbados were combating a movement in favour of Lord Willoughby, which had arisen at Whitehall in consequence of his attempts at conciliation. By this time his emissary George Martin had arrived in London, seeking open trade with the Mother Country and a parliamentary commission for Willoughby, and bearing his appeal for the Roundhead exiles to return. John Bayes, however, and the other Commonwealth men declared in a series of ' humble proposals ' that to continue Willoughby in the Government ' would for the future be destructive to their rights in the island '. They explained away his dismissal of the Walronds and his moderating acts by citing other proceedings such as the proclamation of Charles II. To clinch the matter they petitioned that Edward Winslow, a Puritan of New England and ' a person of approved fidelity to this Commonwealth ', might be appointed Governor of Barbados.[3] So eager were the

[1] A special licence was drafted permitting New Englanders to trade until 31st July 1651 (*Cal. Col.* 1574–1660, pp. 344–5, 347), but did not secure official confirmation. (Cf. chapter vi, below.)

[2] H.M.C. xiii. 1, Portland MSS. i, pp. 542–3. The Parliament fleet in the Downs had been warned to stop a fleet of ten or twelve vessels, due to sail for Barbados from Middleburg and Flushing (*Cal. Col.*, p. 344). It was this trade with the rebel colonies which constituted a chief *casus belli* for the Dutch War in 1652.

[3] ' Humble proposals of several Barbadians ', presented Nov. 22/1650 (*Cal. Col.* 1574–1660, p. 346; C.O. 1/11, No. 25, P. R. O.).

London merchants to re-establish their connexion
with this plantation, now suddenly growing wealthy,
that they asked (and received) permission to send
five or six able merchant ships with the punitive
expedition, in order that, immediately on the submission of the island and its repudiation of Charles
Stuart, they might exchange their goods for cargoes
of sugar.[1]

Thus, Willoughby's policy of conciliation had come
too late. There was now nothing for it but to organize
the island for resistance. Already in August 1650
a premonition of what was to be expected from the
Parliament had been received in the form of a printed
manifesto, declaring the Barbadians rebels and traitors
to the Commonwealth.[2] In February 1651 the news
arrived that Sir George Ayscue with a Parliament
fleet was even now on his way to reduce the rebel
colonies.[3] Various circumstances, in addition to his
natural inclination, decided Willoughby to make a
fight for it. On the one hand he had received word
of the victories of Prince Charles in Scotland, and his
probable triumph. At the same time there was no
hope of pacifying the Parliament. From London he
was informed of ' the violent proceedings of some of
the Planters against him, that Marten was like to be
Hanged for speaking for him ; and in fine That the
Inhabitants were to expect nothing but Fire and
Sword '.[4]

The news of the Parliament's action was brought
by one Mr. Arnold, just when the Assembly was in

[1] *Cal. Col.* 1574–1660, p. 345, signed by Nicholas Blake and thirty-
eight others.

[2] Cf. Tanner MSS. 54, ff. 147–9. Lord Willoughby's letter to his
lady, ut supra.

[3] The fleet (ordered 22nd Jan. 1651) consisted of 2 men-of-war—
the *Rainbow* of 52 guns and the *Amity* of 34 guns, and 5 merchantmen,
with an average of 30 guns each. Total of men 820, with arms,
provisions, &c. (*Commons Journals*, vi, p. 526).

[4] Egerton MSS. 2395, ff. 55–6.

session. Immediate action was accordingly taken. On 18th February, the Barbadians published a Declaration in reply to the parliamentary boycott, which for the eloquence of its expression and the force of its arguments has since been repeatedly used by colonial legislatures against imperial interference. The wording of some of the most important clauses in the American Declaration of Independence bear a striking resemblance to this document.

'Shall we be bound to the government and lordship of a Parliament in which we have no representatives, or persons chosen by us, for there to propound and consent to what might be needful to us, as also to oppose and dispute all what should tend to our disadvantage and harme? In truth, this would be a slavery far exceeding all that the English nation hath yet suffered.'

To the imputation that they had usurped the government, the Declaration reminded the usurpers at Whitehall that their constitution was 'the nearest modell of conformity to that under which our predecessors of the English Nation have lived and flourished for above a thousand years'. The usurping boot was on the other foot, so to speak. The reply to the prohibition of trade with foreign countries was no less firm. The old inhabitants know very well how Dutch assistance saved the life of the colony, and 'what necessary comfort they bring to us dayly', their prices being considerably cheaper than the English. 'But we declare, that we will never be so unthankful to the Netherlands for their former help and assistance, as to deny or forbid them, or any other Nation, the freedom of our harbours and the protection of our laws.' In picturing the Act of Trade in operation, the document points out that the concentration of Barbadian trade into the hands of a few licensed persons would reduce the inhabitants to the position of 'slaves to the companie, who shall have the above said licenses, and submit to them the whole advantage of our labour and industry'. The Declaration accordingly ends on a note of high defiance.

'Wherefore having rightly considered, we declare, that as we would not be wanting to use all honest means for the obtaining of a continuation of commerce, trade, and good correspondence with our country, soe wee will not alienate ourselves from those old heroick virtues of true Englishmen, to prostitute our freedom and privileges, to which we are borne, to the will and opinion of anyone.' [1]

On the following day (19th February) the Barbadian Government enacted that before 20th March every freeholder in the island was to repair to a local justice of the parish and ' cheerefully subscribe ' to a covenant to defend the system of government represented by Lord Willoughby with the utmost hazard of their persons and estates.[2]

Subscription to this ' Engagement ' was strictly enforced. About 8th April 1651 Captain Middleton and four others arrived at St. Christopher, having been forced to leave Barbados ' because they would not consent unto the engagem[t] w[ch] they doe impose upon all the Inhabitants; and those w[ch] doe refuse are brought to the Counsell of Warre and theire goods confiscated '.[3]

In fact the existing situation provided the more violent of the Cavaliers with just that excuse for hard measures which they had formerly lacked. And Willoughby was now obliged to countenance them. ' These men '—a Roundhead planter exclaims, ' are as if y[e] Divell had overpowered them, indeed hee hath

[1] Printed copy of the Declaration (London, 1651) in ' King's Pamphlets ' (Brit. Mus.), E. 644(4). Copied verbatim by Schomburgk, Appendix X.

[2] Tanner MSS. 56, f. 211. The Act and Engagement are also printed in the above pamphlet.

[3] Ibid., f. 44. Colonel Redge (Governor of St. Kitts) to the Earl of Carlisle.

possesd them; their Wiell is extreme, these are y^e
men that Cary ye bussiness, whether it pleaseth my
Lord or noe; And my Lord now dare doe Nothing
Without them.'[1] The same writer describes how a
cargo of his, consisting of 50,000 lb. of sugar and
25,000 lb. of ginger, was commandeered for the public
use with promise of repayment. 'Have it againe wee
shall never, except ye Parlia^t Shipps Come.'

Roused to a sense of their danger, all sections of the
Cavalier party now co-operated in preparations for
defence. For while adopting the policy of the extremists in mulcting the Parliament men,[2] Willoughby
at the same time won the enthusiastic support of the
Moderates by promising that if ever good terms
offered he would accept them.[3]

The first precaution taken was to raise a standing
contingent of horse and foot, to be ready to oppose
a landing at short notice. This force was paid at
monthly rates from a levy assessed proportionately on
the planters.[4] At the same time the forts at Carlisle
Harbour, Speights Bay, and the Hole, as well as the
barricades and other defences along the coast, were
put in good order. And out of every ship that arrived

[1] Tanner MSS. 56, f. 153 a. 'A L^tr from Barbados by ye Way of
Holland conc^g ye condiecon of Honest men there' (ut supra).

[2] On 12th Sept. 1651 the Governor, Council, and Assembly passed
an Act, that whereas it was unfitting to tax the loyal inhabitants
further to pay for the defences, the estates of Alleyne, Drax, and all
others who had stirred up opposition against Barbados in England
should be sequestrated, the proceeds used for public expenses, one-
fifth to be reserved for the relations of those dispossessed. On 3rd
April a previous Act had been passed for borrowing goods for the
defence.

[3] Egerton MSS. 2395, f. 54.

[4] Cf. Tanner MSS. 54, f. 147. Willoughby's letter to his wife,
ut supra. The assessment, however, seems to have been arranged so
as to fall most heavily on the Roundheads. One of them (quoted
above) complained that 25 of his servants were taken as soldiers, and
in addition he paid for the services of 8¼ men, which amounted to
1,530 lb. sugar *per month* (Tanner MSS. 54, ff. 153-4).

at the island, the government commandeered ' one or two pieces of Ordnance to Supplie themselves '.[1] The four per cent. duty on all exports, which had been granted to Willoughby on his assumption of the government, was put to similar uses.

Dutch assistance too, which had proved so valuable in the past, was now relied on more than ever. According to John Scott, Willoughby ordered ' the Mannage of Trade to be onely wth the Hollanders '.[2] And whether this was actually the case or not, Willoughby himself says at this time that, from Holland ' ships come dayly in to us '.[3] Moreover, in order to replenish the stock of provisions which a nine months' drought had brought exceptionally low, a Dutch fleet which was unlading, was ' made to be gone, and to make another Voiage before y[e] Comming of y[e] frygotts '.[4] The Dutchmen also willingly supplied a stock of arms and ammunition in exchange for cargoes of sugar.

Meanwhile those London merchants whose political interests did not specially demand the reduction of the Cavalier element in the island, were viewing with grave concern this proposed dispatch of an expedition, which would ruin all hope of trade with Barbados. Persuaded that the sudden appearance of such a force would cause a violent defence,—' to the disadvantage of the fleet, and the probable ruin of the most improving plantation in the world,' these merchants on 11th February 1651, petitioned that envoys might be sent on ahead, ' to persuade the island to a reasonable compliance to this Commonwealth '. The Council of State was, however, determined on its course of action, and ordered the petition to be ' laid aside '.[5] Another

[1] Tanner MSS. 54, f. 44.   [2] Sloane MSS. 3662, f. 58a.
[3] Tanner MSS. 54, ff. 147-9.
[4] Ibid., f. 154. ' A L[tre] from Barbados by way of Holland.'
[5] *Cal. Col.* 1574-1660, p. 351.

English merchant to Barbados, in a private letter of 11th December, expressed the same view. 'I should be glad'; he wrote, 'that the Island were settled in peace, and that there were a good accord between the Parliament fleet and the Island that we may have an open trade. We are now a prey to all.'[1]

The long delay of the expedition through the summer months of 1651 gave the Barbadians more time to prepare for resistance than they had anticipated. The dispatch of the ' Barbados fleet ' had been ordered by the Council of State as early in the year as 22nd January,[2] Sir George Ayscue and two other commissioners having received formal instructions a week later. Therein they were given a free hand as to peace terms, provided that royal government was repudiated and submission given to the Commonwealth.[3]

But when the fleet was ready to set sail for Barbados, the Council of State decided to take the opportunity of subduing a force of royalists, who were making a last stand at the Scilly Isles.[4]

After the reduction of this royalist remnant, Parliament decided to send Ayscue and his force to Barbados without further delay. Disquieting rumours were reaching Whitehall of the vigorous preparations being made by the islanders, in aid of whom Prince Rupert and his fleet were about to set sail. On the receipt of fresh instructions and supplies, Ayscue's expedition finally set out in July ;[5] and after a fruitless search for Rupert off Lisbon and the Cape de Verd Islands, Barbados was reached on 15th October 1651.[6]

[1] H.M.C. xiii. 2, Portland MSS., ii, p. 30.
[2] Cal. Col. 1574–1660, p. 349.   [3] Ibid., pp. 349–50.
[4] Commons Journal, vi, p. 590 (Major Salwey's report to the Council of State).
[5] Cal. Col. 1574–1660, pp. 358–9.
[6] Tanner MSS. 55, f. 79 (Ayscue's dispatch to the Council of State, 19th October).

It was falling dusk when the Parliament ships first sighted the island. The order was therefore given to heave to for the night, in order that daylight might enable them to seize any foreign vessels in the harbours.[1] For this purpose Captain Pack took a squadron on ahead, while Sir George Ayscue waited with the main fleet a league to windward. In the early morning Pack sailed quietly into Carlisle Harbour, where fifteen Dutch merchantmen were found lying at anchor. Taken wholly by surprise, only three of them succeeded in evading capture by running ashore. They proved however but empty prizes, as the majority of the cargoes had already been unshipped and transported inland.[2]

Upon this success, the remainder of the fleet sailed into the bay, approaching as they did so, to within half a musket shot of the chief fort, where a sharp exchange of artillery fire took place.[3] The skill of the Barbadian gunners, however, was not all that could be desired. One man only of the fleet was killed.

The news of the long-delayed coming of the Parliament force was brought inland to Willoughby, where he had been feasting the night before in honour of the reported triumph of Prince Charles and his Scottish army in England. The island had given itself up to merry-making to celebrate the event, and was consequently caught somewhat unawares.[4]

Willoughby immediately returned to Bridgetown, and distributed his army of five thousand men along

[1] Tanner MSS. 55, f. 79 (Ayscue's dispatch to the Council of State, 19th October).

[2] Ayscue later admitted that the necessity of providing prize crews to take charge proved a source of serious weakness to the Parliament fleet (ibid. 55, f. 85).

[3] Tanner MSS. 55, f. 79 (Ayscue to Council of State, 31st Oct.). Also in C.O. 1/11, No. 87, P. R. O. The Ayscue-Willoughby correspondence is copied by Darnell Davis, *Cavaliers and Roundheads in Barbados*.

[4] *Mercurius Politicus*, number for the week, 12th–18th Feb. 1652.

the coast, to oppose a landing. Within twenty hours his forces had increased to 6,000 foot and 400 horse.

The inhabitants, excited by the report of Prince Charles's success, were determined to put up a stout resistance. Lord Willoughby himself, writing to his wife some weeks later, answered her pleading that he should save himself by submission with—' No, I will not do it, and therefore Dear Heart, let me entreat thee to leave off thy persuasions to submit to them, who so unjustly, so wickedly have ruined thee and me and mine. If ever they get the island, it will cost them more than it is worth before they have it.'[1]

On 11th October Ayscue, whose force was too weak to attempt a regular invasion, sent Willoughby a formal demand to surrender the island to the Parliament of England, which, he declared, was ' willinge that they should be sharers wth them in that Libertye wch by the blessinge of God they have purchased wth such Expense of blood and money '.[2] Within a few hours Willoughby briefly replied that he acknowledged ' no Supreme Authority over Englishmen, but ye Kinges and by his Comission ; and for him I doe, and by God's Assistance, shall defend this place '.[3] The same day Ayscue issued a manifesto to ' the Gentlemen Inhabitants and ffree People of ye Island of Barbados ', calling upon them to submit and not put a vain trust in Lord Willoughby, who was ' Alltogether unable to give y^{ou} protection or Libertye of ffree trade, wthout wch this Island can noe waye subsist '.[4] This and similar pamphlets were scattered at night time up and down the island by Roundhead inhabitants who communicated secretly with the fleet.

Meanwhile Ayscue set to work to starve the island

[1] Tanner MSS. 54, f. 137–9. Cf. *Cal. Col.* 1574–1660, pp. 362–3.

[2] Ibid. 55, f. 70 b.   [3] Ibid.

[4] Ibid., ff. 71–2. Also in C.O. 1/11, No. 38, i ; P. R. O.

into submission. Parliament ships patrolled the coasts, seizing all vessels that endeavoured to approach the island. And the inhabitants were kept in a constant ferment by a series of raids and alarms.[1]

On 5th November a general Assembly, consisting of the Governor, Council, and Burgesses, published a formal declaration in answer to Ayscue's activities. After treating with contempt the papers which had been scattered about the island, ' to poyson y[e] alliegeiance of y[e] good People here,' the signatories declared their unalterable devotion to the King and to his Governor, Lord Willoughby. ' We will adhere and sticke to him, and wth o[r] uttmost power manfully fight under his Command for y[e] defence of this Island, and y[e] Government thereof as it is now settled.' [2]

Ayscue, however, did not give up hope of a voluntary surrender. On 8th November a letter arrived from the Council of State informing him of Cromwell's triumph at the battle of Worcester (3rd September). Following instructions, he made use of the information in a second summons to Willoughby, pointing out the ultimate futility of resistance ; and that the only way to save the island from destruction was by a speedy submission. Willoughby's answer was a noble one. ' I assure you ', he wrote, ' That I never served y[e] Kinge in Expectācon soe much of his Prosperous Condīcon as in considerācon of my Dutye. And if it have pleased God to add this sadd affliccon to his former I will not be a means of increasinge it by deliveringe this place to your keepinge.' [3] Yet hopeless as the royalist cause in England now appeared, Ayscue's

---

[1] On 31st Oct. he wrote to President Bradshaw that the only hope was ' by preventing trade and by continual alarms to keep them in arms '. The Barbadians, he added, thought that the fleet could not long maintain the siege, owing to sickness and lack of provisions. The force on the island was too powerful to attempt anything against them (*Cal Col.* 1574–1660, p. 364).

[2] *Cal. Col.* 1574–1660, p. 365.   [3] C.O. 1/11, No. 38, P. R. O.

force was in no condition to compel Barbados to an
immediate surrender. Ayscue himself reported that
the continuous life on board ship and ' ye want of
necessary refreshm^{te} brought o^r men into ye scurvye ',
which so reduced the numbers that for the time, ' We
had not men Enough to rule o^r shipps much lesse to
annoye ye Enemye on shore '.[1] On 22nd November,
however, a very successful raid was planned and
executed. Captain Morris with 200 men—all that
could be spared from the fleet—delivered a surprise
attack on the Barbadian quarters at ' the Hole '. The
breastworks held by the defenders were captured, four
guns spiked, and thirty prisoners taken, without loss
to themselves.

The Barbadians were further impressed by the
arrival on 1st December of parliamentary reinforcements. It was a fleet on its way to reduce the royalists
of Virginia, which had been ordered to put in at
Barbados in order to give Ayscue a helping hand.
The appearance of this new force caused Willoughby to
increase his guards along the coast. In reality, however, Ayscue was very little stronger than before. The
Virginian expedition was so weakened by sickness and
lack of water, that their stay at the island could not
be a long one.[2] Ayscue's chief hope, therefore, lay
in the chance that the islanders would be overawed
by the formidable appearance of the double fleet.
On 3rd December he sent a further summons of surrender to Lord Willoughby.

This time the reply was not so emphatic. Acting
under pressure from the Moderate party, who reminded him of his former promise to consider any
terms of peace that might be reasonable, Willoughby
replied that though he was unshaken by Ayscue's
added strength he was willing to negotiate. Suggested

---

[1] Tanner MSS. 55, f. 141. Ayscue's dispatch.
[2] Ibid.

terms would be submitted by the Barbadian Government within a few days. Ayscue for his part felt that the royalists did not mean business, and said so. His suggestion of a direct conference between plenipotentiaries was refused ; and there the matter ended.[1] As a matter of fact Lord Willoughby and the extreme Cavaliers realized that their backs were at the wall, and were in no mood for submission. The abortive negotiations had served their purpose in placating the Moderates.

Ayscue now determined to resort to force, while the Virginian fleet was at his disposal. A body of four hundred men was collected, which included a number of Barbadian Roundheads who had joined the fleet, and a hundred and fifty Scottish prisoners, captured at Worcester fight, ' who for a gratuitie tooke upp Armes wth us '. In his graphic dispatch to the Council of State, Ayscue describes the ensuing raid.

' Uppon ye 7th of December at night I gave them order to Land, w^{eh} they did and were notably received at ye Landinge, wth horse and foote, but beinge in ye Night they conceived o^r fforces to be more then they were ; and ye Seamen runninge in uppon ye Enemye wth halloweinge and whoopinge in such a ffeirce disorder y^t ye Enemye was soe amazed y^t after a short dispute they all ran.' [2]

The Barbadian force was computed to be about 1,200 foot and a troop of horse, and their losses about 100 killed and 60 taken prisoner. Eight only of the Parliament men appear to have been killed.

The success of the raid exceeded Ayscue's expectations ; but as he observed, ' it signified Little to o^r Maine designe of gayninge the Island, ffor We had not fforce to keepe the ffeild '.[3] The only useful result was the state of tension in Willoughby's army

[1] Ayscue-Willoughby Correspondence, 2nd, 3rd, 4th December (*Cal. Col.* 1574–1660, p. 366).
[2] Tanner MSS., ff. 141–2b.   [3] Ibid.

of 6,000 men, which in view of possible raids had to be kept continually mobilized.

The sickness and distress in the Virginian fleet had by this time grown so acute that its departure could no longer be delayed ; and with it went Ayscue's only hope of effecting success by force of arms. The scheme which he now adopted was to divide the islanders among themselves. The Moderate Cavaliers were to be won over by an offer of generous terms, thus compelling the extremists to negotiate. His first step was to gain Colonel Modiford, a man whom he considered to be ' very inclinable to Peace and of Considerable power in the Island '.[1] Accordingly Francis Raynes and other Barbadian Roundheads on board the fleet were induced to write to him, ' therein tendring all things of Fairness and Civility ; which the said Colonel received with much contentment and shewed the same to the Lord Willoughby pressing his Promise of Composure upon fair terms '.[2]

Willoughby was thus faced with that split in his royalist coalition, which he had been working to avoid since his first coming. He could not go back on his promise to the Moderates ; and yet the extremists, with whom he largely sympathized, were irreconcilable. Informal conversations were opened and terms offered with which Modiford expressed himself entirely satisfied.[3] The Moderates now applied pressure to bring about official negotiations on the basis of these terms. To that end a member of the party, Lieut.-Colonel Birch, moved a resolution in a General Assembly, which was seconded by Modiford and Henry Hawley. The motion was

[1] Tanner MSS. 55, ff. 141–2b.
[2] Egerton MSS. 2395, f. 54.
[3] Ibid. The statement of Darnell Davis that these negotiations were carried on without Willoughby's knowledge is not in accordance with contemporary evidence. It was the preparations for the subsequent rupture which were kept secret.

carried, and a committee appointed to draw up a statement of terms, which on their first reading were approved by the Moderates. At this point the 'Die-hards' intervened, and inserted a number of clauses which converted the peace propositions into 'nothing but a Defiance'.[1] The first of these emended demands was, 'That yᵉ Legall and Rightfull Gouvernment of this Island remayne as it is now by Lawe and oʳ owne Consent established'.[2]

It is hardly surprising therefore that Ayscue in his reply on 27th December refused to consider the document. He submitted terms of his own which were to serve as a basis of negotiation between chosen representatives of both sides.

The terms which he offered were most liberal, and were in substance the same as those eventually accepted. The Council and Assembly however would have none of them, and wrote on 29th December declaring their unanimous adherence to monarchical government, as expressed in, 'yᵉ ffirst Article in our Proposīcons sent on board; and without a graunt ffirst had of that, we shall not yield to allowe any further treaty'.[3] The extremists had carried their point; no sub-mission to the authority of the Commonwealth in any form was to be tolerated. Moreover the energy with which the Moderates had supported Ayscue's pro-posals caused the Cavaliers to regard them as traitors. The rupture was complete.

Colonel Modiford decided to end the situation. Calling a private gathering of the chief men of his party, among whom were Colonels Colleton and Birch and Captain Hooper, he proposed a resolution, which was unanimously accepted—'to make the Lord Willoughby by Force to perform what by honest persuasions could not be obtained'.[4] That night the

---

[1] Egerton MSS. 2395, f. 54.   [2] C.O. 1/11, No. 38, P. R. O.
[3] *Cal. Col.* 1574–1660, p. 370.   [4] Egerton MSS. 2395, f. 56.

Moderate leaders held a secret conference at a lonely spot by the seashore with Captain Pack, and other emissaries from the fleet, who gave them full satisfaction. There was some delay before the final step was taken ; but after further pressure from Ayscue, Modiford on 6th January 1652, assembled and addressed his regiment. In a short speech he pointed out the absolute dictatorship which had been established by the Walrond party in the Council and Assembly, the reasonableness of the Parliament proposals, and finally Ayscue's promise to supply them with all necessaries from the fleet if they would desert the royalist camp. The regiment thereupon declared its resolution to ' live and die with their Colonel in obtaining Peace upon those Articles '.[1] On receiving news of the triumph of his scheme, Ayscue made a last attempt at a peaceable settlement, informing Willoughby of the defection of Modiford's Regiment and offering the Articles to which the Moderates had agreed. But Willoughby, whose wife and children were now living in great poverty in England owing to the Parliament's action in selling his estates,[2] was in no mood to be bullied. He curtly replied that neither the treachery of one, nor the supineness of others, had weakened him or his followers to accept a dishonourable peace.[3]

Meanwhile Modiford had marched to the seaside at Austin's Bay, where he was joined by the Parliament forces with the promised supplies. The combined army, which numbered 2,000 foot and 100 horse, then marched seven miles inland to Modiford's house, which was converted into a Roundhead garrison.[4]

---

[1] Egerton MSS. 2395, f. 54.

[2] Cf. Willoughby's letter to his wife (Tanner MSS. 54, ff. 147–9).

[3] Ayscue-Willoughby Correspondence, 5th, 6th, and 7th Jan. (*Cal. Col.* 1574–1660, pp. 371–2).

[4] Egerton MSS., 2395, f. 54.

Hither all the Commonwealth men of the island congregated. Satisfied that his new allies meant what they said, Ayscue came ashore from the *Rainbow*, and at a general gathering read his commission from the Council of State, 'wherewth they were very well satisfied and were resolved to live and dye for ye Parliam^t of England '.[1] The Parliament attack was thus converted from a blockade into a definite invasion. Out-manoeuvred as they were, the Cavaliers' only chance lay in obtaining a decisive victory before Sir George Ayscue could establish himself. 'The Lord Willoughby, understandinge of w^t was done, wth all ye fforce he could make, marched towards us,'—so Ayscue relates—'and indeede was upp wth us by y^t time my Commission was read, We understandinge that he beinge ye stronger, especially in horse, intended to have fallen uppon us.'[2]

But Willoughby was not as strong as Ayscue believed. The example of the Windward Regiment had induced so many to desert his colours that only half of the original 6,000 could be mustered to march against the Roundhead army.[3] And the morale of the remainder was becoming unsatisfactory. After holding a council of war, Willoughby retreated two miles during the night.[4] A continual downpour of rain for the next three days prevented Ayscue from following him up and forcing an engagement. When at last the Parliament army was drawn out and ready to march, 'the Lord Willoughbies Trumpet with a Letter earnestly desiring Peace stopt further Proceedings '.[5]

[1] Tanner MSS. 55, f. 141b. Ayscue's dispatch.
[2] Ibid.
[3] Egerton MSS. 2395, f. 56.
[4] Ayscue hazarded a guess as to the reason for the retreat: that it was because a shell from one of his guns had torn off the roof of the house where Willoughby was holding his council of war and killed the sentinel.
[5] Egerton MSS. 2395, f. 567.

The Cavaliers had submitted, realizing that further resistance would only render their cause the more desperate.

In his letter Willoughby provisionally nominated four commissioners to negotiate peace terms, for whom he asked safe conducts, that they might proceed to Ayscue's base at Austin's Bay.[1] The latter replied that despite the superiority of his condition, he was so passionately desirous to preserve Barbados from further devastation, that he would accede to his request.[2] An immediate cessation of hostilities being agreed upon, the royalist commissioners proceeded to the Mermaid Tavern at Austin's Bay, where negotiations were opened with the Commonwealth plenipotentiaries.

The terms finally signed and published by the contracting parties on 11th January 1652 were very generous.[3] The constitutional privileges of the island were guaranteed in a number of clauses, which provided (*inter alia*) that no imposts might be levied without consent of the General Assembly. In return for the restoration of all Roundhead estates, the Barbadian Cavaliers were to receive back their lands and goods, ' which they have in England, Scotland or Ireland', and were to be pardoned for all acts of hostility by an act of oblivion. In particular, Lord Willoughby was expressly guaranteed all his estates both at home, in the West Indies, and in Guiana, and given freedom of movement. The most important concession was that regarding trade. ' All port-towns and cities under the Parliament's power shall be open unto the inhabitants of this Island in as great a freedom of trade as ever and that all trade be free with all nations that do trade and are in amity with England.' In their turn the Cavaliers agreed to hand over the fortifications to Ayscue by twelve noon on 12th

[1] *Cal. Col.* 1574–1660, p. 372 (9th January).   [2] Ibid.
[3] Add. MSS. (Brit. Mus.) 11411, f. 95.

January; 'and that for the safety of the island, the Militia shall be disposed of as to the Parliament, Commissioners, and future Governors shall seem fit'. The authority of the English Commonwealth was to be acknowledged, by whom the Governor would henceforth be appointed.

Both Sir George Ayscue and the two other commissioners, Daniel Searle and Michael Pack, seem to have been apprehensive that Parliament would refuse to ratify these terms, as being too liberal.[1] In his final dispatch Ayscue urges that his own weakness as well as the daily devastation of the island called for immediate peace. Furthermore, he did not know how Modiford's party 'would have liked o^r Refusall of treatinge for it '.[2] He hopes that under these circumstances the enclosed articles ' will not be thought too much'. With regard to trade he is careful to add, ' I shall here humbly take notice to y^or Lopp, That whereas it is sayd in ye part of ye 9th Article " And that all trade be ffree wth all Nations that doe trade and are in Amitie wth England ", it is only to be understood thus under such Restrictions and Limitations as are Enacted by ye Parliam^t of Engld.' He did not like the article, and had desired the parliamentary commissioners ' to Explaine their true meaning in it, wch was according as I have before sett downe'. It is equally certain that the Barbadians understood the clause by its literal interpretation, and were bitterly aggrieved when Cromwell denied them free trade, compelling them to traffic only to English ports. The Articles were ratified by Parliament on 18th August 1652.[3]

[1] Cf. Michael Pack to President Bradshaw (*Col. Cal.* 1574–1660, pp. 374–5).   [2] Ayscue's dispatch (Tanner MSS. 55, f. 141b).

[3] *Commons Journals*, vi, p. 166. The eagerness of Parliament to effect the reduction of Barbados may be estimated by the fact that £10 was ordered to be paid to him who brought the first news of it (*Cal. Col.* 1574–1660, p. 378).

Meanwhile Ayscue proceeded to organize Barbadian institutions on a Commonwealth basis. The regiments of the militia were remodelled and placed under officers of known fidelity to the Parliament. As soon as the new force of five infantry regiments, each a thousand strong, and a troop of four hundred horse had been constituted, it was reviewed by Ayscue, who urged them in a speech to be faithful to the service of the Commonwealth. The Courts of Justice were similarly reorganized, ' all Processe beinge issued in the same forme they are now in England'. The 'Act against Kingship', and similar ordinances of the English Parliament were publicly proclaimed.

Thus supreme, the Parliament commissioners proceeded to violate the indemnity guaranteed in the peace terms. On. 4th March a new Assembly consisting of members carefully chosen for their Commonwealth principles, agreed to an Act proposed by Ayscue, banishing the Walronds and seven other Cavalier leaders for one year.[1] The concluding clause is a quaint piece of sophistry ; ' . . . though it may seem to clash wth the Articles in the Letter, yet it is Cleare and apparent to all Ingenious men that the Articles being made for the benefit and good of this people . . . may uppon the desires of the same people bee discharged or suspended '. Acting on the same principle, Lord Willoughby was ordered on board *The Red Lion* for England under penalty of being treated as an enemy to the public peace, and was not to return without permission of Parliament. All Acts passed during his rule were repealed, ' to the intent that they may be no more seen and perused, but buried in oblivion '.[2]

---

[1] On 17th September another Act was passed forbidding their return at all without Parliament's permission (*Acts of Barbados*, Nos. 52 and 53, edited by J. Jennings, London, 1673).

[2] *Acts of Barbados*, No. 67, edited by J. Jennings, London, 1673.

Before departing to establish the Parliament's authority in the Leeward Islands, Ayscue carried out his instructions by appointing Colonel Daniel Searle as Governor.

Thus was Barbados reduced to submission. In these eventful years of the Civil War the island had virtually become an independent state, owning the direct control of neither King nor Parliament. Reorganized as a constitutional machine by Philip Bell, and converted into a thriving sugar plantation by means of the facilities of free trade with the Dutch, the island had experienced a period of unrivalled prosperity. Then the collapse of one of the disputing parties in England had flooded her with political exiles, who, smarting under a sense of injury, compelled Barbados to take sides in the struggle. The same collapse had freed the hands of the triumphant Parliament to enforce its authority upon that island and to re-forge, both in government and trade, the ties of imperial control.

III

BARBADOS UNDER THE PROTECTORATE
(1652–60)

The Act of 1650 prohibiting all trade with the royalist colonies, also contained a clause which forbade all foreign vessels without special licence ' to come to or Trade in, or Traffique with any the colonies of England '.[1] The colonial market was a perquisite of the Mother Country, to be enjoyed by her alone. It was a policy born of the general mercantilist view. Europe was an armed camp of national units striving for supremacy in the new fields of commerce opened up by discovery. To be dependent on a neighbour for any sort of commodity was considered an economic disadvantage—a tilting of the ' balance of trade ' in the wrong direction. National self-sufficiency was the ideal state.

Consequently each European country looked on its colonies as an invaluable aid to that end. The supply of food, clothing, and equipment to the settlers would stimulate home industries ; while the monopoly of those colonial commodities which the Mother Country herself could not produce, saved her the expense of buying from her European rivals. Just as the medieval town had closed its gates to the ' foreigner ' from the next county ; so now the national community sought prosperity by the same policy of economic isolation.

[1] C.O. 1/11, No. 21, P. R. O.

The Act excluding foreign trade from the English colonies in 1650 merely gave statutory expression to a policy which had been spasmodically pursued under the régime of the Stuarts.[1]

In particular the Act was aimed at the Dutch. As already described, the first care of Sir George Ayscue had been to seize all Dutch merchantmen found at Barbados. For the traders of that nation had reaped a golden harvest during the Civil War. Aided by a financial organization superior to that of other European communities, and favourably situated on the trade routes East and West, they had driven the English from the fisheries of the north, from the Baltic, and from the lucrative trade of the Spice Islands.[2] The international carrying trade of the Dutch had also so expanded, that England was reduced to seeing the commerce of her colonial empire with Europe controlled by her rival. The development of Barbados into a great sugar plantation had been almost entirely the result of free trade with Holland.

As soon therefore as the Commonwealth was firmly established, active steps were taken to attack the Dutch supremacy. In 1651 the 'Rump' Parliament passed the famous Navigation Act, which provided that foreign goods must be brought into England either in English ships or in those of the producing country—thus eliminating the Dutch middleman. The expected result was open war with Holland, which was declared in July 1652.

Upon the colonies the Navigation Act itself had little effect. The Dutch, or any other nation, were still free according to its provisions to barter their own native commodities at English plantations. In this

[1] Cf. *The Origins of the British Colonial System, 1578–1660*, by G. L. Beer, *passim* (New York, 1922).
[2] Ibid., chapter xii.

ordinance there was no attempt to restrict colonial exports to the home market as there had been under Charles I, and as there was again after the Restoration. It was only the punitive Act of 1650—originally passed as a temporary measure—which forbade all foreign intercourse with the colonies. It was argued by the planters of Barbados and elsewhere, and with much reason, that once these outlawed colonies had submitted, the act of outlawry became automatically null and void, with all clauses therein contained. The Barbadians in particular considered their case unanswerable, based as it was on ' Artēs of Warr which are ye ffaith of ye nation, which were given by Sir George Ayscue and Confirmed by Parliament '.[1] In those Articles, Barbados had been granted—' as great a freedom of trade as ever ' ; and the islanders insisted that they were thereby entitled to that free trade which they had enjoyed before the surrender.[2] The United Provinces on their side and the port of Hamburg, made several efforts to obtain permission for a continuance of their former trade.[3] But the Council of State persistently held that the Act of 1650 was in force ; and that therefore all foreigners were debarred from trade with English colonies.

It is evident, however, that for some years Barbados freely ignored these injunctions and continued to trade with Europe as before. The discovery by Sir George Ayscue of seventeen foreign vessels in Barbados harbours, was only an index of the freedom of trade which had been enjoyed by the island during her

[1] Add. MSS. (Brit. Mus.) 11411, f. 3b, ' The State of the Difference as it is pressed between ye merchants and ye planters in relation to free trade att ye Charibee Islands '.

[2] Cf. Tanner MSS. (Bodleian) 55, f. 141b, ut supra. Ayscue had warned them that he only meant it ' under such Restrictions and Limitations as are enacted by ye Parliament of England '.

[3] e. g. H.M.C. xiii. 1, Portland MSS. i, pp. 542-3, ut supra.

period of independence. But when the expedition sent by Cromwell three years later found fifteen more foreign merchantmen riding in Carlisle Bay, the conclusion seems to be that the subjection of Barbados to the Commonwealth had not greatly altered her trade relations. This disregard of the Act seems to have been known to the home authorities. William Penn, the admiral of the expedition, was instructed, ' to seize and in case of resistance to sink, burn and destroy, all foreign ships and vessels trading without license with the Barbados, Virginia, Bermudas and Antigua '.[1] And Penn himself issued similar orders to his subordinate officers.[2] A warrant also was issued to five of the principal inhabitants of Barbados appointing them commissioners, ' for putting in force the laws prohibiting foreign vessels from trading with Barbados to the prejudice of the Commonwealth of England '.[3]

The commanders of this force which touched at Barbados in 1655, discovered that Governor Searle was himself supporting the illegal trade. Writing home on 10th March of that year, Edward Winslow remarked that Searle's behaviour in matters of trade ' hath been very strange and wary, leaving to himselfe in his owne apprehension, a starting hole in every case '. According to Winslow the Dutch captains of the confiscated vessels all pleaded in defence that they had received licences from Searle ;[4] and the latter

---

[1] H.M.C. xiii, Portland MSS., Part II, vol. ii, p. 89.
[2] *Thurloe State Papers*, vol. iii, p. 583.
[3] Portland MSS., ibid., p. 90.
[4] Searle also allowed ships from Hamburg to trade with Barbados. Cf. Rawlinson MSS. (Bodleian) A, vol. 3, f. 135 : ' By the Governor— These are to Lycence the Shipp called the Golden Dolphinn of Hamburgh, Burthen two hundred tuns or thereabouts two line gunns, to come to this Island and here freely to trade with aney the inhabitants hereof provided shee bring noe other than the native commodities of that Country According to an Act of Parliament in

' denies not but he gave them free leave to trade :
but in the tail of all he tells them, if they trade against
the Laws of England, at their peril and fortune be it '.
Under such circumstances it is hardly surprising to
be told that the Dutchmen complained exceedingly of
him. When taxed with having defied the law, as well
as Cromwell's personal instructions to execute the
same, Searle reminded his questioners that he had
signed the Articles of peace, and did not intend to go
back on them.[1]

In this the Governor merely voiced public opinion.
So high did feeling run that in a case at law between
the Customs officials and some Dutch traders whose
goods had been confiscated, no Barbadian attorney
would plead the cause of the State. And when
the jury found for the strangers in defiance of the
Acts, there was general rejoicing. ' The Dutch
were courted and highly prized, and sent home in a
triumphant manner, to invite them freely to the trade
of Barbados, by which means many more of them are
expected before May next.'[2] Indeed Winslow felt
that unless a man-of-war was permanently stationed
at the island, the newly appointed commission for preventing foreign trade would be unable to cope with
the situation.[3]

During the expedition's stay at the island, another

that case made and provided. Given under my hand and seale of
Armes this 7th June 1653. Daniel Searle.'

[1] *Thurloe State Papers*, vol. iii, pp. 249–52 (Edward Winslow to
Secretary Thurloe, 16th March 1655). [2] Ibid.

[3] ' The riches of the island far exceeds England's apprehension, the
Dutch having hitherto reaped all the effects of the peace, and if we
lay not a command upon the militia to be aiding the Commission
office I verily believe, when we are gone, we shall have them stopt
by an injunction from the Governor and the cases referred to the
Common Law '—where, of course, the verdict would be a foregone
conclusion (ibid.).

incident occurred to illustrate the close working alliance between the Hollanders and Barbados. Stuyvesant, the famous Dutch Governor of the New Netherlands, arrived with three ships under his command, with the intention of making a permanent trading arrangement between Barbados and his colony. 'But', remarks Winslow with grim humour, 'we spoilt the sport.' He was seized and his goods confiscated.

On the other hand it is apparent that, although the Acts were freely ignored by the inhabitants, yet Dutch respect for Cromwell and the prowess of the English Navy so deterred those traders that Barbados was to a large extent deprived of her most valued market. Numerous letters and petitions sent from the island to the home government confirm this view. Writing to the Council of State on 8th October 1652, Governor Searle pointed out that hitherto the island trade had been chiefly carried on by Hollanders, and that the Act of 1650 'hath in a great measure taken them off from it, soe that at present the Iland not having binne long since reduced and but few shipps of our nation as yet come hither, there is some scarcity and want of comodities in it '.[1] The sense of grievance which these hardships aroused among the Barbadians, continued to rankle, and if anything to increase, as time went on. English prices were found to be dearer than Dutch, and sugars in consequence dropped in value. In 1655 Captain Gregory Butler, a Commonwealth man lately arrived from England, wrote to Cromwell: 'The islanders heer much desire commerce with strangers, our English merchants trafiquing to those parts being generally great extortioners. I humble represent to your Highness the allowing forreigne commerce, which can be no way prejudiciall, imposing upon them double

[1] C.O. 1/11, No. 68, P. R. O.

custom to be paid in our English plantations in these parts.'[1]

Against this monopoly of the English merchant Barbados offered a vigorous opposition. About 1655 the inhabitants presented to the Council of State a demand for their former freedom of trade, pointing out with uncomfortable candour that the settlement of the island and its subsequent prosperity had been performed with ' little or no encouragement or protection from ye supremacy of England '. In the times of their greatest distress they had — ' found reliefe and advantage by fforreigners; and before the late Defeccon and prohibition of free trade, they bought their negros, Horses and other necessaries and provisions cheaper by more than one half of ye present price '. Furthermore they maintained their rights and liberties as free English subjects, reminding the Parliament that Barbados had a special claim to such freedom by the terms of the Articles of Surrender ; but in their present condition they were no better than ' so many slaves to the merchants, employed and appointed to Drudgerie '.[2] Such a petition seems to indicate that the Acts were operating extensively ; and that foreign trade to Barbados was now reduced to a few occasional vessels, willing to run the risk of confiscation.]

The Barbadian planters were therefore unremitting in their efforts to obtain the repeal of the Act of 1650.

[1] *Thurloe*, vol. iii, p. 142. Butler to Cromwell, 7th Feb. 1654–5.
[2] Add. MSS. (Brit. Mus.) 11411, f. 3b. The answer of the English merchants in support of the Acts was an epitome of the mercantilist view. They stated that free trade was wholly contrary to the policy of foreign powers, and ' That therefore ye English ought to use ye same Pollicies for ye better ballancing of Trade ; ' and also ' That by ye consequencies of this Unlimited Trade those Islands will in a short time be brought to dissert English Interests and become ye Treasure of other nations ' (ibid., f. 4a).

A further petition from the Council and Assembly
was dispatched to Cromwell in 1656, urging the
reasonableness and justice of their former demands,
which if granted would be ' noe diminution to your
Highnes greatness And power ' [1] Again, a year later,
Daniel Searle wrote informing Cromwell that a complaint had been presented at a General Assembly,
' relating to the sufferances which the people of this
colony have of late undergone, by reason of the inter-
mission of all trade with foreigners in amity with
England '.[2] This protest expressed a view which
seems to have originated about this time, and which
became so familiar a feature in the colonial affairs of
the eighteenth century—namely, that if the Mother
Country and its dependency were indeed subject to
one authority, then the same restrictions and the same
privileges must apply to both. If, said the Barbadians,
our island is an integral part of the English Commonwealth, we have a right to that trade with foreign
nations which is enjoyed by England. And notwithstanding the firm refusals with which these petitions
were received at home, the islanders returned to the
charge. After the resignation of Richard Cromwell in
1659, Barbados presented another and more elaborate
petition. In addition to political demands, which if
granted would have revolutionized the relationship
between the colony and the home government,
equality of trade-privilege was again insisted on. The
petitioners called upon the right honourable gentlemen ' to revive the Spiritts of this y^{or} remote colony ',
and to comfort and nourish ' this limb of the great
body of the nation of England '. Since we are obliged
to bear the burdens, caused by political upheavals at

---

[1] Rawlinson MSS. (Bodleian) A, 36, f. 680 ; printed in *Thurloe*,
vol. iv, p. 651.

[2] *Thurloe*, vol. vi, p. 169. Searle to the Protector, 4th April 1657.

home, ' soe we cannot but submitt and humbly crave, to partake of those Immunities, priviledges, and ffree-doms which oᵣ Brethren of England, doe and may receive '. In point of fact they asked for more than their brethren of England at that time enjoyed : ' That all nations in Amity may bring us provisions, Servants, Horses, Slaves, Mares, and Cattle, whether of their owne growth or not.' [1] At the same time the Mother Country in various ways compensated the colonies for their loss. Foreign trade was denied them ; but by means of a preferential tariff they were given a virtual monopoly of the market at home. Furthermore, England allowed her colonists to buy certain home manufactures which were rigidly barred from the foreigner. Considerable numbers of horses, fire-arms, clothing apparel, boots and shoes, which would have found a ready sale at home were sent over-seas for the benefit of the dependencies.[2]

As already indicated, colonial tobacco and sugar received a preference over the foreign product in the English market.[3] This preferential system was now extended as the result of Barbadian pressure, in favour of the colonies.

In the winter of 1655–6, the islanders sent home a most important petition, demanding that they should ' pay no Customs for yᵉ Exportation of necessaries for their subsistence ', and secondly that the import duties in England on their ginger and sugar should be reduced. If Jersey, Guernsey, and New England—all of them less lucrative than Barbados—might be freed of custom, how much more so this great sugar colony. With regard to ginger, the petition pointed out that

---

[1] Egerton MSS. (Brit. Mus.) 2395, f. 182.

[2] See table on next page.

[3] See *Commons Journals*, vi, pp. 333–4, quoted in preceding chapter ;
English white sugars 3*d*. per lb.   Foreign white sugars 3½*d*.
do. ' underwhites ' 2*d*. „   do. ' underwhites ' 2½*d*.

The following is a list of licences granted to Barbadian buyers of goods usually prohibited :—

Date.	Commodity.
1652 Apr. 7	600 dozen pairs of shoes
1652 May 10	500 dozen pairs of shoes
1652 May 26	30 horses
1652 June 1	30 horses and 300 dozen of shoes
1652 July 7	10 horses
1652 Oct. 3	20 horses
1652 Nov. 5	16 horses
1652 Nov. 8	24 horses
1652 Nov. 9	50 dozen of shoes
1652 Nov. 15	30 horses
1653 Feb. 11	600 dozen of shoes and 20 dozen of boots
1653 Mar. 11	40 horses
1653 Sept. 7	800 dozen of shoes
1653 Sept. 27	40 horses
1653 Oct. 18	200 dozen of shoes and 6 dozen of boots
1653 Nov. 16	600 dozen of shoes
1653 Nov. 18	300 dozen of shoes and 8 horses
1653 Nov. 26	20 horses
1653 Dec. 31	5 tons of cheese
1654 May 24	500 dozen of shoes and 5 tons of cheese
1654 July 25	100 horses
1655 Jan. 24	34 horses
1655 Feb. 5	900 dozen of shoes
1655 Feb. 19	500 pairs of shoes and 20 horses
1655 Mar. 12	2,000 dozen of shoes and 300 dozen of boots
1655 Mar. 27	20 horses and 7 tons of cheese
1655 Mar. 27	20 barrels of butter
1655 Mar. 27	500 dozen of shoes
1655 Mar. 27	100 dozen of boots
1655 May 31	600 dozen of shoes and 30 horses
1655 Aug. 29	600 dozen of shoes
1655 Sept. 6	50 horses (200 asked for)
1655 Dec. 11	40 horses
1656 Jan. 22	30 horses
1656 Feb. 8	50 horses (200 asked for)
1656 Nov. 13	30 horses
1656 Nov. 18	740 horses
1656 Nov. 19	(various merchants)
1657 Jan. 6	1,000 pairs of shoes

References : Cal. Col. 1574–1660, pp. 377, 379, 385, 390, 392, 393, 400, 401, 407, 409, 410, 411, 412, 417, 420, 421, 422, 424, 425, 428, 433, 436.

the price had fallen from £5 sterling per 100 lb. to 25*s.* owing to the increasing supply, and 'yet ye Imposition remaynes att ye same height'. With regard to sugar, it was stated that the present tariff enabled Brazilian sugars to undersell the Barbadian product.[1]

Cromwell's reply to this petition was to enjoin the islanders to behave themselves and cease their flouting of the Navigation Act, and he would see what he could do for them.[2]

The result was satisfactory. The system under which English goods were exported to Barbados was revised. A great number of commodities were removed from the list of forbidden exports. A number of articles, including all foodstuffs, were declared free of Customs ; and where the duty was continued, the existing rates were revised in favour of the colony. In the case of exported horses—one of the chief needs of Barbados—the rate of 20*s.* a head imposed in 1654 was now reduced to 10*s.*[3] Furthermore, the demand for the preferential treatment of colonial ginger and white sugars was conceded in a liberal manner. The Barbadian planters thus gained both for themselves and the colonies in general trade concessions of the first importance in encouraging their development.

In reviewing therefore the economic situation with regard to Barbados during the Interregnum, the following general conclusions may be drawn. From 1652 until the arrival in 1655 of the Venables Expedition, the Act forbidding trade with foreigners was almost entirely ignored, and the free trade so long enjoyed by Barbados continued with little interruption. But the temporary presence of a strong naval and military force enabled the home government to bring pressure to bear at Barbados in a way which normally would have been impossible. The sudden

---

[1] Add. MSS. (Brit. Mus.) 11411, f. 9b. [2] Ibid., f. 13.
[3] See *Cal. Col.* 1574–1660, pp. 414, 442.

seizure of seventeen foreign vessels there, and the fact
that after 1655 Barbados became a regular port of call
for vessels on their way to the new colony of Jamaica,
were factors sufficiently deterrent to scare away all
but the most daring of foreign adventurers.[1] After
1655, therefore, it may safely be said that alien intercourse with Barbados dwindled to insignificance. At
the same time this loss was to some extent compensated
by special concessions granted in England—concessions which, owing to Barbadian activity, became
widely extended. Whether Barbadian prosperity was
injured or otherwise by this restriction of colonial
trade to England, it is difficult to determine. The
planters themselves were fond of painting the benefits
of free trade in glowing colours. And during the
Civil War when the English market temporarily disappeared, the traders of Holland and Hamburg had
undoubtedly proved indispensable. Yet in an age when
every nation was barring its gates against its neighbours
by means of high tariffs, it is very doubtful whether
the security and privilege of the home market was not
more advantageous than the uncertain profits to be had
in the ports of Europe.

Meanwhile Governor Daniel Searle had been pursuing his task of trying to reconcile a community to an
authority which had been resisted by force of arms.
It was the case of a small minority holding down the
general mass of the people. Searle found the task
neither pleasant nor easy. The Governor had not
been in his place a month when the long-hoped-for
arrival of Prince Rupert, with his royalist fleet, in the
West Indies took place. The island was immediately
agog with excitement; and royalist hopes revived.
But they were doomed to another disappointment.

[1] That a certain amount of secret trading with aliens still continued, is shown by the seizure of six foreign vessels at Barbados by
Captain Myngs in 1658 (*Cal. Col.* 1574–1660, pp. 120, 121, 467).

The log-book of the fleet describes how that when they were about fifty leagues east of Barbados a ship was spied to the southward and chased. While thus engaged the Admiral's ship sprang so great a leak that they had much ado to keep her afloat. The chase was abandoned; and 'thus being in Confusion wee over runn our reckonings and passed the Barbados in the night without seeing it'.[1]

While the appearance of Prince Rupert was being daily awaited, some of the more ardent spirits allowed too free an expression of their hopes, and were accordingly arrested. Others, perhaps in the hope of furthering an invasion, left the island in boats by night; 'which', Searle remarked with satisfaction, 'is a good riddance'.[2] A certain Isaac Cloake, a sergeant in the militia, was condemned to death for high treason, 'for traitorously rehearsing aloud these wicked seditious and treasonable words, "For God and King Charles, God bless King Charles"'. The gentleman, however, on appealing to the Council of State was reprieved, in that he was drunk at the time.[3] Searle, in spite of his declaration that he was not in the least frightened of Rupert, took the precaution of having guns mounted in the various bays to protect the merchant ships, and of sending home for frigates to protect the shipping routes. These he promised to man with armed troops for close-quarter work under Colonel Lewis Morris.[4]

It seems very doubtful, however, even if Rupert had

[1] 'Prince Rupert's Voyage to the West Indies' (Add. MSS. Brit. Mus. 30307, f. 19). The incident described took place on 8th May 1652. Cf. Governor Searle's account (C.O. 1/11, No. 57, P. R. O.). After missing Barbados, Prince Rupert proceeded to the Leeward Islands, where he spent several months fruitlessly cruising to and fro. Eventually the fleet returned to Europe in a battered condition.

[2] C.O. 1/11, No. 57, P. R. O., op. cit.

[3] *Cal. Col.* 1574–1660, pp. 380–1.

[4] Ibid., p. 383. Colonel Morris had distinguished himself under Ayscue at the Scilly Isles.

attempted anything more serious than a temporary raid, whether the mass of the inhabitants would have given him active support. The experience of civil warfare was too fresh in their minds. Nevertheless the Governor had to deal with explosive material when enforcing the commands of the Commonwealth. On 30th October 1652, he issued a commission to the justices of the leeward parts of the island, directing them at their Quarter Sessions to declare the book of Common Prayer abolished and its further use prohibited, ' whose Efects to make up a dumb and lasie Ministry hath been answerable to what could be expected from their idolatrous original'.[1] The Justices obeyed their instructions and issued a declaration calling in all copies of the forbidden book, which were to be delivered up to them at their next Privy Sessions in All Saints Church. Outward conformity to this order was yielded by all except Charles Robson, the parson of All Saints, ' a canonical creature, formerly a Prebendiary of Salisbury's'. This gentleman, when brought before the court on 18th November, peremptorily refused to deliver up his copy, and said he would dispute the order, ' encouraging the people now to Stand to it or never'. The Court very naturally answered they were not there to argue, but to carry out the orders of Parliament; and therefore placed Mr. Robson under arrest. But to the wrath of the Commonwealth men, Major Bailey, a royalist officer who had submitted to Parliament, ' dismembered himself from the Court, and joyned with the distemper'd multitude wheare many hundreds were gathered together, and rescued the said Robson from the Marshall, animating the people to a mutinous opposition'. He then harangued the crowd, declaring

[1] Pamphlet, Brit. Mus. (488, b. 19), London, 1653. Calendared in H.M.C. xiii, Portland MSS., Part I, vol. i, p. 669.

he was sorry he had ever signed the declaration, that it was the foolishest act that ever he did. This speech so excited its hearers, ' that presently swords, canes and cudgells were upp, and a dangerous disturbance made '.[1] It was only the prompt action of the Governor that saved an awkward situation.

Searle's position, difficult enough already, was rendered still more so by the limitations imposed on his power as Governor. The Council of State when drawing up his commission, had withheld the power of nominating his Council, and had given him no definite power of veto. Consequently, he was liable to be constantly outvoted at his own council table. The purpose of the home authorities seems to have been to keep a more direct control over a colony which had been so recently in revolt. But as it happened this action coincided with a ' home rule ' movement inside the colony itself. This impatience of all external authority, in political no less than economic affairs, was chiefly the result of the conditions under which the colony had developed. From very early times the island settlers had been thrown on their own resources. So complete had been the neglect of the Earl of Carlisle, that the struggling planters had regarded him with the utmost scorn. During the Civil War the proprietorship became a mere name ; and the island under Governor Bell was to all intents and purposes an autonomous state. Consequently, when the shadow of proprietary rule was replaced by the very real and direct control of the Commonwealth, the unaccustomed yoke was bitterly resented. As preceding events have illustrated, the population consisted of a small section of royalist ' Die-Hards ', a still smaller party of extreme republicans, and a large majority of moderates, whose sympathies were with the exiled King, but whose chief care was the peace and prosperity of Barbados.

[1] Ibid.

It was this body of public opinion that had supported
Bell's policy of neutrality—a policy which had brought
the island phenomenal wealth and comparative security
during a period of political upheaval.   It was again
this sober-minded majority which had compelled the
Walrond party to make peace when reasonable terms
were offered.

Now that their prosperity was threatened by the
economic policy of the Protectorate, the Barbadians
by the same rule inaugurated a campaign of independence.   Some openly worked for what would now
be called dominion status, the establishment of a free
state in working alliance with England.   Another
group, consisting chiefly of men who advocated the
existing régime at home, insisted that Barbados was as
much a part of the Commonwealth as any English
county, and therefore demanded a direct representation in the imperial parliament.   The leader of the
latter part was the ex-royalist, Colonel Modiford.
As early as 16th February 1652, before Ayscue had
left the island, he had written to John Bradshaw
declaring his complete adherence to Commonwealth
principles, and urging the government to adopt a
course that would gain the goodwill of the colony.
He pointed out how jealously the planters maintained
their right of equal privilege with their countrymen
at home.   ' The great difficulty is one which your
wisdom will easily overcome.   How wee shall have
a representative with you in your and our parliam^t.
To demand to have burgesses with you to sitt and
vote in matters concerning England may seeme
immodest, but to desire two representatives to be
chosen by this Island to advise and consent to matters
that concern this place, I presume may be both just and
necessary.' [1] If laws were to be imposed without their
consent, they could be accounted no better than slaves.

[1] C.O. 1/11, No. 41, P. R. O.

Modiford's action was not lacking of support. A few months later a number of influential planters residing in London presented various ' considerations ' to the Council of State, in which among other things, it was proposed, ' y^t y^u permitt 2 Gent^s to sitt and have votes in the Parlt of England as Representatives of this Island, Then ther can be no complaint, but y^t we have a Part and as much privilege ther as any County in England.'[1] If these proposals had been generally accepted, the subsequent course of American history might well have been very different.

At the same time the free-state party, which desired secession rather than greater freedom within the Commonwealth, was busily at work. John Bayes, a Roundhead planter, relates that the movement began among the Barbadians in England, before Ayscue set out to reduce the island. He describes the design as an attempt ' to make this Place A free State and not to runn any fortune with England either in Peace or Warr '.[2] Within the island the way was prepared by enhancing the power of the Council and Assembly at the expense of that of the Governor. The action of the Council at Whitehall in restricting Searle's authority thus played into their hands. The ambition of the secessionists seems to have been to emulate the autocracy enjoyed by the Long Parliament just before the Civil War. In imitation of the House of Commons, the Assembly elected a Speaker, their first choice being Thomas Modiford. Their next action was to pass a law abolishing the power of the Governor and Council to sit as a court of equity. By this means appeals to the Governor were prevented, the final decision in all cases now resting with the local judges.

[1] C.O. 1/11, No. 66, P. R. O. ' Considerations to be presented to the Council of State, concerning the present settlement of Barbados.'
[2] John Bayes to the Council of State, 30th June 1652. (C.O. 1/11, No. 59, P. R. O.)

It is significant that the Assembly which was thus laying hold of authority, had been elected under Ayscue's direction. Its first action had been to banish Lord Willoughby and the other royalist leaders from the island.[1] Yet John Bayes declared that the Parliament men were frightened of it, and that the majority of its members were ' old overgrown desperate malignants '.[2] In point of fact the Assembly represented the generality of public opinion, which had a sentimental regard for the Stuart dynasty, but which resented the imposition of any authority but its own. The same persons who so persistently demanded free trade were aiming at an equal freedom in civil government. And in the latter project considerable success was achieved. On 4th February 1653 Bayes wrote to the Committee for Foreign Affairs that the Barbados parliament had ' soe eclipst the Governor's power, that at p̄sent he signifieth litle, only his title—haueing not the fifth part of that power wch all former governors have Had '.[3] The remedy, as the writer indicated, was to give Searle adequate authority over his Council. As matters stood, the councillors were commissioned direct from Whitehall, and considered themselves the Governor's equal. Without their consent he could neither appoint nor remove any officer, military or civil. Accordingly, on 13th June 1653, Cromwell issued a new commission to Searle as Governor of Barbados until further order, in which he was expressly granted the power of choosing and controlling his Council.[4]

[1] See *Cal. Col.* 1574–1660, p. 391.

[2] John Bayes must be taken *cum grano salis*. He was a notorious firebrand, and nursed, moreover, a grudge against the present Council and Assembly for having dismissed him from his post of public treasurer, upon certain articles of charge ' (H.M.C. xiii, Loder and Symond MSS. iv, p. 390, 6th Oct. 1652).

[3] C.O. 1/12, No. 2, P. R. O.

[4] *Cal. Col.* 1574–1660 .p. 404 ; cf. pp. 395–6.

The arrival of this commission, however, only served to intensify the opposition of the royalist majority. Searle's first step was to discuss the nomination of his new councillors, 'with severall persons of knowne integritye and faithfulnes to the Interest and State of the Commonwealth'.[1] The next step was the election of a new Assembly, at which Searle and the Commonwealth party did their utmost to secure the election of candidates of their own persuasion. But the inhabitants chose otherwise. Twenty out of the twenty-two candidates so proposed were rejected; and Searle wrote home complaining that such was the affection of the people to their former interest that they had 'made choice of such as formerly for the most part had bin the greatest Ennimies of the Commonwealth in this place'.[2] The result of the election caused consternation among the Roundheads, who advised the Governor to dismiss the new Assembly immediately.

Searle, however, gained the day. After listening to his inaugural speech the members expressed their readiness ' to submitt to the Authority of the Commonwealth as now established'.[3] But the officers of the militia were not so easily placated. In consequence of their rebellious attitude, the Governor on 18th August issued a stern proclamation declaring that any one using seditious words against the Commonwealth, or any officer assembling men in arms without lawful warrant, would suffer the death penalty. All commissions to field-officers were called in, and those of the disaffected cancelled.

Moreover, the submission of the Assembly was, as Searle himself described it, merely ' a seemeing

---

[1] C.O. 1/12, No. 9, P.R.O.   [2] Ibid.

[3] Ibid. Opposition had primarily centred round the disputed legality of the new commission, which had been issued by Cromwell and the unconstitutional 'Barebones' Parliament. Searle's original commission had been authorized by the 'Rump'—nominally the Long Parliament of 1642.

contentment'. The policy of encroachment on the Governor's power was continued without delay. In its first session the Assembly demanded no less than permanent representative government. Its own existence was to be guaranteed for one year; after which annual elections were to take place, the new Assembly formally commencing its session before the old dissolved. The Assemblymen stated that they made these demands because they were the representatives of the people and the guardians of their laws and liberties.

The Governor's refusal was categorical. ' I know ', he replied, ' of noe other representatives of the nation of England, in what parts soe ever of the Commonwealth they are in, Intrusted with the Lives Liberties and Estates of this People, but the supreame authority which God hath established and sett over us.' [1] To grant such a request was entirely beyond the powers of his commission. When reporting the incident to the Council of State, he expressed the opinion that such a concession, ' were in effect to establish them a ffree state, independent to the Commonwealth, only to remaine under England's protection, but not to owne England's Jurisdiction; ' [2]—an ideal state of affairs from the colonial point of view.[3]

The weakness of the ruling minority in Barbados is well illustrated in one of Searle's dispatches, in which he urges that an Act of Parliament disabling royalists from bearing office or having any voice in elections,

[1] C.O. 1/12, No. 12, P. R. O.

[2] Ibid. Searle particularly blamed Speaker Modiford for leading the agitation, describing him as a royalist at heart, who had only joined Ayscue when the battle of Worcester had made royalist success impossible. He deprived him of his regiment of militia. But Modiford successfully appealed to Cromwell for a reversal of the order. See *Cal. Col.* 1574–1660, pp. 406–7 and 413.

[3] For the further activities of the ' Home Rule ' party in Barbados, see C.O. 1/12, Nos. 12, i and ii.

should not be enforced in Barbados ; for 'the saide Act hath not hitherto bin Publickly put in Execution in this place by reason of the verrie small number of others heare that Come not within the Compass of the Act '.[1] In other words, there were not enough Commonwealth men to run the Government.[2]

Meanwhile Searle's difficulties were increased by the rapid changes of the constitution at home. No sooner had he officially recognized one style of government, when another took its place. On 17th February 1654 the Governor received news that the 'Barebones' Parliament had voluntarily yielded up its powers, and that according to the 'Instrument of Government' Cromwell had assumed the title and authority of Lord Protector, assisted by a Council and duly elected triennial parliaments. Searle therefore immediately wrote to Cromwell, declaring his belief that the hand of Providence was responsible for 'leadeinge your highnes through such wildenesses and seas of trouble' to his present position, where at last he would be able to give the nation peace. To prevent confusion on the island, Searle asked that his 'highnes pleasuer and comands maight be made knowne unto us '.[3] A few weeks later the official proclamations arrived. All

---

[1] C.O. 1/12, No. 13.

[2] On 14th Jan. 1654 several merchants of London, who had trade interests in Barbados, proposed a very drastic method to enforce the Commonwealth authority in the island. Seven persons of known fidelity to the Commonwealth were to be sent over to govern Barbados, with power to elect one of their own number president every year. A special council in England was to control this action. The suggestion was not, however, adopted. News of the petition reached Barbados, and the Governor and Council, on 30th March 1654, drew up and sent a formal declaration to Cromwell, assuring him that the merchants' statement as to the distraction of the government in the island was untrue, and that 'this island is in a generall tranquility, peace, and concord under the administration of the Government of the same' (*Thurloe*, ii, p. 200 ; *Cal. Col.* 1574–1660, p. 413).

[3] *Thurloe*, ii, pp. 99–100.

officials were continued in their offices until further
order. The proclamations were duly published on
8th March at Bridgetown, and publicly read in all the
churches on the following Sunday. Yet the Governor
was obliged to report once again that he found ' noe
other acceptance amongst this people but a generall
seeming contentment '.[1] In the same letter he made
a respectful but pointed request that the Protector
would never allow himself to be swayed in matters
affecting Barbados by petitions from agitators in
England until Searle himself had been consulted.
This colony had but recently been in open revolt
against the Commonwealth; and he must not be
blamed if he takes every precaution to prevent royalist
intrigues both in Barbados and at home, the object of
which was ' to rule with more advantage to themselves and their former interest, and less dependence
on the Commonwealth '.[2]

Cromwell, however, was about to affect the fortunes
of Barbados in a very different way—by an armed
invasion of the West Indies. That energetic statesman
regarded the Spaniard and all his ways with an aversion
characteristic of the Elizabethans. He appears to have
entertained the ambition of driving the Spaniards
completely out of the New World, and of expanding
the empire of the British to take their place. Unfortunately he was grossly misinformed as to the
magnitude of his task. Among others, Thomas Gage,
a veteran pioneer, wrote to Cromwell, urging an
attack on Spanish America in the strongest terms.
According to him the Main was waiting to be conquered. In the greatest cities there was ' not one gun
or field-piece, or wall, castle or any bulwarke '; the
Spanish population was lazy and debauched, ' never
trained up to warres '; and furthermore the oppressed

---

[1] *Thurloe*, ii, pp. 198–9, 30th March 1654, Searle to the Protector.
[2] Ibid.

Indians, if granted their liberty, would join the invader *en masse*. Once the territory was acquired planters would flock there with speed ; and especially from Barbados, ' which may afford to such a worke 10,000 fighting men '.[1] Indeed, the exaggerated importance attached to Barbados, and the undue reliance on that colony for supplies and reinforcements, very largely occasioned the subsequent disasters. Similar proposals were urged upon Cromwell by Colonel Modiford. Like Gage he promised substantial reinforcements from Barbados. ' The general should land in Barbados with 2,000 men, in November if he can, where he shall be sure to double his number.'[2] The main attack should be delivered on the mainland, it being more rich and fertile than the islands, and preferably near the River Orinoco, because of the proximity to Barbados. The island would be a base of supply for the new colony, and a safe retreat in the event of disaster.

As soon as peace was settled with the Dutch in 1654 the Protector began preparations for the enterprise. During the summer and autumn supplies were being voted and collected, and commissions prepared.[3] The arrangements, however, were badly managed. Instead of definite regiments being chosen for the service the force was composed of drafts taken from various units. Any chance of high morale or *esprit de corps*

---

[1] ' Some briefe and true observations Concerning the West Indies, humbly presented to his highnesse, Oliver Lord Protector of the Commonwealth of England, Scotland and Ireland ' (*Thurloe*, iii, pp. 59–61).

[2] *Thurloe*, vol. iii, pp. 62–3, ' A Paper of Col. Muddiford concerning the West Indies ', Dec. 1653. See a former paper of Modiford's on the same subject (ibid., i, p. 537).

[3] Ibid., vol. ii, p. 542 (list of provisions to be put on board); p. 543, (list of persons to be commissioned, including three commissioners from England who were to act in co-operation with the Governor of Barbados and six planters there, and with the various Governors and Councils of the Leeward Islands, as occasion served).

was thus ruled out, for the regimental commanders naturally took this opportunity of filling the drafts with undesirables.[1]   To make matters worse, this nondescript force was hurried on board at Portsmouth without training or even inspection.[2]   Particularly unfortunate also was the system of dual control which was employed.   Independent commissions were issued to Admiral Penn to command the Navy, and to General Venables as commander of the land forces. Putting out from Portsmouth on Christmas Day 1654 the expedition arrived at Barbados on 30th January, having been preceded by the Rear-Admiral's squadron two days before.   In Carlisle Bay eleven Dutch merchantmen were discovered, and promptly seized as prize.   'Heare as soune as we came to an anchor many Boates came off to us, with many of the Chefe of the Illand, whoe did profes that wee ware very wellcom, and that as soune as we came ashore we should find it soe, wee telling them that wee ware resolued to trie them.'[3]

The majority of the islanders, however, were bitterly hostile.   The prompt action of Admiral Penn in seizing the Dutch ships warned them that freedom of trade was at an end.   Moreover, the general purpose of the expedition aroused their jealousy and fear. The establishment of a new colony, whether on one of the islands or on the Spanish Main, involved the creation of a dangerous rival in sugar manufacture. The English market would be flooded ; and prices would drop.   Furthermore, a new colony would require a great number of immigrants.   And Barbados justly feared, what in effect actually took place, a serious drainage of her own white population.   Already the proportion of blacks over whites in the island was rapidly increasing ; and this new scheme of coloniza-

---

[1] Cf. the 'Narrative' of Colonel Venables (ed. C. H. Firth), and *Thurloe*, vol. iii, p. 11.   [2] Venables 'Narrative', ut supra, p. 6.
[3] Whistler's account, in the Venables 'Narrative', p. 140.

tion at her expense threatened to render the situation acute. The islanders therefore had every reason to dislike both the presence of the expedition and its ultimate object.

The commanding officers almost immediately came ashore and interviewed the Governor and Council, who received them with civility, and authorized them to billet their soldiers on the inhabitants, ' with an engagement to pay for what they tooke '.[1] General Venables had been instructed to confer with the Barbadian Government as to the best means of raising reinforcements there. Speeches therefore were delivered before the Assembly, pointing out the advantages that would result from the enterprise, and stating that no less than four thousand recruits were expected from Barbados. To prevent the crippling of plantations by the enlistment of bonded servants, Venables suggested that he should be furnished with a list of the freemen, so that recruits would be accepted from that class alone.

As soon as the Assembly had filed back to their own chamber Speaker Modiford urged the acceptance of this proposal, exclaiming how grateful the island should be for such lenient treatment in not disturbing the white servants. But Modiford was already unpopular because of his active share in promoting the expedition.[2] He merely inflamed minds, already irritated. ' I found such a willfully imbittered party,' he wrote, ' that instead of debatinge calmly they fel a clamouringe against the quarteringe soldyers in ther houses, ther rudenesse and misdemeanours, and would

---

[1] *Thurloe*, vol. iii, pp. 566–7 (Modiford to his brother). Nothing was paid for their lodging.

[2] Ibid., pp. 157–9 (J. Berkenhead to Thurloe): ' Here's in the island one Collonel Moodiford and Mr. Nowell, Secretary of the Island's affairs, who are hugely distasted by this island; for that they two, as the islanders say, did invite our forces over hither, which our islanders are generally against. . . .'

come to no conclusion but this, let them beat up drumes and take their owne course, we will not assiste them.' [1]

After their heat had a little abated, Modiford made another attempt to bring them to reason, urging the futility of resistance. But the Assembly was not to be moved. Let the commissioners conduct their own recruiting; and then, if they failed to obtain the requisite numbers, the Assembly would see what could be done. It was a short-sighted policy; for their own position was only made worse by thus giving the commissioners a free hand. The latter accepted this course very reluctantly, warning the inhabitants that the blame for any injuries inflicted must now lie at their own door. The warning was justified by the event.

The recruiting agents naturally took what they could without asking too many questions. Not only free labourers but also great numbers of debtors, and bond servants, who had stolen away from their masters, were accepted for service and hurried on board. Modiford himself admits that, ' though the Commissioners sent out strickt warrants to ther officers not to list servants, yet ther indentures not being writt in their foreheads, they were by some ignorantly and by others wilfully received; and when once they were got into the huddle there was no findinge them '.[1] One of the officers himself describes the hardships thus inflicted: ' the doing of this hath much injured poor people even to their undoing, and prejudiced many of the rich, some losing ten servants, some fifteen, some more, some less, none escaping us; therefore most men will conjecture, hearing of it, that we dealt very severely with our countrymen '.[2]

---

[1] *Thurloe*, vol. iii, pp. 566–7, op. cit.
[2] Letter of Lieutenant-Colonel Barrington, H.M.C. 7th Report, p. 572 (quoted in Venables ' Narrative ', ed. Firth, pp. 28–9).

The islanders' point of view was very understandable. They saw nearly four thousand of the most valuable of their population, the white artisan and servant class, being taken from the island, probably never to return. The safety of the island in the event of a slave rising or a foreign invasion was being seriously endangered in order to help an English Government which the majority of the planters disliked, in its endeavour to establish a colony, which would in all probability prove the ruin of Barbados. The inhabitants did not like it, and the longer the expedition stayed the less they liked it.

Meanwhile, the blunder of the Protector and his Council in imagining that large supplies of arms and provisions could be obtained on the island was becoming increasingly apparent. About three weeks after the fleet's arrival a letter was sent home, complaining that ' all the promises made to us in England of Men, Provisions and Arms, we find to be but Promises '.[1] The writer realized that to obtain foodstuffs from a colony largely devoted to the manufacture of sugar was impossible.[2] To crown these difficulties the store-ships failed to put in an appearance. So anxious had the Protector been to get the expedition under way that he had ordered its departure before the store-ships were ready.

The absence of ammunition and provisions naturally brought the expedition to a standstill. A precarious food supply was maintained, partly from the private stores of the navy (which could ill afford it), partly from the confiscated cargoes of the Dutch, and finally by commandeering the personal supplies of the islanders. ' And so, we lye still,' wrote a member of the expedition, ' eatinge up the island, and our shipps eating up their provisions.' [3] Finally, it was discovered

[1] Venables ' Narrative ', pp. 8–10.
[2] Cf. chapter vii, below.   [3] *Thurloe*, vol. iii, p. 157.

that the army so hurriedly embarked at Portsmouth, was virtually unarmed. Inspection proved that there were only two hundred muskets for every regiment of a thousand men. And even these were temporarily useless, as the barrels of the muskets had not yet been fitted with stocks. The gunsmiths' tools were in the missing store-ships, and nothing could be done. Admiral Penn moreover refused to jeopardize the safety of his fleet by disbursing anything except a small quantity of ball, shot, and match. 'Wherefore,' wrote Venables, 'I was necessitated to set all hands to work to make half Pikes . . . which yet were so bad that I suppose Tom Tinker or Tom-a-Bedlam in England marches with better weapons.' [1]

In this strait arms, no less than provisions, were exacted from the Barbadians, the Assembly being requested to hand over two thousand muskets from the regiments of militia. When the planters, fearful for their safety, resisted this order, the commissioners commanded their officers to collect the arms by force,—'in which proceeding some misdemeanours were committed by diverse of the soldyers'.[2] Such rough treatment was not calculated to win enthusiastic support for the expedition.

But there was more to follow. The planters did not yet realize how extensive were the powers which Cromwell had delegated to General Venables. In March 1655 the latter notified the astonished Governor and Assembly that he was about to appropriate the excise duties, 'for the carrying on of the Expedition'. For that purpose two-thirds of the money was to be transferred to the Prize Office, the remaining third being left to pay the Governor's salary.[3] The action

[1] Venables 'Narrative', p. 12.
[2] *Thurloe*, vol. iii, pp. 565–6. Cf. H.M.C. 7th Report, p. 572: 'As for fire-arms, we took them where we could find them, without giving any satisfaction to the owners.'
[3] H.M.C. Portland MSS., Part II, vol. ii, p. 90.

was indeed tantamount to the imposition of a special tax on the inhabitants, for the customs duties normally paid for all public expenses.[1] The islanders protested that such a course contravened the Articles of Surrender, which had guaranteed that no tax would be imposed without their own consent ; but the order was enforced notwithstanding.[2]

In fact, the Protector was taking this opportunity of vindicating the authority of the Commonwealth among the recalcitrant Barbadians. For some time he had been watching with growing anger their defiance of the Acts of Trade and intrigues for political independence. In order to suppress such contumacy, Venables was instructed himself to take charge of and reorganize the island militia. Thus the military as well as the civil government of the colony was taken out of the hands of the inhabitants and lodged with the Protector's emissary. Vested with dictatorial powers, Venables made every effort to ensure the supremacy of the Commonwealth party. The militia was remodelled with new officers, all of whom were known adherents of Cromwell.[3] An instrument was thus forged to uphold the officials of the Prize Office in enforcing the Navigation Act, and in general to overawe all opposition. Indeed, Cromwell was applying

---

[1] *Cal. Col.* 1574–1660, p. 404. When Ayscue returned to England he had presented a request from the Barbadian Government that Parliament would allow them to defray their public expenses by ' continuinge the custome of 4 and 2 per cent. upon all goods of the growth of this place exported, 4 upon what goes off on the merchants accompt, and 2 of what goes off from the planters ' (H.M.C. xiii, Loder and Symond MSS. 4, p. 398).

[2] The Commonwealth commissioners retorted that the inhabitants were in debt to England for a large sum of money which Ayscue had realized on the sale of Dutch vessels confiscated at Barbados, and which had mysteriously disappeared (Winslow's dispatch of 6th March 1655, *Thurloe*, vol. iii, p. 250). Cf. his second dispatch of 30th March, ibid., p. 325.

[3] *Thurloe*, vol. iii, pp. 229 and 352.

to Barbados the same drastic methods by which he had tamed his enemies in the British Isles.

Meanwhile, the long delay of the expeditionary force at Barbados was decreasing the chances of eventual success. Every day brought the hurricane season nearer, during which navigation among the islands was a virtual impossibility. Yet still the supply-ships failed to appear. At last a council of war decided that the expedition should proceed forthwith, leaving the store-ships to follow on. ' But truly, Sir,' wrote Winslow, ' we are so weary of wayting, and the season so neer spent as we are resolved to cast our-selves into the arms of Almighty God, whose provi-dence we trust will be ever for good.' [1] Some time previously it had been decided to deliver the first attack against San Domingo; and on 31st March 1655 the fleet sailed out of Carlisle Bay thither bound.[2] Had we prolonged our stay at Barbados, Venables declared, ' we should have eaten up and devour'd that Island, and so destroy'd it and our selves '.[3] As it was Barbados was weakened by the loss of nearly 4,000 of her white male population, many of whom had taken their wives and families to settle in the new colony. All but a remnant of these emigrants perished.

The failure at San Domingo, the terrible sufferings of the soldiers, and the establishment of a plague-stricken settlement at Jamaica, are events which do not directly concern Barbados. Curiously enough, the

[1] *Thurloe*, vol. iii, p. 325, op. cit. It was now learnt that the supply-ship, *Great Charity*, 'with many others in Company was forced back by the fowle weather '.

[2] The fleet sailed by way of the Leeward Islands, where about 1,200 recruits, who had been collected by commissioners, sent on ahead from Barbados, were taken on board. The landing at San Domingo took place on 14th April (Egerton MSS. Brit. Mus. 2395, f. 60).

[3] Venables ' Narrative ', p. 100. See also p. 93.

task of developing Jamaica from a military settlement
to a rich and important colony fell to a planter of
Barbados, Colonel Modiford.[1]

It must have been with feelings of intense relief that
the planters watched their unwelcome guests embark
and put to sea. Writing to his brother in England,
Modiford relates that there was ' such strange cursinge
and raylinge at these men after they were gone, that
it would have troubled your eares to have heard it '.[2]
At the next session of the Assembly in April the
general discontent intensified by news of the disaster
at San Domingo found expression. It was immediately proposed that John Bayes should be sent home
to present a formal complaint against the conduct
of the commissioners. The question of Venables'
authority in Barbados was also disputed by a demand
to the Protector, ' that our government be under no
command but immediately his '.[3] So unanimous was
the resentment felt against their recent treatment,
that even the Governor's Council supported the proposal.[4] Modiford however, whose guiding principle
at the moment was loyalty to Cromwell, petitioned
for rejection, urging the obvious impossibility of the
proposed demands. Cromwell himself could not
possibly execute all business affecting Barbados ; while
to complain against the commissioners and to grudge
help to the expedition would only anger the Protector
and probably incur a further reduction of local
privilege. Following up his attack by a vigorous
speech, Modiford contended in the first place that
Bayes was no fit person to send as envoy, considering
' his last il offices at home ' :[5] that if Barbados had

---

[1] He was appointed Governor of Jamaica at the Restoration.
[2] Thomas Modiford to his brother Charles, *Thurloe*, vol. iii, pp.
566–7. [3] Ibid.
[4] One of the councillors told John Colleton the reason was because
Venables had said they were ' a company of geese ! ' (ibid., p. 565).
[5] Ibid., pp. 566–7. The fact that such a red-hot republican

suffered under the commissioners it was their own fault for refusing to manage the recruiting themselves ; and finally, ' That it would be apprehended saucinesse in us to circumscribe the supreme magistrate either to persons or the way of his Command.' [1] The Assemblymen of course were quite aware that Cromwell had no time to manage the executive business of a colony. What their demand really meant was that he should leave them to themselves, and not send over officials from England to interfere in their internal government.

Modiford's defence of the Commonwealth officers was the last straw to the angry planters. Knowing the excited state of public opinion the leaders of the protesting party called for a general election, which, as they had expected, returned them with a large majority. Thus secured, they were able to vent their wrath on Modiford. But for him, they declared, Cromwell would never have conceived the idea of interfering in the West Indies. He it was who had contrived the raising of a troop of horse to go with the expedition, and who in fine was responsible for all their woes.[2] And yet he had had the audacity to reprove them for their foolish protests. Modiford himself was wise enough to lie low. He had lost his seat at the general election ; and he wrote to his brother that he was glad enough to be out of politics for the time being.

Thus victorious, the new Assembly proceeded to attack the authority which General Venables had assumed over Barbados. On reorganizing the militia he had issued commissions in his own name as commander-in-chief, thus superseding Governor Searle,

as Bayes was proposed as the bearer of the Assembly's protest to the Protector, indicates that even the Commonwealth party were prepared to withstand arbitrary interference from home.

[1] *Thurloe*, vol. iii, pp. 566–7.   [2] Ibid., p. 567.

who was nominated his second in command. On the departure of the expedition therefore, the military government of Barbados was in the hands of an absentee, who had neither the time nor the opportunity to attend to his duties. Moreover the Governor, who had hitherto always directed military affairs, had now no authority to act. The result was confusion. Strenuous opposition was offered to the orders that had been issued by General Venables. The direction of their own defence, they contended, was inherent in the Barbadian Government, and could not be assumed by any external authority.[1]

The arrival on 1st June 1655 of a new Commission from the Protector appointing Daniel Searle as Governor for another three years, gave the latter an opportunity of expressing the same view. His former commissions he explained had granted him military as well as civil authority, and he humbly conceived that the new patent was ' of noe lesse extent '.[2] Venables's action had deprived him of his military jurisdiction, thus nullifying ' all power and commissions by me granted as governor '.

The position however continued in this confusion until the return of Venables to England in disgrace brought the matter to a head.

On 20th March 1656 Colonel Modiford gave the lead in the existing dilemma with a characteristic combination of statesmanship and self-interest. In a formal ' Protestation ' presented to the Government, he charged the royalist party with having engineered the opposition to General Venables's authority in order to discredit the Commonwealth. As for himself he protested—' I doe in yᵉ Presence of yᵉ all seeing God from yᵉ bottome of my heart, abhorre and abjure yᵉ

[1] Ibid., p. 483, Modiford to his brother, 25 July 1655.
[2] Ibid., pp. 499–500, Searle to the Protector, 1st June 1655.

said Interest of ye Stuarts, as inconsistent wth y^e
Peace and Happiness of o^r Nation, and shall wth my
life and fortune Defend ye Present Government'.[1]
Continuing, he called upon the Governor and Council
to decide upon ' some wholesome Expedient whereby
wee may be Justified in our Actinge and an End put
to ye Present Distractions '. In the meantime he begged
to resign his colonelship of horse.

A week later the Council and Assembly complied
with this advice by requesting Governor Searle to
reassume his military powers.[2]

Actual confusion in the government of Barbados
was thus terminated. But discontent still prevailed.
The development of Jamaica, on which Cromwell had
set his heart, was being effected largely at the expense
of Barbados and the Leeward Islands. On the 8th of
October 1656, Governor Searle received instructions
from the Protector to encourage emigration to Jamaica
as much as possible. For this purpose he was desired
to publish in the island an order, declaring Jamaican
goods free of custom and excise for seven years.
Searle obeyed, but sent home a warning that 4,000
had already gone thither; ' and indeed the parting
from so considerable numbers above mentioned hath
much weakened the strength of this place, for that most
of them were freemen, which is the safety of the island '.[3]

When Colonel Brayne arrived at Barbados on 27th

[1] Add. MSS. (Brit. Mus.) 35251, f. 39 : ' The Protestation of me
Tho. Modiford, Presented ye Lieut. Genrll. by ye hands of Seirg^t Major
Tho. Nowell. . . .'

[2] *Thurloe*, vol. iv, pp. 651–2 (27th March 1656). On 1st April
Searle forwarded this request to the Protector, asking for his permission to adopt the course suggested (ibid., p. 665). A few months
later the required permission was given, and the Governor and Council
remodelled the island forces into four regiments of foot, numbering
in all 4,500 men, and eight troops of horse, each a hundred strong.
The repairing of the coast defences was also undertaken (ibid., vol. v,
p. 564).

[3] Ibid., p. 652 (Searle to Sec. Thurloe, 24th Nov. 1656).

November, seeking reinforcements for Jamaica, he received a chilly reception. ' I found the generalty of the island ', he, reported, ' exceedingly prejudiced against the designe of Jamayca.' [1] He seems, however, to have succeeded in persuading a certain number to venture their fortunes there. The floating population of bond servants who had completed their indentures was always ready to emigrate wherever a chance of obtaining land presented itself. It was a standing source of weakness to Barbados that all land was in the hands of great proprietors. Time-expired servants could not hope to purchase small estates in the island ; and thus the most important section of the population was being continually lost. Owing to this fear that Jamaica would drain their population and also under-sell their sugars at home, Barbadian planters continued to regard that colony with jealous eyes for many years to come.

Simultaneously with their efforts to prevent loss of population, the islanders, curiously enough, were becoming alarmed at a tide of immigration that was flowing in upon them. Whenever Cromwell was at a loss to know what to do with an awkward character, he almost invariably ordered him to be transported to Barbados. Prisoners taken in the Scottish and Irish campaigns, British pirates taken on the high seas, as well as ordinary felons for whom the death sentence was considered too severe, were transported to Barbados in such great numbers that the island authorities found it difficult to control them.[2]

---

[1] Ibid., p. 668 (Colonel Brayne to the Protector, 1st Dec. 1656). Cf. vol. v, pp. 778–9 (Colonel Brayne to the Protector, 10th Jan. 1656–7). Major Sedgewicke had experienced a similar reception on August 1655. ' We were in good hope ', he wrote to Cromwell, ' to complete our regiment of foot here, but I think shall hardly do it at this Island. Mens spirits ashore are something dull in their attending to this design ' (vol. iv, pp. 4–5).

[2] Cf. *Cal. Col.* 1574–1660, pp. 419, 421, 447. Also *Thurloe*, vol. v,

On 26th August 1655 Searle received a stern letter
from the Protector, informing him that many ' notorious delinquents and offenders ' sent to Barbados by
express command of his Highness and Council, had
escaped and returned to their native country. Every
possible precaution was to be taken to prevent such
escapes in the future.[1] Accordingly on 29th August,
the Governor issued a proclamation forbidding all sea
captains under penalty of being fined £1,000 to
transport any one from the island without special
license. Every owner also of a ' bark shallop or skiff '
was ordered to give security of £500 not to allow any
one without such permission to make use of his boat.[2]

When however three weeks later a number of distinguished royalist officers arrived direct from con-
finement in the Tower, the Barbadian Government
registered an emphatic protest. It was pointed out
that while Barbados had been weakened by the loss of
her artisans to Jamaica, large numbers of bond servants
remained—men ready at any time to rise against their
masters. Such being the insecurity of their position,
they urged Cromwell to consider the dangerous situation that might arise in Barbados from receiving such
large numbers of prominent rebels. These latest
arrivals were Cavalier officers, ' qualified with parts
and abilities to seduce, corrupt and head our servants
and such others as have no freeholds amongst us, to
raise and join to our destruction '.[3] So alarmed was
the Governor and his Roundhead councillors that the
prisoners were confined under guard in one plantation,
until further orders should be received from the
Protector.[4]

p. 250: ' . . . 26 priests, popish school masters, &c., were ordered
to be shipped from Ireland to Barbados (26th July 1656).

[1] *Thurloe*, vol. iv, pp. 6–7.   [2] Ibid., vol. iii, p. 743.

[3] Ibid., vol. iv, pp. 39–40 (Searle to the Protector, 18th Sept.
1655).

[4] The numbers of those transportees may be estimated by the

Meanwnile Colonel Modiford was entering on the final stage of the intrigue which he had begun on deserting the royalist cause in 1652. Since then he had done his utmost to win the confidence of the Commonwealth authorities by addressing to Cromwell expressions of unswerving devotion, and by suggesting and supporting the ill-fated attack on the Spanish dominions. Having in this way caught the Protector's eye, he was now plotting with Colonel John Colleton in England, to secure the recall of Governor Searle and the promotion of himself in his stead. The story of the intrigue is useful in illustrating the underground influences which played so important a part at this time in the relations of Barbados with Whitehall.

It was fortunate for Searle that he was able to combat the intrigue with the support of Thomas Povey and Martin Noel, two of the most influential merchants in London. He had been brought into contact with them through their action in getting William Povey appointed Provost-Marshal-General of all the courts in Barbados.[1] Such an appointment was considered by Searle a direct infringement of colonial privilege, for hitherto all official posts in Barbados under the Commonwealth had been in the gift of the Governor and Council. Martin Noel therefore hastened to mollify Searle, who was an old friend of his, by assuring him that the appointment would not be taken as a precedent, adding that both he and Thomas Povey were prepared to offer him their services.[2] The upshot was that the two merchants became the Governor's agents in London,

---

statement of the island planters that already in 1655 Barbados had received no less than 12,000 prisoners of war in addition to felons and vagabonds (Add. MSS. Brit. Mus. 11411, f. 9b).

[1] Ibid., f. 39b (T. Povey to Wm. Povey, 20th Aug. 1657).

[2] Ibid., f. 45 (M. Noel to Searle, 27th Aug. 1657). On the same day Thomas Povey wrote to Searle, offering his support (f. 41b).

pledged to support his interests and to counteract and report hostile intrigues.[1]

The personal animosity between Searle and his rivals, Modiford and Colleton, had arisen during the stay of the Venables expedition at Barbados. Searle had taken the part of the planters, while the latter had supported the authority of Cromwell's commissioners. On the departure of the fleet, therefore, the Governor retaliated by depriving Colleton of the military command which he had received from Venables, and also of his judgeship of Common Pleas. But Cromwell on being appealed to, took it upon himself to order Colleton's reinstatement, a step which further incensed Searle and the already angry planters.[2]

Writing to Searle on 8th January 1658, Thomas Povey drew a vivid picture of the intrigues going on in London. On the one side were the friends of the islanders protesting against the successive invasions of their privileges, from the arbitrary authority assumed by Venables to Cromwell's own interference in the appointment of judges. On the other hand were Colleton and Modiford, urging that the island government (and especially Governor Searle) had been disloyal to the Commonwealth. So bitter was the attack against Searle, that it would have gone hard with him, so Povey declared, but for the steady and powerful support of Mr. Noel. Povey then concludes his letter with a piece of advice which sounds curious on the lips of a Commonwealth man, speaking of a Commonwealth government. ' It will bee advisable,' he said, ' that hereafter y^{or} Councell and Assembly bee not soe tender and sencible of everie act of Power wch your Prince shall think fitt to exercize among you ; and will sometimes doe to remember us of their

[1] Cf. *The Colonial Agents of the British West Indies* by Miss L. M. Penson, *passim* (London, 1924).
[2] Probably in Feb. 1657 (*Cal. Col.* 1574–1660, p. 456).

Sovereigntie, and love not to bee told of what they cannot, or ought not to doe, especially when they putt forth their power rarely and with caution.'[1] One might almost mistake the description for that of a Stuart monarch. Indeed it is one of the ironies of history that Oliver was being remorselessly driven into assuming a sovereignty as coercive as that of Charles himself.

On the morning of 9th January Martin Noel and Colonel Drax, the representatives of Searle and the popular party, were received in audience by the Protector. After hearing their case 'verie patiently and favourably', Cromwell promised to observe the wishes of the islanders in managing their own internal affairs without interference, and agreed to cancel his former order for Colleton's reinstatement. At the conclusion of the interview Colonel Drax was knighted as a mark of honour to Barbados. It was a great triumph for the colony. But Povey was careful to warn Governor Searle that so high-handed a course might be disastrous if tried a second time.[2]

As if to prove his words, the Colleton-Modiford party almost immediately succeeded in persuading Cromwell to suspend the transmission of the promised concessions to Barbados, insinuating that Searle was a turbulent spirit aiming at independence, and one who should be speedily removed.

Realizing however that Searle's alliance with Povey and Noel rendered him temporarily impregnable, Modiford decided to make a show of reconciliation, biding his time until a more favourable opportunity should occur. The Governor himself had a shrewd suspicion of his enemy's motive, but accepted his offer of friendship for the sake of peace, receiving both him

---

[1] Add. MSS. 11411, f. 53b (Tho. Povey to Searle, 8th Jan. 1657-8).
[2] Ibid., f. 55b (Povey to Searle, 9th Jan. 1657-8). Cf. another letter (same to same), dated 27th March 1658 (ibid., f. 58).

and Colleton into his Council. Many Barbadians, however, questioned the sincerity of the two plotters, regarding the formal reconciliation as merely a blind on their part to conceal further intrigues against Searle.[1] In the case of Modiford, the latter surmise was justified by the sequel.

Events of the first importance were now beginning to take place at home in rapid succession. On 3rd September 1658 Oliver Cromwell died. In April of the following year his son Richard was hectored by the army into dissolving the parliament which he had summoned, and a few weeks later the new Lord Protector resigned office with a sigh of relief. The army leaders thereupon re-established, as the most compliant instrument to execute their will, that remnant of the Long Parliament known as the 'Rump'.

On 30th April 1659 Povey and Noel dispatched a joint letter to the Governor of Barbados, informing him of what had taken place. They advised him not to take any formal notice of the change until an official notification was sent him. ' Nevertheless it may bee prudente in you to behave y[or] self as one who are [sic] now to bee accountable to a Comon-Wealthe.' The personal influence of Povey and Noel had been greatly decreased by the change of government, but they promised to do their utmost to obtain the continuation of Searle in office.

The desired letter confirming all officers in their appointments was sent to Barbados by the Council of State on 6th June.[2] Writing two days later, Povey

[1] Add. MSS. 11411, f. 71 (Searle to Martin Noel, 10th May 1658).

[2] Ibid., f. 89. 'A Declaration from the Council of State to the Governor and Council of Barbados.' (The date here is wrongly given as 9th June. The date given in *Cal. Col.* 1574–1660, p. 475, namely 6th June, appears to be the correct one, as Povey describes his success in getting the order in a letter written on 8th June.) The letter was received and published by order of the Governor and

warned Searle of the precarious nature of his position, as many rival applicants for the Governorship would now make their appearance. He would have to tread warily both in his relations with Whitehall and at Barbados, 'it being a tender thing for one in y^{or} place to keepe upp a Reverence, and enforce an Authoritie without a Commission '.[1] If Searle hopes to continue in office under the new régime, he must take pains to create a good impression. Later Povey advised him of a proposal on foot to establish a joint stock company for the West Indies. The Government was to provide and equip twenty frigates, which the Adventurers would man and victual, and conduct against the Spaniard ; a monopoly of trade being granted by charter in any ports that the Adventurers might conquer. Povey indicated that in such an official venture the State would ' cast discountenance upon all Places or Persons that shall not endeavour chearefully and industriously to advance them '. The writer went farther : ' And to deal freely with you the clamour from the Governor and all others from Jamaica against y^{or} opposing whatever might tend to their increise or improvem^{t} hath soone raised you more Ennemies then any other suggestions whatsoever.'[2] Indeed Searle's jealousy of Jamaican competition had already nearly lost him his place. Not the least important of Povey's points was his advice to leave the Parliament alone as much as possible. It was busy and therefore irritable.

The islanders, however, saw in the change of government a unique opportunity of pressing their claims for local independence and freedom from imperial

Council. On 8th Sept. they replied to the Council of State expressing their loyalty to Parliament and their joy that the change had been affected without bloodshed (C.O. 1/13, No. 73, P. R. O.).

[1] Add. MSS. 11411, f. 85.

[2] Egerton MSS. 2395, f. 176 (Povey to Searle, 20th Oct. 1659).

restraint. On 11th December an elaborate petition
was sent to Parliament. In addition to the usual
demands for free trade and exemption from customs,
the petitioners asked ' that wee may have a confirmācon
of Liberty here (by A Law, or yoʳ Commission) for the
Representative body of the People to choose a Governor
out of the ffreeholders of this Island and one out of
every p̄ish to bee his Assistants and joyn with· him in
the execuson of Govermᵗ'. The petition also demanded
complete control over the appointment of all officials
in the island, that all legal profits should be at the
disposal of the Barbadian Government for defraying
public expenses, and that they might have the privilege
(already accorded to New England and Jamaica) of
coining their own money.[1] In fact, the status demanded was inferior to complete independence in
little else but name. In reply to objections the
Barbadians indicated that they were willing to abate
something of their first petition, provided that the
essentials of responsible government were granted.[2]

When the contents of the petition became known
to colonial circles in London, a certain faction, probably at the instigation of Modiford and Colleton,
spread the rumour abroad that the island was really
in the hands of rebels, who were ' Inclined to shake off
and Renounce the Authority of the Nation, And
Decline any longer to owne a submission thereto'.
This accusation the Barbadians lost no time in repudiating. On 19th January 1660 the Governor, Council,
and Assembly published a declaration to ' signifie
publish and declare that they now are, and at all times

---

[1] Egerton MSS. 2395, f. 182. ' To the Supreame Authority the
Parliamᵗ of the Comon Wealth of England,—The humble Petition
of the Representatives of the Island of Barbados, for and in behalfe of
the Inhabitants thereof.'

[2] Ibid., f. 184. ' A Reply to the Exceptions taken to the waie of
Proceedings and the Desires of the chiefe Merchants and Planters in
relation to Barbados.'

for the future shall Continue to bee in all one submission and obedience to the supreme Authority of the Nation of England '.[1] At the same time, an Act was passed imposing immediate imprisonment and a heavy fine on all who refused to accept the authority of Parliament or expressed seditious sentiments.

At last the freedom to manage its own affairs for which Barbados had been striving so long, was in a large measure obtained. On 24th April 1660 Colonel Modiford achieved the coveted reward of his long labour by being appointed Governor of Barbados. The Commission which he received was the answer of Parliament to the planters' petition. Although the right of electing their own Governors was not granted, a compromise was effected in that for the first time since the earliest days of the colony, the nominee was a planter of the island. Hitherto the home government had always appointed strangers, men who had little or no knowledge of Barbadian interests. As Governor Modiford said in his inaugural speech to the General Assembly, ' I am the first of this order, planter-Governor, and there is hopes I shall not bee the last . . . but that every one of them that stand before mee this day may according to their merritts have a turne and share at the Helme.'[2]

Furthermore the island Council, hitherto nominated by the home government, was now declared elective, each parish selecting one member.[3] Thus with one of themselves as Governor, and with both the Council and Assembly as their own elected representatives, the inhabitants of Barbados possessed a very con-

[1] Ibid., f. 238. ' The Declaration and Act of yᵉ Governoʳ, Councell and Assembly for the Continuance of yᵉ Peace of this Island.'

[2] C.O. 31/1, P. R. O. (minutes of the Council of Barbados, 31st July 1660).

[3] Egerton MSS. 2395, f. 245. Copy of Modiford's Commission to be Governor of Barbados. The Original is in the P. R. O. (C.O. 31/1, pp. 13–14).

siderable measure of self government.[1] Unfortunately the newly acquired privileges were destined never to be put into execution.

Towards the end of May 1660, news arrived of the great preparations in England for the King's return. It was reported too that the Duke of York might be expected at Barbados in June, and that good terms would be offered if the island would receive him and acknowledge the King. Whereupon the great majority of the inhabitants ' did wonderfully rejoice at the strong probability of his maj[tys] return to his dominions.'[2]

The news of the Restoration must have been received by Colonel Modiford with mixed feelings. His Commission from Parliament, which had just arrived, was now little better than waste paper. However, he took over the governorship on 16th July 1660 from Daniel Searle,[3] and made a bid for continued power by turning royalist again. With the enthusiastic assent of most of the islanders he proclaimed his Majesty's right and title to the dominions of England and her dependencies.[4] The arms of the Common-

[1] Obedience to the Act of Trade and the Navigation Act was, however, specifically insisted on in the commission.

[2] Cal. Col. 1574–1660, p. 486.

[3] The event of the Restoration caused Modiford to ignore the provision in his parliamentary commission to have his Council elected by the parishes (see C.O. 31/1, pp. 13–16, P. R. O.).

[4] After the reduction of Barbados in 1652, the majority of the royalists had devoted their energies to the establishment of the island as an independent state. Wilder spirits, however, had continued to plot for another royalist rising. In August 1658 a Commonwealth spy at The Hague reported that one Colonel Browne of Barbados, ' carries on a design to betray that island to Charles Stuart '. In an intercepted letter Browne had declared, ' that it was an easy matter ; for, besides the Governor and about ten more which had command there, they were all for him ' (i. e. Prince Charles). This spy gives details of Browne's activity in Barbados and the suggestions which he submitted to the Prince (Thurloe, vol. vii, pp. 313–14, 16th August 1658). There is also evidence that many royalist exiles at Bruges, Antwerp, and Amsterdam contrived to carry on a secret trade with Barbados (Thurloe, vol. v, p. 307).

wealth were ordered to be taken down and the royal
arms put up in their place. As a further step to win
the favour of the restored monarch, Governor Modiford on 1st August ' did this day press the Gen^{ts} of the
Assembly to consider and provide for something to
bee sent to the King's most excellent Majesty as a
present '. But the Assembly cautiously preferred to
await developments before committing itself.

The period of the Protectorate had witnessed
changes of the first importance in the constitution of
the Empire. It had been a slow reassembling of
component parts, disunited by the action of civil war ;
and the aspect of the reconstructed edifice was in
many ways different from the original. Economically,
the overseas dependencies were bound to the Mother
Country more strictly than ever before. In political
organization on the other hand, the tendency had
been to delegate to the colonies a large measure of
local independence within the Commonwealth. By
a series of concessions Barbados had been gradually
released from imperial control in her internal affairs.
Enjoying what would now be termed ' dominion
status ', the island was self-reliant and prosperous.
With Cromwell replaced by King Charles II, such
status would have been regarded by the planters as
ideal. But the Restoration entailed the re-establishment of proprietary government, and an increasing
control of the island which hampered its development
as a distinct community. Yet Cromwell had permanently influenced the political, as well as the economic,
future of Barbados. He had officially recognized the
tradition of local freedom which had sprung up in the
colony during the years of war when imperial control
had been in abeyance. That tradition, so established,
proved strong enough to withstand the centralizing
policy of the Restoration government. Unfortunately
the name of freedom was prostituted by planters
whose only aim was self-aggrandisement.

IV

THE RULE OF THE WILLOUGHBYS

§ 1. *Francis Lord Willoughby* (1660–6)

ENCOURAGED by the royal pardon which his kinsman, General Monk, obtained for him, Colonel Modiford cherished a hope that his parliamentary appointment as Governor of Barbados would be continued by the sovereign whom he had formerly repudiated.[1] The chief obstacle in the way of his ambition was the fact of the Carlisle proprietorship, which the restoration of the King would automatically re-establish. Modiford therefore, with the aid of John Colleton and his other allies in London, proceeded to attack the proprietary right of Lord Willoughby, just as he had previously intrigued against the power of Daniel Searle. Such a campaign was calculated to attract the twofold support of the London merchants and the planters in Barbados. On the one hand John Colleton and his party feared the proprietorship as involving diminution of their influence and injury to their financial interests : while on their side the planters disliked the prospect of being again reduced to the status of tenants-at-will, subject to exactions and restraints from which the Commonwealth had released them.

The London party for their part lost no time in bringing pressure to bear. In July two influential

---

[1] On 16th May 1660 (i. e. before the Restoration) Prince Charles had written to Clarendon, undertaking to safeguard Modiford's interests, ' of whom I have heretofore had a very good opinion, that I will pardon and forgett all that is done amisse ' (Clarendon MSS. (Bodleian), vol. 72, f. 408).

petitions were presented to the Government demanding the recall of the King's recent letter which had
required the islanders to obey Lord Willoughby, until
his pretended right should have been examined at law.[1]
Simultaneously Modiford endeavoured to organize
resistance to the proprietor in the colony itself. On
31st July the legislature agreed to his proposal that
they should petition his Majesty to reconsider Lord
Carlisle's patent, and also ' doe something for prevention of his clayme to the island '.[2]

But when required to translate this resolve into
action the planters demurred. Modiford's request
that Peter Watson, about to sail for England with
a petition for free trade, should be given a substantial
sum of money, was refused, despite Modiford's argument that if the Carlisle patent was annulled at law,
money would be necessary to outbid the merchants
in buying a royal charter. They had heard, so the
Assemblymen declared, that a royal governor had
already been appointed to Barbados so that there was
no need to agitate further.[3] In fact the planters as
a whole were suspicious that Modiford was trying to
use them and the situation generally to effect his own
aggrandizement. If the choice was to lie between
Modiford and Lord Willoughby, they preferred to
trust themselves to the latter whom they respected—
and save money on it. Modiford was therefore obliged
to base his hopes of the Governorship entirely on the
support of the London magnates.

[1] *Cal. Col.* 1574–1660, pp. 483 and 486. The King's letter (of
9th July) ordered Willoughby ' instantly to apply himselfe to take
care of the affaires and Governm^t ' of Barbados, and required the
inhabitants to obey him as strictly ' as any you have done before y^e
late interruption ' (C.O. 1/14, No. 18, P. R. O.). Also Egerton MSS.
2395, f. 267 (where the date is given as 23rd June, instead of
9th July).

[2] Minutes of the Council (31st July 1660), C.O. 31/1, p. 17, P. R. O.
[3] Ibid., pp. 24–6.

The latter, indeed, were endeavouring to supplant the power of Lord Willoughby in Barbados by their own. The first attempt however was completely unsuccessful. On 20th August the newly constituted committee for American affairs decided that Willoughby ought to be restored to his proprietorship of the Caribee Islands, of which he had been dispossessed by ' the illegal power of Cromwell '.[1]

John Colleton and other Barbadian financiers however were enabled to continue their attack by the confusion which now arose concerning the original Carlisle patent. In addition to the Earl of Kinnoul, petitioning for his rights as heir to the second Earl of Carlisle, the old creditors of the first Earl came forward with their claims. For they had received nothing of the promised moiety of the profits arising from the Caribee Islands.[2] During the course of this complicated dispute, Lord Willoughby continued to exercise his proprietary authority in Barbados, though remaining himself at home until a decision was arrived at.

The harassed committee failed to effect a compromise among the several claimants, and cut the Gordian knot by referring the original question of the Carlisle patent to the Attorney-General, who reported that he considered it invalid.[3] This was a great step for Colleton and his party. They urged anew the overthrow of the proprietorship and the appointment of their nominee, Colonel Modiford, as royal governor

[1] *Cal. Col.* 1574–1660, pp. 489–90. See previous debates on the case : 26th July (ibid., pp. 483 and 485), 2nd August (ibid., pp. 486 and 487), 6th August (p. 488), 13th August (p. 488), 20th August (p. 489), and 30th August (p. 489). The priority of the Courteen settlement in Barbados was again urged. See T.C.D. MSS. (G. 4. 15), No. 736, pp. 77–118.

[2] For various petitions of the creditors, see *Cal. Col.* 1661–1668, Nos. 44, 45, 47, and 48.

[3] *Acts of the Privy Council*, I, No. 506.

On 1st March 1661 they urged the King that Barbados should be placed under the direct control of the Crown, offering as a tempting bait ' to pay your Matie some rate per cent. on the Commodities in ye Island, as well as the Customes heere '.[1] The praises of Modiford were also sung. He was a lawyer, a man ' full of justice and ability ', who should be continued as Governor, ' untill y^{or} Majesty hath had some further tryall of him '.[2]

The petitioners, however, felt that they had over-reached themselves in offering the King a tax on all Barbadian exports ; and when the committee tried to commit them to definite terms on the subject, they retired behind vague phrases, maintaining that Kendall who had first made the proposal, had done so without authority.[3] But it was too late. [The decision of the Attorney-General and the prospect of revenue had determined Charles II to assume the proprietorship himself, adopting the compromise several times suggested by Lord Willoughby.[4] The latter was to continue to rule Barbados as the King's Governor for the remaining seven years of his lease from Lord Carlisle, receiving one half of the profits and himself bearing all public expenses.[5] The other half was allotted proportionally to pay off the Carlisle creditors. Eventually both portions of the revenue would revert to the Crown.[6]

[1] C.O. 1/15, No. 25, P. R. O.   [2] Ibid., No. 26.
[3] See Clarendon's account in his *Life*, pp. 490–8.
[4] See Willoughby's petition (C.O. 1/15, No. 87).
[5] The lease was accordingly drafted in June 1662 (C.O. 1/16, No. 61), and issued in November, the instructions (which he was allowed to draw up himself) were approved on 25th Sept. 1662 (*Acts of the Privy Council*, I, No. 576).
[6] The allotment was as follows : an annuity of £500 for two lives to the Earl of Marlborough, a perpetual annuity of £500 to Lord Kinnoul, which was to be doubled when the original creditors had been satisfied : the remainder to go to the creditors, and finally to revert to the Crown. The heavy war expenditure in the West Indies,

Thus the activity of the Modiford-Colleton party in endeavouring to oust Willoughby in order to obtain for themselves the chief direction of Barbadian affairs, had resulted in the substitution of royal for proprietary government. It was a bad bargain. Willoughby's influence was still paramount; and a monarch in need of funds was found to be a harder taskmaster than an easy-going proprietor.

Meanwhile, Governor Modiford for his part was in high feather. On 21st October 1660 he had been informed that the King had consented not to remove him from the Government.[1] Until Charles should officially confirm his promise, Modiford decided to maintain himself in power by mustering an armed force.

All appeared to be going well when on 17th December 1660, letters arrived from Lord Willoughby, establishing a new government in Barbados.[2] Humphrey Walrond, the old royalist leader, being therein constituted President, proceeded to nominate a council of six and to publish the orders that he had received. Then, and not till then, he wrote to his old enemy Modiford, informing him of Willoughby's command.

To the latter the position was exasperating. The

however, swallowed up all profits, so that these claimants never received anything. In later years their demands for payment were ignored. The above account of the Restoration settlement of this tangled question is of necessity chiefly concerned with that side of the story which affected Barbados. For a detailed narrative of the matter in all its aspects, see Williamson, op. cit., chapter x. Cf. also C. S. S. Higham, *The Leeward Islands under the Restoration*, Cambridge, 1921, p. 13.

[1] Modiford to his cousin, the Duke of Albermarle (General Monk), C.O. 1/15, No. 2, P. R. O. The King made this promise on the receipt of the Barbadian petition of loyalty, delivered by Peter Watson (see above). Though why he did so when he had already confirmed Willoughby as Governor in July and again in September, does not appear.

[2] *Cal. Col.* 1574–1660, p. 496. See also verbatim copy (Add. MSS. (Brit. Mus.) 11411, f. 28).

King's known determination to dissolve the proprietorship and his promise to continue him as Governor,
were of later date than this letter. Yet he himself
had no valid authority. He therefore decided to play
for time, in the hope that the King would send him
a commission in the meantime. Answering his old
antagonist, the ex-Governor indicated that the politer
course would have been to inform him privately of the
letters before publication, but he was so desirous to
maintain the peace that he was willing to receive his
Majesty's commands in the presence of his Council.[1]
Walrond, however, had employed tricks of that kind too
often himself to be easily deceived. Modiford must
first disband his forces and then come himself for
a view of the orders. His reply was a further attempt
to retain power, demanding that his own camp might
'bee the place of Debate'. Patience, however, was
not one of Walrond's characteristics. An order was
issued forthwith requiring all forces then in arms to
disband under penalty of high treason.[2] Realizing
that, temporarily at any rate, the game was up,
Modiford disbanded his forces and recognized the
new Government.

But Walrond and his partisans of the Council had
never forgiven Modiford for his desertion of the
royalist cause in 1652. In the present situation they
saw an excellent opportunity for their long-awaited
revenge. On 2nd January 1661 he was arrested on
a charge of 'High Treason and divers other crimes
and misdemeanours'.[3] The only tangible charge upon
which they could fasten was that he had acted as
Governor under the Commonwealth. The presence of
Daniel Searle, himself an old Cromwellian Governor,
on the prosecuting Council, sufficiently indicated the
farcical nature of the proceedings. After two hearings,

---

[1] C.O. 3/11, pp. 31-2, P. R. O.   [2] Ibid., p. 35.
[3] Ibid., pp. 38-40.

the case was adjourned, and Modiford was temporarily released owing to lack of evidence. But it
would probably have gone hard with him in the end
had not the influence of his cousin Albemarle induced
the King to intervene on his behalf.[1]

During this period of uncertainty, when the status
of the colony was in the melting-pot, the planters
themselves were divided into three parties. Firstly,
Modiford and his friends who hoped to continue in
power by substituting themselves for the proprietor
as the representatives of the Crown; secondly, Walrond
whose authority depended on that of Lord Willoughby.
While the third party, consisting of the great majority
of the inhabitants, was not particularly enthusiastic
over either Modiford or Walrond, but desired as
always, the maximum of local independence. They
favoured the efforts of the London planters and merchants to overthrow the Carlisle patent, only because
royal rule appeared to involve a lesser degree of
subjection than that of a proprietor. Their ideal, like
that of most dependencies, was a free colony under the
Crown, with the comforting protection of the Royal
Navy.

This point of view, which persisted under all political
conditions, was well illustrated by a petition addressed
to Lord Willoughby by the island government about
1660, which demanded that the titles of rightful landowners should be confirmed, despite the proprietary
claims of the Earl of Carlisle.[2] In other words they
repudiated the position of tenants-at-will under a
proprietary owner, claiming that their lands were
held in common socage. Other demands in this

---

[1] *Acts of Privy Council*, I, No. 509. An order was sent to the
Barbadian Government, ' that the said Colonel Thomas Modiford bee
not disturbed or further persecuted for anything he hath formerly
acted, but that he bee permitted to enjoy the full benefitt of his
Majestys Gratious Act of Oblivion '.

[2] Egerton MSS. (Brit. Mus.) 2395, f. 287.

petition were no less significant. No taxes should be imposed, nor any new courts or offices erected, without consent of the General Assembly; no appeals should be allowed to any court in England; a new Assembly should be elected annually, 'to convene fower times a yeare at Least'. Finally, a modified form of the self-government which had been conceded under the Commonwealth was demanded. The Council should be elective, three candidates being chosen by every parish, from whom the proprietor or his governor was to choose the Council. The islanders were quite prepared to accept proprietary rule, provided that the large degree of responsible government hitherto enjoyed by the colony was not encroached upon.

Knowing by experience the tenacity with which these aspirations were defended, Willoughby endeavoured to show that local rights and privileges would be more secure under himself as proprietor than directly under the Crown. The King's officers, he urged, would be found harder taskmasters than those of a proprietor.[1]

Willoughby's efforts to win over the islanders by illustrating the lightness of the proprietary yoke, were energetically seconded by President Walrond. He was jealous of Willoughby; but upon the vindication of that lord's authority in Barbados depended both his own continuance in power and the defeat of Colonel Modiford whom he disliked intensely. All his energies were therefore thrown into the work of enforcing obedience to the proprietor.

His first step in this direction was to call upon the newly elected Assembly to reimpose the old pro-

---

[1] Cf. Add. MSS. (Brit. Mus.) 11411, f. 28 (letter of Willoughby to the Barbadians, September 1660), and another letter urging similar arguments on 9th February 1661 (ibid., f. 30). See also Egerton MSS. (Brit. Mus.) 2395, f. 329.

prietary dues of 2 and 4 per cent. on all exports. The Assemblymen, however, refused to commit themselves. In their answer they desired a respite, until it should be determined in England in whom the proprietorship lay.[1] A policy of ' wait and see ' having been adopted by the Assembly, Walrond and his Council failed to secure their active support when entering their protest against Kendall's offer to the King of a 4 per cent. duty.[2] But Walrond was not the man to be discouraged. Such an offer was dangerously tempting, and might (as actually happened) turn the balance against a continued proprietorship. That done, his enemy Modiford might win at the last hole, so to speak, and continue as Governor under the King. Accordingly he protested strongly that Kendall and his associates had no authority to represent the island.[3] Also the appointment of Modiford as Governor would be no little discouragement to this loyal colony, ' his treachery in betraying ye island to ye Usurper and his voyolent persecution of ye royalists ever since haveing rendered him odious to all honest people '.

Despite the personal popularity of Lord Willoughby, the planters as a whole viewed the possibility of renewed proprietary government with dislike, and all the efforts of President Walrond could not induce them to intervene in its favour. Rumours of the King's intended assumption thereof were so prevalent that they preferred to hold their hand.

But such divisions never prevented the Barbadians from presenting a united front in defence of their

---

[1] C.O. 31/1, p. 42, P. R. O. (13th March 1661), Minutes of the Council.

[2] Cf. C.O. 1/15, No. 52, P. R. O.

[3] C.O. 31/1, p. 42, P. R. O. (13th March 1661). A resolution was passed that no one should be received as the accredited agent of the island ' without the approbation and consent of the General Assembly for the time being ' (C.O. 31/1, p. 43, Minutes of the Council of Barbados). Cf. also p. 44.

privileges. In 1661 the King took it upon himself to fill the two vacant offices of Secretary and Provost-Marshal in Barbados. Such a course was a direct infringement of their rights, and the Council and Assembly joined in protest. Offices had always been disposed of by the islanders themselves, until ' the usurping tyrant invaded o^{ur} priviledges '. Disorder and injustice would arise, for royal nominees were not responsible to the Barbadian Government. The petitioners, therefore, prayed the King to recall his letters patent. Charles refused to give way.[1] It was the beginning of royal intervention in the internal affairs of the colonies. Barbados was soon to learn what it was to have nearly every office filled by the incompetent deputy of a royal nominee residing in England.

Perhaps encouraged by the united action which had been taken in this matter, Walrond in July 1662 made a final effort to carry the Assembly with him in supporting the proprietorship. As a counter-blast to the extravagant offers made by the merchants, he proposed that the King should be presented with a large sum of money, and a petition protesting against the suggested imposition of the 4 per cent. duty. In reply the Assembly admitted that the propositions were good in many ways, ' but conceive it Convenient they be suspended till further consideration '.[2] The President retorted that the Assembly was dominated by a faction, ' wch will not p̄mitt any proceedings in p̄iudice of the designs of the Agitato^{rs} ag^t the people of this Island at home ; ' and forthwith dissolved them.

Though exceedingly angry Walrond did not admit

---

[1] In March 1662 Cradock (the recipient of the Provost-Marshalship) complained that the islanders had disposed of the office to others. The King thereupon sent a direct order to the Governor, commanding that Cradock be immediately admitted to that office (C.O. 1/16, No. 389, P. R. O.).

[2] C.O. 1/15, No. 69, P. R. O. Propositions of the President and Council of Barbados.

defeat.   On 10th July the President and Council sent
a long address to the King, reporting on the unfit
behaviour of the Assembly, and again protesting
against the threatened impost ; ' wee fearing . . . that
Offers are made to him by some that studie his favor
(for to gett power heere) to raise taxes greater then
this people call well beare '.[1]   They again asked for
Willoughby as Governor, for he would scorn to injure
any loyalist.   At the same time Walrond endeavoured
to secure public opinion in Barbados by issuing a statement of recent events, and the cause of the Assembly's
dismissal.[2]   Freeholders were urged to elect persons
of proved loyalty to the King, and to the interests of
the island.[3]

Despite this manifesto, Walrond's party experienced
a decisive defeat at the general election.   Sixteen out
of the twenty-two former members were re-elected.[4]
And to emphasize the matter Modiford was chosen
Speaker.   Walrond for his part was wise enough to
accept the situation.   Indeed, further action at home
was needless.   It was known that the King had assumed
the proprietorship, and that Willoughby would be
appointed as royal governor for the remainder of his
lease.   The President and Council accordingly united
with the Assembly to obtain the best possible terms
under the new conditions.

Jealous as they were of any invasion of their rights

[1] C.O. 1/15, No. 70, President and Council of Barbados to Secretary
Nicholas.

[2] Ibid., No. 71.   The Assembly, it was stated, had sat for six months
and done nothing but adjourn from time to time in hope of change,
refusing to join with the President and Council.

[3] C.O. 31/1, pp. 56-60.   The extraordinary statement was made
that the old Assembly desired and expected the King of Spain or some
other foreign prince as their proprietor.   But Walrond probably
summed up the situation when he wrote in this same manifesto that
his opponents in the Assembly would rather ' perrish then to have
good done to them whilest *wee* are in the Governm^t '.

[4] Ibid., pp. 61-2.

by the home authorities, the Barbadian planters were
no less fearful of damage to their interests by the
settlement of rival colonies. In this respect, Jamaica
was especially disliked. Having already occasioned
Barbados great loss in men and money, it was threatening by its extensive output still further to reduce the
price of sugar.[1] The arrival then of Lord Windsor at
Barbados on 20th July 1662, seeking recruits to go
with him to Jamaica, was far from welcome, despite
royal instructions received through Willoughby to
assist Lord Windsor in every possible way.[2] On the
following day Windsor published the special terms
offered to all who would make the venture, the President and Council reluctantly promising encouragement to the emigrants, and support to Jamaica in the
event of a Spanish attack.[3] Nor was the situation
improved by Windsor's action in conducting his own
recruiting, and sending volunteers on board ship
without reference to the island authorities—a proceeding which resulted in the departure of numbers of
indentured servants and debtors to the great loss of
the inhabitants. As a protest the Council on 7th
August resolved to send a narrative of all proceedings
to the Secretaries of State, and also to represent to
Lord Willoughby ' the sad condition of this Island,

---

[1] Trade rivalry was the point chiefly considered by the planters,
for in this period the loss of population was not a serious factor,
Barbados having a greater white population than she could well
cope with. Complaints against emigration from Barbados was a later
feature, when the preponderance of blacks over whites in the island
began to assume dangerous proportions.

[2] The King to Willoughby, 14th April 1662 (C.O. 1/16, No. 45).
Willoughby to Walrond, 12th May 1662 (C.O. 1/16, No. 52).

[3] C.O. 1/16, Nos. 73 and 75. A special Act was passed limiting
the usual period during which creditors were free to present their
debts to persons intending departure from twenty-one to seven days
(ibid., No. 76). A further Act was passed enabling Justices in Quarter
Sessions to settle cases not exceeding 4,000 lb. sugar, in order to
obviate delay (ibid., No. 79).

and the sudden ruine, it is like to fall into, if it bee thus perpetually harrassed by all his ma^tys men of warr as they come along '.[1]

On the departure of this unwelcome visitor, the Barbadian Government returned to the more important business of defending their privileges at home. On 18th December 1662 the Council and Assembly addressed to the King a number of demands which if granted would have broken the economic bonds which tied Barbados to the Mother Country. They asked that land should be held of the King in common socage, ' paying such an acknowledgement as the Governor Council and Assembly shall agree ' ; that no tax be levied without consent of the freeholders ; that no custom be imposed on exports from England, but that Barbados should have the same freedom in this respect as Virginia and New England ; and also ' that wee may have a free trade as England hath '. Finally it was demanded that the island should be free to trade on the Guinea Coast, or else that the recently established Royal African Company should supply them with negroes at the same rates as hitherto offered by private merchants.[2]

The monopoly granted to the African Company had been inspired by the same policy which had given rise to the Navigation Acts, namely the erection of an independent and self-sufficient empire of which the colonies were to become complementary parts. Prior to the Restoration there had been a great leakage of capital from the British West Indies to the Dutch in exchange for negro slaves. A monopolistic company had therefore been established to supply that labour, and thus divert the capital spent into the hands of Englishmen. A special exception made in the case of Barbados about this time well illustrates the general principle.

[1] C.O. 3/11, pp. 102–3.   [2] Ibid., p. 77.

In March 1662 certain Spanish merchants of Martinique in co-operation with the Governor of Carthagena had proposed to Walrond that, instead of incurring the expense of transporting negroes all the way from the Guinea Coast to Peru, they should procure them at Barbados. If the privilege was granted, the Spaniards were willing to pay 10 per cent. on the commodities brought in payment.[1] To trade with aliens under any conditions was of course contrary to the Acts of Navigation. But President Walrond, never one to be restrained by the letter of the law, encouraged the proposal. A few weeks later two Spaniards arrived at St. Michaelstown, offering to buy negroes to the value of £100,000. After long debates the Council refused to sanction the transaction; but Walrond was determined. On his authority alone the Spaniards ordered up their ship and bought 400 negroes, paying between 125 and 140 pieces of eight per head; a proceeding which, as Modiford reported, 'hath filled our island wth money'.[2] Since he alone was running the risk of defying the Navigation Acts, Walrond decided that a special reward was due to himself, and accordingly took the high-handed course of charging a fee of eleven pieces of eight on each negro sold.

It was not long, however, before he discovered that he had made a mistake. On 7th May the Assembly voted the imposition illegal and arbitrary. The resolution was presented by Speaker Modiford to the

---

[1] C.O. 1/17, No. 7, P. R. O., 30th March 1662.

[2] C.O. 1/17, No. 8, P. R. O., 30th April 1662. Modiford, with his usual insight, realized the potentialities of such a trade. He interviewed the Spaniards, who informed him that all the Spanish colonies wanted trade with England, and would bring to Barbados goods to the annual value of five million pieces of eight. Modiford wrote home urging that the royal permission should be given, for thereby in his opinion the Dutch carrying trade would 'be beaten clearly out of ye West Indies trade'.

Council, who agreed 'y^t itt was corruption and bribery in him to take anything, much more to enforce it'. It was not within the power of any governor or commander of the island to impose any tax. Modiford gives a graphic description of the ensuing scene in the Council chamber. Walrond tried to justify his action; but 'his right hand men rose upon him, and said in o^r p̄sence, " Come, Come Sir, you have done more then you can justifie; you have done y^t for wch you have noe authoritie or colour of right, and therefore for shame S^r, sit down and say no more of itt ; "— wch with a very pale countenance he obeyed '.[1]

Meanwhile the question of intercourse with Spanish merchants had been discussed and decided upon by the home authorities. The terms under which the Spanish trade was officially allowed were sent to Barbados in February 1663.[2] The Spaniard was permitted to buy negroes and European goods from the Caribee Islands and Jamaica, but no goods of the growth of Europe, Asia, or Africa could be imported by them into the colonies. That was the monopoly of the English merchant. No goods in fact could be brought into Barbados 'Savinge only such as are the proper product of the Spanish American plantations'. Moreover, no native commodities such as sugar were to be taken away from the English colonies by the Spaniard. Thus the principle of the Navigation Acts was not violated. England still retained the sole right of supplying the colonies with everything they needed, and of receiving from the colonies everything she herself required. All that took place was the exchange of the surplus negro supply for goods which the British Empire itself could not furnish.

Walrond's career as President of Barbados was in the

---

[1] It must be remembered, however, that Modiford was Walrond's bitterest enemy, and this picture may be overdrawn in consequence.

[2] Ibid., Nos. 5 and 6 (Feb. 1663). See also *Acts of the Privy Council*, I, No. 597.

meantime rapidly drawing to a close. One more quite arbitrary and characteristic coup remains to be related before his departure from power. Unfortunately for him his scheme was discovered and overthrown. On 10th March 1663 a petition was presented to the Council calling for a stay of all legal proceedings for debt, because of the hardship which the probable failure of that year's sugar crop would inflict upon the planters. The petitioners, however, represented only three out of the eleven parishes, and subsequent inquiry proved that the prospects of that year's crop were as good as usual. Whether the petition itself was pre-arranged does not appear. At any rate Walrond and his Council, many of whom were among the most deeply indebted planters in the island, seized the opportunity. An order was issued to all judges of Common Pleas to adjourn and suspend all proceedings of their subordinates in cases of debt until the matter had been further considered in conjunction with the Assembly.[1] The order was of course obeyed; for there were few planters who were not indebted to the merchants. Some of the latter who had obtained attachments of goods on their debtors were imprisoned for not returning the goods in their possession, and very naturally laid their case before the Council for Foreign Plantations. After due inquiry the latter reported that the story of the crop failure was a fabrication, that the President and Council had made the order to avoid paying their own debts and to ingratiate themselves with the inhabitants. They accordingly advised the King to reverse the order, and permit the injured merchants to take their legal remedy against the framers thereof.[2] Soon afterwards

[1] C.O. 1/17, No. 12, P. R. O. (10th March 1663).
[2] Report of the Council for Foreign Plantations to the King (C.O. 1/17, No. 35, P. R. O. (5th June 1663); see also *Acts of the Privy Council*, I, No. 595 (10th June)).

Francis Lord Willoughby of Parham made his second appearance as Governor of Barbados.

Having at last received his commission and instructions in June 1663, he arrived at the island on 10th August. The three years of government upon which he was now entering were packed with events of far-reaching importance both for Barbados and the West Indies generally. Indeed, the vigorous personality of the man created movement of some sort wherever he went, though not always to the best advantage.

Upon his expulsion from the West Indies in 1652, he had plunged into a series of plots for a royalist rising in England. After watching these activities, of which he received accurate intelligence through his secret service, Cromwell had ordered his arrest and imprisonment.[1] Owing probably to Martin Noel and other friends, Willoughby eventually obtained his freedom, and devoted himself to trade ventures in the West Indies and Carolina. As early as 1659, however, he was working for the Restoration, and reporting to Prince Charles the promising state of public opinion.[2] His private letters exhibit the frank, impetuous nature of the man. All his life he took risks, and often grave risks. But his underlying ideas were nearly always those of sound statesmanship. His great defect was a tendency to allow his enthusiasm to betray him into acts of tyranny and injustice against those who disagreed with him. Any one getting in his path stood in imminent danger of being trodden under. It was this utter impatience of opposition that aroused the hostility of many who admired his capabilities, and who would have been glad to be his friends.

[1] See various reports of the Commonwealth Secret Service Agents : *Thurloe*, vol. iii, pp. 72–5 (3rd Jan. 1655), pp. 82–3 (6th Jan.), pp. 126–30 (March), p. 216 (March), p. 302 (April), p. 336 (April), p. 345 (April), and pp. 377 and 384 (April and May?). Also cf. Captain Butler to Cromwell, 18th Feb. 1656, vol. iv, p. 544.

[2] Clarendon MSS. (Bodleian) 71, f. 437. Cf. H.M.C. x, Lord Braye's MSS. 4, pp. 206, 208, 210, and 211.

Willoughby's first duty in Barbados was to obtain the grant of that permanent revenue which had been so carefully allotted beforehand by the King's Order in Council. Naturally great difficulty was experienced in gaining the assent of the planters, who realized that once the royal Governor was in possession of a fixed revenue the legislature would have no further hold over him. To avoid the delay of a general election, Willoughby summoned the old proprietary Assembly to meet on 25th August,[1] the ensuing fortnight being spent in canvassing the most influential of the inhabitants. ' His Lord^pp,' we are told, ' hath taken a very greate deale of paines in driveing this bargain, for he hath been up early and Downe late in advizing & considering how to make out his Ma^tles intrest against ye Allegations of ye Planters.'[2]

Despite these precautions the Assembly offered a stubborn resistance. When Willoughby had privately suggested to the Speaker, Samuel Farmer, an export duty of 10 per cent., the latter replied that it was as much as the clear profits of the whole island, and that he supposed the Assembly might give about half that sum.[3] When the Assembly did meet, three long weeks were spent in hot debate, ' untill himselfe and they were allmost tired '. Willoughby spared no effort to obtain the fulfilment of the King's desires, but in so doing impaired his own reputation.[4]

[1] Strictly speaking, this course was illegal. The fact was subsequently made use of by the Barbadians when attacking the Act. Willoughby told the King that if this Assembly did not grant his desires, he would call a new one (C.O. 1/17, No. 78, P. R. O.).

[2] Egerton MSS. 2395, f. 383 (Wm. Povey to Tho. Povey, 9th Sept. 1663). A slightly different and less probable account of these proceedings is given in Stowe MSS. (Brit. Mus.) 324, f. 4.

[3] This statement is taken from Farmer's indictment of Willoughby before the King in Council, March 1664, and is therefore open to suspicion. Farmer was as hot-headed and as obstinate as Willoughby himself. The subsequent result was a violent feud between them (C.O. 1/20, No. 28, P. R. O.).

[4] Egerton MSS. 2395, f. 384 (Wm. Povey to Tho. Povey, 21st

At last, however, on 12th September the famous Act, granting the King 4½ per cent. on all exported commodities—an Act which proved a source of complaint and friction for nearly two centuries—was passed by the Assembly.[1] The actual amount of the tax does not seem to have been considered the grievous burden that it was in later years, for Willoughby was able to hold out a promise of a still larger grant in return for a relaxation of the Navigation Acts.[2]

In reality the terms of the Act were favourable to the planters. In the old days, the poll tax of 40 lb. of cotton or tobacco per head and the export duties or 2 or 4 per cent. had always been exacted by the Proprietor. At the same time the Proprietor had never done his share of paying, as he should have done, the expenses of administration and defence. According to the new Act, the planters paid their money, and in return not only received confirmation of their estates but the royal promise to bear all public charges. The expenses from which the inhabitants were thus to be relieved were expressly enumerated : ‘ the public meeting of the sessions, the often attendance of the council, the reparation of the forts, the building a sessions-house and a prison, and all other public charges incumbent on the government ’. ‘ In consideration thereof,’ the Act continued, ‘ . . . upon all dead commodities of the growth and produce of this island, that shall be shipped off the same, shall be paid to our Sovereign Lord King his heirs and successors for ever, four and a half in specie for every five score.’ [3]

October 1663) : ‘ His Lord^ps Endeavo^rs are great to please his Matie though perhaps may not be thought soe at Court, but ye People heere feele it. . . .’

[1] C.O. 29/1, pp. 47–50, P. R. O. Also printed verbatim by Bryan Edwards, vol. i, pp. 335–9.

[2] Willoughby to the King (Sept. 1663, C.O. 1/17, No. 78, P. R. O.).

[3] It has been suggested (G. L. Beer, *The Old Colonial System*, vol. i, pp. 180–2) that this clause did not definitely state that the King was

If the Act had been observed, the planters would have been the gainers financially. But on the other hand they would have had no further control of the purse strings. The royal Governor would have been entirely independent; and Barbados would have been reduced to the dependent position of a Crown colony. As it happened, the Sovereign persistently appropriated this revenue to other purposes. The planters made complaint after complaint, and were obliged to pay extra taxes to carry on the government. But by way of compensation they retained considerable control over the penniless royal Governor. For this reason the struggle of the home authorities to reduce Barbados to a stricter dependence was of much longer duration than it would otherwise have been.

As soon as this important business was settled, Willoughby turned his attention to Humphrey Walrond. The members of the late Council informed Willoughby of that gentleman's misgovernment and

bound to spend the 4½ per cent. on Barbadian expenses, so that both parties to the agreement could make their own interpretation. The English Government certainly afterwards claimed that the tax had been granted merely in return for the abolition of the proprietary dues and the confirmation of titles of land which were admittedly defective. It is equally certain, however, that both Lord Willoughby and the Assembly recognized the obligation of the Crown thereby to undertake all public charges. See Sloane MSS. (Brit. Mus.) 3662, f. 57a, where it is stated that the Assembly only agreed to the tax because of these promised benefits. Cf. also the important narrative of Sir Robert Harley, which seems to have been hitherto overlooked: (My Lord Willoughby) 'has had great contest with the Assembly about settling a revenue for the King. The main point is that they would not confess the King to be proprietor, and so receive confirmation of their estates from him, but would have their possessing it dureing the troublesome times to be a good tittle. But I think this is well over and there will be agreement; my Lord haveing as good as quitted al arreares by referring himselfe wholly to the country to doe what they thinke good. . . .' (Sir Robt. Harley to Sir Edward Harley, 11th Sept. 1663, H.M.C. xiv, Part II, Portland MSS., vol. iii, p. 277 (Harley Papers)).

illegal acceptance of money from the Spanish merchants. On 2nd September 1663 Walrond was accordingly charged at the Council Board, where he acknowledged the receipt of £1,000 from the Spaniards, and promised to hand it over to his Excellency. In spite of many requests, however, no payment was made. Five weeks later, being hard put to it, he definitely refused to pay, declaring ' That the said £1,000 belonged unto him and to noe one else because he alone ran the hazard for granting the said permission contrary to the Act of Trade '.[1] This defiance was promptly dealt with. In the capacity of a Court of Exchequer, the Governor and Council issued a warrant to levy the sum demanded on Walrond's estates, which were seized by the Provost-Marshal. Moreover, Walrond's fraudulent dealing and his forcible resistance to the Marshal, determined the Court to call him to account for other sums of public money and goods which he was suspected of having appropriated. Brought to bay, Walrond resorted to armed rebellion, riding up and down the island in an endeavour to induce his friends to join him. The Court replied by giving the Marshal full powers of search throughout Barbados ; and on 4th November followed it up by a proclamation calling on all officers military and civil to aid in apprehending him, on pain of being considered a fellow rebel.[2] Finding the island growing too hot for him, Walrond decamped in a boat by night for England, vowing he had always been a loyal servant of the King for whom he had fought, and would get justice done.[3]

[1] ' A Narrative of the Proceedings of his Excellency and Councell against Coll. Humphrey Walrond ' (Clarendon MSS. (Bodleian) 80, f. 283). Cf. Willoughby's letter to Clarendon, ibid., ff. 280–1, 30th Nov. 1663.

[2] ' Narrative ', ff. 284–5. Cf. Warrants in C.O. 1/17, Nos. 83 and 87, P. R. O.

[3] His reception in England, however, was far from cordial. His

Willoughby's determination to enforce his authority as the King's representative, which had brought about the merited disgrace of Walrond, now deprived him of one of his best friends. His policy in this direction is well stated in a letter to the Earl of Clarendon. ' Notwithstanding the struglings ', he wrote, ' of the troublesome spirritts of English-men, whoe I find to bee in all parts of the world tanted with that desire of usurpin a power to themselves beyond the boundaryes of the sett rule which our late unhappy troubles hath begott in them ; yett I hope in time to bring itt to that pass here, as men shall not dare to appeare soe presumptious in their undertakings.' [1] Throughout the periods of the Civil War and Commonwealth the Governor had been virtually under the control of the elected Assembly. Consequently Willoughby's process of vindicating the royal prerogative provoked bitter opposition. The quarrel between Lord Willoughby and his friend Sir Robert Harley indicates the course of this constitutional struggle in the island, and the somewhat drastic measures which the Governor felt himself obliged to adopt. Harley and Willoughby had worked together in royalist conspiracies during the Protectorate.[2] When Willoughby was ordered to reassume the government of Barbados in 1662 he promised his former associate the post of Chancellor in the island.[3] Harley accordingly proceeded to Barbados

case was heard on 6th May by the Privy Council, who ordered that until a decision was made, he must be committed to the Fleet Prison, ' for contemning the orders of Lord Willoughby, absenting himselfe when sent for by his Lordship and the Councel there, and for commeing from thence without his Lordship's leave ' (*Acts of the Privy Council*, I, Nos. 619 and 621).

[1] Willoughby to Clarendon, Clarendon MSS. 81, f. 110, 18th Feb. 1633–4.

[2] Cf. Willoughby's letter to Prince Charles, May 1660, in which he praises Harley's zeal for the cause (Clarendon MSS., 72, 437).

[3] Cf. H.M.C. xiv, Part II, Portland MSS. iii, p. 266. Harley to

in March 1663 ; and soon after Willoughby's arrival in August, the Great Seal was formally delivered to his charge.[1] In November he was appointed Chief Judge of the Court of Exchequer.[2]

Yet only three months after these marks of honour, Harley was arrested by order of the Governor and Council for refusing to seal a writ, which ordered the public Escheator to inquire into his Majesty's rights to various estates.[3] Harley was then ordered to deliver up the seal ; and on refusal, was committed to the common jail. This writ was part of Willoughby's campaign to vindicate the King's rights and privileges. Harley's refusal seems to have convinced the Governor that he had deserted him, and was supporting his enemies.[4] The terms of the formal indictment entered in the Council minutes supports this view. He was therein accused of assuming to himself full power of judicature in matters of equity independently of the Governor, and also of ingratiating himself with the inhabitants by declaring ' how much hee was for the libertye of the subject'. It was further stated that he had openly accepted bribes, and on one occasion ' stood up more like a comedian than a Judge, and said: " Gentlemen, now it is in my power to carry it which way I please ; and which of you will give me the lustiest Bribe shall have it " ' ; a charge which may or may not be true.[5]

his brother, 2nd Oct. 1662. Also p. 273, King's letter to Willoughby, approving of Harley's appointment (5th June 1663).

[1] Portland MSS. (ut supra), p. 272. Harley to his brother, 29th April 1663. The seal was delivered to him on 25th August at a meeting of the Council, p. 277.

[2] Ibid., p. 278 ; cf. C.O. 31/1, pp. 84–9, P. R. O.

[3] Portland MSS. (ut supra), p. 280 (11th Feb. 1663–4).

[4] Among other activities in the King's interest, Willoughby had declared the 10,000 acres leased by Carlisle to the merchants to be royal demesne land. The tenants had been ordered to relinquish their estates or make composition—to the intense indignation of all concerned (Portland MSS., p. 278 ; also Egerton MSS. 2395, f. 384).

[5] C.O. 31/1, pp. 84–9.

Harley had evidently felt called upon to vindicate his new authority as Chancellor against Willoughby's high-handed methods ; and opposition indiscreetly applied had aroused his wrath, already rendered explosive by the resistance of the planters. Harley's astonishment however at the Governor's action, his submission, and declaration of unaltered loyalty and friendship, seem to show that less drastic action would have reduced him to obedience, and retained his services. But at all costs Willoughby was determined to enforce his authority. On 18th February he reported to Secretary Sir Henry Bennet that Harley had left Barbados, like Colonel Walrond, to lay his complaint before the King, 'because he could not remaine heere to doe as hee listed '.[1]

While the internal struggle between Governor and inhabitants was taking place, Barbados was bearing an important part in the settlement of new colonies abroad. Perhaps the most interesting of the ventures was that to Santa Lucia ; for in this instance Barbados attempted to found a colony itself, without aid or direction from the Mother Country. The new settlement was intended as an extension of Barbados, to receive her surplus population and to be directly under the government of the parent settlement. Indeed the enterprise bore a close resemblance to the ancient Greek method of colonization. Lord Willoughby, who had been informed of the project on his arrival, wrote on 23rd September 1663 to M. de Laubière, the French Governor of Martinique, that, ' Barbados finding itselfe overburdened with people,

---

[1] Willoughby to Bennet, C.O. 1/18, No. 29, P. R. O. Cf. the following comment : Harley's dismissal ' proved very Prejudiciall to them both, his Lord^p lost a Faithfull Freind and good Councello^r, Sir Robert Harley an Honble and Profitable Imploym^t, wch his very Enemies that he had contracted in espousing the Lord Willoughby's cause, could not but confess was severe. . . .' (Sloane MSS. (Brit. Mus.) 3662, f. 57b).

and willing to enlarge themselves ', had determined to
occupy Santa Lucia, and already before his coming had
made a treaty with the Indians there for that purpose.
The Barbadians, he continued, were much resolved to
settle that island in order to furnish themselves with
a convenient source of supply for wood and provisions.[1]
The curt reply which de Laubière returned, claiming
Santa Lucia as French territory, determined Willoughby
to persist in the venture. ' I will quickly take order
with my Monsieur and cool his Couraige,' he wrote to
the King, adding that he intended to send a company
of settlers thither before the year was out.[2] A large
body of planters were accordingly established there.
But owing to lack of capital and other support the
settlement languished, and was eventually wiped out
by native Indians.[3]

This attempt of Barbados to employ its floating
population for its own advantage was indicative of the
jealousy with which that colony regarded its com-
petitors. The impossibility of obtaining land and the
decreasing fertility of the island compelled time-
expired servants and artisans to emigrate elsewhere.[4]
But it aroused the gall of Barbadian planters to see this
population developing Jamaica and other rival sugar-
producing colonies.[5]

Not only was the labouring population being lost,
but even the landowners of Barbados were being

[1] Willoughby to de Laubière, C.O. 1/17, No. 79, P. R. O.

[2] Willoughby to the King, ibid., No. 89.

[3] H.M.C. xiv. 2, Portland MSS. iii, p. 268.

[4] Ibid. The thin layer of soil which covered the basic rock of the
island was becoming exhausted by the intensive cultivation of sugar.
It was the current opinion of the time that Barbados would in a short
time cease to be of productive value. The system of artificial manuring,
by means of which the island has continued to flourish till the present
day, had not yet been introduced.

[5] For example, in 1664, Colonel Modiford sailed to Jamaica with
800 emigrants from Barbados (Modiford to Sec. Bennet, 20th March
1664, C.O. 1/18, No. 39, P. R. O.).

heavily drawn upon for the various schemes of colonial expansion then afoot. A body of planters, known as 'the Corporation of the Barbados Adventurers', had agreed with the Lords Proprietors of Carolina to take charge of and settle a large area of their territory.[1] Willoughby, who had himself engaged in a previous settlement of Carolina, supported the scheme and encouraged emigration thither, because his friend Clarendon was co-operating in the venture. But at the same time he warned the latter that the consequent exodus of people had so thinned out the white population, 'that I feare our negrose will growe to hard for us'.[2] Indeed the concentration of land in Barbados into the hands of a comparatively small body of great landowners, was driving the poorer class of white men to seek land in other settlements. The movement contributed to a marked expansion of the colonial empire, but gradually reduced Barbados from the position of a populous, virile colony to that of a politically unimportant sugar plantation, owned by absentee proprietors, and worked by negro slaves.

Meanwhile the constitutional struggle between Governor Willoughby and the planters was becoming increasingly intense. After his visit to the Leeward

---

[1] See Correspondence of the Lords Proprietors of Carolina (*Cal. Col.* 1661–8, pp. 153, 161, 162, 267–8, &c.). See also H.M.C. xiv, Part II, Portland MSS. iii, p. 290. The Barbadian adventurers included Modiford, Colleton, and Yeamans. The subsequent history of the enterprise is obscure. See J. A. Doyle, *The English in America* (London, 1882), pp. 468–9, 476.

[2] Clarendon MSS. 81, ff. 129–30 (5th March 1663–4). Later, in June 1668, on the receipt of further commands to encourage emigration to Jamaica, Willoughby sent home a strong protest, requiring 'y* you will bee pleased to divert the King from giveing mee any such Ord^ers, for it is not beginning the right end to improve his Majesty's Interests in these partes, for Hee doth but take out of his right pocket to putt into his left'. Such a policy did not increase the total of Englishmen in the West Indies. England itself was the true source of supply (Willoughby to Arlington, C.O. 1/18, No. 81, P. R. O.).

Islands in the summer of 1664,[1] Willoughby raised a storm of opposition by issuing an ordinance, reducing the five district Courts of Common Pleas to only two, with a judge and four assistants for each. The action was strictly legal, and in accordance with his commission wherein he was granted the sole right of altering or establishing Courts of Judicature. It was none the less unwise. For the organization of the Civil Courts dated from the earliest years of the settlement and was one of its most treasured institutions.

Moreover Willoughby had increased this irritation by omitting to summon the Assembly. Hitherto the islanders had been accustomed to a constant reference to their wishes by means of annual elections and frequent sessions of the elective body.[2] But ever since the stormy scene caused by the passing of the $4\frac{1}{2}$ per cent. Act, he had left that body severely alone. The event of war and the consequent need of money eventually compelled Willoughby to face his angry subjects.

On October 1664 Willoughby wrote to the King expressing his apprehension of the aggressive policy adopted by the French and Dutch in the West Indies, and suggesting that if England intended to declare war ' yor timely Orders and Directions to me, might bee very advantageous, with some convenient Assistance of shipping and men, for to Reduce those Island possest by ye Dutch '.[3] Soon afterwards Willoughby

[1] Cf. Portland MSS., p. 285.

[2] Willoughby explained to the Lords of Council that no Acts had been passed, ' because itt hath not beene my good fortune to find the people in soe good a Temper since theire passing of that Act as that I could thinke it fitt to convene them together ; . . . from their first settlement ' (until Willoughby's arrival) ' they had never been otherwise governed but by their own popular way of governing amongst themselves and as they pleased. . . .' (C.O. 1/18, No. 128).

[3] Clarendon MSS. 82, f. 132. Official warning of the outbreak of war arrived in November (Cal. Col. 1661–8, p. 157).

departed on a visit to settle the affairs of his colony in Surinam, the proprietorship of which at his own request had been granted jointly to Lawrence Hyde, son of the Earl of Clarendon, and himself.[1] War with the Dutch was however more imminent than even Willoughby imagined. Official warning of the event reached Barbados shortly after the Governor's departure. The task of preparing the island for defence therefore fell to the lot of his nephew, Henry Willoughby, who had been put in charge of the government during his absence.

In February 1665 the King sent warning that the famous Dutch Admiral De Ruyter had sailed for the African coast with a fleet of twelve men-of-war, and that his ultimate destination was believed to be Barbados.[2] On receipt of the news, the Deputy-Governor redoubled his preparations. All vessels in port were put in a posture of defence, the forts were repaired, a general muster of the militia ordered, and watches were set on the headlands which overlooked the Atlantic.

At six o'clock on the morning of 20th April, to the intense excitement of the islanders, De Ruyter and his fleet appeared off the coast. Four hours later the Dutch fleet of fourteen ships sailed into Carlisle Bay in battle order. Of the ensuing encounter an eye-witness has provided a graphic account.

'When hee (de Ruyter) came by the ffort, he did not fire one gunn Untill hee came at the *Gift's* sterne. Then hee fired a whole volly of small shott and his broadside, and soe did all the rest. Then the ffort and shipping fired at him, and they shot away all his foresayle, and the Vice Admirall lost his mayne yard and two others lost theyre Topsayles.'[3]

[1] See *Cal. Col.* 1661–8, pp. 131–2. Willoughby had founded the colony in 1650, sinking a great part of his private fortune in the venture.

[2] C.O. 1/19, No. 16, P. R. O.

[3] 'A true relation of the fight at Barbados' (C.O. 1/19, No. 50,

The battle developed into a rapid exchange of broadsides, which seem to have inflicted considerable damage to both parties. At four o'clock in the afternoon, the Admiral's ship ran up red bunting to the masthead, summoning the ship commanders to a council of war. After riding at anchor for about an hour, the fleet withdrew from the bay and mended their sails out of gun shot. Then about six o'clock they stood away for Martinique, ' in the confusedest manner that possibly could bee '.[1]

According to Henry Willoughby's report of the fight, the Barbadian casualties amounted to only three killed and about ten wounded, although considerable material damage had been inflicted on the shipping and the houses in St. Michaelstown.[2]

A month later, Lord Willoughby returned to Barbados, and hastened to explain to the King that his long absence had not been due to negligence, but to a severe wound, received at the hands of an assassin in Surinam.

The fight with De Ruyter, despite its successful issue, had greatly increased Willoughby's difficulties. During the engagement a great part of the island's stock of ammunition had been used up, and he was at his wit's end to know how to replenish it. Before the outbreak of war he had done his utmost to obtain supplies of powder, shot, and cannon from the imperial government, but without success.[3] The difficulties

P. R. O.). De Ruyter himself is described : ' I did see him on the poope, wth a cane in one hand and a cuttle axe in the other, and as he stayed (i. e. yawed) I did see most part of his quarter (deck) carried away ' (printed in *Colonizing Expeditions to the West Indies and Guiana*, ut supra).

[1] Ruyter, however, succeeded in carrying away sixteen ships from Nevis and Montserrat (C.O. 1/19, p. 58).

[2] Henry Willoughby to Sec. Arlington. (This account agrees with the above.) Willoughby asked for six larger cannon. ' If our Gunns had been better some of them had never gon off ' (C.O. 1/19, No. 51). See also No. 73.

[3] Cf. Clarendon MSS. 82, f. 132. On 15th May 1665 Arlington

were increased by the King's refusal to allow him to use the proceeds of the $4\frac{1}{2}$ per cent. for public defence. His action in spending part of the tax on the settlement of Santa Lucia had been strongly condemned, despite the fact that he had remitted the remainder to the Carlisle creditors.[1]   In May, therefore, he appealed to Secretary Arlington, begging him to acquaint the King, ' in what an ill condition I am in to serve his mat^ys Comands, for I have received very severe checks for disposing any of y^t Revenue to y^e Kings Service, in settling y^e island of Sta. Lucia '. The great guns he had asked for had at last arrived, but ' What cann y^e Gunns doe without Powder ? '   If another De Ruyter were to arrive, Barbados would be at his mercy.[2]

With the $4\frac{1}{2}$ per cent. put out of his reach, and no other source of supply at hand, Willoughby was at last compelled on 8th June 1665 to call an Assembly. The election of the headstrong Mr. Farmer as Speaker was a sufficient token of their temper.   The Governor's request for supplies was accordingly ignored, and the angry representatives devoted themselves to airing grievances.   A petition was drawn up and presented to the Governor and Council at the suggestion of Farmer, who told Willoughby ' it was a Petition of Right and that therein he had followed the Example of the Best of Parliaments '.[3]

replied to Willoughby, that as for the fire-arms he had desired, it had always been the custom for established plantations to purchase their own, as in the case of Jamaica (*Cal. Col.* 1661–8, No. 991).

[1] Willoughby complained that the creditors accused him of appropriating the revenue to his own use. He demanded that the accounts which he had sent home should be accredited in order to clear his name (C.O. 1/19, No. 58, op. cit.).

[2] Willoughby to Arlington, 20th May 1665 (C.O. 1/19, No. 60, P. R. O.).

[3] Willoughby to the Lords of Council, 5th July 1665 (C.O. 1/19, No. 78, P. R. O.). Willoughby described the petition as ' soe scandalous and false and soe much contesting with the King's authority

After charging Willoughby with various unlawful
and arbitrary actions in the law courts, the petition,
in the best manner of the Long Parliament, requested
that none of the King's subjects in that island might
thereafter be imprisoned, detained, dispossessed of
their estates, or banished, without judgement of their
peers in due course of law.[1]   The real complaint
behind these specific charges was that Willoughby had
come out to Barbados with a fixed determination to
restore constitutional discipline and enforce the King's
authority, and that in doing so he had ridden over
them roughshod—as he certainly had.   At the same
time it must be remembered on his behalf, that the
imposition of the $4\frac{1}{2}$ per cent. and its subsequent
misinterpretation at home (matters in which Willoughby had had no option) had roused such bitterness that a policy of compromise was virtually impossible.

The Governor's reply to the petition was swift and
drastic.   The Assembly was immediately dissolved, and
an affidavit tendered to the ringleaders of the opposition, those who refused it being thrown into prison.[2]
According to this recognizance, the signatory was
bound to appear at the next General Sessions to
answer any crimes objected against him, and in the
meantime to do nothing against the Government.
Farmer's reply was characteristic.   He was willing to
bind himself to appear at the Sessions, ' but for y^e
other part that he should in ye interime act nor doe
anything ag^t the Governm^t of this island as it is now

as even utterly to subvert and destroy his Majesty's Government and
just rights heere '.

[1] ' Petition of the Representatives of Barbados to Governor Lord
Willoughby ' (ibid., No. 78 (1)).   See also H.M.C. xiv, Part II,
Portland MSS. iii, p. 292 (15th June 1665).

[2] H.M.C. Portland MSS., ut supra, p. 293.   William Porter to
Sir R. Harley.   This writer states that Barbados, ' very much com-
mend Mr. Farmer's bold action ' (2nd Sept. 1665).

established, he would be damm'd and rott where he was, before he would acknowledge any such thing '.[1]

Farmer was accordingly hurried off as a prisoner to England, in order to answer a charge of high treason before the King. At the same time, Willoughby wrote to the King explaining his action. Farmer, he said, was a very dangerous fellow, a great Magna Carta man, and petition-of-right maker, 'the first that started up that kind of language heere,' so that he did not think it safe to allow this Jack Cade to remain on the island any longer. He hoped that the King would not encourage others of a like disposition by showing lenity to Farmer. 'For my back is att the wall, And I find good words and meeke carriage begetts little but contempt where no other can bee used amongst A people, who have beene rough bred, and not used to the yoake.' [2]

Faced by the stubborn opposition of the planters in Barbados, by intrigues against him at court, and by the clamour of the Carlisle creditors for payment out of the bankrupt fund of the $4\frac{1}{2}$ per cent., Willoughby obtained the King's permission to return home, in

[1] C.O. 1/19, No. 78, vi, P. R. O. At the same time, Willoughby, with the advice of his Council, issued a proclamation that any person soliciting signatures to any petition for the alteration of the government, or stirring up the people to think that the Courts were not legally established, should be deemed an enemy of the public peace, and be proceeded against accordingly (Portland MSS., ut supra, p. 292).

[2] Willoughby to the King, C.O. 1/19, No. 92, P. R. O. (8th August 1665). Farmer's case was heard before the King in Council on 16th March 1666. The accused had been kept in prison, awaiting trial, for three months. The case was remanded; Farmer being released on giving security not to quit the kingdom. In January 1667 he obtained permission to return to Barbados with the new Governor, Lord William Willoughby, who though condemning his rebellious attitude, took a liking for him (*Acts of Privy Council*, I, Nos. 566–8, 671, 694; also Portland MSS., p. 296). Cf. *Cal. Col.* 1661–8, Nos. 1046, 1047, 1048. Also cf. Clarendon MSS. 84, ff. 126–7 (Wm. Willoughby to his brother Lord Francis Willoughby, 13th April 1666).

order to vindicate his conduct.[1] His two nephews, Henry and William Willoughby, and Sir John Yeamans were to act as joint Governors in his absence. But Lord Willoughby was destined never to see England again.

On 16th November 1665 the King dispatched to Barbados further instructions with regard to the war. Several merchantmen returning to England from the Caribee Islands had been waylaid by Dutch privateers. To prevent similar losses in the future, all shipping was to be concentrated into fleets, which were to sail at stated intervals, and to make for specified ports. In view of a possible repetition of De Ruyter's raid, Willoughby was strictly commanded to repair all forts on the island, to provide sufficient supplies of shot and shell, and to keep careful watch.[2]

Such orders compelled Willoughby to make the hazardous experiment of calling another Assembly. The election took place in January, and the session opened on 1st February. 'At which time', wrote Willoughby, 'I showed them, that the present necessity of fortifieing this Island against fforreigne Invasion, for the securitie of his Majesties Governm[t] and the Planters Interrest, was the Maine cause of their meeting.'[3]

The menace which threatened Barbados was quite recognized by the representatives, who after having

[1] 'I would be very glad', wrote William Willoughby, ' to heare once from you that Lord Kennoule and the Creditors were in any likelyhood to receive their Money, w[ch] would allay much clamour here' (Clarendon MSS. 84, ff. 127). Cf. Arlington to Lord Willoughby (5th Dec. 1665), *Cal. Col.* 1661–8, No. 1099.

[2] The King to Lord Willoughby, 16th Nov. 1665 (*Cal. Col.* 1661–8, No. 1079).

[3] 'A Narrative of y[e] Assemblyes proceeding in relation to y[e] Taxe' (Clarendon MSS. 84, ff. 138–9 (20th April 1666)). See also 'Journal of the Assembly of Barbados', 23rd Jan.–15th March 1666, C.O. 1/20, No. 3, P. R. O. Cf. Willoughby's speech, C.O. 1/20, No. 9.

solemnly viewed the fortifications, agreed that a complete defence of the island was an obvious necessity in a time of such peril.[1] Yet the election of John Jennings as Speaker, a man of an even more violent disposition than Farmer, was an omen that the Assembly was in no mood to purchase security by submission.[2]

On reassembling a week later the representatives, instead of voting supplies for defence as Willoughby expected, presented a resolution, ' that the King out of y^e 4 and $\frac{1}{2}$ p cent ought to beare that Charge, and their reason was because the makers of that Act had soe intended '.[3] The Governor's reply was that ' noe word in that Act did hold the King to ffortifie '. But none knew better than Willoughby that the planters, when they agreed to the measure, had understood the contrary.

The Governor and Council then prepared a Bill for a levy of half a million pounds of sugar to defray the expenses of fortification. But the Assembly was not to be rushed. More information was desired with regard to the condition of the island, and Willoughby was further annoyed by a demand that his letters patent and other documents should be enrolled among the public records. His answer was not as tactful as it might have been. The King was not only their sovereign, but their proprietor, having purchased them with a great sum ; he might reasonably, therefore,

---

[1] ' Narrative ', ut supra.

[2] See ' Indictm^t of Mr. John Jennings ' (Clarendon MSS. 84, f. 142). Among other things, Jennings was charged with having said ' The Lord Willoughby had lead them alonge (ye late assembly meaning) wth nothing but lyes . . . whereof ye said Jennings scoffingly said hee never before did see or read such a bundle of stuffe. . . .'

[3] ' Narrative '. Cf. account in the ' Journal '. The actual words of the Act were quoted : ' which Implyes that Extraordinarys uppon all Contingencyes whatsoever were Intentionally meant and concluded '.

'have Insisted upon and prayed an Ayd from you, whereby to have Assisted his May^tye^' in this time of war. As to the 4½ per cent. he dare not say what the King might think himself obliged to do, but he will go as far as the King will allow.

'To the Assembly this reply was entirely unsatisfactory. After angrily repudiating the possibility of an aid, the House rejected the Bill for a levy, putting forward instead an audacious scheme of their own. A levy as great as that demanded by the Governor and Council was agreed to, but the proceeds were to be at the disposal of three named planters. Two hundred thousand pounds of the sugar raised was to be utilized for the manufacture of gunpowder, and a further three hundred thousand was to be spent by the directors in purchasing firearms from England, which, on arrival, were to be sold to the inhabitants at fixed rates. The proceeds of the sale were then to remain in the hands of the several parish vestries 'for a constant supply of Arms'. Finally, the remainder of the levy was to rest in the hands of the three directors as a reserve fund, to be used as the Assembly should direct.[1]

The reply of the Governor and Council was unequivocal. If such a Bill were passed 'there would be a greater Magazine in the hands of three Private men (and those such whose Affections to his Majesties Government we have reason to doubt) then now or at any time hath been, in his Majesties Magazine here'. The scheme ' was nothing less then to draw the Militia from the King, and to put it into the hands of his subjects, a designe as unanswerable for us to suffer as for them to project '.[2]

On 4th April Willoughby suddenly convened the

---

[1] ' An Act for the Raising a Present Sume of Goods for the needfull Publique use of this Island' (Clarendon MSS. 84, ff. 131–3 (24th Mar. 1666)).　　　　　　　　　　　　　　[2] ' Narrative.'

Assembly. In his speech he said that his purpose was not to dissolve them, as might have been expected, but to urge them to pass the Supply Bill which he had laid before them. The French had declared war against England, and the Danes had also made an alliance with the Dutch. If Barbados were conquered by the enemy, there would then be no need to contend who should carry the purse or manage the sword.[1]

Notwithstanding their consternation at this news, the representatives were not willing to own defeat. They replied that during the preceding year of war with the Dutch, nothing whatever had been done out of the $4\frac{1}{2}$ per cent. by way of defence, ' and now it is expected that all neglects should be supplied by this Assembly without question or satisfaction '.[2] Yet they were willing to aid his Majesty. If the Governor would pass the Supply Bill which they had presented, they would go still farther and spend 300,000 lb. of sugar on fortifying the four seaports.

Matters finally came to a head on 14th April, when Willoughby definitely vetoed the Assembly's Bill. Whereupon, in view of the imminent peril of the island, the representatives decided to submit. But they were determined to have the last word. An elaborate paper was presented to Willoughby, reciting the entire chain of events since January, from their point of view. The Governor asks for money, and when it is offered, he refuses it. ' Nor doth anything they have presented affect or meane more then the procuring or establishing ye means of bringing Powder and Armes to the strengthning and furnishing the militia as the Laws requir.' [3] There was no intention

---

[1] Willoughby's speech, C.O. 1/20, No. 40, P. R. O. This news had been sent off to Willoughby by the King on 8th Feb. 1666 (ibid., No. 11).   [2] C.O. 1/20, No. 41, P. R. O.

[3] ' A paper Given in to the Ld. Willoughby by the Assembly ' (Clarendon MSS. 84, ff. 134–6). It was therein also requested that Willoughby would not misrepresent the Assembly to the King—

of intrenching on the military power of the Governor ; but since he must have it his own way, and since the danger is so pressing, they agree to a levy of 4 lb. of sugar per acre.

Hitherto, the chief effect of the war felt at Barbados had been the very great decrease in trade and a consequent lack of food supplies. While the Navigation Act excluded foreigners, the hazards of the voyage under war conditions and the personal intrigues of the Barbadian merchants in London had reduced the supply of English goods to vanishing point.[1] The islanders, however, were now about to be brought into direct contact with the war. Already in January 1666 Willoughby had fitted out and personally conducted an expedition consisting of six vessels and 350 men to seize the Dutch island of Tobago, but on arrival had found the work already accomplished by a band of eighty buccaneers from Jamaica.[2]

War with the Dutch had made the Barbadians uneasy, but the intervention against them of France, the greatest European power in the West Indies, spread dismay. Nor was the home government's disregard for the welfare of the colonies calculated to increase their morale. ' I cannot but admire ', wrote Willoughby to Arlington, ' that places of soe great consideration as these Islands are to yᵉ King should be noe more looked after nor regarded, but left to looke to themselves.' [3]

' As if they were . . . to bee terrifyed in themselves against all sense (like children under the Rod) into an awfull subjection of their Estates and fortunes to unknowne ends. . . .' The paper concluded with a repudiation of Willoughby's alleged statement that on emigrating to Barbados, settlers lost their rights as free Englishmen, becoming subject to the limitations of proprietary rule.

[1] See ' A Narrative for yᵉ Councell Concerninge Barbados ', by William Willoughby in England (Clarendon MSS. 84, f. 140)

[2] Willoughby to the King, 29th Jan., *Cal. Col.* 1661–8, No. 1124 ; Willoughby to Arlington, No. 1125 ; J. Reid to Arlington, No. 1126.

[3] C. O. 1/20, No. 59, P. R. O

Despite these discouragements, Willoughby and the planters in general rose to the situation admirably. By commandeering a merchant fleet about to sail for England, the former was enabled to fit out an expedition of thirty vessels and 600 men, under the command of Henry Willoughby, to defend the Leeward Islands.[1] ' Better hee and I ', wrote Lord Willoughby to the King, ' and as many of our name as ever was borne, should be suncke and p̄ish, then those islands lost.'[2] Both French and Dutch, he added, were pouring reinforcements and supplies into the West Indies : unless the King does the like, all will be lost.[3]

On arrival at Antigua with his fleet Henry Willoughby was met with the news that St. Christopher had fallen and that a strong force of French and Dutch men-of-war was there. Panic ensued ; the deep-laden merchant ships did not dare to fight, landed the troops at Antigua, and proceeded on their way for England.[4]

The news of this disaster spurred Willoughby to a final effort. His first step was to write a very plain-spoken letter to the King. St. Christopher had gone, Nevis might go too ; ' and if it once come to run in a blood, God bless Barbados that fair jewell of your Majesty's crown'. He must and will tell the truth. Barbados is one of his Majesty's most valuable colonies, populated by a spirited and industrious people. Yet the island is without adequate means of defence and is faced with starvation, owing to the neglect of those

[1] See Porter's account to Harley, H.M.C. xiv, 2, Portland MSS., iii, pp. 300–1.

[2] Lord Willoughby to the King, 21st April 1666 (C.O. 1/20, No. 58).

[3] Further demands for help were made to the King (*Cal. Col.* 1661–8, Nos. 11, 88, 1189, 1204, and 1205). Cf. Willoughby's remark to the King : ' Hee that stopped your Gracious Warrant for 300 barrells of powder, and converted it into but 50, had wee but the ordering of him heere, I know not how he would be handled' (15th July 1666), C.O. 1/20, No. 120.　　　　[4] Portland MSS., iii, pp. 300–1.

at home. The only remedy is an immediate dispatch of military aid, and the provision of a food supply by permitting free trade with foreigners.[1]

On 24th June two English men-of-war arrived at Barbados with royal orders for the reconquest of St. Christopher. Since the force provided was quite inadequate for the purpose, Willoughby decided to run the risk of once more exceeding his powers by commandeering merchant vessels for active service. By means of a further loan from the Assembly he was able to fit out a fleet of six large vessels, a fire ship, and a ketch, and to enrol a force of nearly a thousand men. He decided to command the expedition in person.

On 18th July[2] therefore, he set sail from Barbados on his fatal enterprise. It was late in the year for such an attempt, as the hurricane season during which vessels rarely ventured abroad, was due to begin. After taking two prizes near Martinique on 23rd July they arrived before the French island of Guadeloupe. Here Willoughby ordered Captain Hill, of H.M.S. *Coventry*, to take his own and four other ships into the harbour, and seize a number of richly laden vessels there. While the prizes were being towed out of port, the main fleet came to anchor. But suddenly one of the terrific hurricanes, so well known in the West Indies, bore down upon them. The anchor cables snapped, and the fleet was scattered. Some vessels were driven ashore at Guadeloupe, while the Rear-Admiral and three more ' arrived at Montserrat a mere wreck, not having a mast standing '. Many

---

[1] Willoughby to the King (C.O. 1/20, No. 92, P. R. O.).

[2] Three days before his departure Willoughby wrote to the King urging the dispatch of more guns and ammunition. Of the planters' loyalty he spoke in the highest terms. ' Notwithstanding theire great want of all necessaryes, haveing but very scanty of bread to putt in theire mouthes, yett they have spared itt out of theire oune bellyes to sett y^{or} ma^{ty} out a ffleete. . . .' (C.O. 1/20, No. 120, P. R. O.).

others were never heard of again. The only trace that was ever found of Lord Willoughby was a couch, recognized to be his own, ' and some peeses of a ship,' that were washed ashore at Montserrat.[1]

The manner of Lord Willoughby's end typified his career, which had known little else but storms. From the opening of the Civil War when he respectfully defied his sovereign until he died defending his sovereign's cause, he pursued a career of strenuous action. The last three years of his life, spent in enforcing the royal authority in Barbados, had been the most difficult, and probably the most distasteful. The interpretation which the imperial government chose to put upon the $4\frac{1}{2}$ per cent. Act placed him in a false position, and set him at odds with the aggrieved planters. On their side the planters were stubborn, and suspicious of any attempt to curtail their former privileges. Willoughby for his part, with a hatred born of experience of all ' Petition-of-Right-makers ', and with a temper easily provoked, often attained his ends by force, when he could have done so much more easily by means of tact and conciliation. Indeed, his most important work was performed not as Governor of Barbados—though he permanently affected the fortunes of that island—but as a colonial pioneer. To him was due much of that development of Carolina which took place in the latter half of the seventeenth century. Again, it was owing entirely to his personal initiative and enterprise that Surinam was settled, which, though eventually lost to the Dutch, attracted British enterprise and capital to adjacent areas which

---

[1] This account is combined from the following sources :

   (i) Henry Willoughby to Sec. Williamson, 28th Aug. 1666 (C.O. 1/20, No. 140, P. R. O.).

   (ii) Sam Barwick to Clarendon, 27th July 1666 (Clarendon MSS. 84, ff. 357–8).

   (iii) Capt. W. Porter to Sir Robert Harley, 11th Oct. 1666 (H.M.C. xiv, 2, Portland MSS., iii, pp. 300–1).

were to constitute the subsequent colony of British Guiana. Similarly, he put into execution the project of sending planters to occupy Santa Lucia, a step which ultimately vindicated the English claim to that island. It is not too much to say that Lord Willoughby did more to extend the British Empire in West Indian regions than any other man of his time.[1]

It is significant that Willoughby, who so vigorously defended imperial authority in Barbados, was yet a consistent opponent of the economic policy pursued by the home government in relation to the colonies. At the Restoration the planters had hoped that the trade restrictions imposed by the Commonwealth would be abolished along with the rest of the works of the usurper. Those restrictions, however, were not the peculiar handiwork of Cromwell, but the expression of current economic theory. One of the first proceedings of the restored government had been to pass the Navigation Act of 1660.

Since sugar—virtually the sole product of Barbados —was included in the enumeration list, the trade of that island was thereby concentrated into the home market. The policy against which the planters had protested from the earliest years of the settlement was thus definitely continued. The only direct communication remaining between the plantations and foreign countries, was the shipment of European goods in English vessels. It was soon felt, however, that

[1] There is something, however, in Sir Jonathan Atkin's criticism ten years later, that Willoughby's schemes of colonization were ' too much for any man's undertaking' though hee had beene a Prince considerable '. He had spent—so Atkins declared—£50,000, thus ruining his fortune, while the population of the Caribee Islands was too small to be able to provide adequate numbers for the new settlements (C.O. 1/37, No. 22, July 1676). Willoughby, it is true, was too much of a gambler to be a successful business man ; but his farsightedness and readiness to take risks led the way for subsequent development. He was essentially a pioneer.

such a concession deprived England of a part of the colonial trade, and by a further Act in 1663 no goods were allowed to be shipped to the colonies until they had first been brought and unladed in England. British navigation and manufactures were increased, but the colonist suffered by having to pay more for foreign commodities. The individual interests of the colonies were subordinated to the ideal of a self-sufficient Empire protected by a powerful mercantile marine. The object was attained to a striking degree, but it was very largely at the expense of the West Indies, the entire productions of which were monopolized by the home market.

In their case the system was an unmitigated evil. The profits obtained on their productions dropped to less than half, while the prices of goods imported rose in proportion.[1]

Writing after one year's experience of the new Navigation Act, the Barbadian Government was emphatic in its denunciation. There had been such a drop in the price of sugar that many planters were contemplating leaving the island. The concentration of their goods into one market had caused a glut, ' as to our very great losse, wee have found by sad experience, sugars being fallen 20 p cent since the said Act was put in Execucon amongst Us '.[2] Three months later (July 1661) the Barbadians renewed their protests. Sugar had fallen to so low a rate that ' the Merchants bring no commodities to us, but draw off

---

[1] It is true, of course, that colonial sugar received preferential treatment in the home market. But this concession was of little value, owing to the keen competition of other sugar-producing colonies.

[2] Petition of the President, Council, and Assembly of Barbados, 11th May 1661 (C.O. 31/1, pp. 45–7). The petitioners also asked for the privilege of recoining foreign money, and also bullion, to any value they might desire, in order to facilitate trade relations in the island.

all their Ingagm^{ts} in sending empty shipps onely, to freight away o^r sugars, wch alsoe if sent upon o^r owne accompts yeilds soe contemptiable a Rate, y^t it is good as nothing, for the merchants haveing us in theire power that wee can sende o^r sug^{rs} noewhere else, and so having the markett in themselves to send it for other Countreys, they sell it for what they list '.[1] As an alternative plan the petitioners put forward a very practicable suggestion. Let the planters be free to send their goods where they will, provided they are shipped in English bottoms, and that the customs, which would normally be paid in London, are paid at Barbados before starting. Then if the island fails to keep its bond in paying these dues, let the Act of Trade be again imposed with all severity. The payment of customs, however, was not the point, but the supposed benefit to the national balance of trade derived from the monopoly.

At the same time it is evident that the fall in sugar prices was not entirely due to the Navigation Act. Every year the expansion of new sugar plantations, such as Jamaica, was increasing the total supply, and consequently lowering the sale price. Moreover, Barbadian sugar was earning a bad reputation with regard to quality; so much so that in July 1661 the London merchants petitioned the King on the matter. Coarse, ill-cured sugars were being sent over, with the result that instead of the former £3 10s. per hundred pounds, only an average of 21s. was being offered.[2]

To what extent the provisions of the Navigation

---

[1] Egerton MSS. (Brit. Mus.) 2395, f. 365; also in C.O. 1/15, No. 70, P. R. O. (10th July 1661).

[2] *Acts of Privy Council*, I, 12th July 1661, No. 524. Also in *Cal. Col.* 1661-8, pp. 46-7. It was suggested that a standard rate of 30s. per 100 should be fixed by the King. This would prevent the planters from being forced to sell at ruinously low rates, and also from daring to bring unmerchantable sugars into the market.

Act were actually enforced in the colonies it is impossible definitely to say. But it is evident that a considerable amount of illegal trading took place. In August 1662 an order was issued to all customs officers, requiring them to take special care that no ship coming from an English plantation should proceed to a foreign country without first unloading at an English port, ' this being grounded upon an Advice given by Sir George Downing that divers English shipps laden in Barbados are lately arrived in Holland without touching in England '.[1] Despite these precautions, the practice seems to have continued. In the following year a sharp letter was sent by the King to the colonial governors, pointing out ' the many neglects or rather contempts of his Majesty's Commands for the true observance of the said Act ', and threatening severe penalties in case of further infringement.[2]

On the other hand, considering the number of protests that were evoked, the regulations must have been widely enforced. In December 1662 the Barbadian Government demanded as great a freedom of trade as England herself enjoyed, and the abolition of custom duties on goods exported to the colony.[3] The campaign was taken up even more vigorously by Lord Willoughby. Unless some relief from the Act is afforded, he wrote in November 1663, Barbados will be ruined. ' I can give y^{or} ma^{tye} an accompt of some thousands y^t are gone off from this Island of Barbados and ye rest of ye Leeward Islands to ye neighbouring Collonyes of the ffrench and Dutch where there is allowed ffreedome of trade with all nations.' [4] A vague promise was extracted from the King to give some ease from the hardships complained of, but nothing

---

[1] *Acts of Privy Council*, I, No. 569, 15th Aug. 1662.
[2] Ibid., No. 601 (19th June 1663).
[3] C.O. 1/16, No. 114.   [4] C.O. 1/17, No. 89.

definite was done,[1] and Willoughby continued his attack. In a series of letters he described the poor condition of the Leeward Islands; how that owing to the Act the ports were empty of shipping, whereas the French and Dutch harbours were full. Barbados itself was in a stronger position to endure the restrictions; but even there the inhabitants lived twice as happily in the former days of freedom. He had lately seen forty ships lie idle for many months, owing to lack of lading.[2]

It was not, however, until the outbreak of the Dutch war in 1665 that the Barbadians began to feel the full loss of foreign trade.[3]

As already indicated, English communication with her distant colonies almost ceased. Consequently, Barbados, which depended on England almost entirely for her supply of food and other necessaries, was placed in a serious predicament. In his last great appeal to the King for help Lord Willoughby urged that the abolition, or at any rate the suspension, of the Navigation Act was the only way to save Barbados from starvation.

Thus the years succeeding the Restoration were for Barbados a time of hardship and discontent. Under any circumstances the enforcement of direct royal control over a colony, which had to a large extent

[1] C.O. 1/18, No. 1. The matter was referred to a committee of the Privy Council, who, on 28th Feb. 1665, reported against any alteration of the Act. The usual arguments of the period were cited (C.O. 1/19, No. 31).

[2] *Cal. Col.* 1661–8, p. 205 (petition of Council and Assembly of Nevis), 29th April 1664; pp. 229–30 (Willoughby to Arlington), 25th Aug. 1664; pp. 234–5 (Willoughby to the King), 20th Sept. 1664.

[3] In view of war conditions, several clauses of the Navigation Act were suspended, English merchants being permitted to employ foreign crews and vessels in the colonial trade, but with the express proviso that England was to remain the staple for all colonial commerce (*Acts of the Privy Council*, I, No. 649, 6th Mar. 1666).

gone its own way since the first settlement, would have been no pleasant business for either party. But the King's refusal to accept the obligations implied in the 4½ per cent. Act—obligations rendered still more pressing by the event of war—intensified the friction between the royal Governor and the stubborn islanders. Finally, the navigation policy, which afforded so striking an incentive to the English mercantile marine, brought very real distress to Barbados and to the West Indies in general.

§ 2. *William Lord Willoughby* (1667-73)

WHEN September came and still no news of Francis Willoughby arrived, his nephew William and the Council of Barbados, who had been left in charge of affairs, wrote to the King, asking for instructions in the event of his Excellency having perished.[1]

On receipt of this news the Barbadian merchants in London began as usual to exert their influence at Whitehall. One of their number, Sir John Colleton, persuaded his friend, Lord Shaftesbury, to have the government of the island established in the hands of four persons, William and Henry Willoughby (nephews of Lord Francis), Henry Hawley, and Sam Barwick, the two former representing the interests of the Crown and the latter those of the planters.[2] The arrangement was essentially a bad one. Hawley and Barwick endeavoured to ingratiate themselves with the people

[1] Lieutenant-Governor William Willoughby and Council of Barbados to the King (29th Sept. 1666 ; C.O. 1/20, No. 143, P. R. O.). They added that so many of the best men of the island had been lost in this and other ventures during the war, that unless liberally supported by the King, Barbados would be at the mercy of the French. They urged also (as Lord Willoughby had done) that freedom of trade and the free importation of negro labour was the only remedy.

[2] They were commissioned on 5th Dec. 1666 (C.O. 1/20, No. 189, P. R. O.).

by opposing the two brothers in everything that tended to increase taxation. It was not long before the Government was at a deadlock, with the planters themselves divided into two hostile factions.

It was unfortunate that friction of this kind should have arisen at a time when the resources of Barbados were desperately needed in order to save the Leeward Islands from falling into the hands of the French. The destruction of the Governor and his fleet in July had deprived Henry Willoughby of that relief which he had been awaiting at Antigua. Moreover, his efforts to rescue four hundred survivors who had made their way to Todos los Santos, were frustrated by the appearance of two powerful French men-of-war, which gave chase and scattered his little fleet. Willoughby himself escaped with difficulty to Nevis, and forthwith reported to the King that the French were masters of the seas, and that the heavy losses sustained compelled him to remain on the defensive until powerful reinforcements should arrive from England.[1]

The position of the English in the Leeward Islands was rendered still more precarious by the fall of Antigua in November. Henry straightway wrote to his brother at Barbados, urging the dispatch of armed vessels to check the operations of the French. But William Willoughby was himself without supplies. All he could do was to write to the King, pointing out the imminent peril with which the British West Indies were threatened. His analysis of the position at Barbados, though possibly exaggerated, is illuminating. The fighting force of that island he declared had

[1] Lieutenant-General Henry Willoughby to Sec. Williamson, 28th Aug. 1666 (C.O. 1/20, No. 140). Cf. Porter's 'Narrative', H.M.C. xiv, 2, Portland MSS., iii, pp. 300–1, op. cit. The latter account concludes : 'If his Majesty ware justly inform'd how much this island (Barbados) is wekened in men, armes and ammunition by setting forth these ships, he would soone take care for streightening us against soe powerfull an enemy.'

shrunk to 7,000 men, of whom only 2,000 could be depended on for a resolute defence in the event of invasion. Only rich landowners with interests at stake were ready to fight. So disheartened were the mass of servants and landless freemen that they were ready to desert Barbados, the loss of which would mean little or nothing to them. In order to restore the colony to its former virility he suggested a drastic remedy, ' the setting out a portion of land, as ten acres in the hundred by the richer sorte to the poorer '.[1] He was indeed striking at the root of the matter. As already stated, it was the concentration of land into large estates which was gradually depriving Barbados of her ' yeomen ' class, and which eventually put an end to her development as a white community.

The advent of the hurricane season brought a breathing-space for the English colonies. And with the spring came the long-awaited reinforcements from England. On 12th February 1667 four men-of-war arrived under the command of Captain Berry, ' an expert Seaman and a Dareing bold commander ',[2] who brought with him a fleet of merchantmen, laden with arms, ammunition, and supplies.[3] Three days

---

[1] C.O. 1/20, No. 194, 8th Dec. 1666.

[2] Sloane MSS. (Brit. Mus.) 3662, f. 56b. Cf. C.O. 1/21, No. 25, P. R. O.

[3] The London merchants had petitioned the King to send these ships, because, owing to ' the fewness of ships that went last year and the plenteousness of crops, there remained behind great quantities of sugar and other goods, more than double what the ships now going can load. . . .' (Cal. Col. 1661–8, No. 1365). This cessation of shipping, together with events at home, had made the need for provisions and other necessaries in Barbados very acute. Cf. Sam Barwick's letter to Clarendon (Clarendon MSS. 84, f. 358, 18th Nov. 1666). ' We are almoste Consumed to ashes with the flameinge newes of London, which hath raysed the small store of English wares we have here to an intollerable prise, and the planter who for the moste parte is tied to his alleageance by the Stringes of his purse then the veynes of his hearte, I feare will make little scruple of his subiection to him

later the commission appointing the two Willoughbys, Hawley, and Barwick as joint Governors, was formally read at a meeting of the Council.

These reinforcements, which revived the hopes of the disheartened planters, arrived none too soon. A few weeks previously the Government of Nevis had asked Henry Willoughby to return to Barbados to make a final appeal for help, regarding any further attempt against the French without such aid as hopeless. The Barbadians themselves were in a state of consternation. A number of French privateers were blockading the coasts, and threatening the island with starvation. The inhabitants had been badly frightened, too, by the appearance one day of four French men-of-war in Carlisle Bay, which had sailed almost within gunshot of the forts, viewed the defences, and put out to sea again before the gunners realized that they were the enemy.[1]

But now that active measures were possible the islanders set to work with a will. The new commissioners ordered a general election;[2] preparations for an expedition to the Leeward Islands were pushed forward, and Captain Berry was dispatched in the meantime with four vessels, on a five days' raid on the enemy shipping at Tobago.

When the letter of the Duke of York, as Lord High Admiral, was read before the Assembly, directing that every effort should be made to recover what had been lost, that body declared its willingness to expend itself

that best supplies him. . . .' See also Henry Willoughby's letter to Clarendon, 2nd Feb. 1667 (Clarendon MSS. 85, f. 48).

[1] Clarendon MSS. 85, f. 48.

[2] The new Government took a summary step to prevent opposition arising in the new assembly. John Jennings, Speaker of the late Assembly, and a violent opponent of Francis Willoughby, was declared incapable of election. 'It is the Judgement of the Governors and Councill that Mr. John Jennings is a person Incapable to bee nominated or Elected a Member of the Assembly of this Island' (C.O. 31/1, p. 99).

in defence of his Majesty's honour. On the following day (7th March) the representatives made good their word by voting a million pounds of sugar for the Leeward expedition.[1] Warrants were thereupon issued for commandeering provisions, arms, and ammunition, and the ships' crews were encouraged by promises of liberal prize money.

At the same time the Assembly did not forget their own danger. When the Governors and Council intimated that the million pounds would probably not be sufficient, the Assembly replied that further help would be forthcoming, but that they could not bear the entire charge of defending Nevis, as the fortification of Barbados would require immediate and considerable expenditure.[2] The preparations, however, were hastened with all speed, as a combined attack by French and Indians against Nevis was expected before 23rd March. Instructions were issued to Captain Berry, as Admiral of the fleet, to endeavour to sink all hostile craft, to co-operate with the Governor of Nevis in an attempt on St. Christopher or any other enemy island, and finally to return to Barbados by 1st June in order to convoy the merchant fleet back to England as directed by the Duke of York.

The fleet, consisting of four men-of-war and six well-armed merchantmen, set sail on 21st March. The success attained was considerable. Nevis, which was in a wretched plight, was preserved from attack; Antigua and Montserrat were partially resettled; and the French ' sorely Gauled '.[3]

[1] At the same time they characteristically declared before the world that the King's gracious letter, ' and you his Governors Readily asserting and confirmeing of theire just rights and Libertyes is the ffoundation of this their cheerfull and ready Aide. . . .' (C.O. 31/1, pp. 109–10, P. R. O.).

[2] Minutes of Council of Barbados, 7th, 8th, 12th–15th, 18th–22nd March (C.O. 31/1, pp. 130–4).

[3] Sloane MSS. 3662, f. 56b. This writer says that Nevis ' had

Having temporarily disposed of external affairs, the Barbadian Assembly returned to its favourite pastime of wrangling with the Government. A novel feature was furnished by the fact that two of the governing body were inclined to support them as against the Willoughby brothers. On 22nd March, among other demands, the disbandment of a standing regiment known as 'the American Brittain'—apparently enrolled by Lord Francis Willoughby—was called for, 'it being a just grievance to the people and unanimously complayned of'.[1] The Barbadians seem to have inherited that almost unreasoning fear and dislike of standing armies which characterized the inhabitants of England.[2] A further cause for complaint was provided by the action of the Governors and Council in issuing an ordinance on their own authority for continuing the work of fortification. When asked to give their approval, the Assemblymen replied that 'there was noe need of makeing this illegall ordinance'; and that if they passed it into an Act, they would thereby punish those who had quite rightly refused to obey, and would 'render themselves to all his Majesty's Loyall and understanding Subjects, betrayers of theire owne Rights and persons and of the just rights and Libertyes of all those they represent'.[3] The incident is, indeed, strongly reminiscent both of the American colonies, and also, in later times, of Upper and Lower Canada before the advent of Lord Durham—the

most certainly been lost had not these Gentlemen of Barbados, both then and the yeare before sent them large supplyes both of Provisions and Ammunition allmost beyond the Bounds of Prudence, considering their own Condition.' He estimates the sum provided by Barbados from April 1666 to August 1667 at £40,000.

[1] Minutes of Council of Barbados, 22nd March 1667 (C.O. 31/1, f. 152).

[2] See the attitude of the planters to Sir Tobias Bridge's regiment, later in this chapter.

[3] C.O. 31/1, pp. 153-4, P. R. O.

ever-recurring struggle between an elective Assembly
and an imperial executive.

Meanwhile, the appointment of a successor to Lord
Francis Willoughby was being decided at Whitehall.
Fortunately, there was a claimant who combined the
qualities of a court favourite with an intimate knowledge of the social and political conditions of the colony.
This man was William Willoughby, younger brother
to Francis, to whom the barony now reverted.[1] The
characters of the two were for the most part in sharp
contrast. The versatile mind and hot impetuous
temper of the elder brother were replaced in the
younger by shrewd common sense and a power of
suave conciliation. Francis was an idealist ; William
a man of the world. Yet the latter, no less than his
brother, possessed a strong will and a determination
to have his own way. Less enthusiastic and more
cynical, he knew better how to manage men. Since
the Restoration he had been his brother's unofficial
agent at court, countering intrigues and pressing the
claims of Barbados. ' You have stript me out of
taffetie, and putt me into a canvas sute ', he wrote to
the King after his appointment ; and it was just this
combination of courtier and colonist which fitted him
so well for his new post.[2]

Willoughby's formal application for the governorship

---

[1] Francis Willoughby had no sons to succeed him. His two daughters, to whom he bequeathed a large part of his fortune, were married
to Lord Brereton and to the eldest son of Lord Ranelagh. See ' The
Will of Fras. Ld. Willoughby of Parham ', C.O. 1/20, No. 122.

[2] The degree of William Willoughby's intimacy with the King
may be judged from the following letter : ' Pardon I beseech your
Majesty that I put you in mind of the good breeder (my good wife)
I leave behind, who hath brought your Majesty 7 he subjects such as
I dare own ; may the two mares prove as justifiable in their kind,
but if they fail she is resolved to supply your Majesty with a handsome
jade of my breed, but not by her ; . . . though out of sight I beseech
your Majesty forget not the humblest of your subjects ' (C.O. 1/21,
No. 28).

was presented to the King in December 1666.[1] And in the same month, that influential body—the Barbadian merchants in London—addressed an almost unanimous petition on his behalf.[2] A commission was accordingly drawn up, appointing him Governor-in-Chief of the province of Carlisle for the remaining three years of the lease granted to Francis, and on the same terms.[3] The King then wrote to the Government of Barbados enjoining obedience to a Governor ' of soe known and approved a Conversation and ffittness for this Considerable charge '.[4]

In consequence of the perilous condition of the English in the West Indies, Willoughby was enabled to secure a valuable supply of men and munitions to go with him. On his departure from Cowes on 11th March 1667, he took in addition to a large number of carbines, firelocks, and cannon, six companies of regular infantry, with a total strength of 800, under the command of Sir Tobias Bridge.[5] After a prosperous voyage, Willoughby arrived at Bridgetown on 23rd April. Such was the state of disorder that if his coming had been delayed for another ten days, civil war would have broken out. ' They had all beene together by the eares ', as Willoughby put it, and at

[1] He therein stated that his brother's rights in the West Indies constituted the only income with which to support the title of baron, Francis ' having in y^{or} Majesty's service in ye West Indies spent his paternall estate to the value of above 4,000*l.* per annum land of Inheritance and is att this present also indebted to y^{or} Petitioner in great somes of money ' (C.O. 1/20, No. 187).

[2] Ibid., No. 188.   [3] *Cal. Col.* 1661–8, No. 1372 (3rd Jan. 1667).

[4] C.O. 1/21, Nos. 1 and 2.

[5] He took 2,000 firelocks, 1,000 pikes, 200 barrels of powder, 800 hand grenades, and 20 cannon (C.O. 1/21, No. 8). Willoughby was ordered to pay the infantry ' out of ye King's Moyetie of the 4½ per cent. ' (*Cal. Col.* 1661–8, No. 1427). Strictly speaking, the King had as yet no share in the 4½ per cent., because the Carlisle creditors had received little or nothing of what they had been promised in the settlement of 1663.

the mercy of an invader.[1] For this state of affairs he
largely blamed the system of government which had
been established. Two of the commissioners, Barwick
and Hawley, had consistently opposed the vigorous
and expensive policy of Henry and William Willoughby
in the Leeward Islands. The result had been the
division of the planters into two hostile camps. ' They
tell me they are all loyal subjects ', wrote Lord
Willoughby, ' nor doe I doubt but in a shorte time to
make them soe, for all the metall'd Lads are on my
sons' side.'[2]

Hearing of his arrival the members of the Assembly
then in session immediately laid down their authority
and addressed themselves to him on board ship, ' with
grave Complements '. This body, as Willoughby
noticed, was composed of ' the highest factious spirits
in the Island, and almost all my Brothers Enemies '.[3]
The new Governor, however, had no great opinion of
those who had professed to be his brother's friends,
and was determined to conciliate the opposition. As
he well knew, the internal politics of the island largely
consisted of a faction fight between the ' ins ' and
' outs ' : the adherence of most of the ' Magna Carta
men ' could be bought by office.[4] Willoughby, therefore, embarked on a policy of general conciliation.
The friendship of the redoubtable Samuel Farmer,
whom he had brought over from England, was already

[1] Willoughby to Clarendon (7th May 1667), Clarendon MSS.
85, ff. 264–5. See also Willoughby to the King (7th May), C.O.
1/21, No. 43 ; and again (22nd July), C.O. 1/23, No. 23.
[2] C.O. 1/21, No. 43.
[3] Clarendon MSS. 85, ff. 264–5.
[4] ' . . . and this is the practice and ever hath beene of Barbados.
And when these insolent treacherous persons ruled, as in my brother's
tyme they did, and almost to his distruction (for they betrayed him
then with the helpe of Sir Thomas Modiford and Sʳ Robert Harley).
Ffarmer and his ffaction endeavoured the like against my Brother,
who since have appeared loyall subjects ' (C.O. 1/23, No. 23).

secured. Philip Bell,[1] a ringleader of the opposition, was made a councillor, other opponents being similarly rewarded. Whereas one person had previously often held three or four minor offices together, each post was now given to a separate individual, thus ' engaging and almost pleasing all '.[2] When, therefore, Willoughby convened the newly elected Assembly, he met with hearty support. ' After my Harangue to the Assembly, with which they seemed satisfied, though but moderately perform'd (for I am no great Orato[r]), to work they went; I holding them to the point of pursuing that charitable Undertaking of relieving their distressed Brethren at Nevis, Montserratt and Antigua being totally lost.'[3]

The powerful fleet, which had sailed from Barbados in March, had turned the scale at the Leeward Islands. Although the French men-of-war, being forewarned, had for the most part made their escape, its presence at Nevis had prevented further attack. Colonel Russel, Governor of Nevis, and Captain Berry, Admiral of the fleet, had then written to Barbados urging the dispatch of 1,000 firearms, and 500 armed men with food and ammunition, to attempt the reconquest of St. Kitts. Nevis, itself, they said, could only furnish 1,500 men, 600 of whom were unarmed.[4] In particular, it was requested that Henry Willoughby should return to conduct the operations in person, ' whose presence I Esteeme as an Addition of ffive hundred more '.[5] Owing to the opposition of

---

[1] Son of the old Governor. [2] Ibid.

[3] Clarendon MSS. 85, f. 265.

[4] Clarendon MSS. 85, Governor and Council of Nevis to the Governor and Council of Barbados, f. 174 (29th Mar. 1667); ibid., Russel to Henry Willoughby (21st March), f. 176; ibid., Berry to Henry Willoughby (1st April), f. 182.

[5] Ibid., f. 176 (Russel to Henry Willoughby, 29th Mar.). Henry had declared his willingness to go with the fleet in March, provided his brother William was allowed to take over his share in the

the Hawley-Barwick faction, the only response had been the transmission of 500 muskets.

The arrival of Lord Willoughby and the reorganization of the Government gave rise to more energetic measures. Preparations for the dispatch of Bridge's regiment on board a well-armed fleet were already in hand, when a rumour reached Barbados that a powerful flotilla of French and Dutch men-of-war had attacked the Leeward Islands. The Barbadians promptly called a halt. ' The Assembly here ', wrote Willoughby to Governor Russel, ' have desired me not to send any Souldiers from hence till such time as I receive an Account of y^{or} present Condition, and if you yett Continue Master of ye Island.' [1] In another letter of 2nd May, he further indicated the public feeling of Barbados, by advising Russel not to be backward in repaying the generous loans which the planters were so freely voting on their behalf. For, he continued, ' I doe Assure you I were not, bearly on the King's Account, able to Afford you such Releife As by the Assistance of your Charitable fellow subjects I intend '.[2] A similar letter was sent to Captain Berry, informing him that powerful aid would be forthcoming as soon as news arrived that Nevis was still holding out.[3]

Disasters, long dreaded, now befell the English colonies in quick succession. Already on 26th February Surinam had surrendered to the Dutch, though the news did not reach Lord Willoughby until May.[4]

Government. But the Hawley-Barwick faction had refused (C.O. 31/1, pp. 130–4, 13th and 14th March). Owing, however, to the urgent request of Governor Russel, who declared that his presence would put new heart into the inhabitants, the required permission was eventually given (ibid., Minutes of Council of Barbados, 11th April, pp. 162–3).

[1] Clarendon MSS. 85, f. 255 (Willoughby to Russel, 2nd May 1667).   [2] Ibid., f. 257.

[3] Ibid. (Willoughby to Captain Berry, 2nd May 1667), f. 254.

[4] See ' Narrative of the taking of Surinam by the Dutch ' (C.O.

' Brewers and Cheese mongers I presume most of them to be ', he wrote of the Hollanders in disgust.[1] After this success, the Dutch fleet proceeded to Berbice and Tobago, where the former Dutch settlements were re-established, and so to Martinique, in order to join up with the French contingent, which had been recently reinforced by six men-of-war from France. The combined fleet, consisting of over thirty vessels, and with nearly two thousand soldiers on board, then decided to attack the English shipping in Nevis road as a preliminary to invasion. The English fleet discovered the approach of the enemy at six o'clock on the morning of 10th May. The fight began two hours later, and continued until two in the afternoon, by which time the English had chased the enemy in disorder as far as the forts of Basseterre in St. Christopher. As Willoughby proudly reported, they fought like Englishmen.[2] At the same time he realized that Nevis would be in constant peril until this French fleet was destroyed.

On 23rd May, therefore, the promised aid was sent to that island, in the form of six companies of Sir Tobias Bridge's regiment on board H.M.S. *Jersey* and *East India Merchant*, the expedition, as a whole, being under the command of Henry Willoughby.[3] As soon as this force arrived at Nevis, preparations were made for an attack on St. Christopher. An

1/21, No. 21). Printed in *Colonizing Expeditions to the West Indies and Guiana*, ut supra.

[1] Clarendon MSS. 84, ff. 177–8 (Willoughby to Clarendon, 25th May 1667). Willoughby blamed the Governor of Surinam, Major Byam, for cowardice. But in the subsequent court martial it was proved that the colony was exhausted from disease, and without arms or sufficient numbers to make a defence. Cf. H.M.C. xiv. 2, Portland MSS., iii, pp. 308–10.

[2] Willoughby to Arlington, 25th May 1667 (C.O. 1/21, No. 50).

[3] 'Major Scott's Relation', 12th July 1667 (C.O. 1/21, No. 75, P. R. O.). Cf. Sloane MSS. (Brit. Mus.) 3662, f. 55a.

army of 3,200 was mustered on 2nd June, the attack being launched five days later in the early morning. Exactly what caused the ensuing confusion is not known. But the landing force was beaten off with very heavy loss, and the enterprise was abandoned.[1]

The news of this disaster roused Lord Willoughby to further activity. It has 'touch't me so neere', he wrote to Clarendon, 'and made such an Impression upon me, that I put on a firme Resolution to goe that way my selfe, taking with me halfe a dozen of the best ships in the Harbo[r]'.[2] It was not until after two or three refusals that the Assembly at last gave their consent. Willoughby found, however, that it would be quicker and better not to wait and collect another fleet under his command, but to send off reinforcements piecemeal as soon as they arrived from England. On 4th June he dispatched Captain Morris with an armed vessel, containing 'good store of soldiers and such Provisions as are most necessary'.[3] Five days later Sir John Harman arrived with seven stout men-of-war, two ketches, and two fireships. And this useful contingent was also sent on to Nevis.

Despite the added strength of these reinforcements and the vigorous appeals of Henry Willoughby, the Leeward men decided to abandon the attempt on St. Kitts for some lesser enterprise. June and the greater part of July were spent in constructing an army out of the new units and the remnants of the original force. In the meantime, Sir John Harman inflicted a severe defeat on the French fleet in Martinique road.[4]

---

[1] Scott's 'Relation', ut supra. See also Henry Willoughby to his father, 15th June (C.O. 1/21, No. 56). For a detailed modern account, see Higham's *Leeward Islands*, pp. 52-4.

[2] Clarendon MSS. 84, ff. 177-8.

[3] Ibid. Cf. C.O. 1/21, No. 47 (24th June), P. R. O.

[4] Sir J. Harman to Lord Willoughby (June 30th, C.O. 1/21, No.

As the hurricane season was now approaching, Lord Willoughby instructed the expedition to return to home waters.[1] Reaching Barbados on 8th August, the leaders decided to proceed forthwith against the French island of Cayenne, which after a short resistance was captured, together with much plunder and military equipment.

This success was quickly followed up by the recapture of Surinam, a colony of which the Willoughbys were the founders and proprietors. Lord William had fumed at its loss to the Dutch and had been determined to regain it.

The attack commenced on 4th October. But it was not until after a stubborn defence that the Dutch garrison surrendered. All property or land previously seized by the Dutch was now declared lawful prize for the English soldiery and divided among them.[2] Well pleased with these victories, which to some extent compensated for the disasters at the Leeward Islands, the expedition set sail again on November 3rd for Barbados.

The news of their success, however, was more irritating than otherwise to Lord Willoughby. He had just been informed of the declaration of peace by the Treaty of Breda, according to which all places taken after 10th May—as Surinam had been—were to be restored. Unable to keep Surinam himself, Lord Willoughby was determined that no one else should. He ordered his son Henry to return without loss of time and to

[1] Lord Willoughby to the Privy Council (' Narrative of Events '), 16th Dec. 1667 (C.O. 1/21, No. 162).

[2] ' Narrative of the taking of the island of Cayenne from the French and the fort and Colony of Surinam from the Dutch. . . .' (C.O. 1/21, No. 90, P. R. O.). Printed in *Colonizing Expeditions to the West Indies and Guiana*, ut supra. Cf. Governor Wm. Byam to Sir R. Harley, 6th Nov. 1668 (H.M.C. xiv. 2 ; Portland MSS., iii, pp. 308–10). See also ' Description of Guyana ', Sloane MSS. 3662, f. 42.

do his utmost to induce the English settlers, who had been re-established there, to embark with all their movables for Antigua. This course, he felt assured, would utterly disable the Dutch from settling that colony.[1] Henry accordingly remained at Surinam until February 1668, busily removing the inhabitants and laying waste the sugar factories. When the Dutch captain, Du Bois, arrived with a fleet and demanded the surrender of the colony, Henry refused, although shown an order from King Charles to that effect, on the ground that no such order had been received by the Governor of Barbados. The delay, thus acquired, was employed in further devastation and the transhipment of settlers with their cattle and goods. Against this unscrupulous dealing the Dutch Government entered a strong protest at Whitehall, which drew from the King an order for the immediate restitution of Surinam and a severe reprimand for Lord Willoughby.[2]

Now that the war was over, Barbados was able to count the cost. The bill was not a light one; for the expense and conduct of the war in the West Indies had fallen almost entirely on the shoulders of the Barbadian planters. Willoughby estimated that the value of the goods and military equipment sent for

[1] Portland MSS., ut supra. Also, Willoughby to the Privy Council (C.O. 1/21, No. 162).

[2] See Willoughby to Arlington (2nd–9th Mar. 1668), *Cal. Col.* 1661–8, No. 1710; Protest of the Dutch Ambassador to the King (*Cal. Col.* 1661–8, No. 1746); further letter of the Dutch Ambassador to the King (*Cal. Col.* 1661–8, No. 1759); King to Lord Willoughby (*Cal. Col.* 1661–8, No. 1785). Willoughby was ordered to pay full compensation to the Dutch for all damage done and all goods taken away. He was also to bear the entire cost of transporting back to Surinam any settlers who had been intimidated into leaving, and who wished to return—all this on pain of the King's ' high indignation '. For a history of the Surinam colony, see J. A. Williamson, *English Colonies in Guiana and on the Amazon*, 1604–88 (Oxford, 1923), pp. 151–77.

the relief of the Leeward settlers amounted to £50,000, and that a similar sum had been expended on the fortification of Barbados itself.[1] To an island whose entire white population numbered less than 20,000, this amount (about £250,000 in modern money) assumed very serious proportions. Nominally this burden was to be borne by the 4½ per cent. But as Willoughby pointed out, the duty, even when nothing was sent home to the Carlisle creditors, was hopelessly inadequate. Within two months of his arrival at Barbados, he wrote that the planters were ready to lend to the King more than he dare borrow ; ' yet borrow I must, for y^{or} ma^{ties} Revenue is allready by y^{or} commands more indebted then will bee payd dureing my life '.[2] Writing again in September he described his difficulties in paying the seamen of the fleet. The Assembly had raised ' as much as they were able without making a mutiny at Land ', and Willoughby was obliged to take the desperate step of inflating the standard value of sugar, by forcing the seamen to accept 100 lb. at a value of sixteen shillings instead of the normal ten ; an action which raised such a storm of protest that, ' had I not engaged by an expedient to give them their sugar, custome free, I know not what might have followed '.[3]

More pressing than financial difficulty was the scarcity of provisions. Partly owing to the Navigation

[1] Lord Willoughby to the King, C.O. 1/21, No. 89 (July 1667).

[2] Lord Willoughby to the King, C.O. 1/21, No. 54 (June 3rd 1667).

[3] Lord Willoughby to the King, 16th Sept. 1667 (C.O. 1/21, No. 108). At the end of the war Willoughby reported to Arlington (2nd Dec. 1667) that he and Sir John Harman had been obliged to pawn themselves to their shirts in order to pay for the victuals and necessary charges for sending the fleet back to England (C.O. 1/21, No. 154). See letter in similar strain to Arlington (26th Nov.), ibid., No. 149. He said that the 4½ per cent. could not pay off the debt in five years, even though the Governor and the Carlisle creditors received nothing in the meantime. The fund had been already overdrawn for war expenses before his arrival.

Act and partly to the necessity of supplying the swarm of refugees on Nevis, the Barbadians had been faced with a serious shortage. In 1666 Francis Willoughby had declared that but for New England they would have starved, and a year later his brother echoed the statement.[1]

Public debts and a scarcity of foodstuffs are the attendant circumstances of every war. In the case of Barbados, the most far-reaching effect was the accentuation of her need for labour. The disastrous expedition under Francis Willoughby and other subsequent losses had severely depleted her male population. Nor could the deficiency be made good by a supply of emigrants from the British Isles. The prohibition of trade with Scotland prevented aid from that country, whence a large supply of industrious servants had hitherto been drawn. English emigrants were few ; and as to the Irish, Barbadian planters had learnt by experience that they were usually lazy and of no value.[2]

The obvious solution of the difficulty would have been an increased importation of black slave labour. But the Royal African Company, which held a monopoly of the Guinea trade, had (like other traders) virtually ceased operations during the war.

Consequently Barbadian demands for labour became more insistent as the war progressed. In July 1667 Willoughby wrote to the King—' Two things there are wch except speedily remedyed, Whither peace or warr, will ruine these Plantations : . . . ffirst the want of ffree trade wth Scotland, by wch formerly this and the

---

[1] C.O. 1/21, No. 162 (16th Dec. 1667). For the important part played by New England in supplying provisions, see chapter vii, below.

[2] ' Notwithstanding Barbados hath beene soe magnifyed for her strength, I find not above 4,000 ffighting men uppon the Place ; here are 2,000 Irish, I wish I had soe many Scotts for them. . . .' (Willoughby to Williamson, 7th May 1667), C.O. 1/21, No. 44.

rest of y^or Islands was Supplyed wth brave Servants and faithfull Subiects, as by experience they have here been found.' Secondly, a free trade in slaves was the only way to secure a cheap and plentiful supply. 'Soe excessive deare are they now here', he adds, 'that the poore planters . . . will bee forced to goe to fforaigne plantations for a livelyhood.'[1]

These demands were strongly reiterated a few months later by the Barbadian Assembly. The dearth of labour was crippling the manufactures of the island. 'The Planter has been reduc'd to a meane estate, his courage brought low, his Labour not recompensed, most much impoverished, and the best disabled to manure above two thirds of their Land.'[2] The remedies urged were an open trade for Scottish servants[3] and negro slaves, and permission to export direct to foreign countries, provided English shipping was employed and the regulation duties paid at Barbados. 'This Liberty will Accomodate the Planters with many needfull Comodities, and to great advantage at reasonable rates wherein (since debarred a free trade) they have not been supplied.' In short the Barbadians had discovered that the imperial policy of restriction which had proved irksome in peace time, was in time of war unendurable.

In one respect their persistence was rewarded, but under such conditions that the concession was value-

[1] Willoughby to the King (July 1667), C.O. 1/21, No. 89.

[2] Petition of the Representatives of Barbados to the King (5th Sept. 1667), C.O. 1/21, No. 102. Willoughby wrote to the King on 16th Sept., supporting this petition (ibid., No. 108).

[3] See 'Letter from William Willoughby to Lord —— ' (16th Sept. 1667): 'Some of y^or Nation (i. e. Scots) I find here and those good subjects, I wish there were more of them. . . . Three or 4,000 Servants would be upon honourable termes Here entertained ; and if in my time they can be supplyed, this Country will be willing to pay for their passage ; and they shall be freemen after one years Service : . . . by such a supply, whether Peace or Warr, I should be able to grapple with mons^r ' (Sloane MSS. Brit. Mus. 1519, f. 19).

less. In July 1668 the King granted them permission
to buy servants from Scottish merchants, provided
the Navigation Act was not contravened ' by coun-
tenancing or contriving any Commerce or Trade
therewith '. The planters discovered that traders
would not come with servants unless they could return
to Scotland with cargoes of colonial products. The
position was therefore unaltered.

Within a few days of the departure of Sir John
Harman and the fleet for England, Lord Willoughby
himself set sail for the Leeward Islands, to settle the
Government.[1] The work of reorganization proceeded
satisfactorally. As it was visited, each island formally
repudiated the intrigues of the merchants in London,
who had been endeavouring to effect a separation
between Barbados and the Leeward Islands. The
former, so the merchants argued, being a trade rival,
had no interest in their welfare.[2] The reply of John
Champante, Willoughby's agent, that but for Barbados
the Leeward planters would have been wiped out,
was sufficient to quash the matter for the time being.
The desired separation, however, was obtained in 1671.
The intrigue was another example of the undue influence wielded by London merchants and financiers
over colonial administration.

After spending seven weeks ' dashing to and again
among the Leeward Islands ',[3] Lord Willoughby
returned to Barbados on 8th February 1668. Having

---

[1] Willoughby to Arlington, 4th Jan. 1668 (C.O. 1/22, No. 2).

[2] Petition of the Leeward Merchants. Champante's answer, 29th
Oct. 1667 (Egerton MSS. 2395, f. 457). Also in Willoughby's speeches
to the Nevis Assembly, 6th–20th Jan. 1668 (C.O. 1/22, No. 4). Declaration of Montserrat (ibid., No. 17) ; Antigua (ibid., No. 30).

[3] Willoughby to the King, 11th Feb. (C.O. 1/22, No. 34). He had
visited De la Barre, the French Governor-General, and discovered
that the French were very anxious to retain St. Christopher. ' If
they would swap for the Granados, I think it noe ill bargaine.' If
his suggestion had been adopted, much friction and wearisome negotiation would have been avoided.

temporarily done all that was possible in those islands, he next decided to subdue the Indians of St. Vincent and Santa Lucia, who during the war had joined the French and became a serious menace. Sir Tobias Bridge was accordingly ordered to bring his regiment to Santa Lucia, there to join Willoughby with several other companies from Barbados, for a joint attack. The threat proved sufficient for the Indians, who on 23rd March agreed to a treaty, acknowledging themselves as subjects of the English King. Liberty was granted them to come and depart at pleasure in the English islands, similar privileges being extended to the English at St. Vincent and Santa Lucia.[1]

Thence the combined force sailed to Antigua, where Willoughby remained for some time continuing the work of restoring order, and endeavouring to compel the evasive De la Barre to surrender St. Christopher.[2] Bridge in the meantime was ordered to proceed with his regiment to Barbados, which was reached on 21st April.

Their coming was distinctly inopportune. Three days previously, the greater part of St. Michaelstown had been laid in ashes by a sudden outbreak of fire. The damage had been greatly increased by the explosion of the public magazine which tore up buildings in all directions. The total loss was estimated at not less than £300,000.[3] Under such circumstances the sudden arrival of a regiment of soldiers demanding quarters was not calculated to receive a very enthusiastic welcome. The friction was aggravated by the fact that the taverns in St. Michaelstown, where they would normally have been billeted, were destroyed. The only other accommodation was private houses.

[1] Copy of the Treaty, 23rd March 1668 (C.O. 1/22, No. 55).
[2] Willoughby to Arlington, 27th April, and again 2nd May (C.O. 1/22, No. 74). Cf. Willoughby to the King, 2nd May (ibid., No. 79).
[3] *Cal. Col.* 1661-8, No. 1739.

' I found ', wrote Bridge, ' verry great difficulty to persuade the Country to receive the Soldiers on any Termes, but at length the Assembly ordered quarters for the Soldiers upon security given them for payment, but refuse to take the least notice of any of the officers.' [1] The Barbadians were notoriously averse to anything approaching a standing army. They had even refused to allow Lord Francis Willoughby to keep a thousand of the island militia in regular pay, during the time of their greatest danger. And in this case they shrewdly suspected that Bridge's regiment had been sent from England as much to overawe Barbados as to attack the French.

The regiment itself was in a wretched state. On leaving England, the King had optimistically ordered their wages to be paid out of the $4\frac{1}{2}$ per cent. But Willoughby, already at his wit's end for money, had told Bridge plainly that it was impossible. During twelve months' arduous active service the soldiers only received one month's pay. On 27th May Bridge and the officers of the regiment petitioned the King, pointing out that both soldiers and officers were in rags and in need of necessaries, that they were detested by the suspicious islanders, and that Willoughby had neither the authority to disband nor the means to maintain them.[2]

[1] Sir Tobias Bridge to Albemarle, April 1668 (C.O. 1/22, No. 78). The Act was passed by the Assembly on 24th April. Whereas all the public houses were burnt down, the soldiers were to ' be entertained and accomodated in the severall parishes of this Island, in such houses as the Gentlemen of the Council of the Assembly, and the Justices of the Peace in the respective pīshes shall appoint . . . for six weeks and no more '. Three pounds of sugar per day were to be paid to the residents for feeding those billeted on them (ibid., No. 73).

[2] Petition, C.O. 1/22, No. 115. On 30th May Willoughby wrote to the Privy Council urging that a regiment should be permanently stationed at Barbados. Bridge's regiment had done more than all their other forces to overawe the French and Indians, and set an example of good conduct to the planter. But adequate maintenance

In point of fact a royal order for their disbandment
had been sent off to Willoughby on 20th May ; [1] but
because of ' the delayes and difficultys the ffrench
King makes in surrendring the Island of St. Christophers ', it was countermanded two months later.[2]
According to the latter instructions the soldiers were
to be paid immediately out of the moiety of the
$4\frac{1}{2}$ per cent., the collection of the duty being put into
the hands of Sir Tobias Bridge for that purpose.
The residue was to be spent on public expenses.
Considering that the entire fund for five years was
due to the planters for their numerous loans, given to
the King in good faith, it is not surprising that the
presence of the regiment became increasingly distasteful.   In vain Willoughby wrote explaining the
bankrupt condition of the island Government.   ' Y[or]
Ma[tie] will be satisfied that the $4\frac{1}{2}$ per cent. is not
sufficient to doe all things, and that as yet I have had
nothing towards my support.   But I live in hopes, for
I know I serve a just master ; but to keep Souldiers in
good order w[th]out pay is impossible.' [3]

It was unfortunate that, when the financial burden
imposed by the war was being felt most keenly, the
situation should have been aggravated by the disastrous
fire at St. Michaelstown.   When news of the accident
reached London, the King ordered a committee of the
Privy Council to confer with the London merchants
on the best means for the relief of the island.   The
merchants' report on 16th June, in addition to repeating the demands already presented by the islanders,
advised the immediate dispatch of a large supply of

should be assured, because whatever Bridge's soldiers had received
had been from his own pocket. ' I have supported my selfe to this
day on my owne credit in all these great expenses which appartaine
to Government ' (C.O. 1/22, No. 118).

[1] *Acts of the Privy Council*, I, No. 775.

[2] Ibid., No. 792.

[3] Willoughby to the King, 21st July 1668 (C.O. 1/22, No. 20).

fire-arms and ammunition to replace the exploded magazine; free importation of black and white labour; that the $4\frac{1}{2}$ per cent. be abolished or moderated; and finally that to the poorer inhabitants who were utterly ruined, some relief should be afforded by means of a public collection.[1]

Indeed Barbados was going through a very trying period, and nerves were strained in consequence. Nor was the temper of the inhabitants improved by the widespread conviction that their hardships were caused by the policy of the home authorities. The unity which, thanks to Lord Willoughby, had characterized the Barbadian Government during the war, now broke up. The old factions reappeared. The new Assembly, elected early in 1668, adopted an attitude of stubborn hostility to the Governor and all external authority. The last Assembly, Willoughby reported, had loyally supported the King's interest; but the new members, 'who are most composed of my brother's pretended freinds, act hitherto counter '.[2] In fact it was the old turbulent 'Home Rule' party that was stirring again. Personal friendship or external danger might range them temporarily on the side of the Governor, but it was not their normal position. The action of Sam Barwick was typical of this party. When Willoughby endeavoured to retain his support by nominating him a Judge of the Exchequer, he held the patent for three months without making use of it, and before the election of the Assembly resigned the office, ' supposing it would prejudice him wth his faction '. When the opposition was returned, as he had anticipated, with a large majority, he came out

---

[1] Order of the King in Council, 12th June 1668 (ibid., No. 122). Report of the Merchants, 16th June (ibid., No. 123). The planters, however, considered that the merchants had asked for less than half the requisite number of great guns (ibid., No. 125).

[2] Willoughby to the King, 21st July 1668 (C.O. 1/23, No. 20).

into the open. At a debate on a Bill providing accommodation for Bridge's regiment, he declared before the Governor and Council, 'that he would neither give nor lend the King a ffarthing if he could helpe it'. His remark voiced the feelings of the inhabitants.

The exasperated planters now launched an attack against the Governor, charging him and Henry Willoughby with extravagance and mismanagement at St. Kitts, and intriguing with London merchants for his recall.[1] The home authorities too were blamed for the distress that had befallen Barbados. Let the King abolish the 4½ per cent. in return for a lump sum, and grant them a charter constituting them an independent corporation with all the powers formerly held by the Earl of Carlisle.[2] Let them also be allowed freedom of trade, for they had been reduced to inconceivable poverty ; while the prosperity of the French and Dutch was drawing settlers away from Barbados, because of 'their owne pinching and heart killing restraints'. The taming of the opposition, upon which Willoughby had so prided himself, was proving somewhat illusory.

All things considered, the outburst was not surprising ; but it aroused Willoughby's wrath. He was prepared for drastic measures. 'I finde that nothing

[1] C.O. 1/23, No. 20. 'Their correspondents in England are Sir Peter Colleton, a chip of the old block, Sir Paul Painter, formerly a worthy cobler, Sir Peter Leare, all Baronets, and subtle Mr. Ferdinando Gorges who pretends kindness, but is only for a planter Governor, in hopes to arrive to that honour, which when his Majesty condescends to, Farewell Barbados, ffor there is at present such an animosity betweene the planter and the merchant That all wayes Imaginable are studied by some of the Assembly to make the Merchants quit the island.' (They had proposed an Act that no merchant should sue for any debts for the next four years.)

[2] 'Address of the Representatives of Barbados to the King', 3rd August 1668 (ibid., No. 33). These demands were repeated in November 1668. Cf. Letter of the Speaker of the Assembly to the Gentlemen Planters in London, 17th Nov. 1670 (C.O. 31/3, pp. 6–14).

will sooner unsinue the faction then a timely remove
of its chiefes at a distance.' His Majesty must pardon
him if he transports ' the most seditious for a time into
some other of his Majesty's adioyning Collonies'.
For he is resolved not to trouble England with such
spirits.[1] When the Assembly forwarded their petition
to the King in August, Willoughby sent his son William,
with two of his supporters, Colonel Drax and Mr.
Bowden, to lay an account of his own behaviour and
the people's temper before the King. ' This Assembly,'
he wrote, ' by theire impudent Address to y[or] Ma[tie]
have fully declared w[t] they aime at.' A sharp rebuke
from his Majesty would strengthn his position.[2]

For some time now Willoughby had been agitating
for permission to come home, in order to put himself
right with the King and personally defeat these
intrigues. In March his request had been refused as
not convenient in the existing juncture of affairs.[3]
But on 7th August the required licence was given;[4]
and Willoughby, after appointing Christopher Codrington as Deputy-Governor, sailed for England early
in 1669.

Codrington almost immediately incurred the disfavour of the planters by strictly enforcing the Navigation Acts. In December 1668 Arlington had sent
word that three ships were on their way from London
to Barbados, ' upon Accompt of the Jews at Amsterdam'. These and all other vessels found trading from

[1] Willoughby to Arlington, 21st July 1668 (C.O. 1/23, No. 21).

[2] Willoughby to the King (11th Aug. 1668). He added: ' The
greate peake these persons have ag[st] mee is for my endeavouring to
enlarge y[or] Ma[ties] Territories, w[ch] is my Duty' (ibid., No. 36).
The Barbadians had willingly done their utmost to preserve their
countrymen in the Leeward Islands; but now that St. Kitts was
lost, they did not appreciate Willoughby's attempts to re-establish
settlements there and elsewhere, which would compete with Barbados,
and still further reduce her trade.

[3] *Acts of the Privy Council*, I (18th Mar. 1668), No. 763.

[4] C.O. 1/23, No. 38. Also *Acts of the Privy Council*, I, No. 794.

foreign countries were to be confiscated.[1] On arrival
the ships were accordingly seized ; and Codrington
replied that he was glad to have official support in the
matter, for his attempts to carry out the regulations
of the Acts had ' gained him an imputation of
severity '.[2]

Some time later Codrington increased his unpopu-
larity by seizing a vessel in harbour for not having a
sufficient proportion of English seamen in her crew,
the majority being Scots who were reckoned by the
Act as aliens. With the support of public opinion the
aggrieved party decided to appeal to the King and
Council. ' The people generally ', wrote a Barbadian
merchant, ' doe wish them well and wilbee in great
expectation to know how they come off.' ' Many ',
he added, ' could and doe wish there weere not this
nice distinction betwixt the two nations, but that
there should bee a free and mutuall intercourse
between us.' [3]

Yet although the Mother Country dealt somewhat
oppressively with her dependencies, the colonies themselves were equally hard on one another. By the
Treaty of Breda the colony of New Amsterdam had
become a British possession, under the name of New
York, and had opened up trade relations with other
English settlements. ' Wee had begun a pritty trade
there,' wrote a Barbadian, ' sending thither o͏ͬ strong
liquors, Sugar, Cotton, Molasses and ginger.' But
subsequently an agent at New York had sent word
for them to stop, ' because the Governor or Governors

---

[1] *Acts of the Privy Council*, I, No. 823.

[2] Codrington to Arlington, 21st April 1669 (C.O. 1/24, No. 42).
At the request of the customs officers the King sent a letter to each
colonial governor strictly requiring him to take the oath to observe
the Act in order to prevent ' all future ffraud and deceipt ' (*Acts of
the Privy Council*, I, No. 827).

[3] Nicholas Blake to Sec. Williamson, 23rd March 1670 (C.O. 1/25,
No. 17, P. R. O.).

have put some Impost on their goods ; and by this means a hopefull trade is like to bee spoyled '.[1]

Meanwhile the necessity for the reorganization of the chaotic finances of Barbados was becoming daily more pressing. In March 1669 the officers of Bridge's regiment again represented their wretched condition to the King, begging him to order some speedy course for the payment of their arrears, and not to suffer so many of his subjects and their relations to perish for want of their pay.[2] In fact Bridge was meeting with considerable opposition in collecting the 4½ per cent., nor would the island Government give him adequate support. In October he reported to the Privy Council that he was heavily in debt both to the country and to Lord Willoughby, and that if not relieved it was likely to fall heavy upon him.[3] Six months later he informed the King that the situation was becoming hopeless. He had done his best to make the 4½ per cent. pay public expenses as well as support the regiment, but in spite of rigid economy 500,000 lb. of their pay for the preceding year was still owing, and he himself was nearly 300,000 lb. in debt for billeting.

The necessity of settling the 4½ per cent. had been one of the chief reasons why the King had allowed Willoughby to return to England. The three and a half years remaining of the lease, which had been granted to the elder brother, was now almost terminated. At the end of that term the moiety of the 4½ per cent., which had been paid to the Willoughbys

---

[1] Nicholas Blake to Williamson, November 1669 (C.O. 1/24, No. 94).

[2] 24th March 1669 (ibid., No. 33).

[3] Sir T. Bridge to the Lords of the Privy Council (9th Oct. 1669). He stated that he owed 197,064 lb. of sugar to the Barbadians, and 113,798 lb. to Willoughby. Willoughby's moiety had been handed over by order of the King to Tobias Bridge to pay his regiment, the residue going to governmental expenses.

in return for bearing the public expenses, was due to revert to the Crown.[1]

According to the settlement of 1662, the other half of the revenue was still to be paid to the Carlisle creditors until their claims were satisfied. The latter, however, were now calmly ignored.

Notwithstanding the representations of Lord Willoughby and the London merchants, the King decided to appropriate this useful source of revenue for his own use. In December 1669 the offer of Sir Charles Wheler and three others to pay the King £7,000 a year for the farm of the duty was accepted. Out of this sum the latter declared his intention of paying the arrears due to Bridge's regiment and of compensating all Barbadians ' who have in those Partes sustained lose of shipps or Goods employed in his Ma[ties] service in the late Warre '.[2]

But after such temporary disbursements, the revenue was the King's own private money ; and the Barbadians were left to bear the charge of government as best they might. Being asked to report on this settlement, Lord Willoughby drew up a reasoned protest. ' The Island ', he reported, ' will be much dissatisfied to see themselves and the Government left naked, without any publique Revenue upon the place.' He then recapitulated the various public charges which according to the Act the King was expected to defray ; yet the deluded planters ' will now see what they have provided for themselves shippt for England '.[3]

---

[1] Nominally, the second moiety went to pay off the Carlisle creditors. But war expenses had swallowed up the entire fund, and they had received nothing.

[2] ' Order Concerning y[e] 4½ per cent. of y[e] Charibee Islands ' (22nd Dec. 1669, Egerton MSS. 2395, f. 463). Also in *Acts of the Privy Council*, I, No. 881.

[3] He added, that ' it is most certaine that in the late Dutch Warr the 4½ per cent. being applyed all to the publique use, and the Creditt had, were principall meanes at that time of preserving this Island and the rest '. In the event of the farm being continued, he suggested

In the light of the political situation at home during this period, when Charles II was desperately in need of money wherewith to appease his creditors and escape the galling control of Parliament, the King's action is hardly surprising. It was none the less flagrantly dishonest, and raised the planters' anger to boiling point. In April 1670 Codrington the Deputy-Governor reported to Willoughby that the Assembly were refusing to do anything, and all he could do was to keep the peace until his arrival. ' The farming of the foure and halfe and dissposing thereof to other uses then first intended by the Country hath very much disstasted all people.' In the preceding year they had given him 200,000 lb. sugar for the governmental charges, this year they were neither willing nor able to give anything ; and as to the soldiers, ' all my persuations would not prevaile the last sitting of the Assembly to quarter them any longer '.[1]

Meanwhile Lord Willoughby had been busily engaged in meeting a series of charges against his conduct in the West Indies and in pressing the claims of the Barbadian planters. In the former his actions had been vindicated in every case,[2] and as a token of his confidence the King granted him a new commission, as Governor-in-Chief of the Caribee Islands. He was now a Governor in the direct pay of the Crown, with no proprietary share in the revenue as before.

various alleviations (C.O. 29/1, pp. 122-4, P. R. O.). Cf. Egerton MSS. 2395, f. 465.

[1] Codrington to Willoughby, C.O. 1/25, No. 23 (18th April 1670).

[2] Nathaniel Kingsland's charge of injustice and extortion at Surinam was dismissed, with a reprimand for Kingsland (*Acts of the Privy Council*, I, No. 856 ; cf. *Cal. Col.* 1669-74, Nos. 53 and 62). Similar vindication was obtained against William St. Barbe, who accused William and Henry Willoughby of mismanagement and cowardice at St. Kitts (*Cal. Col.* 1669-74, Nos. 78, 79, 80). In February 1669 he had requested that all complaints should be heard before the Privy Council, and that his accounts should be examined and audited (*Acts of the Privy Council*, I, No. 936).

In his defence of the planters' interests he was less successful. Although carefully considered by the Committee for Foreign Plantations, the numerous petitions from Barbados had not been acceded to.[1] Moreover the Royal African Company had replied to the planters' charges by initiating a counter-attack. The unjust proceedings of the Barbadian law courts in shielding the planters from paying their just debts had, it was maintained, seriously injured the company. As a result the Privy Council made an order that henceforth the lands as well as the goods of Barbadian debtors should be subject to be sold in payment. Willoughby had succeeded in vindicating the justice of their law for debt, but wrote informing the islanders that their misbehaviour in this respect had brought them into grave disrepute.

Furthermore he informed them that it was useless to kick against the pricks in the matter of the 4½ per cent. They had recently taken the bold step of ordering the gunners' wages to be paid out of that fund. But he warned them such a defiance of the King would bring upon the island a greater inconvenience than they might imagine.[2]

The Barbadians, however, were determined to make a fight for it. On 21st October 1670 the combined Government again petitioned the King. The duty had only been given to the King, 'Provided the Supporte of the Government and other publique charges expressed, should out of the said 4½ per cent. bee satisfied.'[3] By the same mail they sent a letter to their Governor stating that although the King had not yet acceded to their requests, they heartily thanked Willoughby for his support, and as a

[1] *Acts of the Privy Council*, Nos. 840 and 852 (March and May 1669).
[2] C.O. 31/2, pp. 4–6.
[3] Petition of the Deputy-Governor, Council, and Assembly of Barbados to the King (C.O. 1/25, No. 78).

token of gratitude had voted him 100,000 lb. of sugar.[1]

In order to drive their attack home the colonists decided to effect a close working alliance with that powerful body the Gentlemen Planters of London.[2] In November 1670 they sent a formal letter describing the course of action which they had been pursuing with the support of Lord Willoughby, and urging them to assist in applying pressure at Whitehall.[3] Curiously enough, before this letter reached England the London planters had themselves written to the Barbadian Government warning them that the home authorities were about to apply another twist to the screw by imposing a very heavy import duty on colonial sugars. The better to withstand this danger, they suggested that the islanders should entrust them with a fund to be used in defending Barbadian interests, and that some courtier should be allowed a salary to attend council meetings on their behalf. Indeed some such alliance was essential to success, for the islanders were faced by powerful antagonists.[4]

The islanders falling in with these suggestions, the London planters formed themselves into a committee,

[1] This sum, they declared, though little enough, was very considerable, considering their extreme poverty—they not being able to pay their debts—all which had long since been satisfied had the uses of the 4½ per cent. been performed (*Cal. Col.* 1669–74, No. 301).

[2] The most influential members were Sir Peter Colleton, Sir Paul Painter, Henry Drax, Philip Bell, Constant Sylvester, and Ferdinando Gorges.

[3] Symon Lambert, Speaker of the Assembly to the Gentlemen Planters, 17th Nov. 1670 (C.O. 31/2, pp. 6–14).

[4] This letter also sheds valuable light on the process of depopulation which was taking place in Barbados at a rapid rate. They stated they had been informed that 2,000 had left the island during the preceding year and great numbers were still going. They suggested as a remedy that no planter should be capable of buying more land, with a view to upholding the number of freeholders, 14th Dec. 1670 (ibid., pp. 15 and 17).

which set to work. The ill-success of the previous petitions, it was pointed out, had been largely due to their independence of tone. In future, requests should be forwarded to the committee, who would clothe them in language sufficiently humble as to please the court.[1] Minutes taken at the frequent meetings that were held, reveal considerable activity. Within a few weeks £145 was collected in London to act as a central fund until the money should be received from the Barbadian Assembly. It was further arranged that Willoughby should wait on Lord Lauderdale to press for a free trade with Scotland ; that a parliamentary solicitor should be engaged to oppose the proposed imposition on sugars ; and that Sir Peter Colleton and two others should attend daily at Westminster Hall until the matter of the imposition should be decided.[2]

On their side the Assembly appointed a committee to keep up a constant correspondence with the London planters. The influence which this quite unofficial body now began to exercise over Barbadian affairs is remarkable. The Assembly's letters of 7th March and 4th April 1671 show that all the London committee's suggestions had been adopted and embodied in legislation.[3] Writing on 20th April, the Assembly urged that the King, who seemed to be angry with them, should be informed of the true history of the $4\frac{1}{2}$ per cent., and that all possible pressure should be

[1] Gentlemen Planters to the Assembly, 17th Feb. 1671 (C.O. 31/2, pp. 33–5). Cf. Willoughby's letter to Codrington (20th Dec. 1669). He had presented their important petition to the King on 16th Dec. But he had been privately informed that he would have difficulty in convincing the court of the good intentions of the planters (ibid., pp. 17 and 68).
[2] Minutes of the Committee of Gentlemen Planters (consisting of Lord Willoughby, Colonel Middleton, and eleven of the subscribers), 28th Jan. to 28th Feb., drawn up by Colonel Thornburgh (ibid., pp. 35–9, P. R. O.). [3] Ibid., pp. 18–21.

applied to obtain a free trade with Scotland. Unless the Scottish merchants were allowed to bring their goods without restriction, Barbados would soon be destitute of servants, as few or none came from anywhere but Scotland.[1]

The services of the London committee in opposing the imposition of a further duty on sugar proved invaluable. Unsuccessful in stopping the Bill in the House of Commons, they applied themselves to the House of Lords. During the debates it became clear that the inclusion of sugar in the Bill had been the work of the English refiners, who hoped by the added impost to make it impossible for planters to export purified sugar at a profit. It was chiefly owing to Willoughby that the Lords became convinced of this fact, and accordingly reduced the duty on refined sugar to $2\frac{1}{2}$ farthings per pound. Upon this the Commons flew into such a heat against the Lords for having interfered with a money Bill, that the King prorogued Parliament, and the Bill consequently fell through.[2]

Despite this success, however, the committee was unable to make any impression at Whitehall as regards the main desires of the Barbadians. No concession in the direction of free trade with Scotland, the reversion of the $4\frac{1}{2}$ per cent. to its proper use, or (still less) the issue of a charter, was granted.[3]

---

[1] Ibid., pp. 26–31 (20th April 1671). The Assembly also stated that their choice of a permanent solicitor was Ferd. Gorges, who was to receive £100 per annum and act under the orders of the London committee.

[2] Committee of Gentlemen Planters to the Assembly, 1st May 1671 (ibid., pp. 45–6).

[3] Though unsuccessful, the committee, with the steady support of the Assembly, persisted in its endeavour. See subsequent correspondence, ibid. (10th June), pp. 77–8 ; (15th June), pp. 78–9 ; (15th June), pp. 81–6 ; (18th June), pp. 91–3—in this letter the Assembly stated they had sent off 90 butts of sugar, out of which each subscriber was to be repaid, the remainder to lie in the treasurer's hands

Meanwhile, Deputy-Governor Codrington was struggling to maintain his authority over a colony of stubborn and exasperated planters. In January 1671 he reported to Willoughby that the islanders were so angry about the misappropriation of the $4\frac{1}{2}$ per cent., that he doubted whether they would pay anything more towards the government of the island. It had only been after earnest persuasion that they had agreed to quarter the soldiers (now in a wretched plight) for two months more. ' The Council and Assembly ', he added with a touch of humour, ' dined with me when I gotte them into this good humer ; I feare it will not laste.' [1] Referring to the renewed agitation of the Leeward planters in London for the separation of those islands from Barbados, he remarked that it had ' so Netled the people of this place, I doubt if there be a second occasion they will want that reddy and hearty assistance they formerly received '.[2]

At last, one of the standing grievances with which Codrington had had to contend was abolished by the long-awaited order for the disbandment of Bridge's regiment. The soldiers were to be paid off on the spot and land granted to those who desired it in Jamaica or the Leeward Islands.[3] The question,

as a fund for the furthering of Barbadian interests ; (7th Sept.), pp. 94–6.

[1] Codrington to Willoughby, 15th Jan. 1671 (C.O. 1/26, No. 6).

[2] Ibid. This time the agitation was successful. On 25th Jan. 1671 Sir Charles Wheler was appointed Governor-in-Chief of the Lee-ward Islands, as distinct from the Barbadian Government (ibid., No. 7). The charge that Barbados was jealous of the Leeward Islands, and used its position to their disadvantage, was hotly resented by Willoughby, who urged .that local interests were guarded by the Council and Assembly of each island, and that unity of command was necessary against the Dutch and French. See correspondence (*Cal. Col.* 1669–74, Nos. 268, 269, 297, 309, 327, and 340).

[3] C.O. 1/26, No. 36, P. R. O. Nearly all, however, elected to go to England, where many of them were formed into a dragoon regiment.

however, of finding money for public expenses was as acute as ever. In April 1671 the Council made a futile endeavour to force the commissioner of the $4\frac{1}{2}$ per cent. to apply a portion of that duty to the fortification of the island. His reply that he could disburse nothing without orders from the King or the farmers of that duty was only to be expected.[1]

The important results arising from this constitutional deadlock were strikingly portrayed by Sir Thomas Lynch, Governor of Jamaica, while staying at Barbados in June on his way out from England. Such was the effect of the taxation in the island, that two hundred had volunteered to go with him to Jamaica, and as many more were preparing to follow him there. ' They dread nothing lyke y^e $4\frac{1}{2}$ p. cent.,' he declared. Moreover, the methods used to collect the tax were aggravating the situation; ' for besides that they take it for a great grievance to pay itt to any but y^e Islands use, y^e methods they have used and y^e p̄sons they have employed has made it more difficult and uneasy '. Furthermore, he noticed that the transmission of the revenue to England left the Governor helpless, and without any funds, except ' what ye Capricious Assembly will give, which is lyttle, unless they are mightily pleased '. This, in fact, was the key to the constitutional situation within the colony until the repeal of the obnoxious duty in 1798.

On the outbreak of another war with Holland in 1671, Willoughby presented the King with a number of suggestions for the conduct of operations in the West Indies. An armed frigate should continually patrol those waters to prevent Dutch privateers from preying on English shipping, as they had done so extensively in the former campaign. Also Barbados should be allowed to import food and clothing from

---

[1] Minutes of the Council of Barbados (C.O. 31/1, pp. 189–90 (18th April 1671)).

foreign countries, 'the bringing of which to them from England, will undoubtedly be very difficult, if not totally hindered by the Warr '.[1] But all that the Government would grant was the usual war-time dispensation, permitting English merchants to employ foreign crews and vessels.[2]

The King, moreover, considered that Willoughby's proper place in time of war was at the head of affairs in Barbados rather than at the court of Whitehall. On 13th June he was ordered to proceed on board ship at Portsmouth.[3] His departure, however, was further delayed by alterations in a new commission, which constituted him Governor-in-Chief of Barbados and the other Windward Islands.[4] Herein the imperial power made a very important advance in the process of increasing the subordination of colonies. It was now laid down that laws passed in the island were to be in force for two years and no longer, unless confirmed by the King within that time. The power of the island legislature was thus greatly curtailed. Hitherto, Barbadian laws had continued indefinitely, so long as the King did not veto them. Another indication of the same process was to be found in the injunction that the island Government was not to dispose of any offices, 'which now are or have been granted by us or any of our Royall Predecesso[rs]'

[1] 'By the Lord Willoughby—Proposalls Concerning the West Indies ', 8th April 1672 (Egerton MSS. 2395, f. 470). Also in C.O. 1/28, Nos. 38 and 39, P. R. O.

[2] *Acts of the Privy Council*, I, No. 937 (10th May 1672).

[3] See copy of letter from Willoughby to Clifford, Portsmouth, 3rd July 1672 (Egerton MSS. 2395, f. 479) (B.M.). Cf. also, Clifford to Willoughby, 3rd July (ibid., f. 479b) ; Willoughby to Thomas Povey, 4th July (ibid., f. 480).

[4] Commission and Instructions (first drawn up 30th April, clauses added 10th June). The Leeward Islands now being separate, his nominal government consisted of Barbados, Santa Lucia, St. Vincent, Dominica, and the rest of the Caribee Islands windward of Guadeloupe (C.O. 29/1 (Commission), pp. 141-7 ; (Instructions), pp. 147-52).

By this means royal control of the colonial executive was assured.

When Willoughby at last returned to Barbados on 17th October 1672 he found the island in a strong state of defence. The instructions which he had forwarded in July with Sir Tobias Bridge, dismissing Codrington [1] and appointing Sir Peter Colleton as president, had been obeyed. [2] When, however, Bridge presented a royal letter ordering his inclusion in the Barbadian Council, Colleton had refused to admit him on the ground that being ' noe ffreeholder ', he was not eligible as a councillor, according to the Governor's official instructions. [3] But the King was determined to enforce this arbitrary exercise of his prerogative. On 7th January 1673 he dispatched a letter to Willoughby, ordering Bridge's immediate admittance to the Council. [4]

Soon after his arrival Willoughby determined to send an expedition against the Dutch settlement at

[1] He informed Thomas Povey that ' my late Deputy, Coll Codrington hath harrassed them to death wth needless impossitions '. (Willoughby to Povey, 14th Nov. 1672), Egerton MSS. 2395, f. 483. Codrington, however, seems to have fulfilled his duties conscientiously.

[2] Sir Tobias Bridge (at Barbados) to Arlington, 28th Sept. (C.O. 1/29, No. 32). Cf. Minutes of Council of Barbados, 17th Sept. (C.O. 31/1, pp. 198-9).

[3] Minutes, 28th October (C.O. 31/1, pp. 200-1). Cf. Willoughby to Arlington (C.O. 1/29, No. 42 (3rd Nov.)).

[4] *Cal. Col.* 1669-74, No. 1019. Willoughby's action in suspending the royal order for Bridge's admittance, had angered the King. Thomas Povey (the faithful friend and supporter of the Willoughbys both before and after the Restoration) wrote informing Lord William of this, and giving him at the same time a polite but very firm ' wigging ' for not having informed him of the circumstances. Being thus ignorant, he had been unable to defend him before Arlington and the Lord Chancellor, as (being Willoughby's agent) he should have been able to do. He *must* keep in close touch with his representative in England, ' who is, as it were, to stand sentrie, and bee watchfull, and give the Allarum ' (Egerton MSS. 2395, f. 487 (15th March 1673)). Before this letter reached Barbados, however, Willoughby was dead.

Tobago, which, owing to its situation and possession of good harbours, was a constant menace in time of war, and in peace a serious rival to Barbados. His appeal to the Assembly for funds received a ready response. Eighty thousand pounds of sugar was immediately voted, with an additional forty thousand a fortnight later. A committee also was appointed to superintend the preparations.[1]   On 15th December Sir Tobias Bridge, with over 600 soldiers under his command, and Captain Poole in charge of the *Great David* and six smaller vessels, sailed for Tobago.[2]   In spite of stout opposition the attack was successful, and on 21st December the Dutch surrendered on honourable terms.[3]   The island was stripped, and the Dutch settlers shipped away.

Realizing the great strategic as well as commercial potentialities of the place, Willoughby tried to persuade the planters to settle it. He made a present of the island to Barbados, for which the Assembly thanked him. But when pressed to undertake the work of colonization they drew back owing to a lack of the necessary capital and population, acquainting his Excellency, ' that they desired noe people might be

[1] Minutes, 14th, 20th, and 27th Nov. (C.O. 31/1, pp. 204–7). Willoughby, however, reported to his agent, Thomas Povey, that, ' notwithstanding yᵉ Assemblyes readiness to assist me in this Attaque of Tobago, I was forct for the compleating of it to assist them wᵗʰ my Creddit, soe that I am beginning to Govern after the old fashion, and expect to be called ffoole for my paines, but, I cannot hold when my Masters interest and Honor are in hazard. . . .' (Willoughby to Povey, 29th Dec. 1672), Egerton MSS. 2395, f. 484. Willoughby, since the termination of the lease in 1671, had no share in the 4½ per cent., which had reverted to the King, who (nominally) paid him a salary of £800 per annum.

[2] Ibid. Cf. Bridge's letter to Arlington, 15th Dec. (C.O. 1/29, No. 63).

[3] Bridge's dispatch to Willoughby, with documents relating to the peace negotiations annexed (C.O. 1/29, Nos. 6767, i–viii, 69, 70). See Willoughby to the Secretary of the Council for Foreign Plantations, 22nd Dec. (*Cal. Col.* 1669–74, No. 1000).

sent off this Island to Tobago, this place much wanting funds '.[1]

Indeed, this war with the Dutch was injuring Barbados almost as much as the former struggle had done. In addition to the usual scarcity of provisions and the burden of the Tobago expedition, the Barbadians had suffered a heavy blow in the capture of the great merchant fleet which had left Barbados in June laden with sugar.[2] The consequent distress was intensified by the outbreak of another disastrous fire at St. Michaelstown which destroyed a great part of their supply of provisions—all too scarce already. Furthermore, all attempts to obtain satisfaction in the matter of the $4\frac{1}{2}$ per cent. had failed. On leaving England Willoughby had been specially instructed that if he could induce the Barbadians to pay off the load of debt which attached to that duty and to guarantee a lump sum of £5,000 per annum in its place, he was to come to a definite agreement.[3] Considering that the aforesaid debts amounted to nearly £38,000, it is hardly surprising to find that the Council and Assembly refused the offer.[4]

[1] Minutes of Council of Barbados, 18th Feb. 1673 (C.O. 31/1, p. 212). See former meetings, 4th–8th Jan. (ibid., pp. 208–10).

[2] *Cal. Col.* 1669–74 (8th Nov. 1672), Nos. 960, 998, and 1001. An inquiry was ordered into ' the ill Conduct and Cowardice of the fflag Officers of the ffleete of Merchant ships coming from the Barbados to this kingdome. . . .' (*Acts of Privy Council*, I, No. 952).

[3] Additional Instructions to Lord Willoughby (10th June 1672). The debts included £14,500 for Bridge's regiment, £6,000 arrears to Francis Willoughby's daughters, £14,000 for shipping during late war, £3,500 to Lord Kinnoul in satisfaction of his claim to Barbados, as well as £6,000 per annum for five years, and afterwards £1,000 per annum for ever (*Cal. Col.* 1669–74 (10th June), No. 845).

[4] Minutes of Council, 3rd Jan. 1673 (C.O. 31/1, pp. 210–12). Cf. Willoughby's letter to Sir Joseph Williamson, 10th Feb. 1673 (C.O. 1/30, No. 6). He added that the $4\frac{1}{2}$ per cent. only produced £5,000 per annum, and so could do little to pay off the huge debts that were owing. It is, therefore, not surprising that the King desired to exchange that duty for ready cash.

Suddenly, in the middle of his many activities, William Lord Willoughby fell ill. On 6th April he appointed Sir Peter Colleton as Deputy-Governor to carry on the Government. Three days later he died.

The termination of what may be called 'the Willoughby era' was to mark the beginning of a new phase in the colony's relations with the Mother Country. The two brothers had been able to play a double role. On the one side they were intimately acquainted with the temperament and aspirations of the islanders and with West Indian politics in general, and on the other hand, they were courtiers, friends of the King, and in close touch with the leading statesmen. Consequently, they were able to obtain greater concessions for the colony at Whitehall, and at the same time enforce a stricter obedience to the royal authority than any other colonial Governors of their time. When these 'go-betweens' had disappeared, the contest between colonial independence and imperial supremacy became more uncompromising and more bitter. The rule of the Willoughbys had been drastic, sometimes arbitrary, sweeping aside opposition whether it was justified or not; but on the whole it had been just, and in the best interests of Englishmen in the West Indies.

V

IMPERIAL CONSOLIDATION

§ 1. *Sir Jonathan Atkins* (1673–80)

ON 23rd May 1673 the body of the late Lord Willoughby was conveyed on board ship for England, with the solemn pomp of a military escort bearing draped regimental colours and muffled drums.[1] That done, the attention of the island was directed to the nomination of his successor. It had always been the aspiration of the Barbadians to have a planter Governor, one of themselves, whose acquaintance with the needs and circumstances of the island would be able to defend their privileges against imperial encroachment. ' I hope as you have hitherto been our friend ', wrote Sir Peter Colleton to Henry Slingsby in London, ' that you will stand by us in this juncture and gett us a good Governor, and one that will have regard to the p̄servation of yᵉ place as well as his p̄ticular proffit.' [2]

In the persons of the two Willoughbys Barbados had found able and influential defenders. Deprived of their support the planters regarded the appointment of a new Governor with anxiety. The nominee might fail to preserve the former balance, furthering the interests of the Crown and of himself at the expense of the colony.

---

[1] Minutes of Council, 8th and 21st May (C.O. 31/1, pp. 236 and 238).

[2] Colleton to Slingsby, 28th May 1673 (C.O. 1/30, No. 43, P. R. O.). He added : ' I continue still of opinion that a man that hath an Intrest upon the place will bee more certain to doe that than any man that hath nott.'

Imperial administration was in the hands of the Council for Trade and Plantations, of which the Earl of Shaftesbury was at this time President. Consisting of leading statesmen such as Arlington and Shaftesbury, who were themselves taking an active part in colonial expansion, and of merchants and financiers with long experience in plantation commerce, this body consistently worked for a more efficient and more direct control of the dependencies. Statistics and information of every kind was demanded from the various Governors, in order that the central executive might be able to rule this Greater Britain with the same knowledge and authority as the counties of England. Onwards from the Restoration the machinery of imperial administration had been steadily elaborated. From the point of view of the colonies this process meant increasing restriction and subordination. The planters preferred local independence and the right to ' gang their ain gait ' to the benefits of efficient supervision. The long period of freedom from imperial ties which Barbados had experienced before the Restoration had made her peculiarly sensitive to all interference, whether constitutional or economic. Accordingly, as each succeeding year now witnessed some new step in the process of tightening the bond between the island settlement and the Crown, an increasing tide of indignation and protest arose among the planters.

During the interim, before the new Governor was appointed, the Barbadian Government took the opportunity of representing the exhausted condition of the island, and urging by way of relief the return of the $4\frac{1}{2}$ per cent. duty to its proper use.[1] The constant

[1] Already on 21st May the Assembly had agreed to pay the expenses of the General Sessions, &c., but with the express declaration that ' the same and other publique charge ought to bee discharged out of the $4\frac{1}{2}$ ' (C.O. 33/1, p. 241).

expeditions against the enemy and losses by emigration had reduced the militia to such low numbers that the dangerous expedient of arming negroes had been resorted to. Furthermore, they declared, executive government was nearly at a standstill. The public debt amounted to 1,200,000 lb. sugar, yet the forts were lying in decay, and nothing could be raised to support a Governor, to build a public jail, or to provide a session house for the legislature, which was obliged to assemble in taverns. They therefore begged that as soon as the Dutch war should be over the King would allow the $4\frac{1}{2}$ per cent. to be devoted to its proper purpose—a request as vain as it was oft repeated. Meantime, the support of some men-of-war was craved to prevent the Dutch blockading the island and to preserve ' that little Remaynder of trade now left us '.[1] Their desperate plight was further emphasized by Sir Peter Colleton : ' unless the king will assist them out of the $4\frac{1}{2}$ per cent., I cannot well see how they can goe through with their publick charge '.[2] In three months' time the situation had, if anything, worsened. No method had been found of paying off the public debt. ' Some ', it was reported, ' have proposed a Land and Pole Tax, but have again deserted those thoughts, finding the Planter allready mightily impoverished, and many to have Quitted and Sought new Habitations by reason of the great charge of y[e] ffortifications and other Military dutyes.' [3] In fact, Barbados could ill afford to provide a revenue of £7,000 a year by way of the $4\frac{1}{2}$ per cent., and at the same time pay her own internal charges. When in addition the island was called upon to bear

[1] President and Council of Barbados to Council for Trade and Plantations, 28 May 1673 (C.O. 1/30, No. 40).

[2] C.O. 1/30, No. 43, op. cit.

[3] President and Council to Council for Trade and Plantations, 14th August (C.O. 1/30, No. 59).

the financial burden of the war in the West Indies, the position—already difficult—became almost impossible.

In this dilemma the planters unwisely adopted a policy of passive resistance, obstructing every action of the imperial government. The case of Edwin Stede is a fair example of their temper. In January 1673 that gentleman produced before Henry Walrond, Judge of the Austens Court of Common Pleas, a royal warrant appointing him Provost-Marshal of Barbados. Walrond refused to admit him, maintaining that according to the Barbadian constitution the appointment of judicial officers lay with the Governor, and that the royal warrant was therefore invalid. The scene in court grew stormy. Stede demanded that his patent should be read aloud, but was refused. ' He thereupon held up his Patent to be viewed by the whole Court (there being as he believes 500 Persons) desireing them to take notice what had passed.' [1] After great opposition he was eventually admitted to the office, but only to meet the hostility of the islanders who were determined to make his position untenable. Within a few months he appealed to the King to intervene on his behalf. He was obliged (so he declared) to keep a constant watch over the prison, ' it being soe decayed and insufficient that the prisoner escapes out of it at noon day '. The government held him responsible for the debts of all those who escaped, and yet would not repair the prison on the ground that it was part of the King's duty as expressed in the $4\frac{1}{2}$ per cent. Act. Further, he reported that the Assembly had cut down his perquisites and withheld the office of Marshal of the Courts, ' alledging that if his Majesty will appoint officers, he ought to pay them out of the $4\frac{1}{2}$ per cent., as they intended when it was

[1] Petition of Ed. Stede to the King, 19th Nov. 1673 (C. O. 1/30, No. 82).

given '.[1] Indeed the determination of the planters seems to have been to bring matters to such a deadlock by refusing to do anything which they conceived it was the duty of the King to do, that the latter would be compelled to devote the island revenue to its original purpose. It was a futile course to pursue, for the King had the whip hand. If the internal government was reduced to chaos the first to suffer would be, not the King, but the inhabitants themselves.

Unexpectedly, however, a champion of Barbadian rights was forthcoming in the person of the new Governor, Sir Jonathan Atkins. The request for a planter Governor had been refused by the King, who had been informed that ' they were too much inclined to Popular governm^t already '.[2] He had, therefore, pitched on Atkins, a courtier and a man of long experience in both civil and military affairs as a fit person to uphold the royal prerogative. The terms of his commission bear witness to the determination of the home authorities to extend their authority in colonial government. Not only were all Barbadian laws to lapse automatically after two years if not definitely approved by the Crown within that time ; but the members of the Council were to be directly

---

[1] Ibid. Stede declared that the islanders' scheme was to disable all officers appointed by the Crown, so that none but native nominees should hold office, who would exact fees in accordance with the wishes of Barbados. In April 1674 the Assembly made an attempt to have the royal patent suspended ; but the Council replied, that although they were in sympathy with the desire, it was impossible, for ' the King in open Council declared hee would have his Pattents obeyed ', and that with some anger. Also the Governor had been expressly restrained from granting patent offices. Minutes of Council, 8th April 1674 (C.O. 31/1, pp. 265-8). See further correspondence (C.O. 1/31, Nos. 20 and 38). The activity of Stede's friends at home against the Assembly's action roused that body to another unsuccessful attack upon him in April 1675 (C.O. 31/2, pp. 157 and 164-73).

[2] Sir J. Atkins to the Council for Trade and Plantations, 1st Dec. 1673 (C.O. 1/30, p. 84).

commissioned by Royal Warrant, and not by the Governor, as before. The reason for the change was clearly expressed by John Locke, the philosopher ; ' Because ye Governm^t' would thereby more immediately depend upon his Ma^ty, and so ye Island be better secured under his Obedience.' [1] Thus not only the local legislature but even the royal Governor was brought into more strict subordination to the central power.[2]

Before Atkins left England he presented to the Lords of Trade an address, drawn up by the Gentlemen Planters in London. Therein it was demanded once again that the $4\frac{1}{2}$ per cent. should be devoted to its proper use, that all offices should be executed by the patentees themselves and not by irresponsible deputies, and finally that by reason of the serious scarcity of provisions and utensils occasioned by the war a special convoy of ships should be sent by order of the King.[3] Atkins's support of these Barbadian claims was an indication of the strong line of action which he later took on behalf of the planters. But at the same time he was determined to uphold the royal authority.

Arriving at Barbados on 1st November 1674 his first endeavour was to conciliate and unite the inhabitants in loyal co-operation. The two opposing factions which had sprung up under the rule of the President

---

[1] J. Locke to Arlington, 6th Jan. 1674 (C.O. 1/31, Nos. 2 and 3).

[2] Atkins protested vigorously against this : ' The Council thus constituted are established by as good authoritye as mine.' The Governor will be a puppet. ' It were much better that his Majesty would make them a Corporation and leave them to a free choyce of the Council and of the Assembly ' (C.O. 1/30, No. 84). Cf. Atkins's Commission, 19th Dec. (ibid., Nos. 92 and 93).

[3] Ibid., No. 91 (Dec.). In the following March the President and Council of Barbados sent a similar petition. ' We have continued in great peace and health, but by reason of the Interruption of Trade by the p̄sent Warr, in great want of all things, but especially Provisions. . . .' The situation had been aggravated by a severe drought (C.O. 1/31, No. 17, P. R. O.).

and Council were reconciled, and to some extent the
exasperation against imperial interference was alle-
viated by a growing conviction that the new Governor
was their friend.

This spirit of confidence and cordiality became
evident at the first assembly on 1st December of the
newly elected representatives. When Atkins in a
speech urged them to repeal a law in favour of debtors,
whereby the Royal African Company was being scan-
dalously defrauded, they replied with counter charges
against the Company of injustice and neglect. But
the law was repealed nevertheless.[1] A more substantial indication of public opinion was the grant of
200,000 lb. of sugar for the support of the Governor.

In the heat of imperial disputes, however, the gradual
growth of constitutional machinery within the colony
tends to be lost sight of. A quarrel which took place
between the Council and Assembly throws an interesting light on this internal development. On 8th
July 1674 the President and Council had sent down
to the Lower House for its consent a Bill, imposing
a tax on imported liquors. In imitation of the English
House of Commons, the Assembly replied that they
conceived ' that a bill for raiseing of money ought to
move primarily from them, and therefore the House
cannot proceede upon the bill sent them this day'.
The representatives then proceeded to draw up a
Bill themselves on similar lines. The reply of the
Council was equally reminiscent of the House of
Lords. That the initiation of Bills lay with the Lower
House as of right, was vigorously denied. The present
Assembly would therefore do well ' to follow the

---

[1] See Atkins to Sec. Sir Joseph Williamson, 22nd Jan. 1677 (C.O.
1/39, No. 9). Atkins had been ordered to be kind to the Royal African
Company by the Duke of York, who was one of its chief promoters.
For a description of the Company's relations with Barbados, see
chapter vi, below. See also Minutes of the Council, 30th Sept.,
1st and 3rd Nov., and 1st Dec. (C.O. 31/1, pp. 277–84).

Prudent and Modest Stepps of their predecessors, without innovating or intrenching on his Mat^{ies} Prerogative '.[1] The outcome was a wordy warfare between the two chambers. After various abortive conferences it was not until April 1675 that a settlement was reached. The Assembly agreed that the Council should initiate Money Bills as before; but goods so raised were to be at the joint disposal of the Governor, Council, and Assembly.[2] The representatives, though not entirely victorious, thus gained an important constitutional advantage. The liquor excise—the sole permanent revenue apart from the $4\frac{1}{2}$ per cent.—was now largely in their hands.

Thus conciliated the Assembly proceeded to make use of the proffered friendship of the new Governor.[3] On 16th April a petition laid before him the speedy approach of ruin to the island, ' through oppressions unknown to his Majesty and contrary to his intentions', and asked that since the greatest difficulty had been experienced in approaching the King, his Excellency would give his support and advice in their future addresses.[4] At the same time the Public Treasurer was ordered to send twelve butts of sugar to the Committee of Gentlemen Planters in London for propaganda expenses. An accompanying letter stated that they had been encouraged to renew their addresses, in spite of former ill-success, by the zeal of their excellent Governor.

Indeed, the Barbadians were becoming seriously alarmed at the drastic policy of the colonial adminis-

---

[1] Minutes of the Council, 22nd July and 30th Sept. (C.O. 31/1, pp. 275–7).

[2] Minutes of the Assembly, 14th April 1675 (C.O. 31/2, p. 166).

[3] On 17th Feb. Atkins had written to the Secretary of the Council for Plantations that he found the inhabitants ' a very obedient people to the King ', and ' to myself so conformable that they refuse nothing I ask of them ' (C.O. 1/34, No. 13).

[4] Minutes of the Assembly, 16th April (C.O. 31/2, pp. 178–83).

trators at home. The ruin of all West Indian settlements which they so loudly prophesied was probably
not so imminent as was represented. Yet undoubtedly
great material hardship was being inflicted. Despite
the opposition of the Gentlemen Planters a law had
been passed in 1673 imposing export duties on inter-
colonial trade.[1] The effect of this ordinance was felt
severely in Barbados, which exported considerable
quantities of sugar to New England in exchange for
provisions, the price of which was proportionately
enhanced.[2] It was this same policy which, by prohibiting direct trade with Scotland, was depriving
Barbados of her chief source of white labour.[3]

Assured of the Governor's active support the Barbadian legislature lost no time in opening its campaign.
In September 1675 the Assembly moved that the
custom recently laid on goods transported to New
England might be taken off, the island already suffering
great scarcity of provisions by reason of that impost.[4]
Atkins himself had already written to Secretary
Williamson in the same strain. Not only were the
Navigation Acts threatening to ruin the all-important
commerce with New England and Ireland, but they
were undermining trade with the Mother Country
itself. English merchants, he maintained, were finding

[1] ' Act for better securing the Plantation Trade ' (C.O. 29/3, No. 7).
Cf. Minutes of Barbados Council, 8th July 1674 (C.O. 31/1, pp. 272–3).
See also G. L. Beer, *The Old Colonial System*, Part I, vol. i, pp. 80–2.

[2] Cf. chapter vii, below.

[3] Ferdinando Gorges urged the Lords of Trade to give Barbados
every encouragement. The American colonies, he admitted, were
unprofitable to England ; but not so Barbados, which bought nearly
all its provisions, clothing, &c., from England, to the annual value
of £300,000, employing 6,000 seamen and 200 ships yearly. It was,
therefore, to England's interest to encourage the island by allowing
an unrestricted trade with Scotland—' as Ireland hath '. Mr. Gorges
to the Committee of the Council for Trade and Plantations, 17th
March 1674 (C.O. 1/31, No. 21).

[4] Minutes of Assembly, 28th Sept. 1675 (C.O. 31/2, p. 195).

that the decline in sugar prices so lowered their
profits that it was scarcely worth their while to run
the hazard of the long voyage to Barbados. The
consequent want of shipping had raised freightage to
£9 per ton ; and even then the planters ' cannot get
shipps to carry of the one halfe of their effects of this
yeere '.[1]

Two disasters in the form of an attempted negro
rising and a hurricane, which took place about this
time, caused the planters to redouble their addresses
for some alleviation of their condition. The plot of
the negroes was discovered before they were ready ;[2]
but the hurricane was a more serious affair. The
sugar canes for the next year's crop lay twisted and
broken ; houses, works, and mills lay ruined throughout
the island, whole families being buried in the debris.
A torrent of rain during the night had beaten down
all before it, unroofing store houses and spoiling foodstuffs and sugars. So great was the damage that for
some time the disheartened planters were minded to
leave Barbados, and start again elsewhere.[3]

The immediate outcome of the disaster was a strongly
worded petition to the King, begging for relief in the
matter of the 4½ per cent. and the Navigation policy.
Unfortunately for the planters, the trade policy of
Whitehall was controlled by a powerful coterie of
merchants and financiers, whose interests demanded,
not the relaxation, but the more strict enforcement

[1] C.O. 1/34, No. 57. Cf. same to same (3rd to 13th Oct.). Three
months often elapsed without arrival of a single ship, ' and never so
few has come as this year . . . which hath advanced freight to such
a height, as considering the low price of their commodities in England,
tis impossible for them long to continue to make their sugars ' (C.O.
1/35, No. 29).

[2] For a further description of the plot, see chapter vi, below.

[3] Atkins's description to Williamson, 3rd to 13th October, ut
supra. Cf. H.M.C. xii, 7, Le Fleming MSS., p. 123 (14th Dec.). Also
Add. MSS. (Brit. Mus.) 25120; ff. 41–51 (The Coventry Papers),
Sir W. Coventry to Atkins, 21 Feb. 1675–6.

of the Acts of Trade. Their guiding influence is to be
seen in a number of successful petitions which they
presented for tightening up the Navigation system.
In October 1675 the farmers of the customs obtained
the issue of an order requiring plantation governors to
send home a periodic list of all ships homeward bound
with enumerated commodities, in order to prevent
' the fraud used in carrying the Plantation Com-
moditys to other parts '.[1] Again in the following
January a number of London merchants entered an
emphatic protest against the New England traders,
who were importing goods direct from Europe and
selling them to the other colonies at cheaper rates than
those shipped by English traders from the Mother
Country.[2] Thus, faced by the prospect of being
ousted from the colonial market, it is not surprising
that merchants at home upheld the Navigation policy
at every point. The private interests of individuals,
therefore, as well as the economic theories of statesmen
were opposed to the desires of the Barbadian planters.
Consequently, Sir Jonathan Atkins discovered that his
attack on the Navigation Acts had brought him into
sharp contact with a stone wall.

By way of reply the Lords of Trade commanded his
strict obedience to the Acts, which were of so high
importance to His Majesty's service and so penal to
him in the omission, that they were resolved to exact
from him a frequent and punctual account therein.[3]
Nothing daunted, Atkins proceeded to give reasons
why the Acts in question were bound eventually to
ruin all His Majesty's colonies. The only way to
restore Barbadian prosperity was to allow free trade
and an easement from the $4\frac{1}{2}$ per cent. for a period of
years.[4]

[1] C.O. 1/35, No. 31.   [2] C.O. 1/36, No. 10.
[3] *Cal. Col.* 1675–6, No. 872 (6th April 1676).
[4] Atkins to the Lords of Trade and Plantations, 4th to 14th July

The sense of injury inculcated among the planters by economic subordination was deepened by the repeated interference of the Crown in the internal government of the colony. Charles II did not embark upon his career of undisguised absolutism until 1681, but ever since the Restoration his policy had been to extend the authority of the monarch at the expense of local privilege, both in England and overseas.

The case of Mr. Wyatt is an excellent example both of the methods which the King employed to this end, and also of the opposition which Atkins and the Barbadian Government on all such occasions were in the habit of offering. It was a recurrence of the old grievance of English favourites being appointed to colonial offices, a grievance which had been stubbornly, though unsuccessfully, contested in the case of Edwin Stede. On this occasion the King appointed Mr. Wyatt, an aged civil servant, to be clerk of the markets in Barbados. Atkins retorted that the post was not a ' patentable place ', and was in the Governor's gift. Secretary Sir William Coventry then tried to smooth matters over by suggesting that the Barbadian who was in possession of the office should compound with Wyatt,[1] adding a personal promise to make it his future care, ' that the Governor shall be very barely, if at all, entrenched upon in that kind '.[2] Soft words failing however, Coventry adopted a sterner note. ' If you have anything to show ', he wrote in November 1676, ' whereby the King hath deprived himself of

(C.O. 1/37, No. 22). In April the Governor had written in a similar strain to Sir Joseph Williamson. If the Indians do not destroy the West Indian settlements as they threaten to do the American colonies, ' the Act for Trade and Commerce in a short tyme will effect it, for by bringing all their Commodities to one Markett it hath brought down the price of them to soe low an Ebb that it will not countervayle the charge to plant and prepare them ' (C.O. 1/36, No. 39).

[1] Add. MSS. 25120, f. 68 (Coventry Papers), 31st July 1676.
[2] Coventry to Atkins, 16th Sept. 1676 (*Cal. Col.* 1675-6, No. 1033).

bestowing this place, you will have reason to dispute it ; but I doubt your Assembly will be very much mistaken if they think they can erect any Office with power to take ffees of the Kings Subjects and by their power exclude the King from disposing of it.' The King was determined to enforce the full prerogative of the Privy Seal : unless the Barbadians could prove that authority illegal by process of law, Wyatt must be admitted to his post.[1] The islanders thereupon settled down to that form of passive resistance which they knew so well how to employ. It was not until the autumn of 1677 that Wyatt's title to the clerkship was finally admitted. In a letter acknowledging their submission, Coventry definitely stated the King's policy. ' Whatsoever yor Opinion is,' he wrote, ' that it is prejudiciall to Government to have Officers nominated here, his Majesty and Councell are of another opinion ; that it concerneth his Majesty to be a little better acquainted with those that bear Offices in his Plantations than of late he hath been, . . . and to let them know, they are not to govern themselves but be governed by him.' [2] The imperial policy during this period could not have been more clearly defined. During this dispute Coventry stated that he would have tried to induce the King to draw up a definite list of patentable offices in order to define the extent of the royal prerogative, had not the recent insulting petition from Barbados rendered such a course impossible.[3] The petition referred to was the ' Griev-

[1] Add. MSS. 25120, ff. 96–9 (Coventry Papers), No. 28, 1676. Atkins's argument was that since he was responsible for all offences committed by the Clerk of the Markets, he should therefore be able to appoint his own man. Coventry denied this ; the law does not punish a man for another's fault.

[2] Ibid., f. 120 (Coventry to Atkins), 21st Nov. 1677. In April 1679 Wyatt having died, the King emphasized this victory by again appointing his own nominee (ibid., f. 141).

[3] Ibid., ff. 96–9.

ances of the Inhabitants of Barbados ', which had been presented on 24th November 1675 to the King and the Privy Council.[1]

It was not so much the demands themselves which angered the home authorities, as the audacious attitude of the petitioners. It was an unpleasant thing to have cherished economic laws attacked as injurious and suicidal. Touching on the recent quarrel with the collectors of the $4\frac{1}{2}$ per cent., the petition had described the accusations of those officials as ' very frivolous and ill grounded '. The Royal African Company was similarly abused. They have a monopoly of the slave trade, yet their supply is wholly inadequate and their prices excessive. Moreover, the virtual cessation of white immigrants (from Scotland in particular) had made the planters completely dependent upon the Company for their supply of labour.[2] As to the general application of the Acts the same grievance and the same proposed remedy were put forward as so often before. Concentration of colonial exports into the home market raised the freight and lowered the price. Let the planters therefore pay full duties at Barbados, and then be free to export direct to foreign countries.[3]

Such permission would have entirely defeated the ends of the Mercantilist policy. The payment of customs duties was a very secondary matter. While, therefore, the specific grievances were referred to the Customs officials and representatives of the African

[1] C.O. 1/35, No. 45.

[2] ' . . . now Wee can gett few English, having noe Lands to give them at the end of theire tyme, which formerly was theire maine allurem^t.' As to Irish servants, ' Wee find them of small value ' (ibid.).

[3] It was pointed out that the Customs would gain by this arrangement. For full duties would be paid, whereas there was a drawback of 50 per cent. of the duty in the case of goods re-exported to foreign countries from England.

Company,[1] the Lords of Trade proceeded to indulge in some straight talking with their rebellious subordinate Governor Atkins. That gentleman in his July report to the committee had taken the opportunity of again urging the advantages of free trade, and particularly in the case of newly founded settlements. In reply the Lords returned ' their severest censures of these dangerous principles, which he entertains contrary to the settled laws of the kingdom and the apparent advantage of it '.[2]

Having thus expressed themselves to the Governor, they proceeded to deal with the petition itself.

In their final report presented to the King on 8th November 1676[3] the Lords denounced the impudent suggestion of free trade. ' Wee need not lay before y^{or} Majesty the evill consequence it is that any of y^{or} subjects should presume to peti̅con y^{or} Majesty against Acts of Parliament, which are the laws they must live under, and call them Grievances.' The planters, they feel sure, would never have dared so to petition the King, had not Atkins, who had already shown which way his sympathies lay, incited them thereto. Indeed, they wrathfully declared, he ' doth labour with more arguments than ye Inhabitants themselves, when on the contrary it was ye duty of y^{or} Maties Governor to have supprest any such Address'. Atkins therefore ought to be severely reprimanded for encouraging the people in notions which so tended to the ruin of trade.

In accordance with the resolution a royal letter of censure was drawn up for the King's signature and

[1] See Journal of the Lords of Trade and Plantations, 7th April 1676 (*Cal. Col.* 1675–6, No. 878). Answer to the Committee of the Lords of Trade by the R. A. C., ibid., No. 911. Cf. Journal (20th June), ibid., No. 966. Further reply of the R. A. C. (6th July), C.O. 1/37, No. 25.

[2] *Cal. Col.* 1675–6, No. 1084. Journal of the Lords of Trade, 26th October 1676.

[3] *Acts of the Privy Council*, I, No. 1100 (8th November). Also in C.O. 1/38, No. 31.

dispatched to this outspoken Governor. It was the duty of a royal official to uphold and not to undermine imperial legislation. And yet it had been discovered that the very foundations of England's commercial policy had not only been shaken by the presumptuous attacks of planters who represented them as grievances, but also the latter had been ' countenanced and encouraged therein by your patronizing and pleading in their behalfe, whose duty it was to bend all your reason and interest to have diverted such proceedings, and convince them of their error and danger in the attempt '.[1] Continuing, the letter proceeded with a severe criticism of the Governor's attitude in the quarrel with the $4\frac{1}{2}$ per cent. collectors and of his attack against the African Company. In conclusion it was stated that on this occasion a lenient view would be taken of the matter, judging that Atkins had been misled by some rebellious spirits on the island ; but that any repetition of his former actions would bring down upon him the King's ' severe reprehension '.

After such a rebuff most men would have been only too glad to imitate the wary gait of Agag. Not so, however, Sir Jonathan Atkins. Already a new cause of friction was appearing between himself and the Lords of Trade. In accordance with imperial policy the latter were making strenuous efforts to obtain a closer acquaintance with the internal affairs of each colony. In past years ignorance at Whitehall had compelled the Government to let the colonies very largely go their own way in matters of local administration. Now that the clumsy machinery of councils and semi-official committees in London had been gradually organized into efficiency, the way lay open for a greater measure of imperial control. For this reason Atkins's Instructions on his appointment had expressly

[1] The King to Sir Jonathan Atkins, 9th December 1676 (C.O. 268/1, pp. 60–3).

required him to send home copies of all laws, a yearly account of the slaves imported, the various courts and their procedure, as well as the peculiar needs, defects, exports, and general industrial features of the island.[1]

This information Atkins had been slow to provide, having devoted himself to the venting of grievances rather than the supplying of information. Growing impatient, the Lords of Trade in November 1675 sent him a paper containing thirty-two 'heads of enquiry' which he was ordered to answer forthwith, together with an injunction to dispatch all laws immediately upon their passing, so that the King's confirmation or rejection of them might be known before the expiry of the statutory two years.[2]

To this missive the Governor replied in the following July, answering each question in order. But, as already indicated, he roused the wrath of the Lords by therein attacking the Navigation Acts as ruinous to English interests in the West Indies.[3] To increase their dissatisfaction he refused to attempt to answer their questions as to the island's wealth. It was impossible, he declared, to arrive at an accurate estimation of the exports and imports; and the planters, whose existence depended on their credits

[1] Atkins's Instructions, 19th December 1673 (C.O. 1/30, No. 93).

[2] Lords of Trade and Plantations to Atkins, 20th to 30th November 1675 (*Cal. Col.* 1675-6, No. 885). Before this letter arrived Atkins had sent off a fairly comprehensive account of his government—'An Account of His Majesty's Island of Barbados and the Government thereof' (C.O. 29/2, pp. 1-14).

[3] He also complained that the system of placing the Barbadian Council directly under the Crown so reduced his authority, 'that they seem rather to be ordeyned to be my Governors than I theirs'. He further exposed the evils of the King's practice of bestowing Barbadian offices on persons in England, who farmed them to irresponsible deputies, 'to the great discontent of the people, they having received much Damage by the losse concealment and Imbezilling of Records' (C.O. 1/37, No. 22, 4th to 14th July 1676).

in London, refused to compute their estates. In point
of fact the islanders were suspicious that the demand
for all this information was the preliminary to a
further diminution of their privileges. And Atkins
was afraid of incurring their enmity by attempting
coercion.

The tone of his reply after the receipt of the King's
censure clearly indicates this attitude. Bewailing that
he had come four thousand miles away from home and
friends to fall under such misconceptions, he declared
that it was his desire to recover their Lordships' good
opinion. Yet in the same breath he sturdily defended
his former actions. He had supported the Barbadian
' Grievances ', which had caused so much excitement,
because he was ' not willing to resist utterly their
desires, lest it should make them more earnest, and by
shocking with them at my first coming might render
me incapable of doing the service I had done and hope
to do '. The Crown on the one side and the colonists
on the other were for him in the position of Scylla
and Charybdis. ' Thus is the poor Governor exposed
to complaints on both sides ; I have but this choice,
to obey the first and to qualify as well as I can the last,
and so take my fortune.' As the letter proceeded,
however, Atkins evidently warmed to his task. The
deferential tones of the opening sentences give place
to his normal pugnacity. He thought that he had
already fully answered their Lordships' queries, but
will endeavour to enlighten them on what they do
not seem to understand. As to their request for a map
of Barbados he was sorry, but the only person in the
island capable of drawing it was a Quaker gentleman,
whose religious scruples forbade him to mark thereon
anything so warlike as forts or coast defences.[1]

Another demand of the Lords of Trade with which
Atkins found it extremely awkward to comply was

[1] Atkins to the Lords of Trade (C.O. 29/2, pp. 164–73).

that for a copy of all laws passed since the foundation of the colony. This, even more than the inquiry into the island's wealth, aroused the suspicions of the planters, who feared that the imperial government intended to utilize their information by questioning their rights of tenure in common socage in order to reduce them to tenants of the Crown.[1] The Governor in consequence had recourse to shifts and evasions; the transcription of the laws was always on the verge of a completion which somehow never materialized.

The tension already existing between the Lords of Trade and Governor Atkins was scarcely relieved by a tactical victory which the latter scored about this time at their expense. The undue interference of London merchants in the government of Barbados was a constant source of irritation to the Governor. Already in April 1677 he had bitterly complained that 'there is scarce an order made at your own Board that comes not from the Exchange here sometimes two or three months before your orders come to me'.[2] An opportunity now occurred to make both the merchants and the Lords of Trade look foolish, whereof Atkins was not slow to take advantage. On 16th May Sir Peter Colleton and Colonel Thornburgh waited on the Lords with a petition, desiring them to report to His Majesty that the Barbados militia was in urgent need of a supply of pikes.[3] Their Lordships accordingly ordered the immediate dispatch of 1,500 pikes to the island,[4] and wrote to Atkins expressing their surprise at his recent statement that the military

---

[1] Atkins, when emphasizing this difficulty, cited 'the strange jealousies and confusions' that had b.... caused by Lord Francis Willoughby's public inquiry into the validity of certain land rights, 3rd to 13th May 1677 (C.O. 29/2, pp. 175–7).

[2] Atkins to Lords of Trade, 17th to 27th April (C.O. 29/2, pp. 173).

[3] Ibid., p. 155.

[4] *Acts of the Privy Council*, I, No. 1139; also in *Cal. Col.* 1677–80, No. 264 (23rd May).

stores of Barbados were in a satisfactory condition.[1] They admitted that such representations should come from the Governor alone, yet in view of the island's peril (according to the merchants' report) they were sending a supply of pikes.[2] On receipt of this notification Atkins prepared to do battle. For recently their Lordships had been making themselves unpleasant with regard to the Governor's tardiness in supplying a regular ' journal ' of events in the island.[3] On 4th September the letter was brought before the Assembly, who resolved, ' that the 1,500 pikes therein mentioned are wholly useless to the island and would be a great and unnecessary charge '.[4] Instead, it was agreed to buy 1,200 plain firelocks and 200 carbines.

Thus armed Atkins applied himself to the Lords of Trade. In respect of the merchants' report he wonders no less than their lordships that any one, without order from himself and the Council and Assembly, should venture to make such an address, especially considering that pikes were quite useless because of a worm in Barbados, which devoured all wood of English growth. Continuing, Atkins expressed himself with some freedom. The merchants upon the Exchange, of the Guinea Company, and others, seemed to take it upon themselves to be governors of Barbados. Having so many masters he knows not whom to please. All places of profit, too, ·are given away by royal patent, which was never done before. It were to be wished that Sir Peter Colleton and those other gentlemen for the future would mind their own business.[5]

[1] See Atkins to the Lords of Trade, 6th Dec. 1676 (*Cal. Col.* 1677–80, No. 223) ; also *Acts of the Privy Council*, I, No. 1133.

[2] Lords of Trade to Atkins, 31st May 1677 (C.O. 29/2, pp. 171–2).

[3] Cf. Lords of Trade to Atkins, 21st June, and Atkins to the Lords, 4th to 14th July (*Cal. Col.* 1677–80, Nos. 309 and 317).

[4] Journal of the Assembly of Barbados, 4th Sept. (C.O. 31/2, pp. 266–7).

[5] In reply to their repeated requests for information as to the

In order to drive the matter home the Council and Assembly also addressed the Lords of Trade, returning thanks for their care, but pointing out the uselessness of pikes, and praying that in future no such persons might draw any mischiefs upon them or be heard in their behalf, without their sanction or the recommendation of Governor Atkins, in whose prudent government they could with all assurance confide.[1]

The Governor's determined opposition to all encroachments on his own rights as well as those of the islanders was further illustrated on the arrival at Barbados of Sir Thomas Warner. That gentleman, a lawyer and traveller, said that he had orders to inquire into the forts and general military resources of the island, but held no official commission. Whereupon Atkins warned him that he would be wise to forbear his inquiries ; for if he proceeded, he would certainly treat him as a spy.[2]

military resources of Barbados, he was still more caustic : ' Three times, my Lords, already I have given you this account ; . . . the strength and weakness of any place of this importance ought to be kept secret. And therefore, My Lords, His Majesty having been pleased to appoint me here his Captain General for which I am accountable to him, either with the utmost peril of my life to defend it, or if I neglect my duty to answer it with my head ; . . . I beg your Lordships' pardon that I use these expressions. . . . But I fear my papers are neglected, that you are pleased to take no more notice of what I writ before, and that papers of that kind are made more public than the nature of the thing will admit. But to show I will disobey your Lordships in nothing, I have sent you herewith a new list agreeable to your last commands...' 6th to 16th Sept. 1677 (C.O.29/2, pp.185-91).

[1] The Lords of Trade endeavoured to make the best of a bad business. In January 1678 they wrote to Atkins expressing their dislike of the complaints made by himself and the Assembly, especially as Colleton and Thornburgh agreed there was a necessity for them. They therefore must report to the King that the 1,500 pikes be sent, Barbados to pay for the same according to custom. Further Atkins was informed that Colleton did not voluntarily meddle with the proposal, but was called in by their lordships to give his opinion (*Cal. Col.* 1677-80, No. 575).

[2] Atkins to Lords of Trade, 8th to 18th Oct. 1677 (ibid., No. 422).

The planters themselves, too, were similarly watchful of their interests. When Colonel Sharpe, a Barbadian judge, was ordered to England to answer charges of contravening the African Company's monopoly, the Assembly addressed a protest to the King, representing that they enjoyed their own legal system, by which offenders had always hitherto been punished. If inhabitants of so distant a colony were liable to be ordered to England on any accusation, however groundless, their estates would be inevitably ruined, whether they were guilty or no. They therefore prayed his Majesty to guarantee that henceforth no one would be removed from their homes upon the pretence of any crime, before the case had been first heard in Barbados.[1]

Meanwhile Atkins's policy of delay and evasion in sending home copies of the laws was steadily increasing the exasperation of the Committee for Trade. In November 1677 twenty Acts passed in recent years had been received, but none of the fundamental laws passed prior to the Restoration had yet made their appearance. The reason for this omission, moreover, was clearly perceived at Whitehall. Writing in the following April, Sir Robert Southwell warned Atkins that if he persisted in conciliating the planters rather than the committee, he would find himself in serious trouble.[2]

Similarly, Abraham Langford, who had received a royal patent on 8th May 1676, to be clerk of the Naval Office in Barbados, was refused admittance to the office by Atkins, until the Lords of Trade (being petitioned by Langford) sent a direct order to that effect on 27th Nov. 1677 (*Cal. Col.* 1677–80, Nos. 493 and 494).

[1] Journal of the Assembly, 13th Dec. 1677 (C.O. 31/2, pp. 282–8.

[2] Sir R. Southwell to Atkins, 23rd April 1678 (*Cal. Col.* 1677–80, No. 472). Atkins at this time was specially eager to maintain his former cordial relations with the inhabitants, because of the threatened war with France, of which the King had sent him warning, 16th April 1678 (ibid., No. 658). The Assembly had heartily concurred with the Governor and Council in raising money and buying military

For his part Atkins frankly admitted his difficulty.
He was doing his best to obtain all former laws, but
the Council and Assembly were very much averse to
parting with them. They were the foundation of the
first settlement, and upon which they conceived their
proprietary rights to depend.[1] Moreover, what encouragement was there to transmit laws, when the King
neither confirmed nor rejected those already sent, thus
allowing them to lapse? Was the island to be without
laws; and if so, how were the people to be governed?
Under their laws they were easy and submissive, but
without them the most stubborn of subjects, for they
had the arms in their own hands.[2]

Up to this point the Governor had deliberately
braved the anger of the home authorities by siding
with the colonists, representing their grievances and
again and again urging redress. In appreciation of
these efforts the Council and Assembly had worked
in co-operation with them. Unfortunately, the complete failure to obtain any satisfaction decided the
impatient representatives to conduct operations on
their own, and to ally themselves with the London
merchants.[3] The result was that the Governor was

stores wherewith to defend the island. See Journal of the Assembly,
22nd to 24th Jan. (C.O. 31/2, pp. 280-4); 16th April (ibid., pp. 306-8).
Cf. Atkins to the Lords of Trade, 2nd to 12th June (C.O. 29/2,
pp. 233-4), and again in 19th to 29th June (ibid.).

[1] Atkins to Sir T. Dolman, 2nd to 12th June 1678 (ibid.,
pp. 230-2). Cf. Atkins to Lords of Trade, 10th to 20th Nov. (ibid.,
pp. 238-49).

[2] Atkins to Lords of Trade, 10th to 20th Dec. (ibid., pp. 249-51).
To this objection the Lords retorted that absence of the King's
confirmation was no bar to the re-enactment of laws for a further
period of two years (Southwell to Atkins, 10th March 1679, ibid.,
pp. 251-3).

[3] A letter was drawn up by the Assembly, and, after amendment,
agreed to by the Council, to be sent to Sir Peter Colleton and Henry
Drax in London (15th April 1679). The demands which the latter
were to urge included (1) that since free trade with Scotland could
not be obtained His Majesty would license six ships yearly to bring

isolated, and left to grapple with the irate Lords of Trade as best he might.

To complete his discomfiture the Lords caught him tripping in the business of referring laws to England. In June 1679 the farmers of the 4½ per cent. laid a protest before the Privy Council against the Barbadian legislature for passing two Acts which required them to pay back the duty on all goods captured or otherwise lost at sea.[1] The matter being referred to the Lords of Trade, they replied that they doubted whether there were any such laws in Barbados, since Atkins had assured them that all Acts in force had been sent home. When, however, the petitioners produced authenticated copies their Lordships determined to inflict a severe censure upon the Governor, not only for having deliberately misled them into a belief that they were possessed of all Barbadian laws, but because he had failed in his duty in not vetoing these two Bills which were unreasonable and prejudicial to the King's revenue. He was immediately ordered to forward a complete transcription of every law within three months under penalty of being recalled from his Government.[2] Indeed, this incident sealed Atkins's fate as Governor of Barbados.

On 24th July the King's signature was obtained to a letter that censured him in the strongest terms. Little had it been imagined that, after his first reproof in 1676, he would still delay to transmit the laws ; ' nor have the excuses and evasions by which you

white servants thence ; (2) that the Royal African Company should be divided into separate stocks and jurisdictions, thus breaking the existing system of monopoly ; (3) that the 4½ per cent. might be compounded for by a lump sum paid yearly in England, so as to avoid the friction caused by the collection thereof at Barbados (Journal of the Assembly, 15th and 16th April, C.O. 31/2, pp. 338–46).

[1] Order of the King in Council, 18th June 1679 (C.O. 29/2, pp. 261–5).

[2] Journal of Lords of Trade, 26th June (*Cal. Col.* 1677–80, No. 1034).

endeavour to justify yourself had any other effect
with us than to increase the offence'. Touching the
4½ per cent., 'wee require you not to intermeddle
with our revenue, so that any part of it may be thereby
lessened or interrupted without first receiving our
special commands'. Failure to furnish copies of all
laws within three months would be interpreted not
only as ' a supine neglect or weariness of the trust
reposed in you but an avowed disobedience to our
commands ; and shall thereupon find ourselves obliged
to provide in such other manner for our Government
as may better answer all the parts of our Service '.[1]

The letter of the Lords of Trade themselves was
equally severe, and with a touch of the comic about it.
After the usual complaints of his evasions they added—
' But that which we cannot pass in silence is that
although these difficulties arise from yourself, yet you
cease not to impute the blame and evil Consequences
unto us.' [2] The most serious charge herein adduced
against him was that of nullifying the royal power in
Barbados by passing Acts with a short time limit, so
that they lapsed and could be re-enacted before the
King had had time to veto them.

On receipt of this ultimatum Atkins realized that he
had gone too far, and forthwith dispatched a letter of
apology. ' His Majesty's disfavour is more grievous
to me then the deprivation of any Government his
Majesty hath to give.' As to the Acts concerning the
4½ per cent., he had realized his mistake soon afterwards and had stopped them forthwith. Wherefore in

---

[1] King to Atkins, 24th July 1679 (C.O. 29/2, pp. 274–7). Cf.
Report of the Lords of Trade and Plantations to the King, 4th July
(*Cal. Col.* 1677–80, No. 1051).

[2] Lords of Trade to Atkins, 26th July (C.O. 29/2, pp. 277–86).
At the same time Atkins's friend, Sir W. Coventry, wrote, warning
him that his delay in sending the laws ' hath provoked the Councell
extreamely ', 25th July 1679 (Add. MSS. 25120, f. 143, Coventry
Papers).

order to conceal his error (which had been rectified) he had not sent the Acts home. 'I may fail in my judgement but I hope shall never fail in my integrity.' Yet, characteristically enough, Atkins could not refrain from coupling his apologies and promises of future obedience with a parting protest. 'My Lords, I must finish with a request that you will please to consider me as the King's Governor here ; and that you are pleased to put the opinion of merchants and people that are concerned in this Island in balance with me . . . is something hard to bear.' [1]

But the Lords of Trade had had enough of Atkins. His apology and explanation were deemed unsatisfactory. If a stricter obedience to their desires was not rendered by him they would take steps to find a more compliant Governor.[2]

In fact, despite such occasional opposition, the process of imperial consolidation was being rapidly effected. On 14th January 1680 a general letter was sent to all colonial legislatures signifying that the growing importance of dependencies required that the committee, to whom the King had entrusted the care of the same, should have frequent accounts by many hands of all events, and that the King had therefore commanded the colonial governments to furnish the committee with a quarterly journal describing all matters of importance, especially those relating to trade.[3] At the same time the Lords made it clear that their dependence on the London merchants for advice and information had been due to the state of ignorance in which the negligence of Governors like Atkins had left them. 'While you are Governor, we shall always

[1] Atkins to Lords of Trade, 16th Oct. 1679 (*Cal. Col.* 1677–80, No. 1156).

[2] Journal of the Lords of Trade and Plantations, 13th Jan. 1680 (ibid., No. 1259).

[3] See Lords of Trade and Plantations to the Governors and Council of Barbados, 14th Jan. 1680 (C.O. 29/2, pp. 300–2).

consider you as such, and we shall be able, when you Comply with our demands, to distinguish the Statements of merchants, from the more solid Information, which we have constantly required of you in vain.' [1]

Atkins, nevertheless, made genuine efforts to pacify their Lordships. On 26th March 1680 he dispatched an elaborate report, repeating information that he had already sent at least three times, and including such details as christenings, burials, and a census of the white and negro population for each parish.[2] But the Governor's former shifts and evasions had made the committee profoundly distrustful of him. Sir Peter Colleton being called in to examine his figures, reported a number of discrepancies with former returns. For this the Lords required Atkins to furnish an explanation, adding further strictures against his method of passing short-time Acts, that were due to expire before their arrival in England. Such a situation could have but one solution. In July 1680 the King recalled Sir Jonathan Atkins from Barbados, appointing Sir Richard Dutton in his stead.

The methods adopted by Atkins in defending Barbados from the process of imperial consolidation had been short-sighted and unskilful. The Lords of Trade were labouring to organize the machinery of colonial government on a basis of knowledge and efficiency. If Atkins had won their approval and confidence by promptly supplying copies of every law and all other information by them demanded, even at the risk of arousing Barbadian hostility, he would have been in a strong position to urge redress of grievances. But involved, as he became, in long-drawn-out quarrels with the Lords, he lost the close co-operation of the impatient planters. Isolated on both sides his recall was inevitable.

[1] Lords of Trade to Atkins, 16th Jan. 1680 (C.O. 29/2, pp. 305–15).
[2] Atkins's Report, 26th March 1680 (ibid., pp. 313–22).

Yet, even if he had been more diplomatic, it seems doubtful whether he would have attained a greater degree of success in his defence of Barbadian interests. With or without the confidence of the Lords of Trade his attack on the Navigation policy would have been unavailing. The policy of subordinating colonial interests for the benefit of those of the Mother Country was the accepted principle of the age. At the same time the uncompromising attitude of the choleric old Governor probably checked the King's attempt to extend his prerogative in Barbados more successfully than less stormy methods would have done.[1] In Sir Richard Dutton's Commission the system of biennial laws which had placed the island legislature under the direct surveillance of the Crown, was altered. In future all Acts were to continue in force unless the King expressly disallowed them.[2] Furthermore, the abuse of Barbadian offices being held by royal patentees, against which the ex-Governor had repeatedly inveighed, was remedied by a clause in Dutton's Instructions, that no places other than those already granted would be disposed of by the Crown, but would be left in the hands of the Governor.[3]

Constitutionally, then, the history of Barbados during these years was fairly typical of the general process of imperial development. The home authorities aimed at a stricter obedience from the colony, but in return provided a wise and efficient system of law and order.

[1] Atkins was seventy years of age, forty-two years of which, so he informed the Lords of Trade, had been spent in the service of Charles I and Charles II. 'But this is unfashionable discourse and I leave it, placing myself at the King's disposal and willing if he thinks anyone more fit to serve him here, to submit to his Pleasure' (C.O. 29/2, pp. 313–22).

[2] Journal of the Lords of Trade and Plantations, 6th August 1680 (Cal. Col. 1677–80, No. 1477).

[3] Dutton's Instructions, 30th Oct. (ibid., No. 1563). Cf. ibid., No. 1554. Also Acts of the Privy Council, II, No. 16 (20th Oct.).

Charles II had not yet embarked on his career of absolutism.

Economically however the case of Barbados was exceptional, an example of the old colonial system at its worst. For the inclusion of sugar on the list of enumerated commodities restricted the entire commerce of that island to the home market, with the subsequent disadvantages. Barbados received the maximum of injury and the minimum of compensation possible under the regulations of the Acts of Trade.

§ 2. *Sir Richard Dutton*, 1680–5

THE Governor of a colony, enjoying a measure of representative government such as Barbados, was always called upon to fill the difficult role of a go-between. On the one side he was the King's representative, working under the direction of a committee of the Privy Council. On the other hand he was a component part of the colonial legislature. He was thus set between what were often two conflicting forces. The policy of the Mother Country under the old colonial system, was of its nature opposed to the desires of the colonists. The home authorities, while obviously labouring for the good government of the overseas settlements, yet subordinated their interests to those of the Mother Country. They existed, in the opinion of contemporary statesmen, not as English counties at a distance, but as external possessions, the resources of which must be used to support the homeland in the great game of national rivalry.

The colonial governors were thus set between two fires. Under such men as Shaftesbury and Locke, they were bidden to co-operate in the work of extending the imperial authority in order to organize the Empire into a self-sufficient unit. That this process was being effected at their expense, the planters quite clearly realized. As one of their number bitterly remarked, ' The Citizens of Rome, though they lived in the remotest Parts of the World then known, were still Roman Citizens to all Intents. But we poor Citizens of England, as soon as our backs are turn'd, and we are gone a spit and a stride ; are presently reputed Aliens, and used accordingly.' [1] The analogy was inaccurate and somewhat unjust ; but it reveals the sentiment of the planters in respect of imperial policy. Internal feud and faction was a characteristic of Barbados, as of all small communities. But the presence of a Governor endeavouring to uphold this policy had the effect of intensifying the friction.

The two Willoughbys had successively enforced order and obedience with a strong hand, while at the same time vigorously representing the grievances of the planters to the home authorities. Sir Jonathan Atkins, as we have seen, had balanced his conduct less skilfully. Unwilling (whether from fear or conviction) to oppose the turbulent Barbadians, he sealed his own fate by consistently evading or attacking the commands of the English Government.

Yet all three of these Governors had worked wholeheartedly for the welfare of the island. Indeed it is a remarkable thing in colonial history to find a colony so fortunate in its rulers. From Searle's time until 1680 the island had been governed by a succession of men, who were on the whole clever, honourable, and loyal both to the home government and their own colonial subjects.

In the person of Sir Richard Dutton, however, the inhabitants were about to experience the rule of a new type of Governor—that of an adventurer. Dutton's policy was to make himself absolute master within the

---

[1] *The Groans of the Plantations*, by Ed. Lyttleton (of Barbados), p. 24, London, 1688.

colony. The obedience thereby obtained would serve the double purpose of propitiating the powers at Whitehall and of enabling him to amass a fortune at the expense of the planters.

Before leaving England therefore, Dutton demanded that the scope of his authority, as laid down in the Commission and Instructions, should be extended. He asked (*inter alia*) for the old proprietary right of passing ordinances upon urgent occasions without consent of the Assembly ; that special powers might be given him to deal with refractory Councillors, that suspended members might be ineligible for election to the Assembly, and finally that no agents of the inhabitants should be received at Whitehall unless their propositions had been duly endorsed by the Governor and Council : a hit at the Committee of London Merchants, who (as we have seen) were exerting considerable influence in Barbadian affairs.[1] Working under instructions from the Assembly, the Gentlemen Planters, as they were called, were endeavouring to overthrow the patent of the African Company, and to arrange a commutation of the $4\frac{1}{2}$ per cent. duty.[2]

The latter demand had met with some response. In his inaugural address to the Assembly in March 1681, Dutton intimated that he had the King's authority to arrange for an equivalent imposition in place of the obnoxious duty. After some delay the islanders offered a duty on liquors of £5,000 per

[1] Dutton to the Lords of Trade and Plantations, 11th September 1680 (*Cal. Col.* 1677–80, No. 1505). The power of passing ordinances without consent of the Assembly had been granted to the Willoughbys. But the rare occasions on which it had been exercised had aroused violent opposition among the planters.

[2] Governor Atkins and his Council had refused to sanction these proceedings, stigmatizing them as factious, injurious to the interests of the country, and an encroachment on the royal prerogative (ibid., Nos. 1343 and 1558).

annum, which was to be collected by Barbadian officials. But after discussion the matter for some unknown reason went no farther.[1]

If the new Governor was determined to be master of Barbados, the planters themselves were of a humour no less aggressive. Indications of their temper were soon forthcoming. In May the Assembly, imitating the imperial parliament, presented a bill of Habeas Corpus. But Dutton wrote home that he had been saved ' the trouble of using his veto, by the rejection of the bill on the part of the Council '.[2]

More significant still was the refusal of the Assembly to pay off the public debt by settling a regular excise on liquors. It was strongly suspected that the King intended immediately to lay his hands upon it, as in the case of the $4\frac{1}{2}$ per cent., and give it to his favourite the Lady Portsmouth.[3] ' They thought Monarchy was on its last legs in England,' wrote Dutton, ' and I am confident were preparing to set up a Commonwealth here as early as any of the Plantations.'[4] He proceeded to demonstrate that the monarchy was as flourishing as ever. Nor were opportunities hard to discover.

Already for two years suspicion of the King had prevented the Assemblymen from granting the excise, with the result that no jail delivery had been held ; the expenses of a General Sessions amounting to

[1] Minutes of the Council, 20th July 1681 (*Cal. Col.* 1681–5, Nos. 131, 181, 324, and 611).

[2] He regarded the Assembly's action ' as a snare, either to throw me upon the King's just Displeasure, or to make it a cause of Quarrel with me, so as to give me no present, as they usually did to all their Governors' (Dutton to Sir Leoline Jenkins, 30th May 1681, ibid. 1681–5, No. 123).

[3] Dutton accused Sir Jonathan Atkins, who was still in Barbados, of spreading this rumour. ' He had the confidence or malice to tell me that he did think that the King would lay his hand upon any money bill that might be enacted here ' (same to same, 14th June, ibid., No. 141).   [4] Ibid.

nearly seven hundred pounds. Consequently when the
Assembly pressed the new Governor to hold a Session
forthwith, he replied that he would do so when the
necessary funds had been voted. The Assembly
retorted that the necessary and proper fund was the
4½ per cent.[1] For some time deadlock ensued. No
money was forthcoming, and the unfortunate prisoners
were on the verge of starvation. Dutton at length
solved the problem by calling a General Sessions, and
leaving the officers and freeholders to bear their own
expenses.

In the actual trials the Governor adopted the
arbitrary course of imposing sentences without reference to the attendant Councillors and Judges, who
had always hitherto voted in judgements there given.[2]
The General Assembly accordingly pointed out that
they looked on this as a dangerous innovation, likely to
be of grievous consequence under Governors less just
and moderate than himself, and requested him to stay
execution of the sentences so imposed, as being un-
warranted by law.[3] Wrathful at such contumacy,
Dutton replied in a very high-handed tone. The
alleged right of the Judges and Councillors, he declared,
was founded on no law, but on a mere pretended
custom. They must tell him how they came by their
information, or he will look on their assertion as an
insult and a scandal to the administration of justice.
As to the sentences imposed, he will have them carried
out forthwith. At the same time he refused a number
of other demands which the Assembly had been

[1] Journal of the Assembly, 8th June 1681 (*Cal. Col.* 1681–5, No.
132).

[2] Mr. Peers of the Council and Littleton of the Assembly protested
in court. Dutton threatened Peers that if he left the bench without
permission he would be sent to the common jail. He then submitted
(ibid., No. 797).

[3] Address of the General Assembly to Dutton (5th October 1681,
ibid., No. 112).

pressing upon him, concluding with a tirade of some violence.

' I never heard that the King had granted you a new Magna Carta, though you dispute all his commands as though he had ; So I tell you plainly that those who obstinately oppose their Prince's commands (as you apparently do on all occasions) would, if they had power and opportunity, as confidently make war upon him. . . . It is an insolence beyond expression to imagine that the King should be bound up by the petulant and factious humours of some ill-men among you (for I do not condemn all) to lessen or enlarge his Commission.' [1]

Thus confronted, the Asssembly endeavoured to arrange a compromise by asking Dutton to levy the fines, but to spend the money on fortifications. His reply was to the effect that he could not spend the King's money without the royal consent ; and the Assembly was obliged to admit defeat. But as it happened the matter did not end here. One of the accused who had been fined at the Sessions was an influential planter named Hanson. Evidently somewhat of a firebrand and agitator, he had been subsequently imprisoned by order of the Governor for attempting to disembark a private cargo of negroes upon the island in defiance of the African Company's monopoly. The slaves and the ship had been confiscated and sold. According to his own story he had been imprisoned for refusing to take an illegal oath, tendered by Dutton, to the effect that he would answer any questions that might be put to him, thus swearing against himself. At any rate he succeeded in escaping from prison and making his way to England. Dutton immediately dispatched the unfortunate Marshal of the prison in pursuit, at the same time sending a letter to Secretary Jenkins asking that if Hanson appealed to

[1] Dutton's Reply to the Addresses of the Assembly, 22nd December 1681 (*Cal. Col.* 1681–5, No. 345).

the Privy Council this Marshal might be received as a witness on his behalf.[1]

On arrival in England, Hanson although faring somewhat badly himself, succeeded in his main desire of making things uncomfortable for Dutton. In January 1683 his petition was transferred from the Privy Council to the Lords of Trade and Plantations.[2] The case was then considered by the latter on several occasions, but nothing definite was done until the summer, when Dutton himself came home on furlough, and was obliged to make a detailed defence. In October the Lords pronounced the fine inflicted on Hanson illegal; but that the original charge against him of stealing guns, the public property of Barbados, was so serious that the entire case must be re-heard before them. In spite of Hanson's protests, five months' adjournment was granted to allow Dutton to return to Barbados in order to collect further evidence.

Hanson however was determined to bring matters to a head. Being informed that the Committee for Trade and Plantations would not award damages, he now instituted proceedings at Common Law. His petition against Dutton was accordingly dismissed from the Council Board and the scene of the contest shifted to the law courts. Here the indefatigable Hanson presented on 23rd November a series of elaborate accusations, charging the Governor with promoting his relations and friends to all the lucrative posts in Barbados, and with obtaining large sums of money by extortion and fraud. The strenuous denials of the charges which Dutton presented on 5th December carried sufficient weight to prevent the affair going any farther; but they could not quite explain away

[1] Dutton to Jenkins, 2nd December 1682 (ibid. 1681–5, No. 826). Cf. also Dutton to Lords of Trade, 15th and 16th November (ibid., Nos. 791 and 797).

[2] Ibid. Order of the King in Council (26th January 1683), No. 915.

one or two awkward facts such as the acceptance on his part of a bribe of £1,500 from Spanish merchants trading to Barbados for slaves. Hanson had achieved his desired revenge in so far that he had undoubtedly impaired Dutton's reputation in England.[1]

Meanwhile Sir Richard Dutton in Barbados had been vigorously acting the part of a new broom for the benefit of the home authorities, and causing much disturbance thereby. Even at the General Sessions of August 1681, the conduct of which had caused him so much subsequent trouble, he had scored a clear hit by prevailing on the assembled freeholders to address to His Majesty ' an oblation of duty and loyalty '. Anxious that his good work should not go unobserved, he sent by the same mail a letter to Sir Leoline Jenkins, asking that the address might be ' presented as publicly as possible and be inserted in the Gazette '.[2] At the same time he wrote to the King himself, pointing out that this was the first address of its kind ever sent from a plantation. He added that whereas on his

---

[1] See 'An Abstract of some of the many complaints of oppressions and misdemean^{rs} Comitted by Sr Richard Dutton. Gov. of Barbados' (Clarendon MSS., 87, ff. 42 and 43b). See *Cal. Col.* 1681–5, Nos. 1014 and 1015 (24th Mar. 1683); 1167 (27th July); 1310 (15th Oct.); 1334 (26th Oct.) ; 1369 (7th Nov.) ; 1384 (14th Nov.) ; 1390 and 1391 (16th Nov.) ; 1409 (23rd Nov.) ; 1435 (5th Dec.). One of Hanson's charges was that Dutton had caused a special prayer for himself to be drawn up and used in all churches in the island. The action was characteristic, but the prayer itself was harmless enough : ' Almighty God, in whose hands all earthly power doth consist, we humbly beseech Thee to bless his Excellency, Sir Richd Dutton, K^{nt}, Capt Generall, and Governor-in-Chief of this and other ye Caribee Islands and ordinary of the same; Grant that ye Sword wch our dread Sovereign Lord ye King hath committed into his hand he may wield in thy faith and fear, and use according to thy blessed Will and Word. Let thy Grace enlighten him, thy Goodness confirm him ; and thy Providence protect him. . . . Amen. ' An Order by Sir Richard Dutton for a prayer for himself and Council to be inserted for public use ', 11th October 1681 (Tanner MSS. (Bodleian), 36, f. 140).

[2] *Cal. Col.* 1681–5, No. 218.

arrival the Barbadians had been expecting the dissolution of the monarchy and were in a state of faction and disloyalty, he had completely disillusioned them. All rebellious persons had been removed from official posts, the Church and the militia had been regulated, and the colonists generally converted into obedient and repentant subjects of his Majesty.[1]

One of Dutton's earliest activities had been the drastic reform of ecclesiastical organization. The Anglican Church in Barbados although nominally under the jurisdiction of the Bishop of London, was chiefly controlled by the Governor as ordinary. He it was who appointed the parochial clergy and schoolmasters. Dutton determined to make the most of these powers. Early in 1681 he conducted a formal visitation to inquire into the qualifications and orthodoxy of the clergy. One of these—Grey by name— was discovered to have been baptizing, marrying, and performing other priestly offices for the past twenty-four years without holding Anglican orders. The unfortunate man was immediately deprived, and fled the island ; and Dutton reported the case to Henry Compton, Bishop of London. The ex-Governor, Atkins, being taxed with having allowed this irregularity made the characteristic reply, that if Mr. Grey had not received ordination, ' I am sure I could not have ordained him ! '

Among the schoolmasters, too, Dutton found occasion for reform. Many of these were found to be Quakers and Anabaptists. All therefore who refused the oaths of allegiance and supremacy were ejected. It was quite true that this colony, so far removed from the central authority, had become lax in the observance of ecclesiastical usage. There being no regular supply of Anglican clergy from England, many

[1] Dutton to the King, 5th September 1681 (ibid. No. 216).

persons who made no pretence to Anglican orders performed such rites as burial and marriage in out-of-the-way plantations. 'I have made some essay', reported Dutton to the Lords of Trade and Plantations, ' to let them know that I will not tolerate their former liberties, such as marriage by unqualified persons, and between persons within the prohibited degrees.' His action, he added, though hitherto largely unsuccessful, had startled the inhabitants extremely. In order to enforce his desires he begged for formal instructions to establish an ecclesiastical court, ' with full authority to inflict ecclesiastical censures as provided by law in the English ecclesiastical Court.'[1] Part of the same policy was his rigid suppression of ' conventicles', in spite of the fact that religious toleration had been observed in Barbados since the first settlement.[2]

One of the most effective pieces of self-advertisement executed by Dutton was his fitting out of the militia with black helmets and red coats, like the regular foot regiments at home—a luxury which no other colonial government had yet indulged in.[3]

Certainly the factious spirits among the planters had never before been so completely cowed. It will be remembered that on Dutton's arrival in the island, the legislature already for two years had refused to grant an excise on liquors owing to a suspicion that the King would appropriate it to his own use. Yet Dutton persistently returned to the charge. On 4th October 1681 the Assembly again refused; the tax would be granted only when the King had definitely agreed to the commutation of the $4\frac{1}{2}$ per cent.[4] Two

---

[1] Dutton to the Lords of Trade and Plantations, 13th Feb. 1682 (*Cal. Col.* 1681–5, No. 414).

[2] Minutes of the Council, 21st March 1682 (ibid., No. 444).

[3] The Bill was finally passed by the legislature on 16th November 1681 (Minutes of Council, ibid., No. 293).

[4] Journal of the Assembly, 4th October 1681 (ibid., No. 250).

months later financial stress compelled the Assembly
to vote the excise, but only for a period of three
months. In return the Governor declared that his
Instructions forbade him to pass any law of less than
one year's duration. Further debate ensued; after
which the Assemblymen unanimously decided that
their duty to the people prevented them from com-
plying with his demand, and that the Act must be
renewed after every three months.[1] The controversy
thus lapsed into its former state of deadlock. But
Dutton had by no means owned defeat.

Meanwhile the Governor and the Assembly devoted
themselves to a series of contests on other subjects.
On their side the representatives put forward a number of bills and petitions, calculated to increase local
authority at the expense of the royal prerogative.[2]
On his part Dutton replied by using his power of veto
and by administering stern harangues to the Assembly.
Writing home, he declared, ' I shall always refuse them,
whatever the pressure put on me, though as you may
see by the Assembly's late Addresses to me, that
pressure is great.'[3] The crisis came in January 1682.
All members of the opposition throughout the island
were removed from their offices, military or civil,
their places being filled by persons more compliant to
the will of the Governor. A few days later the island
was astonished to hear that the Assembly had been
dissolved and sent home.[4]

All these activities had been carefully reported at
frequent intervals to the home authorities, with the

[1] Journal of the Assembly, 21st December (No. 328).
[2] These Bills included the Habeas Corpus Bill, a Bill restricting
the application of English law to Barbados, and one making all proceedings of the Court of Chancery public, thus imposing a check
on the Governor who was ex-officio president of that court. Cf.
Dutton to the Committee for Plantations, 3rd January 1682 (No. 357).
[3] Ibid.
[4] Dutton to Sir Leoline Jenkins, 2nd February 1682 (No. 394).

desired effect. The Committee for Trade and Plantations were being visibly impressed by the energetic action of this Governor, along lines so well approved, and in such pleasing contrast to the attitude of Sir Jonathan Atkins. In April 1682 the committee presented a report to the King commending Dutton ' for great vigour, prudence, and fidelity, for proposing many things for the benefit of the colony without regard to his private interest, and for his general conduct of the Government '.[1] By way of reward it was somewhat quaintly suggested that the arrears of his salary should be paid.

Sir Richard Dutton, however, like his royal master, soon discovered that while it was quite possible to govern without parliamentary aid in peace time, the additional expenses consequent on a condition of war rendered dependence on the elected representatives inevitable. On 25th April he was constrained to summon a new Assembly. In his opening speech he said quite frankly that he had experienced so much opposition from the former House, that nothing less than pressing need could have induced him to call another. But there was an imminent prospect of war with France, and Barbados was in no state to meet such an emergency. The militia was in great need of muskets and pikes, the forts were unfinished and inadequately supplied with cannon, and the government was burdened with a heavy public debt.[2] The Assembly, putting aside former differences, rose to the occasion. A liberal levy of 6d. per acre and 1s. 3d. per negro was resolved on.[3] Furthermore in the following August the long-outstanding quarrel over the excise

[1] Report of the Lords of Trade and Plantations, 8th April 1682 (*Cal. Col.* 1681–5, No. 463).

[2] Speech of Dutton to the Assembly, 25th April (No. 486).

[3] Journal of the Assembly, 28th April (No. 488). (N.B. Jews and dwellers in towns were taxed proportionately.)

was terminated by the capitulation of the Assembly. In order to make their submission less patent, the representatives designated the proffered tax an 'impost' on liquors instead of an excise. Feeling himself master of the situation, Dutton would now only accept it on two conditions—that it was to be granted to the King according to the style used in the English Parliament, and secondly that it must be given for not less than one whole year. Rather to his surprise they acquiesced in both, expressing sorrow for former miscarriages and offering him a present of £1,500.

Within twenty-four hours a letter was dispatched to the Plantation Committee informing them of the victory. Therein Dutton recounted an incident which illustrates the methods which he sometimes used against his enemies. The leader of the popular party was Colonel Christopher Codrington, the founder of a family which has done illustrious service to Barbados and the Empire in general. This gentleman had been Deputy-Governor in the time of Lord William Willoughby. Dutton now happened to come across some documents which showed that certain public monies had not been accounted for during Codrington's term of office. Seizing his opportunity, the Governor had him proceeded against as a debtor to his Majesty, with the result that verdict was given for £579 10s. to be paid to the King. It was to no purpose that Codrington produced accounts showing that the King was in his debt for £1,200, spent by him as deputy for public purposes. He must seek redress on that score from the Lords of the Treasury. Political incendiaries, wrote Dutton, must be treated like mutineers—with quickness and resolution in seizure. 'I have in some measure,' he added complacently, 'been quick to strike at the head of a factious party, and have been as successful as ever I had anticipated. It makes the hearts of the factious to ache to see the most popular man in the Assembly (i. e. Codrington) in trouble.'[1]

When three weeks later, a most complimentary letter from the Committee for Plantations arrived, Dutton's triumph seemed complete. His care of the Church had been praised by the Bishop of London and all good men ; his zeal for justice and authority had pleased the King ; and the committee in general was greatly satisfied with his conduct. 'Take care of your health,' added Secretary Jenkins, 'for a man~ so valuable as you is not often met with.'[2]

Yet underneath this show of ordered peace and submission, there was much deeply seated discontent and hatred of the Governor. Nor was the resistance of the Assembly by any means broken. On 6th February 1683 Dutton made a speech before the House, informing them that his oft-repeated request for leave to England had at last been granted by the King. After his departure in April the House would not sit, so he trusted they would make good use of their time. Sir John Witham was appointed Deputy-Governor for the interim. To this the Assembly returned a spirited rejoinder. Proceeding to hasten the dispatch of business as directed, they presented for his approval a list of enactments, including the notorious Habeas Corpus Bill, all of which Dutton had repeatedly and angrily vetoed. They acceded to his demand that they should bear the expense of building a 'House of Correction' and a public magazine, but firmly refused to increase the excise or extend the time of its operation. Finally they protested against the closure of the Assembly during his absence. 'Your predecessors did not so limit their deputies.'[3]

On arrival in England Dutton (as already described)

---

[1] Dutton to the Lords of Trade and Plantations, 29th August 1682 (No. 666).

[2] Sir L. Jenkins to Dutton, 12th September (No. 668).

[3] Journal of the Assembly, 22nd February 1683 (No. 962).

was obliged to defend himself against the determined hostility of Mr. Hanson, and to answer the damaging charges of tyranny and extortion which he brought forward.

The rule of Sir John Witham in the meantime was characteristic of that of most Deputy-Governors. It was a constant struggle to maintain order among a number of zealous and turbulent party leaders, who considered themselves as good as he.

The two men with whom Witham almost immediately came into collison were Henry and Thomas Walrond, turbulent sons of their equally restless father Humphrey Walrond, who had been so prominent in earlier years. These brothers Witham stigmatized as the worst of trimmers—men who though in secret alliance with Codrington and the popular party, yet endeavoured to persuade Governors that nothing could be effected in the Assembly without their aid.[1] Quarrels broke out on a variety of subjects. Witham complained that Henry Walrond, in his capacity of Lieutenant-General, behaved as though he were in absolute command of the militia. Another dispute arose in the Court of Chancery. Henry Walrond maintained that whereas bills and decrees had formerly been addressed to the Governor alone, they should have named the Council also. Witham for his part declared that the Court of Chancery was of inherent right in the Crown and devolved on the King's Governor or deputy, and that he would not ' permit this flower of the prerogative to be lightly snatched away '.[2] The upshot was that the Walronds and their party withdrew from all participation in the government.[3]

[1] See ' A General View of the Affairs of the Island of Barbados ', by J. Witham (*Cal. Col.* 1681–5, No. 1177).

[2] ' The Temper of Several of the Council in Barbados ', by Witham (ibid., No. 1093).

[3] Cf. Minutes of the Council, 10th and 11th July 1683 (ibid., No. 1143).

Circumstances more trivial than these contributed to weaken the hands of the Deputy-Governor, and (incidentally) to provide a picture of seventeenth-century etiquette. At the funeral of Anne, Dowager Baroness Willoughby of Parham, Sir Martin Bentley allowed his coach to take precedence to that of Colonel Newton, who claimed seniority of rank. The latter complained to the Council, and Bentley was obliged to apologize. The incident appeared closed, when Sir Timothy Thornhill, a very wealthy and influential planter, put forward his claim to precedence as a baronet. Failing to gain his point he withdrew in high dudgeon from the Council.

In spite of such obvious difficulties Witham succeeded in maintaining comparatively good order.[1] His worst troubles arose from a very unexpected quarter. Towards the end of September 1684, Dutton arrived from England, and proceeded to mark his return by an act of exceptional fraudulence, which exposed his true character and contributed to the ruin of his career. Hearkening to the complaints made against Witham by the Walronds and other disaffected politicians, he conceived the idea of utilizing this discontent to deprive Witham of the half share in the Governor's salary, due to him for his work as deputy. Accordingly he sent a messenger to Witham, who was ill in bed, demanding surrender of the money. Very naturally the latter said he would not part with it.[2] The sum due for sixteen months' service was £812 10s., which was barely sufficient to meet expenses. A few days later (10th October) Dutton appeared before the Council and put a number of questions touching the Deputy-Governor's conduct. Irritated by the unbending attitude which Witham had maintained

[1] Minutes of the Council, 3rd October (ibid., No. 1292).
[2] Cf. Witham to the Earl of Sunderland, 14th October 1684 (ibid. No. 1891).

against them, the Councillors answered adversely, as was expected of them. But when the crucial query was put—'Do you think that the expenses of his Government have been such as to merit the reward of half my salary granted him by the King,' they refused to be drawn. 'He continued,' they replied cautiously, 'his usual thriftness and good husbandry throughout his Government.'[1]

Dutton however had obtained the excuse which he required. Witham was suspended from the Council and from all public employments. An illegal action : for the Governor's Instructions directed that no Councillor might be suspended without his answer and proof of the allegations. On 4th November he went a step farther, and ordered Witham's arrest.[2] The trial at the General Sessions, which began on 16th December, was little more than a judicial farce. With a show of impartiality Dutton refused to take his accustomed place as president of the Court, and appointed in his stead Henry Walrond, late Lieutenant-General and Witham's bitterest enemy in Barbados.[3] The sentence imposed was a fine of £5,000 and imprisonment during the King's pleasure.

Meanwhile Sir John Witham had not been idle in his own defence. Among others he had written to the suave and powerful Earl of Sunderland, begging for his support and describing the proceedings in detail.[4]

[1] Minutes of the Council, 10th October 1684 (*Cal. Col.* 1681–5, No. 1887).

[2] Minutes of the Council, 4th November (ibid., No. 1919). He was on 12th Nov. offered bail, himself in £5,000, and sureties each in £2,500, because of his illness. Cf. Edwin Stede to Sir J. Witham (ibid., No. 1935).

[3] Cf. 'Presentments of the Grand Jury at the Sessions held in Barbados, 14th Dec. 1684' (ibid., No. 2007). Also, Address of the Grand Jury to Dutton (No. 2096). Also, Dutton's order to Th. Jennings for seizure of all letters arriving from England for Sir J. Witham, 4th Jan. 1685 (No. 2040).

[4] Witham to Sunderland, 14th Oct. 1684, and again, 31st Oct. (Nos 1891 and 1912).

A similar defence was sent to the Lords of Trade and Plantations, who accordingly issued an Order in Council, stating that there appeared no sufficient ground for the treatment which he had received, and ordering suspension of sentence until the whole matter had been heard before his Majesty.[1]

Indeed, Sir Richard Dutton, like most clever rogues, had been induced by over-confidence to exceed the bounds of prudence. He had stumbled across a hornet's nest when he attempted to defraud the influential Sir John. When the case was brought before the Lords of Trade and Plantations in March 1685, Witham initiated a counter-attack, charging Dutton with a variety of crimes, including the receipt of bribes, appropriation of public funds, and arbitrary imprisonment.[2] Furthermore he produced a detailed balance-sheet showing that the Governor had made no less than £12,000 profit out of his office.[3] With regard to his trial in Barbados, he proved that the charges of bribery were false, and that Dutton had refused his right of appeal to the King. Eventually after much angry recrimination between the two,[4] the committee on 31st October 1685 pronounced their decision. They found that Dutton's proceedings ' were altogether violent and malicious ', being

---

[1] This Order in Council also noted the receipt of a copy of the Act for an imposition on liquors, which provided for the payment of a present of £2,000 to Dutton. This method (the Order stated) was directly contrary to the King's Order of 15th Dec. 1682 (No. 855) —no entry having been made in the books of the Council or Assembly. The £2,000 was to be reserved till the King should approve the gift or direct its application to other purposes (No. 2048). Cf. Commission of James II appointing Edwin Stede Lieutenant-Governor during Dutton's absence, 27th March 1685 (Rawlinson MSS. A (Bodleian), 257, f. 109). Also draft of James II's letter to the Governor and Council of Barbados concerning the forthcoming trial (ibid., ff. 113 and 115).   [2] Cal. Col. 1685–8, Nos. 94, 95, and 162.

[3] See Note A at end of chapter.

[4] Cal. Col. 1685–8, Nos. 388, 413, 414, 429.

prompted by no other motive than that of depriving
Sir John Witham of the half salary due to him.[1]

Witham was accordingly restored to all his offices ;
and Dutton realizing the game was up pleaded for
pardon.[2] His subsequent attempts to climb back into
favour were answered by the disillusioned committee
with curt rebuffs.[3] The Lords had become thoroughly
suspicious of him.   Further inquiries were made into
the numerous charges of tyranny and peculation which
had been made, with the result that he was recalled in
disgrace.

The governorship of Sir Richard Dutton had been
doubly unfortunate. Not only had his arbitrary
methods exasperated the Barbadians, but the work of
the statesmen at home in reorganizing the government
of the colonies on more direct and more efficient lines
had been greatly retarded. Imperial control, constitutional and economic, was always disliked by the
planter ; but when that control was misused for
purposes of personal aggrandizement, the imperial
system suffered by its representative.   Moreover, the
means adopted by Dutton to become absolute—the
dissolution of Assemblies, the ejectment of popular
leaders from office, and so forth—bore an unpleasant
resemblance to the policy then being pursued so
skilfully by Charles II at home. It was not for nothing that rumours were afoot of the establishment of
colonial commonwealths.

Turning to economic conditions in Barbados at this
period, it becomes clear that the position of the planter
had altered considerably for the worse.

Owing to greatly increased supplies, the price of
sugar in London had gradually fallen from £4 per

[1] Report of the Lords for Trade and Plantations (ibid., No. 439).
[2] Ibid., Nos. 448 and 449.
[3] Cf. ibid., Nos. 454, 455.

hundred pounds of unrefined sugar to an average of 20*s*. ; while the price of white refined sugar had dropped from £7 to £2 10*s*. This depreciation had been felt more severely by the Barbadian planters than most, because of the additional burden of the 4½ per cent. Also there was an import duty on sugar into England of 1*s*. 6*d*. per 100 lb. which had remained constant despite the fall in price.

A comparison of several detailed calculations, worked out by planters, indicates that the total cost of freightage and taxation amounted to roughly 10*s*. per 100 lb.[1] Therefore assuming the selling price to be £1, the planter actually received about ten shillings, from which of course was to be deducted the upkeep of negroes and other plantation expenses. Another planter, Edwin Lyttleton, in his well-known pamphlet *The Groans of the Plantations*, puts the case in a more extreme light. According to him the minimum cost of production was 20*s*. per 100 lb. ; 10*s*. being spent on the making, and 10*s*. on freightage. Taxation on 100 lb. amounted to 2*s*. Thus unless a selling price of over 22*s*. was obtained the unfortunate planter received nothing at all.[2] Such a computation must have been inspired by the author's desire to prove his point ; for sugar manufacturers, like most other people, are not professional philanthropists. Nevertheless the general mass of evidence clearly shows that the margin of profit accruing to the Barbadian planters had shrunk to narrow dimensions.

In 1685 the position had become so much worse that sugar producers were seriously afraid of general bankruptcy. Further taxation of colonial sugar had

[1] See Note B at end of chapter.
[2] Ed. Lyttleton, *The Groans of the Plantations*, p. 3, London, 1688. ' But if the sugar yield only twenty-two shillings, the Duty swallows up the whole profit : if it yield but twenty, the Planter pays the Duty out of his Pocket, and must live by the loss, and there is many a Hundred of Sugar sold under twenty.'

been suggested to Charles II as a useful means of
obtaining revenue. On the accession of James II the
project was executed, an additional impost being
enforced of 2*s.* 4*d.* per 100 on muscovadoes, and 5*s.* on
' whites '. By itself the new duty was substantial
enough, but taken in conjunction with the original
impost and with the 4½ per cent., it was crushing.
The promoters had declared that the duty would be
paid by the consumer ;—a statement which Lyttleton
characterizes as ' Meer Mockery '. ' The Buyer, they
say, must pay the Duty, but sure the seller may pay
it if he please. And he will please to pay it, rather
than not sell his sugar. If he will not, there are enow
beside that will.' [1]

Moreover this high tariff on colonial sugar was
contrary to the spirit of Mercantilism, the aim of
which was to enrich the Mother Country by encouraging the importation of raw material from the
plantations. ' But here lay the mystery. The Pro-
jectors consider'd, that if other Forrainers were hardly
used in England, they would carry or send their
comodities to other Places. But wee poor English
Forrainers are compell'd to bring all Hither, and
therefore they thought they could hold Our Noses to
the Grind Stone and make us pay what they please.' [2]

Writing in 1688, Lyttleton stated that many
planters who had possessed good estates four years
before had by that time been reduced to a condition
bordering on starvation. ' What have we done,' he
exclaimed, ' or wherein have we offended, that we

---

[1] *The Groans of the Plantations,* ut supra, p. 9. This story of the
buyer paying the duty, added Lyttleton, was such ' barbarous non-
sense ', that there was little fear of the duty being adopted, ' had not
the late King (to our great unhappiness) been so strangely earnest for
this Tax. Which yet that Parliament, who then denied him nothing,
had never granted '—if some councillors had not assured them in
the King's name that the duty would be taken off, if it proved
grievous to the plantations.   [2] Ibid., p. 9.

should be used in this manner ? ' [1] And a less excitable writer than Lyttleton remarked that, ' had we known this formerly, we had invested our time and money otherwise '.[2] A long series of protests from Barbados and other sugar plantations were addressed to the authorities at home ; but without avail.

Thus the Barbadians suffered in three ways : from the $4\frac{1}{2}$ per cent. on the island, from the heavy customs duties in England, and from the Navigation Acts which in compelling them to buy in the home market only, placed them at the mercy of the English merchants. With this policy of concentrating the plantation trade most of the inhabitants sympathized, even though it was to their own hurt, because of the resultant advantage to the Mother Country. What they did object to was the clause which compelled the colonist to buy *European* goods from England, instead of bartering directly with those countries. ' Had we been confined to England,' wrote Lyttleton, ' only for those things that England doth produce, we should have been well contented. But that we must fetch from England the Things that are produced elsewhere, seems very hard. We are sure it makes the Prices excessive to us.' [3]

In the case of Barbados it is interesting to note that there was a system in operation which to some extent

[1] *The Groans of the Plantations*, pp. 14–15.

[2] Sloane MSS. 3984, ff. 214–20 (Sept. 1687). Cf. the following protests against the tax :

(*a*) Address of the Lieutenant-Governor, Council, and Assembly of Barbados for Themselves and Inhabitants. The petitioners beg the King (15th Sept. 1685) to think of some expedient, ' that may rayse us from this soe heavy and insupportable burthen, by which only wee can bee preserved from utter ruin . . .' (ibid., f. 221).

(*b*) Another petition (14th Feb. 1687). Petitioners declare their ' utter inability to pay the tax '. We ' lay our former remarks at your Royall ffeet, imploreing your Gratious inspecčon of them . . . that the ruine now rageing and devouring of us, may receive your healing touch ' (ibid., f. 223). [3] *The Groans of the Plantations*, p. 5.

evaded this clause of the Navigation Acts. From early years there had been a settlement of Jewish merchants on the island. In 1681 Dutton had put their numbers at 260, all of whom had been born in Barbados or had obtained denization by letters patent.[1] This group of Jews, it appears, were in close touch with others of their nationality in London and Amsterdam. The method employed was for a number of merchants in Holland to club together and send a cargo of European goods to England. On arrival their associates arranged for the cargo to be entered at the Customs Office in the name of one Englishman, thus avoiding the heavy alien duties. Moreover the ship was usually sent to some small ' out-port ' such as Dover or Falmouth, where the customs officials (being bribed) were satisfied with the unloading of only the top part of the cargo. In the unloaded portion a variety of goods were concealed which thus escaped the duties. The vessel then sailed for the plantations, where the goods were of course sold at prices much lower than those of the English merchants. The return voyage was managed in the same way. A cargo of sugar was taken on board with other commodities concealed in the hold; the vessel, again evading the aliens' duty and the impost on the goods concealed, sailed to Holland where the Jewish owners again undersold the English merchants. Mr. Hayne, a customs official who made a special study of this form of smuggling, declares that ' the Jews in Barbadoes Sell more Hollands there, than all the English merchants do '. At another place he remarks—' if this be granted (which I challenge all the Jews in Europe and America to deny if they can) they may in every

---

[1] Nevertheless they were feared and regarded as aliens. In June 1681 a petition of the inhabitants was presented to the Assembly in which it was stated that ' the presence of Jews is inconsistent with the safety of Barbados ' (*Cal. Col.* 1681–5, No. 134).

Voyage from Amsterdam or Rotterdam to Barbadoes, and back again . . . Sell 20 per cent. cheaper than the English. And this is the main, if not the only Reason, our merchants have to complain of the small advance they make in our Plantation Trade . . . the Jews can undersell us there.'[1] The same system apparently was at work at Jamaica, New York, and a number of other colonies.

From the foregoing statement it would appear that this international league of Jews—so familiar a phenomenon in the Europe of our own days—had secured a virtual monopoly in the supply of European commodities to Barbados. This can hardly have been so, or more would have been heard of the matter. Yet from numerous specific examples taken from the quarter-books of Dover and elsewhere and from his own experience, Mr. Hayne undoubtedly proves that evasion of the Navigation Acts was frequent and that

---

[1] *An Abstract of all the Statutes made Concerning Aliens Trading in England*, &c., by S. Hayne, Ryding-Surveyor for His Majesty's Customs, London, 1685 (p. 13). He quotes a number of specific examples :

(a) A ship from Holland, clearing at Dover for New York, had many Dutch bricks and grindstones for ' ballast ' which were entered, but not unloaded. The ship received the necessary certificate, put to sea, and was wrecked on the coast, where in addition to the ' ballast ', there ' appeared great quantities of Guns, and other goods both prohibited and Uncustomed, which the diligent officers never dreamed of . . .' (p. 15).

(b) In October 1680, Hayne came across a large vessel at Falmouth, clearing there from Barbados on its way to Amsterdam, ' without unloading her Cargo according to Law '. Being suspicious he made a thorough examination, and found that on the general cargo the aliens' duty (amounting to over £84) had been evaded, and that quantities of white sugar, tobacco, ginger, fustick, lignum vitae, and three large copper guns had been concealed from the officials—thus escaping a further sum of over £67. It is significant of the influence possessed by this Jewish fraternity that 'Mr. Hayne was offered large bribes to desist from his prosecution, and that when he refused, his career as a customs officer was gradually ruined by their unscrupulous hostility (see pp. 27 and 38 of the *Abstract*).

Barbadian planters were often enabled by this means to purchase Dutch and other goods at prices little higher than those that would have obtained under free trade.[1]

Despite such alleviation, however, the economic barometer registered a deep depression. For Barbados the Restoration period had been one of increasing burden and restriction. The imposition and mis-appropriation of the $4\frac{1}{2}$ per cent., the enforcement of the Navigation policy, and the increase of the English customs duties, had been successive blows to the planter. Economically (as well as in matters of the Constitution) he realized that his interests were being more and more subordinated to those of the Mother Country. Yet this was not the outcome of a specially repressive policy on the part of the latter. Barbados happened to be unfortunate. The $4\frac{1}{2}$ per cent. tax was peculiar to the Caribee Islands. Again, the Navigation Acts were a much greater burden to sugar plantations, such as Barbados, than to any other dependency. A long list of ' unenumerated ' commodities produced by the American colonies were not restricted to the home market. Also in many cases such generous bounties and preferences were given to colonial products that those colonies benefited rather than otherwise under the system. Unfortunately for Barbados, sugar was in the position of being a declared monopoly of the Mother Country, and being at the same time in excess of the home demand. In the early years sugar had brought great wealth to the island, but already it was beginning to effect that social and economic decay which is so striking a feature of West Indian history.

[1] Cf. the following entry in the Journal of the Assembly for 25th November 1679 : ' On reading a petition of various merchants trading to Barbados, concerning great injuries done to the English nation by the great number of Jews inhabiting and trading in Barbados, it was found worthy of speedy and serious consideration, and to be presented to the Governor and Council ' (Cal Col. 1677–80, No. 1190).

ADDITIONAL NOTES

NOTE A (see p. 258).

	£	s.	d.
'What money Sʳ Richard Dutton hath gott and recvᵈ by the Governmᵗ of Barbados ' :			
'His Sallary from the King for 5 yeares is 6000*l.*, of which Sʳ John Witham is to have 812*l.* 10*s.*, soe remaines . .	5200.	00.	00. (*sic*)
Given him by the Spaniards to allow them trade for Negroes etc. . . .	2000.	00.	00.
Given him by the Assembly before the yeare 1683 and allowed him by the Lords Comʳˢ. of the Treasury . .	3300.	00.	00.
Given him further by the Assembly by Fontabell plantation, 350 pʳ ann. for foure yeares is	1575.	00.	00. (*sic*)
By forfeiture of Ships, etc., Navy Office, gifts, presents, etc., has gott not less than	3000.	00.	00.
	15,075.	00.	00.

	£	s.	d.
'This is besides 2500*l.* lately given him by the Assembly contrary to his Instructions, etc., for which my Lord Treasurer to call him to accoᵗ ' :			
'He had the King's ships alway to carry him and bring him back, and his other expenses were chiefly by what was sent him in wines and provisions by the Inhabitants, and soe it canot be that he hath spent '	3000.	00.	00.
his clear gaines being . . .	12,075.	00.	00.
	15,075.	00.	00.

	£	s.	d.
' Sʳ John Witham Demands.'			
'Halfe of the Navy office being a perquisite of the Government, whilest he was Lieuᵗ. Governoʳ, comes to . .	0140.	00.	00.
'Halfe of the Fontabell plantation, being another perquisite of the Governmʳ. comes to	0233.	06.	08.
Sʳ John Witham's Expenses at his tryal whilest in prison, in comeing for England and disbursements, there be .	0725.	13.	04.

The losses he hath sustained in his owne affaires by his Imprisonment and his speedy leaveing Barbados without settling his Concernes there, and the levying Exec^n. upon all his lands, negroes and chattels, his loss is not less than . 1800. 00. 00.

2899. 00. 00.

' There is nothing reckoned for false Imprisonm^t and other malicious hard useages.'

(Clarendon MSS. (Bodleian) 87, ff. 40–1.)

Note B (see p. 260).

See the following ' moderate Calculation of the annual charge and produce of a plantation in Barbados ', Sept. 1685 (Sloane MSS. (Brit. Mus.) 3984, f. 214). The following figures show that out of 80,000 lb. actually manufactured, 10,000 were spent in charges, thus :

lb. sugar.

' To shipp off seaventy thousand of musco sugar it requires seaventy hogsheads, which with heading gr. cost 4,900

' The Duty of 4½ per cent paid yor ma^{tie} in this Island 3,150

' To store, house Room and shipping it ' . . . 1,950

10,000

(Owing to wastage in transit and in port, only 583 casks out of the original 700 are actually sold, which @ 20s. per cent. = £583.)

' *Out of this £583 are deducted the charges on Sales following* ' :

£ s. d.

' The Seaventy hogsheads shipt makes 17½ tons ffreight, wch at 5l. pr. Tonn (tho' often wee pay unto Seaven pound) is . . . 87. 00. 00.

' To your Majestyes Custome House in London on the Eighteen pence per cent duety . 43. 00. 00.

' To bill money for ffive entryes being adventure Enough for five shipps . . . 01. 17. 06.

' To jetty charges at ten shillings per Tonn . 26. 10. 00.

168. 09. 00.(*sic*)

583. 00. 00. ' The amount of the acco^t of Sales as above exprest.'

168. 09. 00. ' The amount of the charges.'

£414. 11. 00. ' *The produce to the Planter of his* 80,000 *Musco Sugar.*'

VI

TRADE RELATIONS BETWEEN BARBADOS AND NEW ENGLAND

' My Lord, . . . his ma^tys Collonys in these parts cannot in tyme of peace prosper, nor in tyme of War subsist, without a correspondence with the people of Newe England ' (William Lord Willoughby to the Privy Council, 16th December 1667).

THE trade *entente* which gradually grew up between the New England colonies and the island plantations in the Caribbean has been the subject of much generalization, but has not hitherto been subjected to any detailed inquiry from the point of view of the West Indies. In the main, these generalizations are substantiated, but with certain important modifications. [It is however certain that the commercial intercourse enjoyed by the Barbadians with New England was one of the prime reasons for their prosperity in the seventeenth and eighteenth centuries.]

It is hardly surprising perhaps that this important side of New England activity should have been initiated by that great nation-builder, John Winthrop. Even before his arrival in New England in 1630, he had noted with interest the settlement of this rich island in the Southern sea, and had been quick to see the possible advantages of trade therewith. In 1627, that is to say, in the year of its first planting, Winthrop dispatched his son Henry with a company of men and a stock of provisions ' to goe to the Barbethes '.[1] For two troubled years he toiled there raising meagre

[1] *Winthrop Papers.* Collections of the Massachusetts Historical Society (hereinafter referred to under M.H.C.), 5th series, vol. viii, p. 357. Cf. also pp. 334, 337. In September 1628 he was appointed with others ' to be assistance unto Captaine Charles Wolverstone, Gouer, for the Executinge of right and justice unto all men that shall demand it . . . ' (M.H.C., 5th series, vol. i, p. 474).

crops of cotton, tobacco, and indigo, and then departed
to England. From that small beginning the West
Indian interests of the Winthrop family and their
friends steadily grew and expanded. As early as 1631
we find Stephen Winthrop selling Madeira wine at
St. Christopher.[1] Indeed so quickly did the intercourse develop that in this same year the practice
began of sending New England letters to London via
Barbados, thus establishing a postal route which was
regularly employed until the War of American Independence.[2] For many years too the Winthrop family,
particularly Samuel and his brother John Winthrop
Junior, continued to be closely associated with the
West Indian commerce, for the initiation of which
they had been primarily responsible.[3]

The original basis of New England's external commerce was the fishing industry. Attracted by the rich
catches of mackerel and other fish to be had off these
coasts, an increasing number of Bristol adventurers
had become engaged in the trade. In 1620 we are
told that, ' to make triall this yeare there is gone
6 or 7 saile from the West Country, onely to fish, three
of whom are returned, and as I was certainly informed,
made so good a voyage, that every sailor for a single
share had 20 pounds for his 7 moneths work '.[4] The
writer, Captain John Smith, adds that in the following
year about twelve vessels took part in the venture,
and in 1622 thirty-five. At the same time the settlers
themselves began to build ketches and take part in this
lucrative trade.[5] Soon New England fish was buying

---

[1] M.H.C., 5th series, vol. viii, p. 237.

[2] *Mass. County Records*, vol. iii, p. 169.

[3] Cf. *Winthrop Papers*, passim. Samuel Winthrop ran a thriving
sugar plantation in Antigua.

[4] *New England's Trials*, by Captain John Smith, London, 1622
(Force Tracts, vol. ii, No. 2).

[5] *Acts of the Privy Council* (Colonial Series, 1613–80), No. 65.
Cf. Macfarlane's *History of the New England Fisheries*.

cloth and other manufactures from England, brandy from France, wine from Madeira and the Azores, and later (as we shall see) exchanging all these for West Indian sugar, rum, and molasses, which again found their way to Europe, earning profit on profit for the keen, shrewd merchants of Boston.

Together with the coastal fisheries, agriculture in the hinterland was slowly finding its feet. Slowly indeed and with many setbacks ; for in 1634 we find Virginia shipping off 10,000 bushels of wheat to meet the great scarcity in New England.[1] Four years later food was at famine prices owing to the bad winter and ' such access and confluence of people into it '.[2] Such checks however were short-lived. By June 1640 John Winthrop was able to report that ' provision is very plentyful now in the Bay, and very cheape '. The price of cattle had dropped from £28 per head to £5.[3] In fact the pendulum had swung to the other extreme : there was a glut of foodstuffs, and settlers found to their dismay that corn would buy little or nothing. In short, New England needed markets for its stores of fish, beef, and corn. Naturally then Winthrop and his colleagues looked to the West Indies, where, as they knew, practically all food supplies had to be imported.

The New England merchants, however, found themselves confronted at Barbados and elsewhere by keen competition both from London traders and even more from the Dutch, who were supplying the Barbadians with all kinds of European commodities at cheap rates.[4]

---

[1] *Cal. Col.* 1574–1660, p. 184.

[2] *History of Plymouth Plantation*, 1620–47, by W. Bradford (*c.* 1650, reprinted 1919 in M.H.C., vol. ii, p. 269). The planters of Connecticut petitioned the Privy Council that special supplies of provisions should be permitted to be shipped thither, but the request was ' denyed ' (*Cal. Col.* 1574–1660, p. 284). Cf. *Acts of the Privy Council*, No. 387.

[3] *History of Plymouth Plantation*, ut supra.

[4] Cf. Ligon, op. cit., p. 33. At the same time the Dutch, who

An illustration of the difficulties which beset the New Englanders is to be found in their attempt to build up a trade by exchanging their provisions for West Indian cotton. John Winthrop evolved a scheme to obtain a large and regular supply of this cotton, with which to establish the manufacture of textiles in Massachusetts.[1] For a time his scheme made some headway. In October 1642 he wrote that 'two of our vessels . . . returned home with a good supply of cotton, and brought home letters with them from Barbados and other islands in those parts '.[2]

Two circumstances however doomed the attempt to failure. In the first place the mercantilists in London were determined to prevent the colonies from competing with the home market by establishing their own manufactures ; and secondly, the Barbadian planters found that cotton-growing was not a paying proposition, and almost entirely abandoned it in favour of sugar.

The situation as it stood in 1645 is indeed well reviewed by Sir George Downing in a letter to John Winthrop Junior, then about to embark upon his commercial enterprises in the Caribbean.

'If you intend ', he writes, ' to see the Indyes, it would not be convenient (as I thinke) to venter much till you have seen it. New England servants (I fear) will be noon of the fittest for those parts. The certainest comodityes you can carry for those parts (I suppose) will be fish, as mackrill, basse, drye fish, beefe, porke, if you can procure them at reasonable rates ; and if you be there in the Spring, it 's the best time because the fewist ships are there. Linnen cloath is a certaine comodity, but that is deare in New England.' [3]

were above all things carriers and middlemen, sometimes assisted New England trade in the West Indies. In 1639, for example, a Dutch ship of 300 tons brought a cargo of salt from the West Indies to Boston and returned thither laden with timber (Mass. Archives LXI, quoted by Weeden, *Economic and Social History of New England*, 1620–1789).

[1] Cf. *Connecticut County Records*, vol. i, p. 59.

[2] *Winthrop's Journal*, 1630–49, vol. ii, p. 74.

[3] M.H.C., 4th series, vol. vi, p. 538.

In other words the New Englanders had won a footing at Barbados and other islands ; but as yet that footing was slight and precarious.[1] John Winthrop Junior must be careful to buy cheap, and he must go in the Spring to avoid powerful rivals from London and Amsterdam.

Just at this juncture the economic and political life of the colonies was violently disturbed by the Civil War in England. The effect of that upheaval upon Barbadian trade with the Mother Country and Holland has already been noted. No less far-reaching was its influence as regards trade with New England. The latter, with its rapidly increasing population, was badly in need of English manufactures. But, apart from its fish, the colony had little to offer the home market. Beef, pork, timber, and corn had little sale in a country such as England, which at that time was almost self-supporting in food-stuffs. On the other hand Barbados was suddenly leaping into phenomenal prosperity by means of its sugar crops : its numerous white population and its swiftly growing numbers of negro slaves needed food. What happened is aptly summarized by John Winthrop in 1647. ' As our means of returns for English commodities was grown very short, it pleased the Lord to open to us a trade with Barbados and other islands in the West Indies, which as it proved gainful, so the commodities we had in exchange there for our cattle and provisions, as sugar, cotton, tobacco, and indigo were a good help to discharge our engagements in England.'[2]

[1] In 1640 eleven ships cleared from New England ports to the West Indies (Mass. Archives, LXIV. 89). It is noteworthy that Downing does not mention corn. On this point, see pp. 274, 282–5, below. The trade with Barbados in wine, which the New Englanders obtained in Europe in exchange for their fish and victuals, continued to grow in proportion as the Barbadian planters grow richer and more able to afford such luxuries. Cf. *Records of the Governor and Company of the Massachusetts Bay in New England*, edited by N. B. Shurtleef, vol. ii, p. 129 (case of *Smith* v. *Kaesar*, A. D. 1645).

[2] *Winthrop's Journal*, 1630–49, pp. 328–9.

Everything in fact conspired to cement this trade alliance. Commerce between the Mother Country and the colonies was thrown into confusion and finally almost brought to an end by the attacks of Cavalier and Parliament privateers and by the possibility of seizure in English ports. New England and the island plantations thus became more and more inter-dependent during these years. Barbados simultaneously building up wealth and population at an enormous rate, bought where she could ; utensils and manufactured goods from the Dutch, food from New England.

An interesting commentary on the importance with which this new West Indian trade was regarded in New England, was provided in 1648 when a plague, which accounted for six thousand deaths in Barbados alone, raged through the islands. Immediately upon receipt of the news the Massachusetts Court, ' ord^{r}ed y^t all our own or other vessels come from any pts. of ye West Indies to Boston harbor shall stop and come to an anchor before they come at ye Castle, und^r ye pœnalty of 100l. . . .' No one was to leave any such ship, nor was any one to go on board without special order of the Council. A copy of this order was to be immediately dispatched to constables ' of every port towne in this iurisdiction '.[1] Equally prompt was the repeal of the embargo in the following year, ' seeing it hath pleased God to stay the sickness there '.[2]

The sugar industry moreover created a demand for commodities not hitherto required on a large scale. Sugar mills, for example, had sprung up for crushing the canes, but Barbados possessed no water power to

[1] *Records of the Governor and Company of the Massachusetts Bay in New England*, ut supra, vol ii, p. 238. Cf. M.H.C., 5th series, vol. i, p. 36. Lucy Downing to John Winthrop Junior, Salem, 17th December 1648 : ' My 2 sonns Jo and Robin I bless God are safe returned, but Robin in respect of the loss of his master, and Jo in respect to the sad Sicknes still at Barbados are both now gone to Boston to see wich waye Providence will dispose for them.'   [2] Ibid., p. 280.

drive them. The alternative was to use tread-mills worked by horses ; and horses were accordingly obtained from New England.[1] Casks and barrels too were needed in which to pack the sugar. These were provided from the abundant forests of Massachusetts and Connecticut. As a visitor to the island in 1648 reported, ' they want rivers to turn their sugar mills, so that New England sendeth Horses, and Virginia oxen to turn them, at excessive rates . . . and at Barbadoes they buy much Beef and Meal and Pease and Fish from New England and other places '.[2]

' And other places.' That is to say it must not be assumed that the merchants of Boston and Salem had by any means obtained a monopoly of the food supply. At this very time Ligon tells us that ' Barrels of meal close put up . . . comes to us very sweet from England and Holland '. The Dutch also imported wines from France and Spain, and salted meat and flour even from Russia.[3] Indeed it seems probable that the extent of the corn trade from New England to Barbados has been greatly exaggerated. The bulk of the population of the island consisted of indentured servants and negroes, who were fed exclusively on cassava roots, peas, potatoes, and the cheapest grades of fish. Only the shrinking population of planters used wheat-

---

[1] *Rhode Island County Records*, vol. i, p. 338 ; M.H.C., 2nd series, vol. vii, pp. 16–17 ; *Essex County Records*, vol. iv, pp. 176, 409, 410. Rhode Island and Connecticut were the colonies chiefly engaged in horse-breeding, the export of mares being expressly forbidden. In 1700, a toll-book was instituted at the Massachusetts ports to prevent horse-stealing. The New England colonies did not, however, furnish a sufficient supply, large numbers of horses being obtained from England (see table above, chapter iii, also cf. *Acts f the Privy Council*, I, Nos. 533 (A. D. 1661), 588 (1663), 870 (1669), 880 (1669)). Also in 1670, one Morgan Lewis obtained permission to transport from England to Barbados, 100 horses, of which there was great want in the island (*Cal. Col.* 1669–74, No. 370).

[2] Force Tracts, vol. ii, No. VII, p. 5.

[3] Ligon, op. cit., pp. 33 and 37.

flour and beef, and much of that was obtained from sources other than New England.[1]

It is indisputable, however, that the trade in other commodities was very considerable. It was therefore a serious matter when in 1650 the victorious English Parliament laid an embargo upon all trade with Barbados, Virginia, and other hostile dependencies. The Massachusetts Council on 7th May 1651 obediently gave order that the enactment was ' to be of force untill the complyance of the afforesd places . . . with the common wealth of England, or that this Court take further order therein '.[2] But in some cases the attractions of pecuniary gain seem to have outweighed sympathy with the Puritan cause in the minds of the worthy merchants of Boston. Stories began to leak through to Westminster that the New Englanders were secretly supplying the royalist colonies with provisions and even with powder and shot, and to such an extent that Parliament contemplated reprisals.

The trade complained of had, it is true, taken place before news of the embargo had reached Boston ; but the ' Rump ' resented the idea that royalist dependencies should be able to obtain the means of resistance from Puritan New England, and even when the Massachusetts Council had formally ordered compliance with the Act, there is evidence that trade with Barbados still continued.[3]

[1] It is noteworthy that Samuel Sewall, a prominent New England merchant, who in his letter-book (printed in M.H.C., 6th series, vol. i) deals minutely with many sides of the West Indian trade (c. 1660–1700), hardly mentions corn at all. See further discussion on this point below.

[2] *Records of the . . . Mass. Bay in New England*, ut supra, vol. iii, p. 224.

[3] M.H.C., 3rd series, vol. ix, p. 292. ' They tell me of a ship of 300, come from Barbados ; Mr. Wall the master stood upon his guard while he staid there. He brought some passengers, former inhabitants from London, whose case was sad there because of the

Realizing the danger, Mr. Edward Winslow set to work at once to pacify the home government and also to put a stop to the obnoxious trade across the water. 'Heere is a great murmuring', he warned his friends of New Plymouth, 'at the great provisions of powder and shott the severall shipps get licence for; . . . tis layed to our charge that being Custome free wee enrich ourselves by furnishing Barbathoes, Verginia though ennimies etc. with that and other cómodities; and there hath been upon that very account a serius debate about Revoking our free Custome and excise.' By great labour he had persuaded friends in the House of Commons and the Council of State of the honesty of the colonial authorities. The danger had been averted for the time being, but a more stringent control must be exercised in future.[1]

An interesting parallel with this illicit provisioning of the royalist colonies is provided in the Seven Years War, when the New Englanders persistently supplied the French in the West Indies and Canada with foodstuffs.[2]

posture of the island . . .' (Roger Williams to John Winthrop Junior, last of July or first of August 1651).

[1] *Plymouth County Records*, vol. ix, p. 198 (letter from Mr. Winslow, 17th April 1651). A reply was sent to Winslow in the following September, admitting that 'the Trad of powder . . . hath been to exorbitantly managed by somm, though the wellfare of the Collonies in many respects is deeply conserned and hazarded'. A trade in fire-arms, dangerous to the safety of New England, had been opened with the Indians, but the Plymouth Council was unaware of such shipments to Barbados or Virginia from ports in their jurisdiction (ibid., p. 199). On 28th Nov. 1650 a licence had been drafted, 'for the inhabitants of New England to trade to Barbadoes . . . until the last day of July 1651, notwithstanding that Act of 3 October 1650, prohibiting such trade, by reason that the distance being so great they cannot have any certain knowledge of that Act as to observe the times therein limited' (*Cal. Col.* 1574–1660, p. 347). But this concession cannot have received official confirmation, otherwise Parliament would not have taken up the attitude described by Mr. Winslow.

[2] See G. L. Beer, *British Colonial Policy*, 1754–65 (New York, 1922), pp. 72–127.

The hopes of the New England merchants now concentrated upon the Ayscue expedition. Once the revolting colonies were reduced by Parliament, the embargo would be lifted and trade with the West Indies reopened. It must therefore have been very irritating to them when Ayscue's expedition was diverted to the Scilly Isles. When at last Ayscue did reach Barbados on 15th October 1651, the merchants were ready to recapture the lost market. A petition had been laid before the Massachusetts Council, and granted, ' for libertie to sayle forth of these parts to the sd phibited places ' on depositing security ranging from £1,000 to £2,000, according to the size of the vessel, not to land any goods in or trade with any of the said places until they were reduced to the obedience of the Commonwealth of England.[1] Similar arrangements had been made with the Council of State by merchants at Southampton, who owned vessels trading between New England and Barbados.[2] Thus re-established the New Englanders steadily increased their sales of fish, pipe staves, and provisions until by about 1658 they were easily the largest exporters of these commodities to the island.[3]

A striking illustration of Barbados' dependence upon New England in this respect was provided in 1655, when Cromwell embarked upon his ill-advised scheme of mastering the West Indies and Central America. As already noted, the Penn-Venables expedition arrived at Barbados fully expecting not only 10,000 recruits but enough provisions to supply the entire force. The Barbadians naturally had only sufficient food in stock to meet their own needs. For three

[1] *Records of the ... Mass. Bay in New England*, ut supra, vol. iii, pp. 240–1.
[2] *Cal. Col.* 1574–1660, p. 350 (3rd Feb. 1651).
[3] English traders, and to some extent the Dutch still, of course, retained the commerce in all manufactured goods.

months the expedition remained inactive, ' eatinge up the island,' as one of their number expressed it.[1] When at last the force moved off for the attack on San Domingo and Jamaica, the troops were fed almost entirely with supplies regularly brought from New England for the purpose.[2] Thus instead of buying second-hand, the newcomers had been obliged to go to the supply store itself.

An approximate estimate may be formed of the trade done in timber during these years by reference to the following table, which consists of a list of sales at Barbados by one Salem firm alone during the first three months of 1659.[3]

Date of sale.	Name of purchaser.	Description of goods.	Price paid. lb. sugar.
13 January	James Murrow	2,350 pipe staves 412 Hogshead staves and heading 5 boards (100 ft.)	2,700
,,	Edward Harrison	200 hhd. staves and heading	130
,,	Thomas Wiltshire	120 boards (2,699½ ft.)	2,296½
,,	Peter Partiboe	83 bds. (2,039 ft.)	1,834½
,,	Roger Lovell	332 bds. (7,138½ ft.)	6,425
,,	John Sampson	38 bds. (922 ft.)	830
16 ,,	Jonathan Ridgeway	14 bds. (299 ft.)	270

[1] *Thurloe*, vol. iii, p. 157, ut supra. Cf. Venables's narrative, pp. 93 and 100.

[2] *Cal. Col.* 1574–1660, pp. 429, 432, 434, 437. Cf. *Thurloe*, vol. iv, p. 157. ' The first of this moneth arived the *Faulkon* flyboate, one of your highnes fleete commanded by General Penn, which was sent from Jamaica to New England for provisions. . . . The commander of saide shipp acquainted mee, hee had on board for the use of the army at Jamaica 150 thousand of bread, and some 300 tonnes of pease and flower ' (Daniel Searle, Governor of Barbados to the Protector, 7th November 1655).

[3] Compiled from *Records and Files of the Quarterly Court of Essex County, Mass.* (ed. G. F. How, vol. iii, p. 170 et seq.).

Date of sale.	Name of purchaser.	Description of goods.	Price paid. lb. sugar.
17 January	Thomas Page	66 bds. (1,487 ft.)	1,343
18 ,,	Henry Feake	21 bds. (454½ ft.)	410
,,	Giles Ellene	25 bds. (532 ft.)	532
19 ,,	John Pearce	53 bds. (1,106 ft.)	993
21 ,,	Jeremiah Eggenton	153 bds. (3,612½ ft.)	2,705
,,	Thomas Butcher	6 bds. (110 ft.)	110
23 ,,	Timothy Crowther	53 bds. (1,062 ft.)	852½
25 ,,	Thomas Read	23 bds. (499 ft.)	499
,,	George Birkehead	55 bds. (1,258 ft.)	1,132
,,	Robert Pickford	153 bds. (3,254 ft.)	2,929
26 ,,	Thomas Burnham	74 bds. (1,534 ft.)	1,381
2 February	Thomas Hooper	71 bds. (1,506 ft.)	1,506
3 ,,	Henry Batson	45 bds. (962 ft.)	866
9 ,,	Barth. Washington	18 bds. (388 ft.)	388
11 ,,	James Cacill	19 bds. (434 ft.)	392
15 ,,	Thomas Gloyne	5 bds. (100 ft.)	100
,,	William Craly	11 bds. (203 ft.)	203
,,	John Crisp	25 bds. (600 ft.)	540
17 ,,	Andrew Patton	45 bds. (1,000 ft.)	1,000
18 ,,	Richard Glascock	30 bds. (597 ft.)	597
,,	Lt. Coll. John Read	45 bds. (992 ft.)	893
25 ,,	William Phillips	1 bd. (18 ft.)	18
27 ,,	Thomas Hinchman	1 bd. (12 ft.)	12
,,	' by cotten woole '	4 bds. (74 ft.)	74
2 March	Thomas Powdrill	67 bds. (1,326 ft.)	1,194
15 ,,	Henry Stroude	4 bds. (77 ft.)	70
26 ,,	John Creeke	5 bds. (50 ft.)	50
,,	Humphrey Davenport	50 bds. (950 ft.)	618
,,	' by sugar '	6 bds. (116 ft.)	93

Total : 1,731 boards (37,512 ft.), 2,350 pipe staves, 621 hhd. staves and heading—35,986¼ lb. of sugar.

Similarly a cargo shipped on board the *Black Lyon* in August 1659 was sold as follows :—

	£	s.	d.
1,727 boards (37,216 ft.) @ 50s. per 1,000 ft. . . .	93	1	0
1,890 pipe staves @ £4 10s. per 100	7	1	9
630 hogshead staves and heading	1	11	10
	101	14	7

After deducting 570 lb. sugar for ' landing and piling ',
and 1,799½ (commission of 5 per cent. for freightage),
the vendors received 33,617 lb. of sugar.[1]

Even before the Restoration the New England trade
with Barbados had assumed a two-fold aspect. Not
only was there direct exchange of goods, but the
island also came to act as a clearing-house whereby
other commodities such as salt were drawn to the
northern colonies. For example : in 1659 two merchants, by name John Carter of Madeira and John
Allen of Barbados, went shares in buying 17,250 white
oak pipe staves from a Bostonian rejoicing in the name
of Mahaleel Munninges. The consignment was
shipped from Boston to the island of Madeira in a
ketch named the *Rebecca*. Arriving at Funchal in
January 1660, John Carter disposed of 16,812 of the
pipe staves, and loaded up the *Rebecca* with butts of
Madeira wine. With this and the remainder of the
pipe staves she thereupon made her way to Barbados.
Instead then of returning to Boston with sugar as
payment, the ketch was fitted out by John Allen ' for
a voyage for salt '. Unfortunately she began to be
leaky and the voyage was abandoned. But the arrangement was a typical one.[2] Munninges disposed of his
pipe staves partly at Madeira and partly at Barbados,
and intended to receive in return salt from Tortuga or
elsewhere, a cargo which would bring in high prices at
the fisheries along the Massachusetts coast.

Again when New England fish or timber was paid
for directly in sugar, molasses, or rum the latter were
almost always re-shipped to London to exchange for

[1] i. e. taking the value of sugar at about ½d. per lb. (*Essex County
Records*, ut supra, vol. iii, pp. 168–70).

[2] Another example was that of a Barbadian firm, named Captain
Thomas Clark & Co., who regularly exported molasses to Boston at
40s. per ton, receiving in return cargoes of wine brought by New
England ships from Madeira and Spain (see *Essex County Records*,
vol. iii, pp. 324, 369, &c.).

English clothing, leather and iron goods, and all the products of Europe. Thus, starting with fish, timber, and meat, the New Englanders by a clever, complex system of sale and barter in which the West Indies (and Barbados in particular) formed the connecting link, drew to themselves any sort of commodity from the Old World of which they had need.[1]

The fish trade with Barbados consisted of two kinds : mackerel and oysters for the wealthy planters ; cod, bass, and herring of the worst grades to feed the negroes and indentured servants.[2]

Mackerel was much sought after, and throughout the latter half of the seventeenth century realized a steady price of fifteen to sixteen shillings a barrel.[3] The trade in cheap fish, however, was much the more important, and increased rapidly in proportion with the growing number of negroes on the island. Indeed in 1672 the importation had become so extensive that the market was glutted, and merchants experienced a difficulty in effecting sales. One factor reported to

---

[1] The chief ports for the West India trade were Boston and Salem, minor ports being Ipswich, Newport, New London, Newhaven, and Windsor.

[2] Cf. Weeden, *Social and Economic History of New England*, ut supra, p. 245: The best was sent to the Canaries and Malaga, the second grade to the Portuguese islands, and the worst to Barbados.

[3] The following is a typical shipment :

' Invoice of Goods shiped on Board the Brigenteene *Friendship*, Mr. Nathll. Green Commander, Bound for Barbados, (to) goe consigned to—for sales and Returns for the proper account and Risque of Mr. Samuel Sewall, under mark and number as pr. Margent Cost with charges, viz. :

	£	s.	d.
To 24 bb. mackrill att 16s.	19	4	0
To Naills and nailling 3s.		3	0
To literage, porterage, &c. 6s. primage 4s. 6d.	10	6.'	

Similar consignments were at the same time (1663) dispatched to the Leeward Islands and Jamaica (Letter-book of Samuel Sewall, M.H.C., 6th series, vol. i, p. 3). Cf. *Essex County Records*, vol. vii, p. 78, July 1678.

his ' loving Cousin ' at Boston, that his ' Fish came to a very bad markett, here being so much ; and a man may buy as good cod fish as neede to be spent for a pd. of sug^r. a pound . . .' But if he could contrive to send some barrels of pickled oysters, ' I shall ', he promises, ' make y^u honest returns, wch. is ye needfull at p̄sent.' [1]

As to the extent of the trade in provisions, it is not easy to form a just estimate ; as already noted the tendency seems to have been somewhat to exaggerate its importance, at any rate as far as Barbados is concerned. On the one hand we are told in 1662 that New England ' doth send out great store of biscott, flower, peas, beife, porke, butter and other provisions to the supply of Barbados, Newfoundland and other places . . .'.[2] On the other hand we find a merchant of London declaring that, ' in our trade to the Plantations wee carry not onely all sorts of Irons, Brass, tinn, and leaden manufacture wth severall others of Leather, Silks, and woolen, *but all sorts of provisions*, and drinke and all other necessaryes, which wee cannot, with any profitt carry into other countreyes '.[3] At the same time, too, large quantities of beef and pork were being imported into Barbados by English merchants from Ireland. Indeed, so important was this latter trade that when an Act in 1672 passed the Commons prohibiting plantation goods from being imported into Ireland without first paying customs in England, the Barbadian planters in London offered a strenuous

---

[1] *Essex County Records*, vol. v, pp. 48–9. Cf. also pp. 340, 341.

[2] M.H.C., 5th series, vol. viii, p. 65. Cf. Force Tracts, vol. iv, No. 11. ' The other American Plantations cannot well subsist without New England, which is by a thousand leagues nearer to them than either England or Ireland ; so that they are supplied with Provisions, Beef, Pork, Meal and Fish, etc. It is then in a greater part by means of New England that the other Plantations are made prosperous and beneficial ' (A. D. 1689).

[3] Rawlinson MSS. (Bodleian) A, vol. 478, f. 48 (c. 1670).

opposition, and induced the Lords to delete those clauses which adversely affected the provision trade.[1]

Moreover it is significant that whenever war broke out with France or Holland and trade with London was in consequence interrupted, the Barbadians always complained of a shortage of provisions on that account. For example in May 1666, Francis Lord Willoughby wrote to the King warning him that, ' Barbados and ye rest of ye Caribee Islands belonging to y^{or} Majesty ... have not Clothes sufficient to hide their nakedness, nor food to fill their bellies '. ' I need give no certifficate of this,' he adds, ' the few Shipping from England this yeare is too evident a Testimony.' [2] Similarly in November of the following year the island of Nevis was so hard pressed for food because of the war that the Council and Assembly waived the Navigation Acts and bought provisions from two ships of Hamburg which had arrived there. Again in 1673 the merchants of Barbados petitioned Governor Atkins that the King might detail a special number of London ships to sail thither ' by reason there is great want of Provisions on the Island '.[3] In 1674 the complaint was repeated.[4] Thus it seems apparent that Barbados received a considerable proportion of her food-stuffs from England and Ireland, or she would not have suffered to this extent when war conditions rendered the sailing of English ships precarious.

Furthermore there was a third source of supply, namely Virginia. It has often been stated that the export of agricultural produce from this colony to the

[1] *Cal. Col.* 1669–74, No. 852 (12th June 1672). Cf. ibid., 1675–6, No. 526; also *Acts of the Privy Council*, I, No. 1275.

[2] C.O. 1/29, No. 92, P. R. O. Cf. similar statements, ibid., No. 120; C.O. 1/21, No. 71 (10th July 1667).

[3] C.O. 1/30, No. 91.

[4] ' We have continued here in great peace and health, but by reason of the Interuption of Trade by the present warr in greate want of all things, but especially provisions ' (C.O. 1/31, No. 17).

West Indies declined to vanishing point with the increasing production of tobacco. Such, however, was not entirely the case. Tobacco did, of course, become the staple export, and the sale of Virginian meat and cereals was intermittent and small compared with that of New England. Nevertheless there is much evidence to show that throughout the seventeenth and eighteenth centuries Virginia exported these commodities to Barbados.[1]

At the same time it is equally certain that New England controlled a large proportion of the trade. The grateful tributes which the Barbadians paid to her merchants for timely succour in periods of distress is striking evidence of this fact. In November 1663 Francis Lord Willoughby reported that the produce of the island (i. e. cassava and other roots) had been eaten up by 'strange and unusual caterpillars and worms, like Lucusts in Egypt', and that the poorer sort of people must have perished had not special supplies of provisions been hurried thither from New

[1] For example :
  (i) *In* 1656. 'From this industry of theirs (i. e. Virginians) and great plenty of Corn (the main staffe of life) proceeded that great plenty of Cattel and Hogs (now innumerable), and out of which . . . much advantage is made, by selling beife, porke, bacon, and butter &c. either to shipping or to send to the Barbadoes and other Islands ; and he is a very poor man that hath not sometimes provision to put off' (Force Tracts, vol. iii, No. 14, pp. 9 and 19).
  (ii) *In* 1673 *and* 1676. Virginia is coupled with New England as being one of the sources of food supply (*Cal. Col.* 1669–74, No. 1029 ; ibid., 1675–6, No. 973).
  (iii) *In* 1740. A cargo of 1,000 bushels of wheat, 1,000 bushels of Indian corn, and about 100 barrels of beef, with some pipe-staves, was shipped from Virginia to Barbados (Rhode Island Arch. MSS., quoted by Weeden, op. cit., p. 906). At the same time the supply was intermittent. In October 1676 we are told that New England was sending all her available food-stuffs to 'starving Virginia' (*Cal. Col.* 1675 and 1676, No. 690).

England.[1] Again in December 1667, when William
Lord Willoughby was toiling heroically to save Barbados and the Leeward Islands from the French and
Dutch, he warmly acknowledged the vital aid rendered
by New England. ' My Lords,' he wrote to the Privy
Council, ' You see our condition, which yet had beene
much worse had not the freindship and bounty of the
people of Newe England given reliefe in our greatest
necessitye.' [2] They had presented him, he adds, with
provisions to the value of £1,200 for the fleet operating
at Nevis. As a result of his representations a royal
letter of thanks was specially dispatched to New
England.[3]

To sum up then, the conclusion appears to be this :
that while the New Englanders furnished Barbados
with the major part of her food, a very considerable
share was also supplied by English merchants, and
a much smaller, though by no means negligible, portion
came from Virginia. In fact, the position was aptly
described by Lord Willoughby when he stated that
without intercourse with New England, ' his ma^{tys}
Collonys in these parts cannot in tyme of peace
prosper, nor in tyme of War subsist '.[4]

One point more. It was frequently stated during
the latter half of the seventeenth century that New
England was the avenue by which the English in the
West Indies successfully evaded the Navigation Acts ;

---

[1] C.O. 1/17, No. 92 (Willoughby to the King, 4th Nov. 1663).
Cf. a similar statement by him to Sir Henry Bennet (C.O. 1/18,
No. 29, 18th Feb. 1664).

[2] C.O. 1/21, No. 152 (16th December 1667).

[3] *Cal. Col.* 1669–74, No. 58 (April 1669). Cf. the following letter
written at Barbados to John Winthrop, 1st Feb. 1674 : They ' doe
account themselves obleidged to New England for the supply of
provuition they had dureing the warr, consid^{r}ing ye greate risque they
rann by transporting them in such mean vessells of burthen and
without forse ' (M.H.C., 2nd series, vol. vii, p. 16).

[4] C.O. 1/21, No. 162, ut supra.

that Boston merchants flouted the law by buying all kinds of manufactured goods direct from the producing country, and then exchanged them at Barbados and elsewhere for sugar, rum, and molasses. How far were these accusations true? That the New Englanders did in fact persistently violate the Navigation Acts is well established, it being one of the excuses for the voiding of the Massachusetts charter in 1683. To what extent the West Indies indirectly participated in this illegal trade is not so clear however. In 1676 Edward Randolph, that redoubtable champion of the law, roundly asserted that the Boston merchants traded ' directly with foreign countries, even to the Hanse towns, Guinea, and Madagascar in direct viola-tion of the Act of Navigation, so that there is little left for the merchants residing in England to import into any of the plantations, those of New England being able to afford their goods much cheaper than such who pay customs and are laden in England. By which means . . . they abound with all sorts of com-modities, and Boston may be esteemed the mart town of the West Indies.' [1] He further asserted that by means of such violation they had ingrossed the greater part of the West Indian trade, ' whereby his majesty is damaged in his customs above 100,000 yearly and this Kingdom much more '.[2]

It may be said at once that here (as elsewhere) Randolph almost certainly exaggerated. It seems equally clear, however, that an extensive system of evasion in collusion with Barbados and other islands was in operation.

The Navigation Laws of Charles II hit the New Englanders very badly in their West Indian trade. Before the Restoration they had been in the habit of including in their cargoes consignments of manu-

[1] *Randolph Papers*, vol. i, p. 68.   [2] Ibid., p. 78.

factured goods.[1] But by the Act of 1663 this very
lucrative branch of trade became illegal. To make
matters worse, the profits accruing from the sale of
provisions were in 1673 seriously decreased by the
imposition of duties on inter-colonial trade. Indeed,
the Massachusetts merchants talked loudly of refusing
to accept Barbadian molasses and rum altogether. In
February 1674 a Boston factor in Barbados reported
to John Winthrop that the islanders were ' much dis-
sattisfyed with the Custom imposed of 18*d.* on y*e*
hundred, I haveing informed them that our merchants resolve to shipp the greatest part of theire
effects for England, whereby theire rum and molasses
heere will become of noe use or vallew to them, with
which they have hitherto supplyed their plantations
with provision and horses '. The Barbadians, he
proceeds, are ' all sensable of the greate prejudis
which will accrue to them yf they loose the benefitt
of those two commodyties, which are vendable
in noe part of y*e* world but New England and
Virginia ': New Englanders are not dependent on
their food exports, and if they cease to buy sugar
and its by-products, they ' will be improved in
raising manufactures, haueing good wooll, flax, and
hempe '.[2]

Bluff, of course, this last : but the general tenor of
the letter reveals the seriousness of the situation.[3]
The northern colonies could not afford to lose the

[1] For example, in 1658, ' the ship *Brocke*, afterwards called *Providence* sailed from Salem to Barbados with " 100 tons of iron, and about
70 small pots and great kettles of marmelettes " as well as a supply
of mackerel ' (*Essex County Records*, vol. ii, p. 94).

[2] M.H.C., 2nd series, vol. vii, pp. 16–17.

[3] On 28th September 1675, the Barbadian Assembly moved ' that
the late custom laid on the growth of Barbados transported to New
England may be taken off, the island already suffering great scarcity,
the former trade in provisions from thence being much decayed by
reason of the impost ' (*Cal. Col.* 1675 and 1676, No. 682).

West Indian market for their food-stuffs, an exchange upon which the greater part of their commerce was built. The trade naturally continued,[1] but under a heavy handicap. As a writer in 1689 puts it : ' they pay Customs in the Plantations for the goods they export from thence into New England, they pay the same again the second time, when those goods are brought into England '.[2]

Legitimate trade, then, with the West Indies was not such a paying proposition as formerly. At the same time the harbours of Boston and Salem were thronged with ships from Holland, France, Spain, and elsewhere.[3] What more likely than that the New Englanders added to their profits by shipping the products of these countries direct to the Caribee Islands ? The English merchants at any rate repeatedly complained that they did so, and sold at cheaper rates than any who paid the legal duties in London.[4]

Alongside such general accusations it is instructive to place some definite statistical evidence. The following is a list drawn up by Randolph of ships entered and cleared at Boston in the half year between 25th March and 29th September 1688.[5]

[1] For details, cf. *Records of the Court of Assistants of the Colony of the Massachusetts Bay*, vol. i, pp. 39, 130–1, 340 ; M.H.C., 5th series, vol. v, pp. 82, 403, 431 ; *Randolph Papers*, vol. i, pp. 133, 205 ; vol. ii, pp. 19, 172, 209, 248, 249, 266 ; vol. iii, p. 166 ; vol. vi, pp. 90, 212, 249 ; vol. vii, pp. 364, 417, 435, 483, &c.

[2] Force Tracts, vol. iv, No. 11.

[3] Cf. Chalmer's *Political Annals*, p. 433 (quoted by Weeden, p. 237).

[4] For example, in January 1676, it was complained that all sorts of European merchandise was imported directly into New England, ' and from thence are carried to all the other of y^or ma^tys Dominions in America, and are sold at far cheaper rates than any that can be sent from hence (i. e. London) . . . so that New England is become the great mart and staple ' (C.O. 1/36, No. 10).

[5] ' Naval Office Returns Massachusetts, No. 35 ', quoted in Palfrey's *History of New England*, vol. iii, p. 566, note 2. Almost all these vessels were owned in Boston and were ' plantation built '.

From this table it may be estimated with fair accuracy that the total number of ships engaged in the whole of the West Indian trade from New England's leading port was not more than about 150 per annum ; and most of these were small coasting vessels of from 10 to 30 tons each. On the other hand, in 1680, we are informed that the annual sailings to London from Barbados alone was no less than 200 large ocean-going barques.[1] Obviously, then, New England's illegal dealings with that island were very far from having captured the market as regards European commodities.

Ships cleared.		Ships entered.	
To	*Number*	*From*	*Number*
England (all to London) .	7	England	21
Ireland	—	Ireland	1
Fayal	1	Fayal	4
Madeira	2	Madeira	2
Holland	1	Holland	—
Bilbao	11	Bilbao	—
Canary Islands . . .	1	Canary Islands . . .	—
Barbados, Jamaica, and the Leeward Islands . .	84	Barbados, Jamaica, and the Leeward Islands . .	89
Other North American Colonies	32	Other North American Colonies	37
Portugal	1	Portugal	—
Cadiz	1	Cadiz	—

Evidence pointing to the same conclusion is furnished by Barbadians themselves. In April 1675 Governor Sir Jonathan Atkins summed up the situation as follows :

' But in breife the act of navigation lyes so strictly heavie on all these plantations that wee shall loose all Commerce from New England and Ireland . . . the strictnes of the Act

[1] *Cal. Col.* 1677–80, Nos. 1390 and 1427. One year the number of ships had been as high as 270. The usual size of ships plying between London and Barbados was from 100 to 200 tons each.

imposing so, that though they are the Kings naturall borne subjects, yet if they bring but a piece of ffrize or anything of their own manufacture not being first had in England, it is forfeiture of ships and goods, when the bare bringing of provisions so long a voyage cannot answer the charge.'

It had been found impossible, he adds, to induce London merchants ' to carry of the one halfe of their effects of this yeere '.[1]

The statement is indeed doubly illuminating. On the one hand it admits that the New Englanders attempted to eke out their profits on food by also importing manufactures. Moreover, such illegal trade would be much more extensive than Atkins would admit to the home authorities. As indicated in previous chapters, the usual treatment meted out to offenders against the Navigation Laws was not by any means ' forfeiture of ship and goods '. On the other hand it is equally evident that when a reduction in English sailings entailed the non-departure of half the sugar crop, London must have been the staple and not Boston.

To sum up the whole matter then, as regards corn and meat, New England was easily the greatest, but not the sole source of supply. In the fish and timber trade she held a virtual monopoly. And finally, in respect of manufactured goods, there was smuggling on a fairly large scale, but not to the extent of diverting the main stream of the trade from London to her own ports. Barbadian intercourse with New England was thus continuous from the beginning, and of great importance. Instead of being a dependency, standing alone, and entirely dependent on the irregular transport service to London, Barbados was, by her connexion with New England, also linked up with a large international trade organization. By this means the basis of her commercial system was broadened

[1] C.O. 1134, No. 57.

and deepened, and her finances invigorated by an extended credit, thereby creating a reserve of strength with which to face the frequent crises brought about by hurricanes and other disasters to which the tropical colony was prone. To-day negotiations are afoot by which it is hoped that Canada will assume the position in the Barbadian economy which during the seventeenth and eighteenth centuries was held by New England.

VII

THE LABOUR PROBLEM

THUS far has been traced the growth of Barbados from a small band of struggling settlers to a flourishing and virile community, possessed of a considerable share of representative government. Yet constitutionally this island colony is in virtually the same position to-day as in the early years of its settlement. Instead of following the normal course of development from the crown colony stage to that of representative government, and finally to responsible rule, the British settlements in the West Indies have risen to the intermediate stage, and have then sunk to their original state of dependence. Gradually these white communities have been displaced by a vast negro population from Africa. At the present time, Barbados alone retains its elective chamber in the legislature ; and even in this case the island parliament has but the shadow of its former virility. The reason for this almost unique retrogression lies in the problem of labour.

Manual labour is largely governed by climatic conditions. Successful white settlements can only take root in regions where the climate is sufficiently temperate for the European to work, and to work hard. The American colonies, enjoying natural conditions very similar to those of Europe, have attracted an increasing tide of white immigrants, which have moulded themselves into a distinct and healthy stock, and become a world power. On the other hand, the West Indies are subject to a climate as tropical as Central Africa. Here the white man was an alien—

an unnatural importation. Soon the planters discovered that the labour of negro slaves, accustomed
as they were to intense heat and sudden cold, was
more efficient and less expensive than that of white
servants. Consequently, the British labourer in these
islands gave place to the negro. It was the triumph of
geographical conditions. The constitutional rise and
fall of the British West Indies is an index—the outward
and visible sign—of this gradual ousting of white labour
by black.

The normal method of obtaining white servants for
the plantations was by indenture. An intending
emigrant (man or woman) who was too poor to go
overseas independently would sign a contract in
England agreeing to serve a planter for five or seven
years, in return for a free passage, maintenance, and a
strip of land or a sum of money at the end of the term.[1]

Such terms appear reasonable enough on paper.
But during the agreed period the indentured servant
was a chattel, at the absolute disposal of his master.[2]
Cases of cruelty and ill-treatment (as will be shown
later) were only too common, especially during the
earlier years of the settlement when white servants
were plentiful.

[1] For example, see copy of an indenture between Sir James Modiford
and a servant, named John Wright, made on 16th February 1663.
The document concludes with the following clause : ' In witness
whereof, the said Sir James Modyford doth hereby covenant and
grant to and with the said John Wright to pay for his passage, and to
find and allow him meat, drink, apparel, and lodging, with other
necessaries during the said tearm, and at the end of the said tearm
to give him the value of tenn pounds sterling in sugar. . . .' (Davis
Collection, Box 4, Royal Colonial Institute).

[2] See, for example, the following document :
' I, William Marshall of the Island aforesaid ' (Barbados) ' Merchant, do by these present assign, sett, and order, all my right, title
and interest of one Maide Servant, by name Alice Skinner, for the
full term of four years from ye day of her arrival in this Island, unto
Mr. Richard Davis, or his assigns . . .' (Re-copied Deeds of Barbados,
vol. ii, p. 47, Davis Collection, Royal Colonial Institute).

Occasionally freemen, already living in the colony, were constrained to pay off their debts by selling themselves into temporary servitude. For example, in 1640, a certain Richard Atkinson owed another planter named John Batt the sum of two thousand pounds of cotton. He accordingly entered into an agreement, ' that if the said two thousand pounds of Cotton shall not be paid upon the day aforesaid, that then and immediately upon default of the said payment, it shall bee for the said John Batt, or his assigns, to take the body of me Richard Atkinson, servant for the terme of sixe yeares, without any further trouble or sute of lawe. . . .' [1]

Again, if a colonist had the temerity to elope with a woman servant, he was compelled by law to become the servant of her former owner for the unexpired portion of her service. One George Haddock found himself in this unpleasant position, and was obliged to sign the following covenant :

' Lett all men know by these present that I, George Haddock, doth Covenant and promise to and with, William Light, Gent., for to serve him for and dureing the terme of two yeares fully to compleate and end from the day of the date hereof ;— which two yeares I am and doe serve for Anne Mitchell, who is now my Wife, being the remainder of her four yeares for which she came over for, as by her Indenture. . . .' [2]

Such was the system of voluntary agreement by which indentured servants were obtained. More important from the point of view of numbers and also of ultimate effect were the various methods of compulsory transportation, adopted by the home authorities to satisfy the demands of the planters for labour, and at the same time to get rid of unwelcome citizens. The founder of this particular traffic seems to have

[1] Deeds of Barbados, 14th December 1640 (vol. ii, p. 359, Davis Collection, Box No. 1).

[2] Ibid., vol. i, p. 746, 3rd June 1640 (Davis Collection, Box No. 4).

been Oliver Cromwell. After a parliamentary victory royalist prisoners (some of them officers of high rank) were sold in batches to London merchants, who conveyed them to the West Indies, and there sold them by auction to the planters.[1] In September 1651 an order was issued that no lieutenants or cornets of horse, or any above that rank, were to be shipped to the plantations, and if any such had already been disposed of, private soldiers were to be sent out to take their place.[2] But the order seems to have been generally ignored. In 1655 Colonel Gardiner, Major Thomas, and a band of other royalist officers arrived at Barbados, after being imprisoned in the Tower.[3]

Cromwell's ruthless suppression of the Irish rebellion in 1649 had already occasioned the transportation of great numbers of that nationality to a like servitude. In his letter describing the storming of Drogheda, Cromwell wrote that, ' When they submitted, these officers were knocked on the head, and every tenth man of the soldiers killed, and the rest shipped for Barbados.' [4] ' A terrible Protector this ', remarks Thomas Carlyle, ' . . . he dislikes shedding blood, but is very apt to Barbados an unruly man : he has sent and sends us by hundreds to Barbadoes—so that we have made an active verb of it, " barbadoes you ".' [5]

[1] For example, large numbers of Scots were transported after the battles of Dunbar and Worcester (*Cal. Col.* 1574–1660, pp. 363, 421, 433).

[2] Ibid., p. 360.

[3] Thurloe State Papers, vol. iv, pp. 39–40.

[4] See *Life and Letters of Oliver Cromwell*, by Thomas Carlyle. Letter CV, Part V. Although it was given out that this severity was employed because the defenders had continued to fight after the place had surrendered and quarter had been given, it is now certain that they had not surrendered (see Gardiner, *Commonwealth and Protectorate*, i. 132 et seq., 3rd edition, 1901).

[5] Ibid., Part IX (11th March 1655). Some of these royalist gentlemen were able to buy themselves out and return to England—to the great indignation of Cromwell, who soundly rated Governor Searle

This practice was continued after the Penruddock rising at Salisbury in 1655. On suspicion of complicity, about seventy royalist gentlemen were arrested and brought for trial. Owing to lack of evidence, the jury could not convict them ; ' yet your petitioners and others ', in the words of their graphic appeal, ' were all kept prisoners for the space of one whole year, and then on a sudden (without the least preparation) snatcht out of their prisons, . . . and driven through the streets of the City of Exon . . . none being suffered to take leave of them, and so hurried to Plymouth aboard the ship *John of London.*' [1] The petition goes on to describe the terrible conditions of the voyage out to Barbados, and their sufferings as servants on the plantations, ' grinding at the Mills, attending the furnaces, or digging in this scorching land, having nothing to feed on (notwithstanding their hard labour) but Potatoe Roots, . . . being bought and sold still from one Planter to another, or attached as horses and beasts for the debts of their masters, being whipt at the whipping posts, as Rogues, for their masters pleasure, and sleep in styes worse than hogs in England.' [2]

One of these captives was an old gentleman seventy-six years old. He (according to the petition) had been standing before his house in Tiverton, when a troop of Cavaliers came trotting by. ' Marry, they are very brave Gentlemen ', he cried with enthusiasm. ' Were I as young as I have been I would goe along with them.' [3] His punishment was field work in Barbados.

for allowing it. The latter replied that he had received no instructions to prevent it (see Searle's Proclamation, *Thurloe*, iii, p. 743 ; also Searle to the Protector (September 3rd 1655) ; ibid., iv, pp. 6–7).

[1] *England's Slavery or Barbados Merchandize, Represented in a Petition to the High and Honourable Court of Parliament by M. Rivers and O. Foyle* . . . (London, 1659).   [2] Ibid.

[3] Ibid. Another version in Rawlinson MSS. A, 62, f. 638.

At the same time it is clear that want of power alone prevented the royalists from similarly transporting parliamentarians. In 1647 Edward Hyde (later Earl of Clarendon) wrote to the King's secretary, expressing approval of the proposal to send Roundhead prisoners to the West Indies.[1] Cromwell, it is interesting to note, also made use of this expedient to get rid of pirates who had been caught on the high seas and lodged in the jails of Dorchester and Plymouth.[2]

After the Restoration great numbers of Nonconformists were transported to the plantations for refusing to comply with the injunction of the so-called ' Clarendon Code '.[3] The system, however, reached its most flagrant stage under James II. After the Monmouth rising, Judge Jeffreys alone ordered the transportation of nearly nine hundred prisoners. His Majesty granted these unfortunates in batches to his favourite courtiers, who made a handsome profit by selling them to the merchants for £10, and sometimes £15, apiece. It has even been stated that the Queen shared in this disgraceful traffic.[4] Of these nearly four hundred were sent to Barbados, with a royal letter to the Governor, ordering their detention as servants for ten years.[5]

[1] Hyde to Sir Edward Nicholas, 28th Jan. 1646–7 (Clarendon's *Life*, p. 42).

[2] They were a mixed crew, including English, Irish, French, and Dutch (*Cal. Col.* 1574–1660, pp. 419, 427, 428).

[3] They were not allowed to go to New England because of the sympathy which that Puritan settlement would have extended to them.

[4] By Macaulay ; but convincing contemporary evidence is lacking. The statement has been much questioned by subsequent historians (cf. Inderwick, *Sidelights on the Stuarts*, and Hamilton, *Quarter Sessions from Elizabeth to Anne*).

[5] The letter, after giving a nominal roll of 397 prisoners dispatched, concludes : ' And to the end that theere punishment may in some manner answer to theire Crimes, Wee doe think yet hereby to signify our pleasure unto you, our Governor, and Council of Barbados, that you take all necessary care that such convicted Persons . . . guilty of the late Rebellion, that shall arrive within that our Colony . . . be

Transportation was again resorted to after the Jacobite risings of 1715 and 1745.

Rebellions, however, proved an uncertain source of supply. Two very different methods arose to satisfy the colonial demand for labour, namely, the transportation of felons and kidnapping. Owing to the medieval harshness of the English law, which provided the death sentence for cases of petty theft and other minor offences, transportation became a popular form of punishment in the courts. And felons were naturally only too glad to accept such an alternative. In August 1663 five notoriously bad characters, not being convicted of the crimes laid to their charge for want of proof, were ' remitted to Prison as sturdy and Incorrigible Persons '. It was then ordered that if they so desired, they would be handed over to ' such merchants as will be willing to transport them to the plantations '.[1]

In Bristol (the most convenient port for the plantations) a regular trade developed. A minor offender would, on conviction, be persuaded by an officer of the court to beg for transportation in order to avoid hanging. These transportees were assigned to the mayor and aldermen in town, who sold them to the planters, and grew rich. Macaulay describes how on one occasion Judge Jeffreys descended upon the

kept there and continue to serve their masters for the space of Ten Yeares at least . . .', 11th Oct. 1685 (Davis Collection, Box 2, Royal Colonial Institute).

[1] *Acts of the Privy Council*, I, No. 607 (24th August 1663). Cf. petition of Thomas Devenish, keeper of Winchester House Prison, praying that he may be allowed to set at liberty certain prisoners committed for petty misdemeanours, upon security from Captain Wm. Fortescue that he will transport them to Barbados, who if detained till the end of the next Quarter Sessions will then be discharged in course to the danger of the country (House of Lords MSS. 6th Report, p. 106). This practice had been in operation under the Protectorate, but not on an extensive scale (cf. *Cal. Col.* 1574–1660, p. 447, also Egerton MSS. 2395, f. 167).

borough court, ordered the mayor into the prisoner's
dock, crying, ' See how the kidnapping rogue looks ! '
and there abused him in language characteristically
vile.[1]

Transportation of minor offenders seems to have
become as prevalent in Ireland as in Great Britain.
Numerous examples of the practice are to be found in
the records of the Earl of Ormonde. In 1669, one
Margaret Little, stole the sum of £3 18s. and ' some
pieces of linen '. Upon examination she confessed
the theft, and expressed ' passionate sorrow ' therefor.
She then petitioned the Earl of Ormonde that, ' being
a very poore woman and destitute of friends ', he
would be merciful enough to inquire of the local
justices, ' if they doe think your Suppliant a fit object
of his majesty's mercie, to be transported for the
Barbadoes, or elsewhere beyond the Sea '. The report
of the justices, we are told, was favourable, and
Ormonde gave the required permission.[2]

Of a different nature was the supply of white labour
by means of kidnapping. One of the most cruel
features of this traffic was the ' spiriting away ', as it
was called, of young children. Distressed parents

---

[1] Macaulay, *History of England*, vol. i, p. 836 (1854 ed.).

[2] H.M.C. x, Ormonde MSS. 5, pp. 91–2 (7th May 1669). Another
example : The Justices of the Peace for the County of Meath petitioned the Earl of Ormonde (3rd May 1667), ' that Owen MacDaniel
and six others, now prisoners, committed to the gaole of Trim, who
upon their examinacions confessed themselves guilty of severall
fellonys . . . for want of further evidence were acquitted at the General
Assizes held at Trim, . . . yet they still remaine in prison. And your
petitioners, considering the evill consequence of such notorious and
knowne robbers to be sett at liberty will tend to the further destruction of the Country, they therefore pray your Grace will be pleased
to grant your order to transport the aforesaid prisoners to the Barbados, it being there desire, and there being a ship now in the bay
of Dublin bound for that island . . .' (ibid., p. 26). See also p. 35
(a case in 4th September 1667) ; p. 47 (16th December 1667) ; p. 73
(19th January 1669) ; and p. 94 (26th May 1669). Cf. H.M.C. xii,
Le Fleming MSS. 7, p. 35 (25th April 1665).

would often follow a ship down the Thames in an endeavour to recover their stolen children. Yet even when overtaken, ship masters who had bought their human freight from kidnappers on land, would refuse to surrender their spoil without a substantial ransom. In consequence, such violent tumults broke out in London in 1660, that the Lord Mayor and Aldermen addressed the Privy Council on the subject. After inquiry the latter issued an order, in which the practice of child stealing was described as ' a thinge so barbarous and inhumane that nature itself, much more Christians cannot but abhorre '. The instance was quoted of a ship named *The Seaven Brothers*, ' lately fallen down to Graves End . . . in which there are Sundry such children and Servants of severall Parents and Masters so deceived and enticed away, cryinge and mourninge for Redemption from their Slavery '.[1] Accordingly, official searchers were ordered to board all vessels bound for the plantations, to release any forcibly detained, and, in case of resistance, to place the ship under arrest and bring the master before the Council.

In addition to child stealing there existed in London and Bristol an extensive system of ' trepanning ' unwary men and women. The methods employed were similar to those of the press-gang. The victim, after being plied with liquor or struck insensible, was hastily conveyed on board ship, where returning consciousness revealed a fast disappearing coastline and the prospect of a long period of slavery in the tropics.[2]

[1] *Acts of the Privy Council*, I, No. 486 (26th July 1660).
[2] These abuses were to some extent remedied by the establishment of an office of registration at Bristol. But kidnapping and trepanning continued for many years. Cf. the petition of the Mayor of Bristol to the King (1662). Those who come to Bristol (the Mayor stated) from all parts to be sent as servants to the plantations, included deserting husbands, deserting wives, children and apprentices running

It is pleasing to discover that occasionally these unscrupulous procurers were themselves duped in turn. It became a habit of vagrants and loafers to pretend acceptance of their plausible offers. For days, and sometimes weeks, they would be supported until a vessel was ready to sail. Then when the Government searchers came on board, they roundly declared they had been trepanned and were being forcibly detained. Whereupon they were released, and went their way content, having obtained food and lodging gratis.

Such were the varied sources from which the British plantations, and more particularly Barbados, drew their supply of labour. With regard to the treatment received by servants in their new homes, it is difficult to form a general estimate. There is evidence of cruelty no less than of kindness. On the whole it seems that during the years before the Restoration, when Barbados was flooded with transported political offenders in addition to the large numbers of regular indentured servants, brutal treatment and miserable conditions were prevalent. But as economic circumstances made the white labourer scarce in proportion to the rapidly increasing population of negroes, the planters became afraid of the slave menace, and endeavoured to re-attract the white element by means of better conditions.[1]

The daily routine of servants on a plantation is well described by Richard Ligon, who lived in Barbados from 1647–50. At six o'clock in the morning a bell was rung, summoning the labourers to work in the open fields, in the grinding mills, and boiling rooms.

away from parents or masters, unwary persons tempted on board by ' man stealers ', and men pursued by hue and cry for robberies, &c., thus escaping justice. He therefore begged for power to examine all out ships and keep a register of emigrants (*Cal. Col.* 1660–8, p. 98).

[1] e. g. *before* the Restoration the usual period of service was from five to seven years; after that date it became reduced to three or four years.

At eleven o'clock, the tropical heat becoming too intense for work, they were given a meal of ' lob-lolly '—a mixture made from crushed Indian corn worked up into a paste with water and served cold on trays. At one o'clock work recommenced, and continued until six in the evening, when they returned to their huts for a supper of lob-lolly or of potatoes mashed in water.

' To this ', Ligon remarks, ' no bread nor drink but water. Their lodging at night a board, with nothing under, nor anything on top of them. . . . If they be not strong men, this ill lodging will put them into a sickness ; if they complain they are beaten by an Overseer ; if they resist their time is doubled. I have seen an Overseer beat a Servant with a cane about the head till the blood has followed for an offence that is not worth the speaking of.' [1]

The most significant feature of this question of treatment is the general agreement among contemporary writers, that the European servant was in a less-favoured position than the negro slave. A slave was a permanent possession. It was therefore to the advantage of the master to preserve him for as long as possible. On the other hand, a white labourer was

---

[1] Ligon's *True and Exact Account of the Barbadoes*, p. 44, London, 1657. He adds that in later years servants were better cared for. This writer also gives an interesting list of the usual annual supply of clothing issued by the planter to his servants, with the current prices of each article, e. g. :

	£	s.	d.
' To each Women Domestick Servant ',			
' Six Smocks, at four shillings apiece . . .	01	04	00
' Three Petticoats, at six shillings apiece . .	00	18	00
' Three Waistcoats, at three shillings apiece .	00	09	00
' Six Coifs or Caps at eighteen pence apiece .	00	09	00
' Twelve pair of shoes at three shillings apiece .	01	16	00
	04	16	00.'

A woman field labourer received four smocks, three petticoats, four coifs, and twelve pair of shoes.

A man servant received six shirts, six pair of drawers, twelve pair of shoes, and three monmouth caps (ibid., pp. 114–15).

only available for a restricted period, during which his master worked him to the utmost.[1]

When a labourer became too ill to work he was often ejected from the plantation as a useless burden. A law, enacted in Barbados in 1661, stated that ' many Masters, when their servants grow sick, and unable to perform their daily Labour, will seem to remit some part of the Time to be cleared of them, or turn them off, to the intent they may not be chargeable to them for their Recovery, whereby many of the said Servants most miserably perish, or become a charge to the Parish where they first happen to be laid up. . . .'[2]

Cases of murder and torture were not infrequent. ' It is much feared ', runs another clause of this Act, ' that some Persons within this Island have exercised Violence and great Oppression to and upon their Servants through which some of them have been murdered and destroyed, and the Authors and Causers of such their Destruction have gone clear, undiscovered and unpunished, by reason of the sudden Interring of Servants, so destroyed and murdered. . . .' For future prevention it was enacted that no body of a servant might be buried until viewed by the nearest Justice of the Peace or constable.[3] In 1640 a servant named Thomas declared before the Council that his master, ' did inhumanly and un-christianlike torture the sayd

[1] In December 1656 Colonel William Brayne wrote to the Protector from Jamaica urging him to have negroes imported from Africa, ' because, as the planters would have to pay for them, they would have an interest in preserving their lives, *which was wanting in the case of bond servants*', numbers of whom were killed by overwork and cruel treatment (*Thurloe*, vol. v, p. 473). Cf. Ligon, p. 43.

[2] *Laws of Barbados* (1648–1718), ' By Order of the Lords Commissioners for Trade and Plantations ', by John Baskett, London, 1732, Law No. 21, Clause X (27th Sept. 1661). For prevention of the like cruelty in future it was enacted that any master not using ' all lawful means of Recovery of such their servants ', should forfeit 2,200 lb. of sugar to the overseers of the poor for the maintenance of the sick servant. [3] Ibid., Clause XIII.

James Thomas by hanging him upp by the handes and putting fired matches between his fingers, whereby he hath lost the use of the severall joynts, and is in great danger to loose the use of his right hand '. For this piece of inhumanity the master was ordered by the Governor and Council to give his servant by way of compensation five thousand pounds of cotton, to set him free, and pay for medical attention, and himself to remain in prison during the Governor's pleasure.[1]

Thus the law afforded a certain degree of protection to the servant. He could appeal to the local justices at Quarter Sessions, or to the central authority of the Council, and justice was usually obtained. But, as was natural, the law was mainly concerned to vindicate the authority of the owner. If a servant's complaint was deemed to be frivolous, he (or she) was given

[1] Minutes of the Council (7th May 1640), Davis Collection, Book 4, R. C. I.

For similar cases, cf. (i) Minutes of the Council (2nd Dec. 1656). ' Upon reading the Petition of Daniell Duncombe, Servant unto Capt. John Simmons, alleging that he had shewed the Governor's Order unto him the said Simmons (which was that ye said Simmons should give ye Petitioner Liberty to sue for his wages), and that the said Simmons did not only refuse to obey the said order, but did beat and abuse the Petitioner with blows . . .', it was ordered that Simmons be accordingly arrested and brought before the next General Sessions (ibid.).

(ii) Minutes of the Council (2nd Dec. 1656). ' Upon the complaint of Patrick Cornelius shewing that he was by his said Master inhumanly beaten and bruised, in so much that he is incapable of doing any service for the present, the Complainant alledging that it was without any cause ', it was ordered that two (named) Justices of the Peace should make strict inquiry, ' and, if they find the Beating to be Excessive and without any just and good cause, that they release the said Servant from any further servitude . . .' (ibid.).

(iii) Minutes of the Council (24th Nov. 1657). ' Whereas information hath been given to ye Right Honourable ye Governor that a Maid Servant late belonging to William Trattles, did about three months past *come to an untimely end* . . . ' it is ordered that the two nearest Justices make inquiry and report thereon (ibid.).

thirteen lashes and sent home.[1] Cases of stealing
a master's property were punished by a two years'
extension of servitude.[2] Runaways, if caught, received
three years, and had their hair shaved off.[3]

Under such conditions, it is not surprising to learn
that in 1649 these white servants, who in pre-Restora-
tion days constituted a considerable proportion of the
inhabitants, organized a rebellion. On a given day all
masters were to be massacred by their servants, who
were then to seize control of the island. At the last
moment the plot was frustrated by one of the conspirators warning his master, Judge Hethersall, of his
peril. Prompt measures were taken by the planters,
eighteen of the ringleaders being executed. ' And the
reason why they made examples of so many was,
they found these so haughty in their resolution and
so incorrigible, as they were like to become Actors in
a second plot.' [4]

Although the position of the labouring class improved
as increasing scarcity raised its value, harsh treatment
continued. In 1681 Sir Richard Dutton received
special instructions to urge the Barbadian legislature
to pass an Act ' restraining bad masters and overseers
from cruelty to their christian servants '.[5] Yet the

---

[1] ' An Act for the Good Governing of Servants, and Ordering the
Rights between Masters and Servants ' (September 1661), *Laws of
Barbados*, No. 21 (ut supra), Clause X.   [2] Ibid., Clause V.

[3] Ibid., Clause XXII. If a woman servant was discovered to be
pregnant, the man concerned was compelled to serve the injured
master for three years, and the offending woman had to undergo an
extra two years (Clause VI). As to the morality of masters with
regard to their female servants. I have not been able to collect any
direct evidence. But the general scarcity of European women in the
colony would seem to increase their chances of honourable treatment
in this respect. There was, however, no legal protection.

[4] Ligon, *True and Exact Account*, ut supra, pp. 46–7. Cf. George
Frere, *Short History of Barbados*, p. 12, London, 1768.

[5] Cf. ' Minutes of the Assembly ', 29th March 1681 (*Cal. Col.*
1681–5, No. 59).

only response of the Assembly was that masters should be protected against malicious complaints as well as servants against severity.[1]

It is true, of course, that many planters treated their servants with kindness, not forgetting that the toilers among their sugar-canes were fellow-country-men. 'I give to all my Christian Servants', runs a planter's will of 1657, 'Desmond O'Doyle and Hannah, six months a piece of their times, provided that they doe continue Dutyfull Servants to my Wife; but, if they bee anyways disobedient or refractory, then this bequest to bee voyde and of none effect. And unto Desmond O'Doyle, I give my best Sute of Clothes and my best Hatt.'[2]

Generally speaking, however, the weight of evidence proves incontestably that the conditions under which white labour was procured and utilized in Barbados were persistently severe, occasionally dishonourable, and generally a disgrace to the English name.

As has already been described,[3] the establishment of sugar culture in Barbados during the fourth decade occasioned a phenomenal increase of wealth. The same factor produced important social results, the more immediate of which was the disappearance of the small landowner. Planters with a restricted acreage and little capital found themselves unable to afford the heavy initial outlay or the upkeep necessary for a sugar plantation. Gradually this yeoman class was bought out by richer neighbours, and migrated

---

[1] Journal of the Assembly, ibid., No. 250 (4th October 1681). This pressure on the part of the home authorities was not without reason. On 8th July 1673, the grand jury at the General Sessions in Barbados had presented 'yᵉ cruell severity of some Masters and Overseers towards their Christian Servants by whose undue and inhuman correction some have lately been destroyed' (C.O. 1/30, No. 150, P. R. O.).

[2] *Deeds of Barbados* (vol. ii, p. 300), 1st May 1657, Davis Collection, Box 4, R. C. I.   [3] See chapter ii, above.

to Jamaica or the newly settled Carolina.[1] More
important still was the effect of sugar manufacture on
labour. Cultivation of large plantations necessitated
the use of manual labour on a large scale. Soon
planters discovered that negro slaves, imported from
Africa to a climate very similar to their own, were
more efficient than labourers from Europe, and also
cheaper. For the money which procured a white man's
services for ten years could buy a negro for life.

Moreover, this substitution of white labour by
black was in part making a virtue of necessity. For
a number of different circumstances had combined to
stop the supply of indentured servants from the British
Isles. Chief among these was the fact that after a time
there was no room for the servant after he had completed his period of service. In the early years the
time-expired servant had received an allotment of
three to five acres, wherewith to begin life as an
independent planter. But as soon as 1647, the Earl
of Carlisle, as Lord Proprietor, was obliged to issue
a proclamation, that as there was no more available
land in Barbados, such servants would in future be
provided with the usual acreage in the less thickly
inhabited Leeward Islands.[2] It was not long before

[1] Although the theory that the original settlers received allotments
of ten acres and no more, has been disproved by Mr. Darnell Davis,
who quoting from *Memoirs of the First Settlement of Barbados*, 1741
(q.v.), shows that in 1628, 6,400 acres were granted to only 64 persons,
and that in 1638 there were 766 possessors of more than ten acres,
yet later statistics prove that the concentration of land into the
hands of a small wealthy oligarchy was a pronounced feature. In
1670 Sir Peter Colleton and other London merchants wrote to the
Council and Assembly that they had been informed that 2,000 people
had left Barbados during the preceding year, and more were still
going. To prevent further exodus and to maintain the number of
freeholders, a law was passed (at their recommendation) providing that
no estate owner in Barbados could purchase any more land (*Cal. Col.*
1669-74, No. 357 (14th December 1670)).

[2] Carlisle's proclamation (22nd Nov. 1647): 'Whereas divers People
have been transported from the Kingdom of England to my Island of

these smaller islands were also supporting their maximum of population, and the tide of emigration from England became diverted from the West Indies to the more promising settlements on the American continent. ' In former times ', wrote the Barbadian Governmènt in 1675, ' this island was plentifully furnished wth Christian Servants from England and Scotland, but now Wee can gett few English, having noe Lands to give them at the end of theire tyme, which formerly was theire maine allurem^t.' [1]

As already noted, another factor preventing Scottish servants from coming to Barbados was the Navigation Act, which forbade direct intercourse between that country and the colonies. Repeated representations of the Willoughbys on behalf of Barbados, secured for the planters in 1668 a royal permit to obtain servants from Scotland and Ireland, as well as England. But since trade with Scotland was still debarred, the permit was of no value. Merchants naturally would not ship over a cargo of servants unless they were

Barbados in America, and have there remained a long time as servants, in great labour for the profits of other persons, upon whose account they were first consigned thither, expecting that their faithful services according to the Covenants agreed upon at their first entrance there to make some advantage to themselves by settling of Plantations for their own use ; but . . . the land is now so taken up as there is not any to be had but at great rates, too high for the purchase of poor servants. In consideration hereof . . . I have thought fit to declare that each freeman who is unprovided of land, and shall therefore desire to go off from the Barbados, shall have a proportion of land allotted to him in my Islands of Nevis, Antigua, or any other island under my command . . .' (Thomasson Tracts. Brit. Mus. 669. 11 (115).)

[1] Petition of the Council and Assembly of Barbados to the King (C.O. 1/35, No. 45, P. R. O.). Cf. Atkins to Lords of Trade and Plantations (26th October 1680). 'People no longer come to Barbados, many having departed to Carolina, Jamaica, and the Leeward Islands in hope of settling the land which they cannot obtain here.' Again, ' since people have found out the convenience and cheapness of slave labour they no longer keep white men, who formerly did all the work on the Plantations ' (*Cal. Col.* 1677-80, No. 1558).

allowed to reload with colonial products.[1] Thence-
forward the demand for free trade with Scotland
regularly appeared in every Barbadian petition of
grievance.

Of servants from Ireland the planters apparently
had had more than enough. 'They grow weary of
them', wrote Atkins, 'for they prove commonly very
Idle, and they do find by Experience that they can
keepe three Blacks, who work better and cheaper than
one White man.'[2]

For some time the negroes were chiefly used for
manual work in the fields, British servants being still
employed as skilled artisans. Freemen, too, who had
previously been indentured, were able to secure a
livelihood in that capacity, but not for long. Intelligent
negroes were picked out and taught the various trades
and crafts. 'I have seene', wrote an observer, '30
sometimes 40 Christians, English, Scotch and Irish at
worke in the parching sun w^{th}out shoe or stockin,
while theire negroes have bin at worke at theire
respective Trades in a good condition.'[3] Already, in
1667, this substitution of the negro slave for the white
servant had reached an advanced stage. In that year
Major Scott stated that after examining all the
Barbadian records he found that since 1643 no less
than 12,000 'good men' had left the island for other
plantations, and that the number of landowners had
decreased from 11,200 smallholders in 1645 to 745
owners of large estates in 1667; while during the
same period the negroes had increased from 5,680
to 82,023. Finally, he summed up the situation
by saying that in 1667 the island 'was not halfe soe

[1] *Acts of the Privy Council*, I, No. 790 (29th July 1668).
[2] Sir Jonathan Atkins to Lords of Trade and Plantations, 15th
August 1676 (C.O. 1/37, No. 48, P. R. O.).
[3] 'Some observations on the Island of Barbados', 1667 (C.O. 1/21,
No. 170).

strong, and forty times as rich as in the yeare 1645 '.[1]

Two main factors, therefore, combined to effect the transformation of Barbados from a populous British colony into a settlement of negro slaves governed by a small band of planters and overseers—lack of space and a tropical climate.

The means adopted by the Mother Country for supplying Barbados and the West Indies generally with negro slaves, gave rise to considerable irritation on both sides. As already indicated, the demand for black labour in Barbados did not become prominent until the fifth decade, when the manufacture of sugar became universal. Prior to the Restoration, slaves were shipped over by private English merchants,[2] and (more often) by the Dutch traders, whose low prices had almost secured a monopoly of the Barbadian market. Indeed, the English Government in 1660 found that the United Provinces were within an ace of securing the carrying trade of the world. Among other activities the Dutch West India Company had succeeded in driving all rivals from the African coast, where a chain of forts and bases of supply had been established. The alternative before the English statesmen was either to allow the Dutch to enjoy their monopoly of the slave trade to British settlements or to find some means of throwing the weight of national resource into the task of forcing an entry into the African trade. The uncertain finances of a seventeenth-century government forbade the establishment of an

---

[1] Sloane MSS. 3662, f. 54a, ' John Scott's Description of Barbados '. Scott's computation of the negro population as being 82,000 in 1667 is, however, exaggerated. It was about 50,000.

[2] Cf. H.M.C. xiii, Portland MSS., Part II, vol. ii, p. 29. Letter from Rowland Wilson and others of the Guinea Company to James Pope, merchant, aboard the ship, *Friendship*, in the Gambia River, directing him to sell the spirits brought out by the *Supply*, and then to buy as many ' lusty negroes ' as possible, and send them to Barbados (9th December 1651).

elaborate system of naval and consular protection. The method adopted, therefore, was the formation of a Royal African Company, armed with a considerable capital and with the sole right of trading on that coast.

The bitter hostility, however, with which the English Adventurers were received by the Dutch, made it obvious that success could only be attained by a much richer and more powerful corporation. The charter of 1660 was therefore surrendered. In January 1663 a new and large 'Company of Royal Adventurers trading to Africa' was formed, subscribers to which included members of the royal family and many of the leading statesmen and financiers.[1]

The new company set to work with vigour, promising a regular and liberal supply of negroes at £17 per head. Unfortunately for the plantations, the Adventurers again found the opposition of the powerful Dutch Company rather too much for them. Open conflicts took place between English and Dutch, developing into a war which did not terminate until England's entry to the African coast was formally recognized at Breda in 1667.

Under such conditions it was only to be expected that the Company's consignments of slaves to Barbados, and elsewhere, would be neither frequent nor cheap. The following table of cargoes sold at Barbados in 1663 and 1664, shows that instead of the promised £17, the average price per head had risen to over £20. Exceptionally cheap lots consisted either of children or of 'refuse negroes', who being diseased, were unfit for work.

[1] C.O. 1/17, No. 2, P. R. O. (10th January 1663). The aim of both this and the original company was not only to furnish the British West Indies with slaves, but also to use the British settlements as bases of supply for the Spanish colonies on the Main. In 1662 the Spanish merchants began to buy slaves at Barbados, but had been discouraged by the rapacity of Humphrey Walrond, President of the Council. For Spanish trading at Jamaica, see G. L. Beer, *Old Colonial System*, Part I, chap. 5, pp. 329-31.

COMPANY OF ROYAL ADVENTURERS (1663 and 1664).

Date.	Number of Negroes.	lb. Sugar.	Sterling.			Average price per head.		
1663.			£	s.	d.	£	s.	d.
August 11th	175	—	—			—		
„ 13th	88	3,790	1,662	0	0	19	4	0
„ 28th	17	90	325	0	0	19	17	0
„ „	61	19,400	724	0	0	14	5	0
September 3rd	160	—	—			—		
December	8	9,360	—			8	15	0
1664.								
January 11th	71	· 49,870	801	0	0	16	11	0
„ „	175	34,880	2,700	0	0	16	19	0
„ 14th	14	26,500	—			14	4	0
(same cargo)	12	37,620	—			23	10	0
„ „	32	68,300	164	0	0	21	2	0
„ „	23	21,000	8	0	0	7	4	0
„ „	67	110,500	358	0	0	17	14	0
January 26th	163	299,620	1,014	0	0	20	0	0
„ „	274	258,700	3,455	0	0	19	14	0
February 10th	14	39,200	—			21	0	0
„ „	1 woman	1,200	—			9	0	0
„ „	38	—	760	0	0	20	0	0
„ 16th	2 men	—	42	0	0	22	0	0
„ „	21	32,300	154	0	0	19	16	0
„ „	209	175,350	2,298	0	0	17	5	0
March 17th	130	220,400	1,264	0	0	22	8	0
„ „	140	276,000	615	0	0	19	4	0
— —	13	13,000	17	0	0	8	16	0
— —	48	50,525	78	9	0	7	9	0
— —	19	11,750	153	0	0	12	13	0
— —	2 men	—	42	0	0	22	0	0
— —	19	43,600	100	0	0	22	9	0
— —	38	27,000	234	0	0	11	10	0
— —	17	12,000	156	8	0	14	12	0
— —	60	9,600	494	0	0	9	8	0
— —	210	323,895	1,938	12	6	20	16	0
— —	43	20,700	608	0	0	17	15	0

N.B.—These figures are taken from the 'Barbados Ledger' of the Company (T. 70/646, P. R. O.). Payment was made partly by sugar on the spot, and partly by bills of exchange drawn on merchants in London. The average prices (worked to the nearest shilling) are based on a sugar value of 15s. per 100 lb., at that time the approximate current price in Barbados. The ledger concludes with a long list of planters in debt to the Company, including Lord Francis Willoughby for 95 negroes, to be paid for by instalments at the rate of £20 2s. per head.

Thus the total number of slaves imported by the Company into Barbados during these two years was only about 2,400, while the price of an able-bodied negro had risen to over £20. Moreover, during the latter half of 1664 (when De Ruyter was sweeping the English Adventurers before him on the African coast) the arrival of an increasing number of refuse cargoes sold at nominal prices is apparent. During the Dutch war the Company's supply of slaves diminished almost to vanishing point.

Complaints were soon forthcoming. Already in December 1662 the Council and Assembly, in a general petition to the King, had included a demand for ' ffreedome of Trade upon the Coasts of Africa ; or else that Wee may be furnished with negroes at such rates from the Royall Company as Wee have had formerly from the Merchants, least by want of negroes our workes doe decay. . . .'[1] Five years later the planters had far more cause for complaint, war conditions having forced up the price of negroes to exorbitant heights. Writing on their behalf to the King in 1667, Lord William Willoughby urged the opening of a free trade to Guinea, ' by wch the Inhabi-

[1] Minutes of the Council and Assembly, 18th Dec. 1662 (C.O. 31/1, p. 77, P. R. O.). The statement (frequently repeated on subsequent occasions) that the price of slaves had been cheaper before the establishment of the Company, does not appear to have been generally true. Lyttleton (*Groans of the Plantations*, p. 6) certainly states that ' heretofore we might send to Guiney for negroes when we wanted them, and they stood us in about seven pound a Head '. But this statement appears in a tirade against the system of monopoly, and so must be received with reserve. Richard Ligon, on the other hand, states that (about the year 1650) the price for best male negroes was £30, and £25–£27 for women (Ligon's *Account*, p. 46, London, 1657). This computation is supported by other authorities. See H.M.C. xiv, Round MSS., 9, p. 273. A bill of sale at Barbados in 1652 of ' one negroe woeman by name Phoebe, together with her younge childe named Cherry, and one breeding sow ' for 3,885 lb. of ' good muscovadoe sugar '. Calculating the value of sugar at the then current price of 20s. per 100 lb., the woman with her child and the pig brought nearly £40.

tants may bee as plentifully and at as easy rates furnished as formerly. Soe excessive scarce and deare are they now here that the poore planters . . . will bee forced to goe to fforaigne plantations for a livelyhood.'[1] Following this up in September, the Assembly petitioned the King that either the African monopoly might be abolished, or that the Company 'be obliged to supply therein at yᵉ Prices mencõned in their first printed Declaration'.[2] In the same year the Gentlemen Planters in London reinforced the attack by a petition to the House of Commons.

In reply, the Company issued an elaborate defence.[3] Whereas the petitioners had stated that the average price in the days of open trade had been £12 to £16 per head, the Company maintained that £17 had been the standard, and that according to their promise, they had endeavoured to maintain that rate. The Dutch war, however, had, it was admitted, forced prices up as far as £30 per head.

In January 1668 Sir Ellis Leighton, secretary to the Company, addressed a further reply to the Barbadian petitions. With commendable frankness he pointed out that slaves could not be supplied unless the planters paid for them. To prevent such debts in future, he suggested that Barbadians should give security in London to pay at an agreed rate on notice of their delivery at Barbados, 'which it is conceived the only way to secure the Company from being first not paid, and then loaded with complaints not founded on solidity of reason or truth of fact'.[4]

This evasion of payment on the part of the planters naturally weakened their case against the Company,

[1] Lord Willoughby to the King (C.O. 1/21, No. 89).

[2] C.O. 1/21, No. 102 (5th September 1667).

[3] 'The Answer of the Company of Royal Adventurers of England trading into Africa', London, 1667 (Bodleian and Brit. Mus.). The charges and replies are treated in detail by G. L. Beer, *Old Colonial System*, pp. 335–7 (q.v.).   [4] C.O. 1/22, No. 21.

and incidentally forced up the price of slaves. The Barbadian law with regard to debt provided that after the debtor's property had been formally attached by the marshal, it was then left in the hands of the former for a further eighty days. At the end of that period, if the debt had not been paid in the meanwhile, the attached goods were sold in open market. 'But', declared one of the Company's factors, 'it most commonly happens y^t dureing these 80 daies, those negroes etc.' (which have been attached) 'are made away, and ye Marshal told by ye D^r y^t they are either runn away or dead; and there is an end of all ye charge and delay.' [1]

In response to vigorous protests from the Company, the Privy Council in 1669 ordered that henceforth the lands as well as the goods of debtors in Barbados 'shall be lyable to be sould outright by an out Cry'.[2] Yet despite the advice of Lord William Willoughby, the Barbadian Assembly refused to alter the law as directed, maintaining that it was as efficient as that in England.[3]

This policy on the part of Barbados and the other island plantations largely contributed to the bankruptcy of the Company in 1671. As the Government was unable to face the expense of maintaining the African forts itself, the only alternative was to form another monopolistic corporation. The new Com-

[1] C.O. 1/18, No. 39 (20th March 1664). On 24th August 1664 the Company stated that Barbados owed them £40,000, of which there was little prospect of payment. For ' the present Forme of judiciary proceedings in that Island afford no Remedy, but what is worse than the disease, so that unless some better Constitution and Execution of Justice be suddenly established in that Island, The Petitioners whole Stock will be exhausted, buryed in the hands of the Planters . . .' (*Acts of the Privy Council*, I, No. 629).

[2] Ibid., No. 872 (28th September 1669). Cf. ibid., No. 865 (27th August).

[3] The Assembly took this opportunity of making further complaint against the Company, alleging that they ' sold the best to the Spaniard, the refuse here at near double that sum ' (C.O. 31/2, pp. 5-7, 17th November 1670).

pany, established in 1672, offered 40 per cent. to former creditors, and 10 per cent. in new stock to the old shareholders.[1]

LIST OF NEGROES SUPPLIED TO BARBADOS, May 1673–May 1684.

Date.	Negroes.	lb. Sugar	Sterling.			Average price.			Description.
			£	s.	d.	£	s.	d.	
1673 May 6	204	281,545	1,828	17	0	17	11	0	
1674 Feb. 12	220	401,200	1,577	10	0	18	0	0	
,,. Mar. 11	292	431,425	3,792	6	8	22	4	0	
,, April 6	214	193,250	2,983	10	0	19	11	0	
,, April 8	280	305,950	3,233	15	0	18	7	0	
1675 Feb. 5	322	346,300	3,951	0	0	18	19	0	117 being women.
,, May 20	115	139,800	738	15	0	14	0	0	70 being women.
,, July 15	448	571,400	4,731	11	4	18	10	0	
,, July 26	231	415,750	940	19	8	15	6	0	'Sickly and dying.'
,, Nov. 1	317	494,500	2,709	10	0	18	5	0	
,, Dec. 2	73	69,500	863	5	0	17	15	0	
1676 Mar. 24	281	243,494	3,155	9	11	16	13	0	
,, Aug. 10	10	—	80	0	0	8	0	0	Condemned interloper.
,, May 25	372	156,400	4,844	7	6	15	13	0	
,, June 2	198	125,400	2,063	10	0	14	7	0	
,, June 22	220	79,100	2,689	5	0	14	9	0	
,, Oct. 26	178	212,800	1,521	10	0	16	0	0	
,, Nov. 10	574	593,050	6,532	0	0	17	16	0	
1677 May 1	152	41,100	1,434	15	0	11	2	0	
,, May 4	14	—	262	0	0	18	14	0	
,, April 24	391	351,200	4,189	10	0	16	2	0	
,, June 14	329	185,100	3,812	5	0	15	2	0	
1678 Jan. 5	107	—	900	0	0	8	4	0	Condemned interloper.
,, Jan. 29	452	505,600	4,587	5	0	17	2	0	
,, April 17	244	86,400	2,595	15	0	12	16	0	'Sickly' from ship Arcore.
,, May 28	202	250,000	1,684	0	0	16	1	0	
,, Oct. 17	234	—	2,040	15	0	8	14	0	
,, Nov. 1	281	244,098	3,017	15	0	16	3	0	
,, Dec. 4	281	120,300	3,670	0	0	15	14	0	
,, Dec. 5/10	252	52,100	3,473	10	0	15	1	0	
1679 Jan. 16	151	60,100	2,051	0	0	16	0	0	
,, April 8	40	—	640	0	0	16	0	0	
,, April 24	60	7,000	758	0	0	13	7	0	
,, Nov. 12	134	52,900	1,474	0	0	13	9	0	
,, Oct. 28	184	74,400	2,112	0	0	14	0	0	
1680 Mar. 26	319	123,500	3,597	17	6	13	13	0	
,, Mar. 30	266	—	3,274	0	0	14	9	0	
,, Aug. 5	144	37,900	1,702	2	2	13	9	0	

[1] New Charter, 27th September 1672 (Cal. Col. 1669–74, p. 934).

Date.	Negroes.	lb. Sugar	Sterling.			Average price.			Description.
			£	s.	d.	£	s.	d.	
1680 July 20	300	97,000	3,894	15	0	15	0	0	
,, Oct. 5	58	26,200	622	10	0	13	11	0	
,, Oct. 21	253	101,300	3,543	0	0	16	10	0	
1681 Feb. 18	66	—	1,156	0	0	17	10	0	29 sold to a Spaniard at £25 per head.
,, Mar. 23	157	—	2,543	0	0	16	3	0	
,, May 26	54	—	766	0	0	14	3	0	
,, May 28	19	—	200	0	0	10	10	0	
,, May 13	302	—	3,487	10	0	11	10	0	
,, May 18	122	28,800	1,407	10	0	13	0	0	
,, Aug. 30	100	13,334	1,295	15	0	13	15	0	'Mostly children.'
,, Sept. 27	363	20,000	4,849	10	0	13	14	0	
,, Sept. 27	129	—	1,477	10	0	11	9	0	
,, Sept. 28	134	—	1,528	0	0	11	8	0	
,, Sept. 30	55	—	706	0	0	13	0	0	
1682 Feb. 7	121	—	1,550	5	0	12	16	0	I.O.U.'s to pay in a few months.
,, Mar. 1	18	—	204	10	0	11	8	0	
,, Mar. 1	133	10,800	2,082	0	0	16	3	0	
,, June 15	138	—	1,903	0	0	13	15	0	
,, July 18	229	2,800	3,641	10	0	15	19	0	
,, Aug. 18	86	—	1,307	5	0	15	3	0	I.O.U.'s.
,, Nov. 7	290	150,000	3,594	17	3	15	12	0	
,, Dec. ?	18	—	148	19	4	11	8	0	'Refuse.'
1683 Jan. 3	188	—	2,713	11	9	14	8	0	
,, Jan. 27	429	—	6,435	0	0	15	0	0	Private Contracts.
,, Jan. 27	30	—	300	0	0	10	0	0	'Refuse.'
,, Jan. 31	213	—	3,369	0	0	15	16	0	
,, Feb. 20	303	—	4,535	0	0	14	19	0	
,, Mar. 22	92	—	1,345	1	10	14	12	0	
,, April ?	95	—	1,425	0	0	15	0	0	Private contract.
,, April 4	126	—	1,665	9	3	13	4	0	
,, Mar. 20	133	—	1,995	0	0	15	0	0	Private contract.
,, May 3	145	—	1,715	10	3	11	16	0	
,, Oct. 13	168	—	2,082	10	0	12	7	0	I.O.U.'s.
,, Dec.	360	?	?			?			
,, May 8	91	—	1,020	18	6	11	5	0	
,, July 31	178	—	2,462	15	2	13	16	0	
,, Aug. 29	93	—	1,085	15	0	10	12	0	
,, Sept. ?	185	—	2,775	0	0	15	0	0	Private contract.
,, Sept. 18	15	—	60	0	0	4	0	0	'Refuse.'
,, Sept. 24	119	—	1,785	0	0	15	0	0	Private contract.
1684 Jan. 21	168	—	2,333	10	0	13	18	0	I.O.U.'s.
,, Jan. 22	184	—	2,502	0	0	13	12	0	I.O.U.'s for 3 and 6 months.
,, Feb. 13	429	—	5,935	15	0	13	16	0	I.O.U.'s for 3 and 6 months.
,, Mar. 4	306	—	3,872	10	0	12	13	0	I.O.U.'s for 2 and 6 months.
,, April 15	222	—	2,803	0	0	12	12	0	
,, May 30	71	—	914	0	0	12	18	0	

(N.B.—These averages are calculated on a sugar value of 12s. 6d. per 100 lb.)

Although the new Company (as indicated in the foregoing table) soon began to furnish Barbados with increasingly large supplies of negroes, the first two years of its existence was a time of difficulty and weakness. Governor Atkins reported that in 1673 and 1674 very few negroes had arrived in Barbados.[1] Irritated by the consequent scarcity of labour and by the fact that they had at last been obliged to alter their law concerning debt,[2] the islanders in March 1675 dispatched a strongly worded petition to the King. The supply of negroes they complained was scanty, and the price excessive, the best slaves bringing £20 to £22 per head. Moreover, the Company was now offering lots at £15 per head, taking ' one wth another ', that is to say, healthy and refuse negroes lumped together. ' Wee hold it much worse then to give them theire price of two and twenty pound for good negroes.'[3]

It was unfortunate from the point of view of the petitioners that several large consignments of negroes arrived at Barbados shortly after the dispatch of the petition;[4] and still larger supplies arrived in 1676. At the subsequent inquiry, therefore, before the Lords of Trade, Colonel Thornborough the Barbadian representative in England, was compelled to admit that the

[1] Atkins to Sec. Williamson, 22nd Jan. 1677 (*Cal. Col.* 1677–80, No. 11).

[2] The eighty days of execution had been abolished on 25th March 1675 (*Cal. Col.* 1675–6, No. 451). A series of royal letters had been addressed to the Governor of Barbados demanding redress of this abuse. See also *Acts of the Privy Council*, I (22nd Nov. 1671) : ' Wee are resolved to apply the utmost and most severe remedies Our Royall authority is furnished with to compell the refractory to pay their just debts, and to lett them see, That distance of Place shall shelter none from our Justice and Power.' Another similar letter was sent on 25th May 1672 (*Cal. Col.* 1669–74, No. 840). On Atkins's appointment as Governor in 1673, he was definitely instructed to have this law altered.

[3] C.O. 1/35, No. 45.

[4] Cf. Atkins to Williamson, 22nd January 1677. Also Table II, above.

island was now adequately supplied, and that the complaint referred to the years of scarcity during the Dutch war.[1] Whereupon the Lords of Trade ordered that Atkins should be severely reprimanded for encouraging groundless complaints.[2]

Henceforward it was the quality of the imported negroes, rather than their numbers that the planters grumbled at. 'Whatever the matter is wee know not', wrote the factors in Barbados, 'but within these two or three yeares the negroes have generally proved bad and come in Ill Condition in respect of what they did before.'[3] The frequent appearance of the term 'refuse' against cargoes, and the drop of the average sale price to about £12 per head, show that the deterioration was general.

In 1679 the Barbadian Assembly instructed the Gentlemen Planters in London to represent this grievance, 'how bad and useless the sorts that are brought, and invincible is the trouble, slavery, and attendance to the planter to procure them after they come'.[4] The latter remark indeed reveals the real feelings of the planters. It was the Company itself, not so much its terms, that they disliked. In this same letter it was asked, 'whether the Royal African Company cannot be divided into sundry and separate stocks and

[1] *Acts of the Privy Council*, I, No. 1100 (8th November 1576); also *Cal. Col.* 1675–6, No. 1125. Some of the figures quoted by the Company were, however, inaccurate. They stated that 2,000 negroes had been delivered in 1674; yet actual sales to Barbadian planters amounted to about half that number. Three thousand negroes, it was stated, had been sent to the island in 1675, whereas the number sold was only about 1,500 (see Table II, above).

[2] Journal of the Lords of Trade, 7th November 1676 (*Cal. Col.* 1675–6, No. 1106).

[3] African Coy. Papers, i, f. 64, P. R. O. (18th August 1660).

[4] Cf. *Groans of the Plantations*, Lyttleton (London, 1688), p. 6: 'We are forced to scramble for them in so shameful a Manner, that one of the great Burdens of our Lives is the going to buy negroes . . .'.

jurisdictions . . .'.[1] Nothing, however, came of the projected attack.

Long irritation against the Company and the prospect of saving money both contributed to the encouragement of 'interlopers' at Barbados. The private traders could always undersell the Company, because they paid nothing towards the heavy upkeep of the African forts. They were in fact parasites of the Company; for without the indirect protection from savage tribes and European rivals which the forts afforded the interloper could not have carried on his trade. Such considerations, however, did not trouble the mind of the planter when a cheap line in negroes came his way.

The method of the interloper, after having run the gauntlet of the Company's ships, was to land his human cargo on the 'windward' and unfrequented side of the island. Hither came those planters who were in league with the smugglers, and quickly disposed of the negroes in their several plantations before the Company's agents at Bridgetown could obtain armed assistance to seize them. The case of Captain Pepperell in 1665 indicates how deeply the planters were implicated in the illegal traffic. This captain, who was a servant of the Company, arrived at Barbados with a prize ship in tow, the *William and Susan*, caught interloping on the Guinea coast. Hearing of this, the owners of the interloper (who were Barbadians) sued the captain in an action for damages of 500,000 pounds sugar at common law. The factors immediately bailed out Captain Pepperell, and petitioned Governor Willoughby to transfer the case to the Admiralty Court from that of Common Pleas, 'where they say we can expect no favour from a jury of their neighbours'.[2] The judges in the Admiralty Court were no

---

[1] Journal of Assembly (*Cal. Col.* 1677–80, No. 969).

[2] Factors of the R. A. C. to Sec. Arlington (14th September 1666), *Cal. Col.* 1661–8.

less hostile to the Company. They refused to condemn the interloper on the ground that it had been sent out of their jurisdiction to Jamaica, and would not stay the quite illegal proceedings against Pepperell at common law.[1]

Under such favourable conditions it was not surprising that interlopers grew and flourished. For the Company's factors, opposed as they were by the hostility of the inhabitants, were almost helpless. In 1675 they reported a typical incident which had taken place in Bridgetown. For some days an unknown vessel had been anchored outside the harbour, daily taking in stores and other commodities. Suspecting (because of her former history) that the vessel was intended for a voyage to Africa, the factors obtained a Governor's order that she should either come in or depart the island. The order being disobeyed, Edwin Stede, one of the factors, thereupon led a party on board. A scuffle ensued, in which shots were fired, and the officers were forced to retire on shore. The incident was finally brought to a close by the oppor-

[1] On appeal to the King the whole matter was ordered to be re-heard before the Privy Council (*Acts of the Privy Council*, I, No. 674, 6th April 1666). Despite this order, the Company complained in December that Lord Willoughby had failed to comply, and petitioned for the dispatch of a second order to that effect (ibid., No. 692). Cf. Treas. 70/16, P. R. O. This encouragement of interlopers by Barbadians brought its own Nemesis. The following letter of August 1709, signed by seventy-eight planters, is interesting and significant : ' . . . we have signed a Petition to the Honourable House of Commons representing that unless the Trade to Africa be carried on by a Company of a sufficient Joint Stock, we have not the least ground to expect that we shall have either a sufficient number of slaves imported here, or at such rates as we may be able to purchase them, . . . And we are by Experience convinc'd, that the late high Prices given for negroes has risen from no other Cause but the Liberty given to separate Traders . . .' (Bromly's Parliamentary Papers, vol. 3, p. 23). For a number of similar petitions against the proposed free trade to Africa, see ibid., vol. 2, pp. 51a and b, and vol. 3, p. 12.

tune appearance of two British men-of-war in the bay, at which the interloper discreetly sailed away.[1]

Already, in 1674, a royal proclamation had been issued, recounting that in spite of letters patent granting a monopoly of the African trade to the Company, 'divers who are not members of the said Company doe endeavour to Reep the benefitt, and fruit thereof', and calling on all His Majesty's officers to assist in the maintenance of the Company's privileges.[2] In Barbados the injunction was so ignored that in 1676 the Company informed the King that the planters were conducting a regular trade of their own, and were even refusing to buy the Company's negroes. It was impossible to stop these interlopers, ' all people appearing against us, and are ready to help Interlopers all they can '.[3] Governor Atkins was accordingly reproved for his slackness, and ordered to be diligent in repressing this traffic in future. But without the continuous presence of a strong naval patrol, the Governor was as helpless as the Company's agents.

The difficulty of the position may be gauged by the fact that in 1677 the joint owners of an interloping ship consisted of Colonel Sharpe, a chief judge of Common Pleas, two of his assistant judges, and two commissioners of the customs. ' Sure it would discourage the whole fraternity of interlopers ', wrote the Barbadian factors in indignation, ' if some of

---

[1] *Cal. Col.* 1675-6, No. 670 (15th September 1675).

[2] Ibid. 1669-74, No. 1393 (25th November 1674).

[3] C.O. 268/1, pp. 32-42, P. R. O. ' These offenders ', they added, ' being only bound to the peace, and to answer this outrage at yᵉ General Sessions, seem not at all concern'd, assuring themselves (as we guess by their discourse) they shall not undergoe any severe censure there. . . .' An example of the unscrupulous methods sometimes employed is to be found in the action of three Barbadian merchants, who on having their vessel seized as an interloper by Edwin Stede, brought an action against him for treble damages on the specious ground of a medieval English ' Statute of Monopolies ' (C.O. 1/38, No. 60, 22nd Nov. 1676, P. R. O.).

these be displaced for disobedience to the King's commands.'[1] The dismissal of Colonel Sharpe had already been ordered before the arrival of this letter, but it does not appear that the confidence of the interlopers was greatly shaken thereby.

Indeed, Edwin Stede reported in 1681 that private traders were so numerous along the Guinea coast that the Company were unable to obtain their usual cargoes, ' and that during the time of the Interlop^{rs} being there the natives would keep noe contract wth the Comp^{as} ships '.[2] And a few months later the same writer declared that unless the home government took active steps to support the Company, their trade would be ruined.[3]

The energy, however, of Sir Richard Dutton, and still more of Edwin Stede himself, as Deputy-Governor, succeeded in re-establishing the Company's supremacy to a large extent. The interloper became once more a secret smuggler, instead of a rival bidding open defiance.

Such were the sources, official and unofficial, from which Barbados drew her supply of negro slaves. Their treatment and general condition of life was, if anything, rather worse in that island than in the majority of slave-owning plantations. The fact that

---

[1] *Cal. Col.* 1677–80, No. 266.

[2] Treas. 70/16 (2nd July 1681), P. R. O. The ships and cargoes of condemned interlopers were sold by auction, half of the proceeds going to the King, and half to the Company.

    e.g.   (i) Ship *Marigold*, with 37 negroes, was sold in 1680 for £800 (£400 for ship, £400 for negroes).

T. 70/238   (ii) Ship *St. Paul*, with 31 negroes, was sold in July 1680 for £527 (negroes at £17 each).

             (iii) Ship *Speedwell* and negroes was sold in November 1680 for £658.

In May 1679 the King instructed Governor Atkins to pay all sums arising from his share in the property of interlopers convicted at Barbados, to Anne Countess Dowager of Bristol (*Cal. Col.* 1677–80, No. 993).   [3] *Cal. Col.* 1681–5, No. 306 (29th November 1681).

after about 1680 such a small island as Barbados consumed an annual supply of over 5,000 negroes, points
to a very high mortality. It was cheaper to have them
work out than die out. The sufferings of the negro
during the terrible 'Middle Passage' from Africa
have been frequently portrayed. The high mortality
which obtained was partly the result of insanitary
conditions, and partly owing to the habit of ship
masters herding on board gangs of private slaves of
their own, in addition to the normal cargo of the
Company, thus causing overcrowding.[1] There were,
of course, extreme cases, such as *The Lady Francis*,
which ' had not above 20 or 30 negroes liveing of ab^t
160 Taken in at the Bite '.[2] But the average mortality
of cargoes arriving at Barbados seems to have been
about 11 per cent.[3]

The repressive policy which the planters adopted
towards the slave population was largely dictated by
fear. Every year the mass of negro labourers increased,
while the number of Europeans steadily diminished.
On a small island, often isolated from the outside
world for months together, the danger of a sudden

[1] 'On y^e *Ruth*, Capt. Someroy, wee resolved to tell over these
Negroes, in counting of which wee found in ye ship 180 or thereabouts,
—60 more than they owned to be the Comp^{as}, nor would anybody owne
to whome they belong . . .' (Barbados, 14th May 1679, T. 70/15).

[2] T. 70/16 (1681), P. R. O.

[3] This table is compiled from the R.A.C. ledgers (T. 70/938 and
939):

Date of Arrival.	Original Cargo.	Dead in the Voyage.
1670 Jan. 10	198	19
1680 Oct. 26	89	12
1681 Jan. 21	596	58
1681 Dec. 6	264	42
1682 Jan. 24	290	32
1683 Dec. 7	216	22
Total :	1,653	185

Average mortality—11·2 per cent.

rising and a general massacre of Europeans was a very
real one. As early as 1650 elaborate precautions had
been taken. 'If any tumult or disorder be in the
Island,' wrote Ligon, 'the next neighbour to it
discharges a musquet, which gives the alarum to the
whole Island ; for upon the report of that, the next
shoots and so the next and next, till it go through
the island ; upon which warning they make ready.' [1]

Care also was taken to prevent the negroes of one
plantation from communicating with those of another.
Immediately it was reported that a number of negroes
had run away and were at large, a contingent of the
militia was called out to take them dead or alive.[2]
As early as 1648 a visitor reported that there were
'many hundreds of Rebell negro slaves in the woods '.[3]

The chief circumstance upon which the planters
based their hopes of security was the diversity of
language and race among the negroes. Coming from
all parts of Africa, they represented such totally
different tribes that they were often unable to understand one another. For this reason the planters
always strongly opposed any attempt to educate or
convert the negro to Christianity. Such a step would
give the various elements a common bond of unity.
The Gentlemen Planters in London, when approached
on this subject in 1680, reported that 'the dispro-
portion of blacks and whites, being great, the whites

[1] Ligon, *True and Exact Account*, p. 29 (London, 1657).

[2] Cf. Minutes of the Council (8th June 1657) : 'Complaint of
Thomas Moore, as to Runaways in St. Joseph's (parish) Colonel Lewis
Morris to direct Captain Weston, of his Regiment to levy six file or
more, to apprehend the Runaways. But if the said Negroes shall
make opposition, and cannot otherwise be taken and subdued, that
such as so resist may be lawfully killed and destroyed' (Davis Collection, R.C.I.). If caught they were usually executed as an example
to others. Cf. 'Order for payment of £20 17s. 6d. to Sir T. Thornhill in compensation for a negro executed for running away ' (*Cal.
Col.* 1681-5, No. 1995).

[3] Force Tracts, vol. ii, No. 7, p. 5.

have no greater security than the diversity of the negroes' languages which would be destroyed by conversion, in that it would be necessary to teach them English '.[1]

Notwithstanding these precautions a plot was organized in 1675 to massacre the entire white population on a given day, and was only just discovered in time. A negro woman named Fortuna, belonging to Judge Hall, happening to overhear the conversation of two of the conspirators, reported the news to her master.[2] The latter immediately informed Sir Jonathan Atkins, who had all the ringleaders secretly arrested. At a summary court consisting of a dozen field officers of militia and the island judges, ' seaventeen were found guilty and executed, viz. six burnt alive, and eleven beheaded, their dead bodies being dragged through the streets . . . and afterwards were burned with those that were burned alive '.[3] Subsequently, twenty-five more executions took place.[4]

Indeed the conspiracy confirmed the suspicions and heightened the nervous ferocity of the planters. In December 1683, a Barbadian writer describes how a messenger had come knocking loudly at his door in Bridgetown, at two o'clock one morning, saying that the whole of the leeward part of the island was in

[1] Journal of the Lords of Trade (8th Oct. 1680), *Cal. Col.* 1677–80, No. 1535. Exactly the same argument had been used to Ligon when he broached the subject about 1650 (see Ligon, pp. 52–3). Cf. ' An Act to prevent people called Quakers from bringing negroes to their meeting' (*Laws of Barbados*, No. 198 (23rd Nov. 1675); also *Cal. Col.* 1675–6, No. 712).

[2] For this she was given her freedom (Minutes of Assembly (23rd November 1675), *Cal. Col.* 1675–6, No. 712).

[3] ' *Great Newes from Barbados : A True and Faithfull Account of the Grand Conspiracy of the Negroes against the English, And the happy Discovery of the Same* ' (London, 1676, pp. 10–11).

[4] More still were probably executed later. Cf. ibid., p. 12 : ' Three score and odd more are in custody at the Hole, . . . and are not as yet brought to tryal.'

arms because of a rumoured slave rebellion. Yet on inquiry nothing was discovered but that four or five blacks had used threatening language. For this they were lashed, and one of them was burnt alive.[1] It was not for nothing that in the following year Sir Richard Dutton received instructions from the home authorities to have a law passed 'for the punishment of wilful and wanton murder of negroes '.[2]

Unfortunately, slave conditions on the island in the eighteenth and nineteenth centuries became progressively worse.[3] Reforms adopted in other slave-owning plantations were rejected at Barbados, with the result that a general rising in 1804 was only suppressed after more than a thousand negroes had been slain.[4]

Thus the transformation was complete. A populous British colony had become a settlement of African negroes, ruled by a small band of European overseers, nervous for their safety. Geographical conditions

---

[1] *Cal. Col.* 1681–5 (18th December 1683), No. 1475. One of these, seeing Christians thrashing their negro slaves, had said that ere long the negroes would serve the Christians so.

[2] Ibid. 3rd (May 1684), No. 1661.

[3] Cf. H.M.C. xiv, Round MSS. 9, p. 300 (1767) : ' As for the negroes I think Dr. Campbell argues more forcibly when he proves that a little more humanity would enable the Island of Barbadoes to save 2/3rds of the purchase money for slaves. . . .'

[4] *The Insurrection in Barbadoes*, p. 8 (London, 1816). In Jan. 1805 Lord Seaforth, Governor of Barbados, wrote to Earl Camden giving a long list of atrocities committed by planters upon their slaves. He then adds that although individual examples are no proof of general cruelty, yet, ' In the West Indies . . . we not only hear of the greatest crimes escaping with impunity, but we find the laws themselves conspiring to shelter criminals from justice ; we find the most respectable and enlightened part of the community sanctioning the perpetration, even of murders by their refusal to recognize the commission of it as a felonious act ' (' Debates on the Slave Trade ', 1806, Appendix, pp. 13–15). The murder of a negro in Barbados, unless it could be proved to have been committed ' without any provocation ', was only punishable by a fine of £11 14s.

working through economic circumstance had prevented the permanent establishment of a white community.

Here then, as in Australia and South Africa, a problem has emerged which is exercising the minds of all statesmen and students concerned with imperial development. Upon its solution the future of the Empire to a large degree depends.

In tropical regions where the white man cannot himself perform manual work, the introduction of coloured labour is inevitable. What, then, are to be the relations in the new community between the two elements representing as they do entirely different grades of civilization? The day has passed when a subject race could be imported, and treated as being politically non-existent.

In Barbados, and the West Indies generally, modern evolution is slowly moving towards some form of political fusion between black and white. Before the emancipation of slaves a large half-caste population came into existence. Under the influence of religion and education, this coloured race, possessing something of the European mind in an African body, has constituted a middle class between the negro and the European. They are furnishing an increasingly large proportion of the men to the professions, particularly medicine, law, and journalism.

This class, together with the black peasant proprietors of the land, have been influenced by the general wave of democratic aspiration which has resulted from the Great War. They are demanding political recognition and a voice in the management of their own affairs. The home authorities, for their part, have realized that since the Empire imported this alien element, it thereby incurred responsibility for its future development.

In response to numerous requests the British Colonial

Office in December 1921 sent out to the West Indies a parliamentary mission, under the Hon. E. F. L. Wood, to inquire into the constitutional and economic desires of the inhabitants. In his official report Mr. Wood advises constitutional reform before it be ' robbed by delay of most of its usefulness and of all its grace '. Although the demand for direct representation is described by him as ' far less substantial than its champions would profess ', he yet advocates a system of gradual evolution, whereby the elective element in the legislatures will slowly increase, until eventually it predominates.[1]

The movement, of course, is in its infancy, for the purely black population has very far to travel along the road of civilization. Moreover, there are serious difficulties to be solved. Modern visitors to Barbados report the existence of a widespread bitterness against the white man. The black labourer, whose wage is only a shilling a day, finds it hard in these days of high prices to avoid starvation, and nurses resentment accordingly.[2] On the other hand, the planter maintains, and with much truth, that the average negro labourer does so little for his money that a higher wage would be an economic impossibility. Nevertheless, the course of future development, slow and fraught with difficulty though it must be, is clearly foreshadowed. Purely white communities in the British West Indies no longer exist ; they have de-

[1] Official Report, issued 12th June 1922. In the constitutional section, the report deals only with the Crown Colonies of the British West Indies, thus omitting Barbados. But in that island the franchise (under the above scheme) would be extended to include the more educated of the coloured population.

[2] All the islands are at present suffering from a severe slump in sugar prices (now only £14 per ton), which is due partly to the late war and partly to the competition from beet sugar. A more generous degree of imperial preference is being demanded to relieve the situation.

parted elsewhere. But in their room is a coloured race, which, despite maltreatment in former times, is proud of its allegiance to the Mother Country. It rests with the planters on the islands themselves, no less than with the authorities at home, to guide and encourage the development of this people, until it is fit and ready to assume responsible membership in the commonwealth of nations known as the British Empire.

APPENDIX A

LOCAL GOVERNMENT

I. *The Parish Vestry.*

Parochial government in Barbados, while being an accurate copy of the system developed by the Tudors, was in regard to poor relief and education, in advance of the average parish in England. 'The poor', wrote Sir Jonathan Atkins in 1677, 'are provided for so well that not one will be seen asking for alms.'[1]

Vestries were probably first established in the year 1629, when Governor Sir William Tufton divided the island into six parishes. Every year on the Monday after Lady Day the freeholders of the parish assembled and elected the 'trustees', as they were called, for the ensuing twelve months, who were empowered to levy rates for the relief of the poor, the upkeep of the highways, the maintenance of the minister, and so forth. Indeed, so burdensome did these rates become— 'whereby many a one's Estates have been exhausted and taken from them to make Payment'[2]—that a law was passed about 1655, enacting that no levy might be imposed without the previous confirmation of the Governor and Council.[3] The parochial machinery was also used to collect direct taxes imposed by the central legislature.

Until recent years there was preserved at Bridgetown the original minute book of St. Michael's parish for the years 1658–78, which contains illuminating information concerning local government in the colony. Fortunately, the late Mr. Darnell Davis carefully copied out numerous entries; for the book itself has since been destroyed by fire, and Mr. Davis's transcripts are the only ones extant.

[1] Atkins to Lords of Trade (*Cal. Col.* 1677–80 (31st January 1677), No. 187).

[2] *Memoirs of the First Settlement*, p. 11 (Barbados, 1741).

[3] *Laws of Barbados*, No. 13 (ed. J. Baskett, London, 1732).

'*Minutes of St. Michael's Parish, Barbados* (1658–78).' [1]

(a) *Poor Relief.*

1666, *July 9th.* 'It is ordered for maintenance of the Minister, for defraying of the present Parish debts, the finishing of the Church, and building of two Pest Houses, and Maintenance of the Poor, with all other necessary Parish charges, that a levy be made for this present year of 15 lbs. of sugar per acre, the land itself being valued at 1,050 lbs. of sugar per acre, a year Rent ; and, that the Houses pay 10 per cent. according to the Rents now taken in ' (1,050 lb. was at that time equivalent to £5 5s.).

1666, *October 23rd.* 'That the house built for the Parish be, when finished, made *an Alms House of the Parish ; and the Poor kept at the Parish charge, be all kept there* ; and poor persons appointed to look after them.' [2]

1663, *April 6th.* 'The Vestry being informed that one Bragge, a Rope maker, is willing to employ severall poor people, that are chargeable to yᵉ Parish, and yᵉ vagrants, and idle persons lye about the Town as seeming mad men ; which persons yᵉ said Bragge is willing to employ to pick ocum, and find them in necessary provision for yᵉ ease of yᵉ Parish. It is yᵉ desire of yᵉ Vestry yᵗ yᵉ Justices do take a compassion on such persons, and send them to yᵉ Towne House at yᵉ Cage, there to be employed by yᵉ said Bragge.' (On 6th June 1670 the vestry decided to lay out 3,000 lb. of sugar yearly upon old cables to employ the poor of the Alms House.)

1669, *September 20th.* 'It is ordered that yᵉ Poor at the Almshouse have their accomodation for victuals according to yᵉ King's Allowance at Sea. The Poor to be kept at work by picking ocombe, or such other reasonable work, as yᵉ Church Wardens, or the Overseers of the Poor shall see fitt.'

1670, *September 19th.* 'Leolin Lloyd (again) appointed to look after the Poor at the Almshouse ; to receive 5,000 lbs. of sugar a yeare for that Service.' He is directed to visit the poor at the Alms House twice a week, and oftener if required,

---

[1] Davis Collection, Box 4, R.C.I. Only a number of the more important entries transcribed by Mr. Davis are quoted above.

[2] In 1673 the Grand Jury at General Sessions requested, 'yᵗ in *every* P̄ish within this Island, houses may bee erected and a stock provided for setting to work of impotent and poore people, to prevent yᵉ daily increase of idle and wandring beggars ; for we presume if yᵉ publique did make a beginning other good and charitable persons would contribute theire assistance . . .' (C.O. 1/30, No. 50 (8th July 1673), P. R. O.).

and to send his men daily to administer to the inmates according to their necessities.

(a) *Treatment of Vagabonds and Sturdy Rogues.*

1668, *January* 20*th*. 'Church Wardens to build a new Cage for Vagabonds and others of that kind ; and to be erected neer unto the place as it was formerly.'

1668, *March* 8*th*. 'It is ordered that a plott of ground that was laid out for the building of a Cage, to be in length 14 feet, and in breadth—? feet ; and that Lieutenant William Sidney doe make ye said of strong and substantial timber, with two doors and a partition in the middle, and boarded under foot and over head also ; and upon that to be shingled, and to be 7 feet high floor to floor.' In payment thereof Sidney was to receive, ' the whole profitt for duties of all that shall be putt into the said Cage, both Whites and Blacks ', provided he undertook the duties of parish beadle.

1676, *January* 17*th*. 'The Church Wardens, in pursuance of order of 24th Septr last, to take speedy care to rebuild the Cage, and now erect a polstocke Whipping Post, with a Pillory upon the Cage, and then erect, at the upper end of the Market Place, where it may most conveniently stand ; and also to build a Duckinge Stool, and the same to be erected at the Indian Bridge in St. Michael's Town.'

(c) *Ecclesiastical Organization.*

1661, *June* 20*th*. 'Agreement between the Vestry and Capt. Robert Gullimore for building a Parish Church for 250,000 lbs. of sugar (£1,250), payable in three instalments, a third within the current year ; a third when the walls are bearing up to the battlements, and a third when the Church is wholly finished.'

1663, *September* 27*th*. 'His Excellency' (Lord Francis Willoughby) ' having presented to ye Vestry of ye Parish Mr. William Frith, Clarke, Master of Arts, to officiate as Minister, they are willing to give him 20,000 lbs. of Muskovody Sugar per annum, provided ye said Mr. Frith do allow and confirm ye lease of ye Parish land let to John Trusteene for the tearme of one yeare ; and his Executor' (i. e. *congé d'élire*) ' is desired to ye said Frith's institution and inducttion, accordinge to ye lawes and customs of England.' The Governor thus acted as Ordinary, ' having the only Episcopal power in this place '. Frith was to be provided with a horse, ' for his riding as a gentleman '.

1678, *January* 21*st*. 'At a meeting of the Vestry of this Parish, His Excellency (Sir Jonathan Atkins) being present. His Excellency, upon many complaints made, and proved against Mr. Wm. Frith, late Minister in the said Parish, suspended him yᵉ exercise of his office and function in said Parish, (and) proposed to the said Vestry the nomination of a person fit and well qualified to supply the said place.'

(d) Education.

1662, *August* 21*st*. '. . . It is further ordered that Mr. W. Heynes, Schoolmaster, have license to teach school in Parish Church.'

Prior to 1661 the maintenance of the public highways had been entrusted to the general body of vestrymen. In that year, however, neglect of this duty had become so prevalent, that the legislature established a system of special surveyors. 'Four able and substantial Freeholders', seised of at least twenty acres of land, were to be elected annually by each vestry.

After being sworn in by the local justices of the peace, they were within ten days to make a thorough view of all roads and streets within the parish, then to report to the vestry, who would thereupon 'make an assessment of goods or mens Labours, or of both at their Election, for mending and repairing the said Highways and Streets'.[1] Heavy penalties were inflicted for neglect.[2]

[1] 'An Act for the better amending, repairing, and keeping clean the Common Highways etc.' (*Laws of Barbados*, No. 23, London, 1732 (9th January 1661)).

[2] Absence on the part of any vestryman from a meeting was punished (except in cases of sickness) by a fine of 100 lb.; for a churchwarden the fine was doubled. Such fines helped to pay vestry expenses, not the least of which was a substantial dinner. Cf. *Minutes of St. Michael's*, 1685-6, 18th January, 'The Gentlemen of yᵉ Vestry':

	l.	*s.*	*d.*
'To a Dish of Corn'd Pork and Yames	00.	03.	09.
'To 2 Turkey hennes and 2 capons	00.	15.	00.
'To a Shoulder of Mutton	00.	02.	1½.
'To Gerkins and Capers	00.	01.	03.
'To Cheese and Butter	00.	01.	10½.
'To a Dish of fruite	00.	03.	09.
'To Bread Dressing and fowleing lining	00.	17.	05.
'To Madeira Wine	00.	15.	00.
'To Clarett Wine	00.	05.	07½.
'To Beere	00.	01.	10½.
'To Corne Drink and Sack	00.	03.	09.

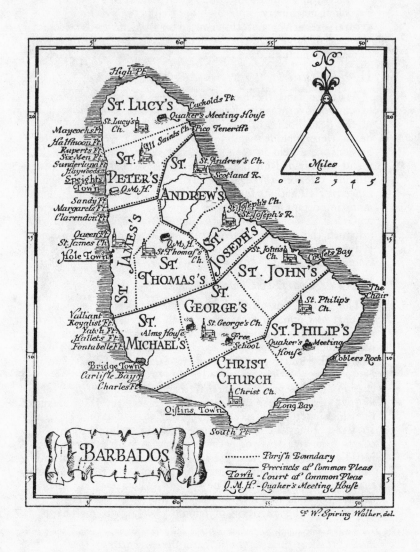

BARBADOS

- - - - - - - - Parish Boundary
───────── Precincts of Common Pleas
Town - Court of Common Pleas
Q.M.H. - Quaker's Meeting House

F. W. Spring Walker, del.

Indeed, in a small community such as that of Barbados, the parochial machinery came under the direct supervision of the central executive, and thus worked more efficiently than in the case of large countries, where great intervening distances impeded communication.

II. *The Justices of the Peace.*

As in England the local justices bore the chief burden of executive government. Every kind of task from the inspection of the dead bodies of Christian servants to trials of life and death were included among his duties. Courts of Quarter Sessions were held in each of the five districts into which the island was divided for judicial purposes. In addition to minor criminal offences, these courts (by an Act of 1669) took cognizance of civil actions for sums less than 1,000 lb. sugar.[1] The more important criminal cases were referred to the General or Grand Sessions held at infrequent intervals at Bridgetown, in which the justices joined with the Governor, Council, and Judges. Larger civil cases were dealt with by the Courts of Common Pleas.

III. *The Courts of Common Pleas.*

The island was divided into five districts or precincts, a Court of Common Pleas being established in the chief town of each. With a chief judge and two assistant judges and other officials, the courts sat for two (and in some cases) three days in the fourth week of each month, from January until September. Notice has already been made of the frequent evasion of debts practised in these courts, and of the abolition in 1675 of the eighty days' grace, which was the chief means by which merchants seeking payment were defrauded.[2] In 1673 Sir Jonathan Atkins suggested the reduction of the courts from five to two, because a planter with lands in two jurisdictions, when a marshal came to distrain his goods and negroes, would withdraw them to the other precinct, thus evading condemnation. 'The Judges', he remarks, 'have neither stipends nor fees, so that if they gett anything it is by favoring the parties Condemn'd.'[3]   English merchants,

[1] 'An Act appointing Bench Actions, and the manner of proceeding therein' (*Laws of Barbados*, No. 128, 12th December 1669).

[2] See Chapter IV, §ii, above. Also *Laws of Barbados*, No. 188 (25th March 1675).

[3] The suggestion was not adopted. Lord Francis Willougby in 1663 had

and in particular the Royal African Company, frequently complained of injustice. But the islanders themselves appear to have known the tricks of the trade too well to be deceived by their fellows.

COURTS OF COMMON PLEAS IN THE YEAR 1683.[1]

	Judge.	Clerk.	Marshal.
Precinct of Bridge Town (for the parishes of Sts. Michael, George, and John).	Henry Walrond, and four assistants.	Wm. Rawlins, and two deputies.	Wm. Gould, and three deputies.
Precinct of Oistens Town (for Christ Church and St. Philips).	Richard Sewell, and four assistants.	Tho. Gleave, and one deputy.	Jn. Gasely, and two deputies.
Precinct of Hole Town (for Sts. James and Thomas).	Wm. Howe, Esq., and four assistants.	G. Payne, Gentleman, and one deputy.	Fra. Chamberlane and one deputy.
Precinct of Speights Town. (for Sts. Peter, All Saints, and Lucies).	John Reid, Esq., and four assistants.	John Le Gard, Gentleman, and one deputy.	Archibald Carmichael, and two deputies.
Precinct of Scotland (for Sts. Andrews and Josephs).	John Daniel, Esq., and four assistants.	Arch. Carmichael Gentleman, and one deputy.	Arch. Carmichael Gentleman, and two deputies.

IV. *Other Courts.*

The Courts of Chancery, Exchequer, and Admiralty consisted of the Governor and the Council, acting in the various capacities.[2]

mortally offended the islanders by the same suggestion. Atkins also declared that, ' The Marshalls for money comply with the debtors and give them notice when they will distrayne ; the debtor makes over his Estate before hand and purchases some small peice of Land in Scotland, as they call it '' (a waste district in the North of the Island), ' which is praised att som small rate. The creditors must be contented with that or non . . . ' (C.O. 1/30, No. 90 (December 1673)).

[1] Sloane MSS. (Brit. Mus.) 2441, f. 22.

[2] For a sketch of the development of the Cnancery Court, see ' The Temper of the Council in Barbados ' by John Witham (*Cal. Col.* 1681–5, No. 1093). For details of the Exchequer Court, see Sloane MSS. 2441 (ut supra), f. 21.

V. *The Legislature.*

The Council and Assembly corresponded roughly to the two chambers of the English Parliament. An assembly of freeholders, under various forms, had existed from the days of the first settlement.[1] Each of the parishes elected two members, the franchise being restricted to landowners of not less than ten acres. Thus the constitution was a close oligarchy of planters. The power of the Council (chosen by the Crown at the suggestion of the Governor) was considerably curtailed by the fact that the Governor was present at every meeting, even when the Council was acting in a legislative capacity.[2] The two Houses deliberated separately, except when called together by the Governor on special occasions.

[1] See Chapter II, p. 25, above.

[2] In Jamaica such intervention on the part of the Governor would have been considered unconstitutional. In that island the Grand Sessions, Courts of Common Pleas, and Exchequer were 'united and blended in one supreme court of judicature'. See Bryan Edwards, *History of West Indies*, i. 349.

APPENDIX B

POPULATION

Year.	Whites.	Blacks.	Authority.
1628	1,400	—	Rawlinson MSS. (Bodleian) C. 94, f. 28.
1629	1,800	50	Egerton MSS. (Brit. Mus.) 2395, f. 602.
1636	6,000	?	Cal. Col. 1574–1660, p. 240. Cf. Memoirs of the First Settlement, p. 20.
1643	(37,200)	6,000 (approx.)	Cal. Col. 1661–8, No. 1657.
1645	(36,600)	5,680	Sloane MSS. 3662, f. 54 a.
1653	30,000	?	Egerton MSS. 2395, f. 48. Cf. T. C. D. MSS. (G. 415).
1655	23,000	20,000	Add. MSS. (Brit. Mus.) 11411, f. 9b. Egerton MSS. 2395, f. 625.
1655	25,000 'at least'	?	Cal. Col. 1574–1660, p. 446.
1668	20,000	40,000	Cal. Col. 1661–8, No. 1788.
1669	20,000	40,000	Acts of the Privy Council, I, No. 853.
1673	21,309	33,184	Cal. Col. 1677–80, No. 1101.
1675	21,725	32,473	Cal. Col. 1675 and 1676, No. 812.
1680	?	38,352	Cal. Col. 1677–80, No. 1386.
1681	(20,000)	40,000	Cal. Col. 1681–5, No. 136.
1684	23,624	46,502	Sloane MSS. (Brit. Mus.) 2441, ff. 1–22
1786	16,167	62,115 (and 838 half-castes)	From Bryan Edwards, History of the West Indies, Appendix IV.
1792	—	64,330	From Bryan Edwards, History of the West Indies, Appendix IV.
1809	15,566	69,119	From Bryan Edwards, History of the West Indies, Appendix IV.
1835	—	82,000	From Bryan Edwards, History of the West Indies, Appendix IV.
1922	15,000	180,000	Parliamentary Report of the Honble. E. F. L. Wood, issued 12th June 1922.

The above table illustrates the sudden growth of the white population in Barbados in the early years, followed later by a steady decline, simultaneously with the rapid increase of the negro population. Prior to the census of 1673 the figures quoted are only approximate computations by contemporary observers. But the general agreement found among the various writers gives to these figures a comparatively trustworthy character. Bracketed figures indicate that the original authority only gave the male population. In these cases the total population has been obtained by doubling the number, on the basis

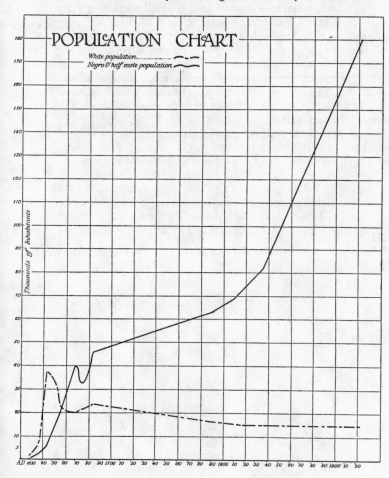

of the census returns of 1673 and 1675, which show that the women and children were together approximately equal to the men.

The decrease in the white population was chiefly attributable to the concentration of land into the hands of a few great landowners and the ousting of white labour by black. A writer in 1667 gives a striking picture of the tide of emigration from Barbados. At least 12,000 former landholders and tradesmen have gone off, ' wormed out of theire small settlements by theire more suttle and greedy neighbours. . . . Between 1643 and 1647 to New England, 1,200 ; to Trinidado and Tobago, 600 ; between 1646 and 1658 to Virginia and Surinam, 2,400 ; between 1650 and 1652 to Gudaloupe, Martinique, Marie-galante, Grenada, Tobago, and Curazoa, 1,600 ; with Colonel Venables to Hispaniola and since to Jamaica, 3,300.' [1] More than 5,000 left Barbados on the various expeditions to the Leeward Islands during the wars with the French and Dutch, very few of whom ever returned. After 1667 the exodus of time-expired servants and others to Carolina and elsewhere consistently outnumbered the arrivals in Barbados from the Mother Country. In 1670 no less than 2,000 colonists left Barbados for other plantations.[2] In these latter years the emigrants included established planters, in addition to the usual floating labour population, driven out by the competition of French and Portuguese sugar manufacturers.

[1] *Cal. Col.* 1661–8, No. 1657.   [2] Ibid. 1669–74, No. 357.

INDEX

INDEX